The church today faces a serious dilemma; it exists within a global social and economic system that is profoundly unjust and excludes those who find themselves on the margins of the modern world. Rather than making disciples of Jesus who speak truth to power and work for justice, Christianity is all too often complicit with and controlled by this culture. Through careful exegesis of the biblical text and of Christian history, Smith shows how Mammon has manifested itself over time, while also describing the extraordinary and unexpected ways in which God has called his people to live as salt and light in the face of this recurring challenge. This is, quite simply, one of the most important books I have ever read. A summons to the church to retrieve its prophetic calling in a world of injustice and pain.

Edwin Arthur, PhD
Former CEO, Wycliffe Bible Translators, UK
Member, OMF International Global Vision Council

This is a ground-breaking book that examines the contemporary global polycrisis from a Christian perspective. Drawing upon personal experience of multiple cross-cultural exposures and utilizing contemporary scholarship from a range of academic disciplines, Smith wrestles with difficult questions concerning the relationship between Christianity, mission and imperialism. He asks how and why British Christianity changed in the course of the nineteenth century, using the spread of imperial power to facilitate its mission, and even at times embracing colonialism itself as a component of that mission. Smith demonstrates both intellectual honesty and moral courage in reflecting on the inexorable growth of the worship of Mammon, while issuing an uncompromising call to world Christianity to display the justice, mercy and love which flows from the worship of the living God. This important book is addressed to a global readership while also demanding the attention of scholars in a range of academic disciplines from which the author has drawn.

Gaofeng Meng, PhD
Lecturer in Law,
SOAS University of London, UK

This is a serious book for serious times. I can't think of one like it. David Smith combines an extraordinary breadth of reading, the wisdom of a lifetime's learning and hard-won experience in global mission, to construct a prophetic critique of the injustices and environmental catastrophe spawned by Western capitalism. His thinking is deeply Christian. By that I mean it not only has remarkable biblical, historical and theological depth, but also demonstrates a passion for justice and a love for the church. David's heart is to help Christians think self-critically about what it means to live faithfully today within the destructive barrenness of a capitalist world. Yet he does this without resorting to simple dichotomies or easy answers. He writes with compassion and humility, giving us a fresh vision of the beautiful yet profoundly radical nature of the Christian faith.

Patrick Mitchel, PhD
Senior Lecturer in Theology,
Irish Bible Institute, Dublin

I wish I had read a book like this twenty years ago. I particularly benefited from the historical, social and political backgrounds it provides, since they bring to life the stories of the Bible and illuminate the work of mission over two thousand years. The powerful conclusion of the book moved and encouraged me in a context in which many of the versions of Christianity we witness do not give hope for a future shaped by the messianic world-changing gospel. I affirm the book's conclusion that the decision for God or Mammon has never been more urgent and the consequences of that choice never so crucial for the future of humankind and its planetary home.

Aako Ugbabe, PhD
University Lecturer, Naturalist and Promoter of the Arts,
Jos, Nigeria

God or Mammon

The Critical Issue Confronting World Christianity

David W. Smith

© 2025 David W. Smith

Published 2025 by Langham Academic
An imprint of Langham Publishing
www.langhampublishing.org

Langham Publishing and its imprints are a ministry of Langham Partnership

Langham Partnership
PO Box 296, Carlisle, Cumbria, CA3 9WZ, UK
www.langham.org

ISBNs:
978-1-78641-058-0 Print
978-1-78641-189-1 ePub
978-1-78641-190-7 PDF
DOI: https://doi.org/10.69811/9781786410580

David W. Smith has asserted his right under the Copyright, Designs and Patents Act, 1988 to be identified as the Author of this work.

All rights reserved. No part of this publication may be reproduced, stored in a retrieval system or transmitted, in any form or by any means, electronic, mechanical, photocopying, recording or otherwise, without the prior written permission of the publisher or the Copyright Licensing Agency.

Requests to reuse content from Langham Publishing are processed through PLSclear. Please visit www.plsclear.com to complete your request.

Scriptures taken from the Holy Bible, New International Version®, NIV®. Copyright © 1973, 1978, 1984, 2011 by Biblica, Inc.™ Used by permission of Zondervan.

British Library Cataloguing-in-Publication Data
A catalogue record for this book is available from the British Library

ISBN: 978-1-78641-058-0

Cover & Book Design: projectluz.com
Cover art: Mammon, 1884-5. George Frederic Watts. Tate, Presented by the artist 1897. © Tate, Photo: Tate

Langham Partnership actively supports theological dialogue and an author's right to publish but does not necessarily endorse the views and opinions set forth here or in works referenced within this publication, nor can we guarantee technical and grammatical correctness. Langham Partnership does not accept any responsibility or liability to persons or property as a consequence of the reading, use or interpretation of its published content.

This book is dedicated to the memory of
Peter Rowan
who eagerly anticipated its publication but departed
this life without seeing it in print. With heartfelt gratitude
for the friendship of this visionary leader whose tragic
loss to the cause we promoted together is keenly felt.

Contents

Preface xi

Chapter 1 1
    The Question of the Twenty-First Century

Part 1: Biblical Roots

Chapter 2 15
    Tracing the Roots of Mammon
        A New Religious Movement in Canaan? 21
        The Mosaic Revolution 23

Chapter 3 27
    Resisting Mammon: Prophets and Wise Men
        From Tribal Society to Monarchical State 28
        The Message of the Hebrew Prophets 31
        Coming to Terms with Endings 44
        Beyond the Abyss 46
        Counterpoint: The Voice of Wisdom 51
        The Emerging Culture of Mammon 57

Pause for Reflection: The Lament of Isaiah 61

Chapter 4 65
    God or Mammon: The Ultimate Decision
        Israel in the Time of Herod the Great 69
        The Galilee of Jesus 74
        The Elite Evangelist 78
        The Manifesto of the Kingdom 86
        The Sermon on the Plain 88
        Two Lukan Parables 95
        The Mystery of Golgotha 102

Chapter 5 107
    The Original Revolution
        From Galilee to the Roman Urban World 111
        Turning the World Upside Down 115
        The Collection 130
        The End of the Beginning 136

Pause for Reflection: Paul's Lament 145

Part 2: Historical Struggles

Chapter 6 151
   Through the Eye of a Needle
      Following Christ in a Hostile World 153
      The Age of "Mediocrity" 164
      The Pursuit of Perfection 173
      Your Kingdom Come 180

Chapter 7 183
   The Age of Reform
      The Resurgence of Mammon 185
      The Power of the Medieval Pulpit 191
      Apocalyptic Spirituality 195
      The Protestant Reformation in Context 201

Chapter 8 211
   Expanding Europe
      The Great Migration 212
      The Forgotten Holocaust 220
      Puritans and Capitalists 223

Chapter 9 233
   Mission and Empire
      The Great Century? 235
      Resistance, Reform, Renewal 244
      The Cross and the Flag 260
      The End of Christendom 268

Chapter 10 275
   From Pillar to Post
      Mammon, Globalization and "The End of History" 277
      The Fall of Icarus 287
      Living through a "Long Saturday" 291

Chapter 11 295
   World Christianity and the Great Unravelling
      Christianity in the Majority World 297
      "Come Out of Her, My People" 304
      Joining God in the Great Unravelling 319

Bibliography 325

How to live without grace – that is the question that dominates the nineteenth century. "By justice," answered all those who did not want to accept absolute nihilism. To the people who despaired of the Kingdom of Heaven, they promised the kingdom of men. The preaching of the City of Humanity increased in fervour up to the end of the nineteenth century when it became really visionary in tone and placed scientific certainties in the service of Utopia. But the kingdom has retreated into the distance, gigantic wars have ravaged the oldest countries of Europe, the blood of rebels has bespattered walls, and total justice has approached not a step nearer. The question of the twentieth century . . . has gradually been specified: how to live without grace and justice?

(Albert Camus, *The Rebel*)

Preface

This book has been a very long time in the making. Elsewhere I have explained how, on my return from service in Nigeria in 1982, I found myself wrestling with the quest for an understanding of the future of Christianity and its mission. Subsequently this search passed through different stages, beginning with the reality of secularization and the collapse of European Christendom, moving on to the phenomenon of "the endless city," and then to the question of the articulation of the message of the gospel in a world changed beyond recognition from the one in which I had grown up. Each of these stages of intellectual and spiritual struggle gave birth to books which were reports on progress, but in writing this culminating volume it has often seemed to me that those previous strands were somehow all coming together.

There is a very long list of debts I owe to the many people who have taken an interest in this writing and have encouraged me to persist at times when I feared I could never complete it. My colleague Eryl Rowlands offered very helpful feedback on the discussion of the history of early Israel, while Patrick Mitchel, Eddie Arthur and Alan Donaldson each read the completed manuscript and urged its publication. I am grateful to Vinoth Ramachandra both for astute comments on my early chapters, and for the friendship and comradeship we have shared over the past years; his courageous calling out of Western Christianity's moral failure in a period of mounting violence is an example of what "prophecy" looks like today. I am privileged to call Gaofeng Meng my friend and his detailed feedback on my manuscript not only challenged me to rethink certain things, but encouraged me to believe that this work has cross-cultural relevance far beyond a Western readership. The same can be said about Aako and Kanchana Ugbabe whose fellowship across many years and enthusiasm for this book means much to me, not least because of their faithful witness in Nigeria. My closest and beloved friend, Wesley White, completed the reading of the final chapters during an eleven-hour train journey returning from Ukraine, and immediately asked for permission to use those chapters for teaching on his return. Alas, it was almost my last contact with Wes, who was so suddenly and tragically taken from us. The example Wesley set of loving and devoted service to all kinds of people, but especially to the stranger and the marginalized, will remain with me as a beacon for the rest of my life.

The book is dedicated to the memory of Peter Rowan of the Overseas Missionary Fellowship who has been a wonderful dialogue partner and whose lifelong involvement in cross-cultural mission resulted in a bold vision of the response needed to meet the challenges now facing the Western missionary movement. I have been blessed by a wider circle of thoughtful Christians who have read parts of the book and responded in ways which encouraged me to think that it could resonate with a general Christian reading public. I thank John Jackson, Elizabeth Swain, Sam Nwokoro, Lamboi Haokip and Siobhan Wheeler for their encouragement. Richard Morrison and Michael Manning expressed enthusiasm for this project from the start and my gratitude to both of them is immense. I must also mention Michael and Elizabeth Middleton, and Heber Martin, who departed this life just as I completed the book. Not only have they been treasured friends throughout my life, but they have exemplified what it means to live and work in an economistic culture without compromising the values of the kingdom of God; my debt to them is huge.

Finally, I am deeply grateful to Mark Arnold at Langham Publishing and his editorial colleagues for their patience and kindness in relation to this project, and I owe an enormous debt to Pieter Kwant, who read the entire work at short notice, gave me the benefit of his acute critical acumen, and then recommended that the book be published. To all of these friends, and to a much wider circle of folk who have followed progress via postings on the Internet, I offer warmest thanks and pray that, notwithstanding the points at which this work may provoke disagreement, it might make a positive contribution to the evolution of world Christianity at one of the most critical points in history.

David Smith
Glasgow, December 2024

CHAPTER 1

The Question of the Twenty-First Century

The statement by Albert Camus on the opening page of this book is taken from one of the most remarkable discussions of contemporary Western culture to have appeared during the twentieth century.[1] First published in 1951, in the aftermath of the horrors of the Second World War and the German occupation of France, *L'Homme révolté* might be described as a secular lament over a broken world in which both normative ethics and an agreed understanding of the meaning of existence appeared to have been lost. Camus confronted the consequences of the loss of transcendence in European culture with unflinching honesty and integrity and searched for a justification for continuing to live in a world which had become (to use a word central to his argument) *absurd*. "When man submits God to moral judgement, he kills Him in his own heart. And then what is the basis of morality? God is denied in the name of justice but can the idea of justice be understood without the idea of God? Have we not arrived at absurdity?"[2]

This existential question dominates all of Camus's work. Like so many contemporary intellectuals, he discovered analogies between the tragic figures in Greek mythology and the plight of modern people, and for him the figure of Sisyphus, condemned to endlessly rolling a rock to the summit of a mountain, only to witness it tumble back down again, mirrored the toil and labour of modern people whose lives had become devoid of purpose.

---

1. Albert Camus, *The Rebel* (Harmondsworth: Penguin, 1971), 117.
2. Camus, *Rebel*, 57.

"His scorn of the gods, his hatred of death, and his passion for life won for him that unspeakable penalty in which his whole being is exerted towards accomplishing nothing."[3]

The widely read novel *The Plague*, first published during the Second World War and attracting new readers during the latest "plague" which bore the name COVID-19, brilliantly articulated these concerns. The story is built around the outbreak of a terrible disease which ravages the population of a town in North Africa, resulting in its isolation and shutdown. The narrative describes the struggle to resist the disease, to cope with a veritable tsunami of suffering and death, and to confront the existential and spiritual dilemmas which this context presents. Camus had read reports of sermons preached by Catholic priests in the cathedrals of occupied France, so that the character of Father Paneloux in this novel, "a stalwart champion of Christian doctrine at its most precise and purest," was realistic and reflected a common response of Christians in a time of extreme crisis and human suffering. However, the novel describes the way in which the horrors of the plague, and especially the priest's repeated exposure to the tragedy of the deaths of *children*, softened his rhetoric and brought about a change in him, so that he "spoke in a gentler, more thoughtful tone than on the previous occasion" and "instead of saying 'you' he now said 'we.'"[4]

Such is the integrity of Camus's thought that while he describes the apparently insurmountable challenges which the plague presents to theology, he is equally clear that those who have consciously rejected faith are faced with profoundly troubling questions of their own. A conversation between two of the characters who play central roles in fighting the terrible disease illustrates this:

> "It comes to this," Tarrou said almost casually, "what interests me is learning how to become a saint."
>
> "But you don't believe in God."

---

3. Albert Camus, *The Myth of Sisyphus* (Harmondsworth: Penguin, 1975), 108.

4. Albert Camus, *The Plague* (Harmondsworth: Penguin, 1960), 182. It is important to note that one group of French Jesuits founded a movement called *la Nouvelle théologie* and, according to Paul Lakeland, developed "a form of resistance that suited perfectly their identity as Christian intellectuals, French patriots, and courageous activists." We shall return to this group later in this book. See Paul Lakeland, "Spiritual Resistance: Theology in the Age of Neoliberalism," *Commonweal* 144, no. 6 (June 2020): 24–29.

"Exactly. Can one be a saint without God? – that's the problem, in fact the only problem, I'm up against today."[5]

Albert Camus died tragically in a road accident in January 1960 at the age of forty-seven. Sixty years later, and into a new century, the question he believed to have been thrust to the centre of concern by the history through which he had lived remains to be answered: *how to live without grace and justice?* In fact, as I attempt to demonstrate in this book, the historical and cultural developments which have occurred during the six decades since Camus's passing have increased the urgency of his question, while at the same time providing evidence which might enable us to offer a credible response to it. To my knowledge, no one has presented a more comprehensive and brilliant description of the post-war period in Europe than the historian Tony Judt. Writing at the beginning of the twenty-first century, he described Western Europe as "an imposing edifice resting atop an unspeakable past."[6]

Post-national, welfare-state, cooperative, pacific Europe was not born of the optimistic, ambitious, forward-looking project imagined in fond retrospect by today's Euro-idealists. It was the insecure child of anxiety. Overshadowed by history, its leaders implemented social reforms and built new institutions as a prophylactic, to keep the past at bay.[7] Judt's massive history of Europe since 1945 won widespread acclaim but within five years of its publication, as he himself lay dying, he completed a book with a title based on the lines of Oliver Goldsmith: "Ill fares the land, to hastening ills a prey, / Where wealth accumulates, and men decay."[8] The very first sentences spelled out Judt's concern: "Something is profoundly wrong with the way we live today. For thirty years we have made a virtue out of the pursuit of self-interest: indeed, this very pursuit now constitutes whatever remains of our sense of collective purpose."[9]

After a lifetime of teaching the history of Europe on both sides of the Atlantic, Judt reported that a constant stream of students had complained to

---

5. Camus, *Plague*, 208.
6. Tony Judt, *Postwar: A History of Europe Since 1945* (London: Vintage Books, 2010), 3.
7. Tony Judt, 6.
8. Oliver Goldsmith, "The Deserted Village."
9. Tony Judt, *Ill Fares the Land: A Treatise on Our Present Discontents* (London: Allen Lane, 2010), 1.

him: "It was easy for you." In Oxford and Cambridge, at the École Normale Supérieure in Paris, and at the universities of New York and California, Berkeley the feedback was everywhere the same: "Your generation had ideals and ideas, you believed in something, you were able to change things. We have nothing."[10] I am reminded of the report of a student of mine from Eastern Germany who raised the question of God in a series of open dialogues with his peers in Leipzig and was told, "We had forgotten that we had forgotten God."

Such reactions on the part of the young suggest that Albert Camus's sense of anguish, his openly expressed anxiety and apprehension at the absurdity of a world whose creator was dead, may have faded in the following decades as a culture without transcendence came to be accepted as the new normal. The vacuum created by the death of God was filled by an onrushing tide of technological transformations, cultural shifts in the form of an ideology of economism, and the invention of a plethora of sophisticated forms of distraction which made possible the suppression of concerns about justice, meaning and the reality of death. As Tony Judt pointed out, "thirty years of growing *inequality* have convinced the English and Americans in particular that this is a natural condition of life about which we can do little."[11]

In fact, this development had been foreseen by perceptive critics much earlier in the twentieth century, and even before that. At this point I want to focus on the work of another key analyst whose insights remain of great significance when we pose the question: *how did we get here?* What were the forces at work, perhaps concealed from view at the time, which prepared the ground for the intellectual and cultural transformations which have remade our world? At the beginning of the twentieth century the German sociologist Max Weber published an article which was eventually to grow into a book destined to become hugely influential in the quest for an understanding of the modern world. Translated into English and published under the title *The*

---

10. Judt, *Ill Fares the Land*, 3.

11. Judt, 21–22. On the very day this sentence was typed it was reported that Jeff Bezos, the founder of Amazon, had increased his personal fortune in one twenty-four-hour period by $13bn. This resulted from Amazon's "soaraway share price as hundreds of millions of people trapped at home by coronavirus lockdowns turned to online retail service to keep themselves fed and entertained." Bezos's fortune is estimated to be $189bn, dwarfing the gross domestic products of nations such as Hungary, Ukraine and Qatar (*The Guardian*, 22 July 2020).

Protestant Ethic and the Spirit of Capitalism, the thesis presented by Weber has been endlessly debated and critiqued, yet his work has remained a key text in discussions concerning modernity for well over a century after its first appearance. The book comes from one of the major figures in the discipline of sociology and its title already suggests that it deals with historical, economic and cultural developments which should be of deep interest and concern to Christian believers, especially with regard to theology and mission.[12]

Having traced what he believed to be the connection between certain aspects of the Protestant Reformation and the growth and eventual dominance of modern capitalism, Weber concluded that a central characteristic of the contemporary, industrialized world, what he significantly called "the *spirit* of modern capitalism," was related to the Reformation concept of the "calling" of Christians to view their daily work as itself a sacred activity carried out for the glory of God. Weber paid particular attention to the English Puritans whose approach to life in the world he described as one of "worldly asceticism." However, the material prosperity which resulted when economic activity was released from the ethical restraints previously placed upon it had unintended consequences as the result of which, to quote a famous phrase, Protestantism "became its own gravedigger." Here is Weber's conclusion:

> When asceticism was carried out of monastic cells into everyday life, and began to dominate worldly morality, it did its part in building the tremendous cosmos of the modern economic order. This order is now bound to technical and economic conditions of machine production which today determine the lives of all the individuals who are born into this mechanism, not only those directly concerned with economic acquisition, with irresistible

---

12. Among Weber's many critics, A. G. Dickens described his work as based upon a "specious theory" for which it "is difficult to construct any defence." (*Reformation and Society in Sixteenth-Century Europe* [London: Thames & Hudson, 1966], 178). By contrast, a recent study of the Reformation acknowledges Weber's "pioneering work" which "made modern capitalism's relationship to the Reformation an issue in multiple academic disciplines." The author notes Weber's "divergences from Marx on matters of economics, politics and culture," but adds that Weber "was hardly less appalled by the effects of modern capitalism on human beings" (Brad S. Gregory, *The Unintended Reformation: How a Religious Revolution Secularized Society* [Cambridge: Belknap Press, 2012], 240–41).

force. Perhaps it will so determine them until the last ton of fossilized coal is burnt.[13]

Weber's conclusion is expressed in a powerful image which remains in the reader's consciousness long after the book has been laid aside. The hope of the Protestant Reformers, and especially their Puritan followers, that secular work might become a sacred calling, and that the acquisition of material goods resulting from this would be like a "light cloak, which can be thrown aside at any moment," was confounded since "fate decreed *that the cloak should become an iron cage.*" In the course of the eighteenth and nineteenth centuries, with the rise of industrial society, the mass migration from the countryside to burgeoning cities, and new philosophical and intellectual developments, material goods "gained an increasing and finally inexorable power in history."[14]

It is not my purpose to discuss, even less to attempt to evaluate, Weber's thesis in detail. His work is of compelling interest in relation to this study for two reasons: first, because it deals with a major transition within Western culture, and in describing the human experience under modern conditions as like life in an iron cage, Weber identified a characteristic of contemporary culture which must be of fundamental concern for us.

Second, Weber's conclusion is clearly pessimistic with regard to the human future in a capitalist world (and one wonders what he would say more than a century later when the developments he described have spread across the globe, drawing nations and peoples everywhere into the same conflicted and often painful experiences of modernity?). However, at the very end of the book there is a hint of hope that an alternative future just might be possible. He describes the pursuit of wealth, especially in the United States, as being "stripped of its religious and ethical meaning" and associated with "purely mundane passions." Modern people appear to be "unable to give religious

---

13. Max Weber, *The Protestant Ethic and the Spirit of Capitalism* (London: Counterpoint, 1985), 181.

14. Weber, *Protestant Ethic*, 181. Weber's work has often been spoken of alongside that of the English scholar R. H. Tawney, whose *Religion and the Rise of Capitalism* (London: John Murray, 1926) explores the same issues from the perspective of social history. Tawney's closing words are relevant to our concerns: "The quality in modern societies, which is most sharply opposed to the teaching ascribed to the Founder of the Christian Faith . . . consists in the assumption . . . that the attainment of material riches is the supreme object of human endeavour and the final criterion of human success. Such a philosophy . . . is the negation of any system of thought or morals which can, except by metaphor, be described as Christian" (286).

ideas a significance for culture and national character *which they deserve*."[15] Yet despite this sober verdict, notice the open-ended character of this crucial sentence:

> No one knows who will live in this cage in the future, or whether at the end of this tremendous development entirely new prophets will arise, or there will be a great rebirth of old ideas and ideals, or, if neither, mechanized petrification, embellished with a sort of convulsive self-importance.[16]

Ever since I first read those words the fact that Weber had left open the possibility that *entirely new prophets* might appear, able to challenge the dominant, all-pervasive ideology of the modern world and articulate an alternative vision for the future of humankind and the whole of creation, has haunted me. I want to pursue that possibility in what follows, but I do so in full awareness of two major obstacles.

First, the possibility that there could yet be a reappearance of prophecy seems to be reduced almost to vanishing point by the fact that contemporary religion, including Christianity, is itself embedded within the structures of the "iron cage" of which Weber spoke, so that a perspective apart from that context appears to be almost impossible to achieve.[17] The obstacles which seem to block the possibility of prophecy in the twenty-first century arise from both the immense ideological power of the system which now rules over our world, and the tragic compromises which Christianity has itself made with that ideology, amounting to a form of syncretism by which the

---

15. Weber, *Protestant Ethic*, 183. Emphasis added.

16. Weber, 182. The American sociologist of religion Robert Bellah wrote an important evaluation of Weber's work titled "Max Weber and World-Denying Love: A Look at the Historical Sociology of Religion." See Robert N. Bellah and Steven M. Tipton, eds., *The Robert Bellah Reader* (London: Duke University Press, 2006), 123–49.

17. A more recent social critic made this same point. Theodor Adorno concluded that the only philosophy which could confront the challenges of our times was one which would "contemplate all things as they would present themselves from the standpoint of redemption." Such a perspective would expose the reality of the condition of the world, "reveal it to be, with its rifts and crevices, as indigent and distorted as it will appear one day in the messianic light." But he then concludes that this is "an utterly impossible thing, because it presupposes a standpoint removed . . . from the scope of existence, whereas we well know that any possible knowledge must not only be first wrested from what is, if it shall hold good, but is also marked, for this very reason, by the same distortion and indigence which it seeks to escape" (*Minima Moralia: Reflections on a Damaged Life* [London: Verso, 2005], 247).

radical message of Jesus Christ has been neutered and faith-as-praxis has become almost impossible.

In the second place, if we assume that, notwithstanding the obstacles just discussed, a prophetic stance towards the culture of economism might be possible, it would inevitably be radically countercultural and would consequently meet massive resistance and hostility from the guardians of the status quo. In other words, it is almost impossible to exaggerate the scope of what is at stake here; the emergence of "entirely new prophets" in a world in which the iron cage is being replicated among every tribe and nation on earth would result in the announcement of a vision for a different kind of world, involving a historical transformation so radical and all-embracing as to surpass all previous paradigm shifts in human history. And that same history repeatedly alerts us to what happens to those who dare to voice such prophetic dreams.

However, the fact that so insightful an analyst of human behaviour and social history as Max Weber could recognize prophecy as a distinct category and remain open to the possibility that a new generation of prophets might yet appear and point a way out of the catastrophe towards which humankind was heading compels us to reflect on the biblical witness concerning prophets and prophecy. Dietrich Bonhoeffer, facing imminent execution by the Nazis in 1945, wrote from prison at a time when the symbol of the "iron cage" had taken on a deeper and more sinister significance. To what extent he may have been influenced by Max Weber's work I do not know, but he certainly grasped the fact that (to use another key term in Weber's analysis) the modern world had been "disenchanted" and human beings had learned "to cope with all questions of importance without recourse to God as a working hypothesis." What Christians named "God" was "being more and more edged out of life, losing more and more ground."[18] In the final days of his life Bonhoeffer wrote to a young relative who was about to be baptized and predicted that the young man would live to see the form of the church "changed beyond recognition." The churches of Europe, he said, were still "groping after something new and revolutionary without being able to understand or utter it yet," but Bonhoeffer predicted (and here the parallel with Weber becomes almost uncanny) that "the day would come *when men will be called again to utter the word of God with such power as will change and renew the world*." It

---

18. Dietrich Bonhoeffer, *Letters and Papers from Prison* (London: Fontana, 1959), 106–7.

would be "the language of a new righteousness and truth" announcing the peace of God with men and the advent of his kingdom.[19] In other words, in the very shadow of a firing squad, Bonhoeffer glimpsed a future in which genuine prophecy would re-emerge to challenge a culture of death and offer the world a credible alternative bearing the hope of the flourishing of the whole human family and the renewal of all creation.

I will argue in this book that the history of the more than half a century since the death of Albert Camus has demonstrated with ever-growing clarity that it is impossible to live without grace and justice. Our world has been reshaped within that period by a series of earth-shaking events and the emergence of new ways of understanding human identity and purpose. We will explore these transformations in detail in what follows, but we note here the conclusion of Zygmunt Bauman that the 1970s marked a "genuine watershed in modern history" because by the end of that decade, "the setting in which men and women faced up to life challenges had been surreptitiously yet radically transformed, invalidating the extant life wisdoms and calling for a thorough revision and overhaul of life strategies." Three decades of post-war reconstruction, the creation of the social state, and the optimism accompanying the end of colonial empires and the emergence of new nations began to give way to a very different world characterized by "information deluge, rampant globalization, consumer feasting in the affluent North, and a deepening sense of desperation and exclusion on a large part of the rest of the world arising from the spectacle of wealth on the one hand and destitution on the other."[20]

For some readers of these pages it may seem odd and anachronistic that I should characterize the culture that has emerged from that period by reference to the term "Mammon." The word is, of course, found on the lips of Jesus of Nazareth at the conclusion of what has been called "The Sermon on the Mount," a manifesto encapsulating the very core of the teaching of the gospel. Unfortunately, this term has often been translated as "money," whereas in its context it is evident that it relates to a phenomenon far more extensive and all-embracing than mere coinage. Money as such acts as an agent and symbol

---

19. Bonhoeffer, *Letters and Papers*, 160. Italics added.
20. Zygmunt Bauman, *Liquid Times: Living in an Age of Uncertainty* (Cambridge: Polity, 2007), 49.

of this ideology, but Mammon is a *system*, a total worldview which comes to dominate society and penetrates to the inner core of the lives of individuals, reshaping their values and desires. The choice presented by Jesus makes it perfectly clear that Mammon extends its reach and influence as far as that claimed by God himself. As the French scholar Jacques Ellul says, "we absolutely must not minimize the parallel Jesus draws between God and Mammon." Christ is speaking of a power which rivals God and "makes itself our master and has specific goals."[21] We may say therefore that "Mammon" refers to an ideology, a system, which dominated the first-century Mediterranean world and thus appears to be *an ancient anticipation and forerunner of Weber's iron cage*.

My argument in what follows will be that there is an analogy between our own times and the first centuries of the Christian era when imperial Rome dominated most of the ancient world, including the Galilee of Jesus, and imposed by force its ideological and economic values on subjugated peoples. The parallels between that world and the one in which we exist more than two thousand years later are striking and suggest that the life and message of Christ has a far more profound relevance to contemporary realities than is generally recognized, both within and beyond the Christian movement.

I need to make it very clear at this point that my aim is not to deploy the question in my title in the service of Christian evangelism, as though its primary point of reference is an unbelieving world. On the contrary, Jesus's message is directed to his own followers and is above all a warning to them of a form of syncretism involving attempted harmonizations between God and Mammon, Christ and Caesar. Today, at a point in history at which Christianity has become a global faith, with millions of its adherents living on the underside of a globalized world, often in conditions which leave them on the margins of life and death, it is imperative that the whole body of Christ hears afresh the challenge of its Lord and articulates the gospel in words and deeds demonstrating the power which sets the prisoners free. This liberation cannot be restricted to individual experience and conversion, but must impact the broader social, economic and political realms, so that the bars of Weber's iron cage are torn asunder, creating the possibility of a new way of being a human family, living in harmony on our shared and cherished planetary home.

---

21. Jacques Ellul, *Money and Power* (Downers Grove: InterVarsity Press, 1984), 76.

On the final page of his history of Christianity in the twentieth century, Brian Stanley writes that since the 1980s the fabric of Christian belief and practice has been fundamentally redesigned "in the interests of the pursuit of individual material prosperity." Consequently, "the most serious challenge confronting the religion in the twenty-first century looks likely to be the preparedness of some sections of the church in both northern and southern hemispheres to accommodate the faith to ideologies of individual enrichment."[22] The worship of God or Mammon will be the question of the century for world Christianity, and only if it can escape the confines of the iron cage of a culture of economism will it have a chance of offering its own prophetic perspective to the wider human family.

I end this chapter as it began, with Albert Camus. In 1948 he accepted an invitation from the Dominican monks at the Monastery of Latour-Maubourg to speak to them on the subject of "The Unbeliever and Christians." He began by saying that he did not speak on the assumption that Christian truth was illusory, "but merely from the fact that I cannot accept it." He continued:

> I feel like telling you today that the world needs real dialogue, that falsehood is the opposite of dialogue as is silence, and that the only possible dialogue is the kind between people who remain what they are and speak their minds. This is tantamount to saying that the world of today needs Christians who remain Christians.[23]

He concluded with a warning that contemporary Christianity might lose "all the virtue of revolt and indignation that belonged to it long ago," in which case Christians would survive "and Christianity will die." Yet he longed that the voices of Christians, "millions I say, throughout the world would be added to the appeal of a handful of isolated individuals who, without any sort of affiliation, today intercede almost everywhere and ceaselessly for children and for men."[24]

---

22. Brian Stanley, *Christianity in the Twentieth Century: A World History* (Princeton: Princeton University Press, 2018), 366.

23. Albert Camus, *Resistance, Rebellion and Death* (London: Hamish Hamilton, 1961), 58.

24. Camus, *Resistance, Rebellion*, 52–53.

Part 1

Biblical Roots

CHAPTER 2

Tracing the Roots of Mammon

The decision to serve God or Mammon with which Jesus confronted his first followers has a significant precedent in the story of biblical Israel as this is told in the Hebrew Bible. The book of Joshua contains an account of the entrance of former slaves, liberated from the bondage of imperial Egypt, into the land of Canaan. The narrative is bookended by statements which accent the distinctive character of these people and impress upon them the imperative of their embrace of the unique identity which they now possess. At the beginning of the story Joshua is reminded of the Torah he had received from his predecessor, Moses, and is told that the practice of the personal and social ethic contained within the Book of the Law is absolutely crucial to the well-being and survival of the people he leads (Josh 1:7–8).

At the other end of the book, following the tumultuous (and sometimes puzzling) events which are recorded as having taken place between times, the now-settled tribes are gathered at Shechem and solemnly reminded of their origins "beyond the River." They are presented with a crucial decision: whether to serve Yahweh or to embrace the way of life of the cities whose kings and priests they had just overthrown. "Now fear the LORD and serve him with all faithfulness. Throw away the gods your ancestors worshipped beyond the River Euphrates and in Egypt, and serve the LORD. But if serving the LORD seems undesirable to you, *then choose for yourselves this day whom you will serve . . .*" (Josh 24:14–15).[1]

This biblical book, together with its companion, Judges, has presented readers and interpreters of the Bible with difficult challenges and its account

---

1. All emphasis in Scripture quotations has been added.

of what appears to be a "conquest" of the original inhabitants of the land has, alas, been used to justify crusades, "holy wars" and even genocides. The history of the reception of this text within Christendom has created serious barriers to faith on the part of many thoughtful and sensitive people, and for contemporary Palestinian Christians its interpretation as an ethnically based conquest has seemed to justify their own expulsion from their ancient homelands in the modern state of Israel.[2]

There are, I want to suggest, two issues which have contributed to the misinterpretation of these narratives. First, a significant part of the problem has been that these texts have invariably been read without serious consideration being given to the wider historical context to which they relate in the ancient Near East. According to the report in Numbers 13:28, the land which the freed slaves were to enter contained cities which were "fortified and very large." This should alert us to the fact that the events we are concerned with here occurred following a major era of *urbanization* during which the entire Fertile Crescent had witnessed the rise of many of the earliest cities in human history. Then, as now, urbanization was accompanied by significant cultural and social transformations.[3]

Lewis Mumford suggests that "the most important agent in effecting the change from a decentralized village economy to a highly organized urban economy, was the king, or rather, the institution of kingship."[4] He notes that modern archaeology has uncovered the remains of cities throughout the Tigris and Euphrates valleys and that everywhere they reveal traces of what

---

2. Peter Craigie comments that perhaps the most terrible example of the use of Old Testament texts to justify Christian violence is seen in the Crusades. The first Crusade in 1099 culminated in the capture of Jerusalem amid terrible bloodshed: 10,000 Muslims were beheaded in the Great Mosque and Christian chroniclers reported this with joy and applauded "the 'justice' that was done" (*The Problem of War in the Old Testament* [Grand Rapids: Eerdmans, 1978], 28). William Dever points out that "revisionist rhetoric from biblical and archaeological scholarship is now being subverted to serve nationalist agendas, whether extreme forms of Zionism or those of Muslim Fundamentalists" (*Who Were the Early Israelites and Where Did They Come From?* [Grand Rapids: Eerdmans, 2003], 237–38).

3. Ernest Becker observed that ancient people lived in a world devoid of clocks, calendars and years. "Nature was seen in her imagined purity of endless cycles of sun risings and settings, moon waxings and wanings, seasons changing, animals dying and being born, etc. This kind of cosmology is not favourable to the accumulation of either guilt or property, since everything is wiped away with the gifts and nature is renewed with the help of ritual ceremonies of regeneration. Man did not feel that he had to pile things up" (*Escape from Evil* [New York: Free Press, 1975], 87).

4. Lewis Mumford, *The City in History* (Harmondsworth: Penguin, 1966), 47.

might be called the iconic buildings of that age: the palace, the granary and the temple. Mumford concludes that these interconnected structures reflect the emergence of an alliance between the political, economic and religious agencies. "With this came vocational differentiation and specialization in every field. The early city, as distinct from the village community, is a caste-managed society, organized for the satisfaction of a dominant minority: no longer a community of humble families living by mutual aid."[5]

Whether life in pre-urban villages was as idyllic as this suggests we may doubt, but Mumford's description of the cultural, political and economic changes taking place at this time sheds significant light on the context of our texts and the violent conflicts which they describe. Old Testament scholarship has paid increasing attention to the world-shaping events which were taking place within the wider Near East at the time of the action described in the books of Joshua and Judges and, in doing so, has opened up fresh understanding of these narratives. As George Mendenhall observed:

> The context of early Israel was one of disintegration of power structures; the mid-thirteenth century saw the whole civilized world divided among four great empires. After less than two generations, little was left of any of them; widespread destruction had taken place from Troy to the borders of Persia, and the toll in human life must have been incalculable. An economic and political dark age set in which was to last for over two centuries; but it was during this period that the new religious community called Israel developed its distinctive patterns of thought that were normative even for early Christianity over a thousand years later.[6]

---

5. Mumford, *City in History*, 50. Describing the typical pattern of sacred kingship in the ancient Near Eastern cities, George Mendenhall says that "the king and his bureaucracy had a surplus of funds sufficient to support an ambitious building program – of temples, palaces, fortifications, a sumptuous and expensive art in ivory, gold and silver. His royal glory had to be magnificent to convince the peasants that they should be proud to have such a king. His prestige was based on divine right; his power derived from the gods whose rituals he supported both in the building of elaborate temples and in the maintenance of an elaborate priestly organization, and of course from an army and often a navy" (*The Tenth Generation: The Origins of the Biblical Tradition* [Baltimore: Johns Hopkins University Press, 1973], 222).

6. Mendenhall, *Tenth Generation*, 64.

Second, the threat which the wandering band of migrants encamped on the eastern bank of the River Jordan posed to the fortified cities of Canaan was *not* the result of superior military force. It arose rather from their vision of a new kind of society based on the Book of the Law which they had received from Yahweh. Mendenhall insisted that the story of early Israel is conceivable only within the framework of the cultural forms of the Later Bronze Age and that, when viewed from that perspective, it appears as a *revolution* in which the ethical concerns enshrined within the Book of the Law became the basis for both the critique of existing political and social arrangements, and the vision of a new kind of human community. This is confirmed by the choice presented to the liberated slaves at both ends of the book of Joshua, as we have already seen. The exodus from Egyptian bondage, the covenant made with Yahweh, and the vision of a community practising "justice and justice alone" provided the impetus for what amounted to a historic turning point in the history of humankind. As Mendenhall says:

> What happened at Sinai was the formation of a new unity where none had existed before, a "peace with God" among a "mixed multitude" and tribally affiliated families who had in common only deliverance from an intolerable political monopoly of force. Perhaps for the first time in history, a real elevation to a new and unfamiliar ground in the formation of a community took place – a formation based on common obligations rather than common interests – *on ethic, rather than on covetousness.*[7]

Archaeological discoveries made during the twentieth century have enhanced our knowledge of this period, while posing some difficult questions regarding certain aspects of the biblical texts. For example, we have to account for the fact that the relatively small group of slaves freed from Egypt appears to have been rapidly transformed into a large community within

---

7. Mendenhall, 21–22; emphasis added. Mendenhall's book is not as widely known as it should be. I have found his scholarship immensely stimulating and, notwithstanding controversial aspects, it remains a key text for the study of the history of early Israel. Note Jonathan Sacks's description of sacral kingship in the ancient world: "At the apex of Mesopotamian or Egyptian society was a ruler, king or pharaoh, seen as a god, or child of the gods, or the prime intermediary between the people and the gods. Below him ... was the cognitive elite, the administrative class. Below them was the mass of people, conceived as a vast work- or military force" (*The Dignity of Difference: How to Avoid the Clash of Civilizations* [London: Continuum, 2003], 132).

Palestine. As long ago as the 1950s John Bright had raised this issue and wondered where "all these Israelites came from if they did not all march in from the desert?" The "conquest," he suggested, must have been "an inside job"; there must have been Hebrews long settled in Palestine who now united with the incomers from Egypt and "their joining struck the spark that ignited Palestine." From the fusion of the liberated slaves with groups of earlier immigrants who had long been settled in Canaan, "the Israelite tribal league in its normative form emerged."[8] Subsequent studies were to develop Bright's suggestion of an "inside job," but challenged his assumption that these people shared a common ethnic identity. In fact, they were all described by the term *'Apiru*, which signified people of a particular *social* status: slaves, casual labourers, prostitutes. William Dever has shown that the term relates to a kind of underclass, people living "on the fringes of urban society as refugees from the Canaanite city-states, rebels, highwaymen, sometimes mercenaries, but always underminers of the Establishment."[9]

References to such people and the threat they posed to the authority of the rulers of the city-states in Canaan are to be found in the famous Amarna Letters which were discovered by a peasant woman in the ruins of Akhenaten's palace in Middle Egypt in 1887. This remarkable correspondence flowed from troubled puppet rulers in the cities of Canaan to their Egyptian overlords, and provides us with a vivid picture of social unrest during this period. Embattled kings plead repeatedly for the support and assistance of their imperial sponsors. Here is an example:

> Let the king, my lord, learn that the *'Apiru* has risen (in arms) against the lands which the god of the king, my lord, gave me; but I have smitten him. Also let the king, my lord, know that all my brethren have abandoned me, and it is I, 'Abdu-Heba (who) fight against the chief of the *'Apiru*. And Zurata, prince

---

8. John Bright, *A History of Israel*, 3rd ed. (Philadelphia: Westminster, 1981), 138.

9. Dever, *Early Israelites*, 73. See also Francesco de Magistris, "The *'Apiru* and the Egyptian Domination of Late Bronze Age Israel" (MSc diss., University of Edinburgh, 2014). He notes that more than two hundred documents refer to the *'Apiru* in the Late Bronze Age and that they represented a social phenomenon "composed of 'disenfranchised urban dwellers' who, lacking the possibility of paying their debts and taxes, took to the hills to live as marauders and mercenaries."

of Accho . . . it was they who hastened with fifty chariots – for I had been robbed by the *'Apiru*.[10]

The letter clearly indicates the gravity of the situation from the perspective of one urban ruler, and the reference to the arrival of fifty chariots points to the deployment of what was a new form of military technology to which these embattled kings frequently had access. Walter Brueggemann has pointed out the reference to "horses and chariots" in Joshua 11:4–5, and notes Yahweh's instruction to "hamstring the horses" (v. 6), a command which confirms that the God who had liberated the slaves from Egypt is now "allied with the marginalized, oppressed peasants against the monopoly of the city-state."[11]

Elsewhere in the Armana Letters the king of Shechem assures the pharaoh of his undivided loyalty: "I have not rebelled, I have not sinned. And I do not withhold my tribute, and I do not refuse the request of my commission." This is a ruler under huge pressure from two different sides because Egyptian doubts concerning his reliability have been aroused by the extraordinary revelation that his own son had gone over to the marauding *'Apiru*: "I did not know that my son associates with the *'Apiru* and I have verily delivered him into the hands of Adday. . . . If the king should write to me 'Plunge a bronze dagger into thy heart and die!' how could I refuse to carry out the command of the king?"[12]

What these quotations demonstrate is, first, that the political system of the city-states within Canaan was displaying indications of grave crisis prior

---

10. Quoted in Dever, *Early Israelites*, 171.

11. Walter Brueggemann, *Divine Presence amid Violence: Contextualizing the Book of Joshua* (Eugene: Cascade, 2009), 24. He goes on to say that the narrative in the book of Joshua reveals that "the world of the city-kings is not closed. It is the purpose of 'horses and chariots' to close that world and so to render the peasants hopeless and helpless. But the world ostensibly controlled by oppressive city-kings is now dis-closed, shown to be false, and broken open to the joy of Israel. The revelatory decree of Yahweh breaks the fixed world of the city-kings" (30). Much later in the history of biblical Israel the prophet Zechariah reports hearing the Lord Almighty declaring to the nations which had plundered Jerusalem: "I will surely raise my hand against them *so that their slaves will plunder them* (Zech 2:9).

12. Quoted in Dever, *Early Israelites*, 173. De Magistris says that, whereas earlier kings are portrayed as "just, rightful, loving fathers for the sons of their lands," under Egyptian domination the nature of kingship changed and the model of the "strong, brave, courageous general, who no longer cared about the freedom of his subjects," became widespread ("The *'Apiru* and the Egyptian Domination," 14). As we shall see, it was precisely the fear of such a change in the concept of kingship which prompted Samuel's later opposition to Israel's demand for a king "such as all the other nations have" (1 Sam 8:5).

to the entry of the liberated slaves under the leadership of Joshua. Second, they also suggest that internal movements of protest and rebellion had already erupted and were shaking the foundations of the authority of the privileged elite who could no longer rely upon the forced labour of a docile peasantry taught that the established social order was willed by heaven.[13]

A New Religious Movement in Canaan?

The crucial question which now comes into focus is how did the slaves liberated from Egypt relate to their fellow 'Apiru within the promised land? An important clue to the answer to this question is provided at the very beginning of the Joshua narrative which describes how, when Joshua despatched spies across the river to investigate conditions within Canaan, they found refuge in "the house of a prostitute" (Josh 2:1). This remarkable woman, Rahab, sheltered them and informed them that "great fear" had gripped the local populace. She reported that the inhabitants of the land were "melting in fear," a terror provoked, not because the migrants posed a military threat to the ruling elite, but because she and her people had "heard how the LORD dried up the water of the Red Sea for you when you came out of Egypt" (Josh 2:8–11). That the news of the exodus from Egyptian bondage had spread throughout Palestine, and that this information had profoundly impacted the ruling class, is not surprising since, as we have seen, local rulers held power only with the permission of the pharaohs. Egyptian agents monitored life in the city-states of Canaan, supporting their client rulers in return for the regular supply of goods and services. Consequently, the realization that the liberated slaves had migrated northwards would have set alarm bells ringing in the royal palaces, *while we may imagine it triggered hope among the oppressed underclass, of whom Rahab is surely a representative.*

Rahab's reception and shielding of the spies, her confession that "the LORD your God is God in heaven above and on the earth below," and her courageous identification with the liberated slaves, may be described as a form of *conversion*. Her status as a prostitute locates her within the underclass

---

13. While this present book was being completed I became aware of the important two-volume work of Gregory Boyd, *Crucifixion of the Warrior God: Interpreting the Old Testament's Violent Portraits of God in Light of the Cross* (Minneapolis: Fortress, 2017). This widely praised work is clearly an important contribution to a theological understanding of this subject.

of the city of Jericho since urban prostitutes shared with other groups an identity as "occupational outcasts." That is to say, their services were desired and used, but "because of their demeaning work and the social taboos, codes and conventions which they breached, [they] bore a scapegoating stigma and worked under decided disabilities."[14] Later in the narrative we are informed that Rahab, her family "and all who belonged to her" had begun a new life, living "among the Israelites to this day" (6:25).

If the first person the Yahweh community encountered in Canaan showed a clear understanding of the religious foundation of the social revolution they promised to bring about, and if she identified with their cause in a manner which revealed knowledge of the revolutionary nature of the new faith, might she and her people have been the harbingers of a much wider turning to Yahweh among the oppressed population of the Canaanite city-states? This question has been asked by contemporary Old Testament scholars such as Norman Gottwald who suggests that we may indeed "entertain the logical possibility of the conversion of substantial segments of the Canaanite population to Yahwism."[15] If Rahab and her extended family became integrated within the liberated community, why should her response not be replicated and multiplied elsewhere within this "stress-torn Canaanite society"? Such a new religious movement in which liberated slaves bearing the vision of a new kind of society attracted the sympathy and support of an internal, oppressed underclass would explain the "sudden appearance of a large community in Palestine and Transjordan only a generation after a small group escaped from Egypt under the leadership of Moses."[16]

---

14. Norman K. Gottwald, *The Tribes of Yahweh: A Sociology of the Religion of Liberated Israel, 1250–1050 BCE* (Sheffield: Sheffield Academic, 1999), 557.

15. Gottwald, *Tribes of Yahweh*, 211. Gottwald's book is complex and controversial, but his summary of the different approaches to the early history of Israel is very helpful, pp. 192–219. Gottwald's work is described and critiqued in Leo Perdue's *The Collapse of History: Reconstructing Old Testament Theology* (Minneapolis: Fortress, 1994). He helpfully concludes: "Theologically conceived, it is not the experience of freedom that is exalted in the Bible but rather the love of God and neighbour practiced by a servant people. Liberation is the instrument or means by which obedience and service in the name of love are enhanced, but not the ultimate and final objective of human striving" (107). See also Pekka Pitkänen's "Ethnicity, Assimilation and the Israelite Settlement," *Tyndale Bulletin* 55, no. 2 (2004): 161–82.

16. These are the words of Mendenhall, *Tenth Generation*, 25. I have used the phrase "new religious movement" deliberately here since it suggests an analogy between the conversion of 'Apiru peoples in ancient Palestine and the phenomena given this label by historians of religion seeking to understand mass conversions in primal societies today. See A. F. Walls and Wilbert

I suggest that we discover at this point the deepest roots of what Jesus will, centuries later, identify as "Mammon." There is a direct analogy between Christ's demand that his followers choose between God and Mammon, and the insistence of Joshua that the liberated slaves must decide whether to remain faithful to Yahweh, the covenant God who had set them free, or fall back and embrace the form of sociopolitical life which would continue to fascinate, allure and tempt them. Israel became the community whose life together constituted a religious and social experiment of a people ruled by Yahweh. The later, passionate concern of the Hebrew prophets for social justice was driven, as we shall see, by the catastrophic consequences of precisely such a "falling back." The rejection of the kingship of Yahweh for a "political power structure" which eroded "the old religious ethic in favour of 'being like all the rest of the nations,' obsessed with power, concentration of wealth, and competition in the insane world of power politics," anticipated the conflict between God and Mammon of which Jesus speaks.[17]

The Mosaic Revolution

We have referred a number of times to the events of the exodus, the gift of the Torah, and the creation of a new community devoted to the worship of Yahweh, as a *revolution*. There is a danger that in using this terminology we may be understood to suggest that these events are analogous to the political upheavals of modern times which have been described by such language. That the earliest history of biblical Israel may legitimately be compared to such contemporary historical turning points is granted, yet it is vital to recognize the *differences* between the ancient and modern contexts in order to appreciate the uniqueness of the Mosaic revolution.[18]

Shenk, eds., *Exploring New Religious Movements: Essays in Honour of Harold W. Turner* (Elkhart: Mission Focus, 1990). For a specific example, see Aurélien Mokoko Gampiot, *Kimbanguism: An African Understanding of the Bible* (University Park: Pennsylvania State University Press, 2017).

17. Mendenhall, *Tenth Generation*, 28.

18. Note, however, the important work of Michael Walzer, who argues that the exodus story remains the source of "messianic politics." He quotes a radical English writer who claimed in 1657: "It is a common received opinion; in the Lord's bringing Israel out of Egypt was shadowed out his deliverance of his church and people from all tyranny and oppression in the last days." Walzer concludes that the revolutionary political tradition in Western history belongs especially to Jews and Christians in the West, "and its original source, its original version, is the Exodus of Israel from Egypt" (*Exodus and Revolution* [New York: Basic, 1985], 133, 146).

The world within which that revolution erupted was dominated by imperial powers, so that no significant population group anywhere could escape the political, economic or cultural shaping of "the network of empires which divided the fertile crescent among themselves."[19] As we have seen, for early Israel this meant the dominance of Egypt, but the whole history of this people was to be played out in the shadow of successive empires, each one more powerful and expansive than its predecessor, up to and including the Roman imperium which transcended them all in its reach and power.

What distinguished the biblical revolution from the imperial powers which shaped the ancient world was the perception of the source and nature of political power and the fundamental emphasis upon ethical behaviour in both individual and social life which lay at its heart. "In other words, the covenant-Decalogue established common norms binding on all members of society – and society consisted of those who accepted the common norms. The first, foremost, and most revolutionary of which was the rejection of all obligation to 'other gods.'"[20]

Clearly, we cannot explore in detail the content of the Book of the Law, but we may sum up its entire thrust in the statement of Walter Brueggemann that it revealed Yahweh to be a God "committed to the establishment of concrete, sociopolitical justice in a world of massive power organized against justice." It gave to the exploited, landless and oppressed 'Apiru the possibility of the creation of a "stable, institutional form to the social possibilities engendered by the Exodus."[21] At the same time, while this obviously required concrete laws and social structures intended to ensure the practice of distributive justice, it was also profoundly concerned with what might be called the "spiritual" dimension of the community and of the individuals who belonged to it. This can be seen in the classic example of the Ten Commandments in Exodus 20 which, while they relate to issues concerning property and possession, so creating "a communal disposition to watch for the economic endangerment of other members of the community," conclude with the prohibition

---

19. Mendenhall, *Tenth Generation*, 176.

20. Mendenhall, 194, 196.

21. Walter Brueggemann, *Theology of the Old Testament: Testimony, Dispute, Advocacy* (Minneapolis: Fortress, 1997), 736.

of *covetousness*.[22] In other words, while external structures and practices are crucial to the establishment and maintenance of social justice, the underlying causes of antisocial behaviour are located in the interior realms of human *desires*, and they must also be addressed.[23]

Patrick Miller has studied the Hebrew law codes intensively and notes that the commandment against coveting is sometimes treated as though it provides protection for the rich and privileged against "the encroachment of the poor." One thinks of the way in which in modern societies radical political options proposing structural, economic transformation in the interests of justice are invariably branded as the "politics of envy" by the defenders of the status quo. Miller comments:

> Where one encounters instances of coveting in the Old Testament, they are largely acts of royalty and the wealthy. Coveting is not a problem of the poor. It is the king and the wealthy who lust after and take (for example, David's coveting of Bathsheba and Ahab's coveting of Naboth's vineyard). When the prophets inveigh against those who commit this sin, they clearly have in mind the wealthy who want to acquire more. . . . This does not mean that the poor do not steal. But the cultural problem is the acquisitiveness of the rich and powerful and the development of means – legal and illegal – to appropriate the property of others.[24]

The theme of disordered and misdirected human desire, here discovered to be at the very centre of ancient Israel's religious and ethical concerns, could hardly be more relevant to the context of the modern world. That context is one in which, as we shall see, Mammon expands its domination of an age in which the release of human desire from all traditional restraints and controls has become both culturally acceptable and economically crucial. The Mosaic revolution, far from being a form of legalism which can play no part in the

---

22. Patrick D. Miller, "Property and Possession in Light of the Ten Commandments," in *Having: Property and Possession in Religious and Social Life*, eds. William Schweiker and Charles Mathewes (Grand Rapids: Eerdmans, 2004), 29.

23. In *Money and Possessions*, Walter Brueggemann describes the focus on coveting as the essence of the core narrative of biblical Israel (Interpretation: Resources for the Use of Scripture in the Church [Louisville: Westminster John Knox, 2016], 15ff.).

24. Miller, "Property and Possession," 45.

practice of Christian discipleship, contains resources which will prove vital to those who are determined, like Joshua, to say, "But as for me and my household, we will serve the LORD" (24:15).[25]

I conclude this chapter with the wise words of John V. Taylor:

> Unless, as we have a perfect right to do, we dissociate ourselves entirely from the religion which takes the Bible as its scriptures, we are bound to take seriously the unifying thread which runs through all those scriptures and binds them together. And that thread is the idea that when God set about redeeming the whole of his creation he chose those Hebrew people, liberated them from slavery and gave them a pattern to live by in order that through them all the nations of the world might be blessed. Christians say that this promise was fulfilled in Jesus Christ. But when Jesus came preaching the kingdom he was opening up to the entire world that Kingdom of right relationships which long ago God had invited that one special nation to enter and enjoy. If we take the Bible seriously at all, then we must take seriously the idea that what was first offered to Israel was meant to be a model of the salvation that was to be experienced in the end by all.[26]

---

25. See Samuel E. Balentine, *The Torah's Vision of Worship* (Minneapolis: Fortress, 1999).

26. John V. Taylor, *Enough Is Enough* (London: SCM, 1975), 52. I must add that the "pattern to live by" is that which is described in detail in the Pentateuch and that this vision of the world that God intends is expressed and enabled by the worship prescribed by the Torah. Samuel Balentine discusses this subject at length and concludes that "within the Hebrew Bible the Torah constitutes the founding vision of God and of God's design for the world and for humankind" (*Torah's Vision of Worship*, 34).

CHAPTER 3

Resisting Mammon: Prophets and Wise Men

In the opening chapter of this book we drew attention to Max Weber's recognition of the possibility that "entirely new prophets" might appear in the modern world, capable of challenging the culture of the "iron cage" and offering humankind an alternative vision of individual and social life. Since Weber could envisage the *return* of prophecy, the question arises as to which historical examples of this phenomenon he might have had in mind. Who were the "old" prophets whose impact on their particular times had been significant enough to have resulted in major transformations which reshaped their own era and left a significant legacy within world history? This is an important question since by answering it we may be able to clarify the nature of prophecy and appreciate why a modern intellectual like Weber could recognize the possibility of its reappearance today as a source of hope for the future.

The answer to the question is not difficult to find. Between 1917 and 1919 Max Weber published a series of articles which later appeared in a book with the title *Ancient Judaism*.[1] He suggested that the distinctive character of Christianity, in contrast to the religious traditions of Asia, was its determination to change the world; it was what might be called world-transformative religion. It had received this core characteristic in the first instance from Jesus and Paul, but its true origin had to be traced much further back to the great Hebrew prophets of the eighth, seventh and sixth centuries before Christ.

---

1. Max Weber, *Ancient Judaism*, trans. H. Gerth and D. Martindale (Glencoe: Free Press, 1952).

Weber paid careful attention to the social aspects of this tradition of biblical prophecy and concluded that it had left an indelible mark on the Jewish people and, when inherited and developed within the Christian movement, significantly shaped Western civilization.[2] Weber would, I suspect, have agreed with a recent scholar that biblical Israel's prophets constituted "a great disruptive force in its life and economy" since their outrageous poetic images and metaphors undermined "what had seemed to be a settled, well-ordered society."[3]

From Tribal Society to Monarchical State

It is not my concern here to offer a detailed study of the Hebrew prophets; they are significant for this book as the founders of a tradition of social and economic criticism, courageous and brilliant communication in the public square, and, above all, as the bearers of inspired visions of a different world, shaped by the ethics of the kingdom of God. As such they anticipate and presage the conflict between God and Mammon which is our primary concern. Having said that, it is necessary to take notice of the circumstances within which this revolutionary tradition came into being.[4]

The period of the tribal confederacy of ancient Israel came to an end as the result of the demand of the people for the creation of a state and the appointment of a king "such as all the other nations have" (1 Sam 8:5). There is obviously deep and tragic irony here; we have seen that it was precisely the office of kingship in the context of urbanization which resulted in the social divisions which confronted the '*Apiru* peoples and led to suffering, violence and warfare. Samuel, who is described as "a prophet of the LORD" (3:20), resisted this demand and spelled out the long-term consequences of such a

---

2. In his *General Economic History* Weber said that Judaism "made Christianity possible and gave it the character of a religion essentially free from magic," thus rendering an important service "from the point of view of economic history." Extract in George Dalton, ed., *Tribal and Peasant Economies: Readings in Economic Anthropology* (Austin: University of Texas Press, 1967), 448.

3. Walter Brueggemann, *Money and Possessions*, Interpretation: Resources for the Use of Scripture in the Church (Louisville: Westminster John Knox, 2016), 139.

4. Matthew Coomber's *Re-Reading the Prophets through Corporate Globalization* (Eugene: Cascade, 2022) came into my possession too late to be used in this discussion. It is clearly important in relation to this subject and I note his warning that no one "can claim to have a full understanding of the societal contexts of the prophetic texts attributed to eighth-century Judah or even to know with certainty the period in which they were written or modified" (39).

decision: "the king who will reign over you . . . will take your sons and make them serve with his chariots and horses . . . and others to plough his ground and reap his harvest, and still others to make weapons of war and equipment for his chariots" (8:10–18). In other words, monarchy would inevitably lead over time to the centralization of power, to ever-widening socio-economic divisions, increased militarization, and the creation of a system of taxation to fund the royal lifestyle and glory. But underlying all of these external changes was the conscious rejection of the rule of Yahweh and the ethics of the Torah which demanded "justice and justice alone." Samuel is reported as having communed with God concerning this development and he received from Yahweh the response: "it is not you they have rejected, but they have rejected me as their king" (8:7).

A leading scholar of the prophetic literature in the Hebrew Bible describes the shift in the character of Israel at this point in its history as follows:

> With the break up of the tribal organization and the dissolution of collective solidarity the individual and individual interests were more in evidence. The right to hold private property and to amass possessions was both recognised and practised. Thus the foundation was laid for a fatal class distinction between the rich and the poor, between those who were able to enjoy luxury and plenty and those who had to toil for the barest necessities. The poor and defenceless were often oppressed and fleeced by the wealthy. The judges were bribed to pronounce unjust judgements in favour of those who had power and influence.[5]

This sets the scene for the appearance of the classical Hebrew prophets. We might add that it already suggests a striking analogy with the world of the twenty-first century in which small, traditional communities across the globe, often described as "tribal societies," are everywhere under massive pressure as the result of the spread and dominance of global capitalism. Indigenous peoples on every continent today might read the words we have just quoted and feel that they mirror their experience with an extraordinary clarity at the present time.

---

5. J. Lindblom, *Prophecy in Ancient Israel* (Philadelphia: Fortress, 1962), 347.

Despite Samuel's opposition and warning, the demand for kingship proved irresistible and resulted in the erosion of the covenantal values of the Torah and what would today be described as the "privatization" of religion. The crucial turning point was the reign of Solomon who, despite his reputation for wisdom and the apparent success of his expansionist economic and political policies, adopted a model of kingship and urbanization which involved the enactment of key elements of the systems of governance and centralization of power from which the Israelites had been delivered at the time of the exodus and the overthrow of the Canaanite city-states. His reign began with the intrigue and violence typical of dynastic successions in the ancient world and involved both the banishment of the elderly priest Abiathar to the rural backwater of Anathoth, and a political alliance with Pharaoh, sealed by marriage to the Egyptian ruler's daughter. William Foxwell Albright went so far as to describe the construction of the temple in Jerusalem, notwithstanding Solomon's prayer at its dedication, as "the climax of the Canaanization of Israel."

> The Temple was not intended primarily to be a public place of worship for all Israel, but rather . . . a royal chapel into which the palladium of Israel was brought as a sign that the worship of Yahweh was thereafter to be under the special protection of the king. It was built by a Canaanite architect from Tyre, undoubtedly following Phoenician models, since there was none in Israel to follow.[6]

The negative social consequences of this tremendous development became evident very rapidly in the growing concentration of wealth and privilege among the urban elite of Jerusalem, the heavy taxation of the common people, which later resulted in an uprising and the division of the kingdom, and in the employment of slave labour and the amassing of a military force which included "four thousand stalls for chariot horses" (1 Kgs 4:26). The subsequent history involved a tragic descent into deepening ethical confusion until, by

---

6. William Foxwell Albright, *From Stone Age to Christianity: Monotheism and the Historical Process* (New York: Doubleday, 1957), 293–94. The Jewish philosopher Martin Buber described Solomon's prayer at the dedication of the temple as an "unreserved expression of the aim of the early kingdom to confine YHWH's sovereignty within the cultic sphere alone" (*The Prophetic Faith* [New York: Macmillan, 1949], 82).

the eighth century, "the economy had developed into an unbearable mismatch between the wealth of the *urban elites* in Samaria and Jerusalem and the *vulnerable agricultural peasants* who were reduced to near subsistence existence."[7]

The Message of the Hebrew Prophets

Traditional religions throughout the world rely upon people described by anthropologists as "religious specialists," individuals possessing gifts which enable them to make contact with the realm of the spirits and to "divine" the causes of events such as sickness or death. The world of the ancient Near East was no different, and besides the diviners who communicated messages from the underworld there were also prophetic figures who claimed gifts of discernment and foresight. The Hebrew prophets emerged from this broad religious context, yet their messages alone have remained in circulation across all the centuries up to the present day. According to Klaus Koch, the reason for this is that "they tower far above all comparable intuitive diviners or soothsayers . . . in the acuteness of their thinking and the precision of their language, as well as in their concentration on the one God and the unity of human responsibility."[8]

The historical period during which the classical Hebrew prophets appeared is divided into two very distinct phases by the great catastrophe of the destruction of Jerusalem and the termination of the state by the invading Babylonians in 587/586 BCE. This has been described as the pivotal event in the entire history of biblical Israel, and as such it created two contrasting contexts for prophetic ministry. Prior to that cataclysm the message was shaped by the need to address apostasy and its social, ethical and spiritual consequences. As a result, the pre-exilic prophets sounded the note of urgent warning and anticipated the destruction and loss which would result from the violation of the covenant stipulations. Koch describes the messages of Amos, Isaiah,

---

7. Brueggemann, *Money and Possessions*, 143 (emphasis original). Elsewhere he discusses Solomon's significance in detail, concluding that his perspective "came to dominate urban Israel's imagination," supplanting "the neighbourly demands of Sinai. . . . It is as though Pharaoh, through his son-in-law, had come to rule in Israel as in Egypt. Jerusalem becomes a place that re-enacts Pharaoh's acquisitiveness that is rooted in Pharaoh's anxieties" (*Journey to the Common Good* [Louisville: Westminster John Knox, 2016], 54).

8. Klaus Koch, *The Prophets*, vol. 1, *The Assyrian Period* (Philadelphia: Fortress, 1983), 12.

Hosea and Micah as concerned above all else with the fact that "far too many people are getting on far too well, and that in the near future this is going to lead to an inescapable catastrophe." The prophetic exposure of the ills of society and the pessimistic expectation of the future is "new and unique in the ancient world."[9]

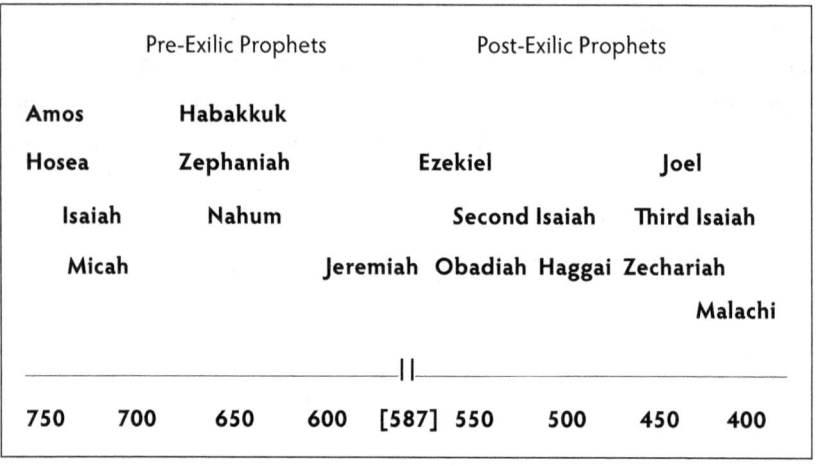

Table 1: Two phases of Hebrew prophecy: before and after the destruction of Jerusalem in 587 BCE[10]

It is important to keep in mind the fact that the foundation of the prophetic message was located in the memory of the exodus and the tribal confederacy when a generation that had known the experience of oppression and slavery had been gifted a new vision of human community and the summons to model this in the sight of other nations. The pre-exilic prophets evaluated the existing society of their times in the light of the demands of the law and covenant and, from that perspective, announced that the social and economic practices they observed around them were *unsustainable* and would inevitably

---

9. Koch, *Assyrian Period*, 4. It is worth quoting at this point from Max Weber's study of Hebrew prophecy: "The possibility of questioning the meaning of the world presupposes the capacity to be astonished about the course of events. Now, the experiences which the Israelites had before the Exile, and which gave them cause to ask such questions, were the great wars of liberation and the rise of kingship, the development of the corvee state and of urban culture, the threat of the great powers" (*Ancient Judaism*, 206–7).

10. The dating of many of these prophets is uncertain and disputed, but there is broad agreement concerning their locations in one or other of the two phases.

result in disaster. Their critique was inspired by Yahweh's declaration to the assembly of ancient Israel: "Be holy because I, the LORD your God, am holy" (Lev 19:2). What this meant in practice is immediately spelled out in the following verses where holiness is defined, not by some ethereal, other-worldly concept, but in terms of the concrete practices of neighbourliness within and beyond the community. The edges of the fields were *not* to be harvested; gleanings were *not* to be gathered up; fallen grapes in the vineyards were *not* to be picked up, but all were left "for the poor and the foreigner." The wages of hired men must *not* be withheld even for one night; the deaf and the blind were to be shown compassion and mercy. Negatively, slander, hatred, revenge or the harbouring of grudges were all actions or dispositions inconsistent with the divine holiness which is then encapsulated in the climactic statement: "love your neighbour as yourself. I am the LORD" (19:18).[11]

The mention of love alerts us to the fact that the underlying cause of ethical failure must be traced back to the tragic loss of memory and of devotion to the God who had elected Israel to be his servant in a broken world. Martin Buber insisted that in the relationship between God and Israel, "love comes first": "Because they love Him with all their heart and with all their soul, they do what they do for Him with all their heart and all their soul. Moreover the love between a man and his neighbour flows from the love of God."[12]

What Leviticus 19:18 reveals is that the command to love the neighbour, far from limiting this obligation within the narrow confines of a particular community, opens it up to the world and to the recognition of "an equal neediness of all human beings for environments that support life." Love here comes into view, "less as an affect or emotion, and more as a special form of

---

11. Andreas Schüle points out that the Hebrew of this text is ambiguous and can be rendered literally as "Love your neighbour – like you." This would justify a translation such as "You shall love your neighbour *as a man like yourself.*" He describes this as one of the most fundamental statements in biblical ethics and says that it contains a concept of equality that is "simply not guaranteed by national, cultural or religious affiliation. To be part of a people group with a given tradition . . . does not yet attain the idea of equality intended in Leviticus 19:18" ("Sharing and Loving: Love, Law, and the Ethics of Cultural Memory in the Pentateuch," in *Having: Property and Possession in Religious and Social Life*, eds. William Schweiker and Charles Mathewes [Grand Rapids: Eerdmans, 2004], 64–67). We may add that this is precisely the point made by Jesus in the parable of the good Samaritan in Luke 10:25–37 where the issue at stake was, "And who is my neighbour?"

12. Buber, *Prophetic Faith*, 160–61.

creativity, which can apply transformative and always new ways to all regions of social life."[13]

The detailed and distinctive messages of each of the pre-exilic prophets cannot be discussed here, but we may identify three central themes common to them all. *First, they all engaged in a sociopolitical critique of a culture which had suppressed the Mosaic prohibition on covetousness.* Beginning with Amos, the consequences of the uncoupling of human desire from the worship of Yahweh and respect for his law is spelled out in the most explicit and dramatic language, exposing the greed and injustice of those who "store up in their fortresses what they have plundered and looted" (3:10). Images of luxury and abundance abound: the powerful who feel "complacent" and "secure" (6:1) move between their "winter houses" and "summer houses," all of which are adorned with ivory (3:15). They consume the finest food and wine while musicians "strum away on your harps like David" (6:5)! Amos repeatedly makes mention of music as though it plays a central role in distracting the elite from the terrible consequences of their lifestyles, deadening the voice of conscience as they "lie on beds adorned with ivory" and "dine on choice lambs and fattened calves" (6:5). In fact, this perversion of the gift of music is linked to one of the great poetic statements of this prophet:

> Away with the noise of your songs!
> I will not listen to the music of your harps.
> But let justice roll on like a river,
> righteousness like a never-failing stream! (5:23–24)[14]

This prophetic demand for justice is persistent, passionate and urgent because while the excessive wealth of the powerful elite is one defining feature of this society, the other is the condition of the common people who paid a very heavy price in the form of poverty, despair and humiliation. The organic connection between these two aspects of social life is made clear when Amos accuses the rich of trampling on the poor and depriving them of justice in the courts (5:11–13). Later, Isaiah will make this structural connection even

---

13. Schüle, "Sharing and Loving," 68.

14. Gerhard von Rad describes Amos as portraying "a thoughtless upper class complacent in its material security." He adds that "all asceticism and any kind of suspicion of material good was really quite alien to Yahwism," so that it can only have been "extreme indulgence which necessitated the raising of such complaints about the enjoyment of material things" (*The Message of the Prophets* [London: SCM, 1968], 107–8).

clearer when he announces God's judgement "against the elders and leaders of his people" because "the plunder from the poor *is in your houses*" (Isa 3:14). Here is a classic example of prophetic language designed to communicate meaning and truth in the most direct manner possible:

> "What do you mean by crushing my people
> and grinding the faces of the poor?"
> declares the Lord, the LORD Almighty. (3:15)

This concern with issues related to property, ownership and the distribution of scarce resources is evident as Isaiah announces a series of woes, beginning with people who

> add house to house
> and join field to field
> till no space is left
> and you live alone in the land. (5:8–9)

The directness of the prophetic proclamation created a *scandal* among the privileged and powerful classes, especially when Isaiah identified the authorities in Jerusalem as "rulers of Sodom . . . you people of Gomorrah!" (1:10). This palpably shocking language was intended to expose the fact that the distinction between Israel and the nations had not just become blurred, but was effectively obliterated! It is not often noticed that this stunning accusation originated earlier with Amos (4:11), while much later, addressing exiled survivors in Babylon, Ezekiel was to draw even starker parallels between Jerusalem and Sodom:

> As surely as I live, declares the Sovereign LORD, *your sister Sodom and her daughters never did what you and your daughters have done.*
> Now this was the sin of your sister Sodom: she and her daughters were arrogant, overfed and unconcerned; *they did not help the poor and needy.* . . . You have done more detestable things than they, *and have made your sisters seem righteous by all these things you have done.* (Ezek 16:48–51)

Language of this kind highlights the fact that the calling to prophetic ministry was an invitation to a life involving loneliness, suffering and the threat of violence and death. With few exceptions the kings surrounded themselves with priests and advisors who were incapable of speaking truth to power and these defenders of the regime regularly identified the prophets as madmen and traitors. Amos was denounced by a court priest who accused him of "raising a conspiracy against you [King Jeroboam] in the very heart of Israel. The land cannot bear all his words" (Amos 7:10–12).[15] This charge, which is repeated time and again by the defenders of the status quo, shows the inevitability that prophetic preaching, faithful to the vision of God's shalom, was bound to be interpreted in royal circles as treasonable, so bringing prophecy into serious conflict with the holders of political and religious power. We are given few glimpses into the personal lives of the prophets, but where they do occur, as most movingly in the case of Jeremiah, the personal price paid by such individuals becomes painfully clear.[16]

There is a sobering warning for us at this point: if Max Weber's "entirely new prophets" were to emerge in the twenty-first century and were able to mount a credible challenge to the global dominance of Mammon, including a fresh articulation of an alternative vision of the future for the human family, the resistance they could expect to meet and the vilification they would face would likely mirror the experience of the pre-exilic prophets of biblical Israel.

Which brings us to the *second* feature common to them all, namely *that the sociopolitical critique of the culture of their times was accompanied by, and inseparable from, the critique of the form which religion had taken during and after the reign of Solomon*. At the risk of pointing out the obvious, we should note that the distinction between politics and religion, so characteristic of the modern world, was unknown at this time. These were societies in which

---

15. Gerhard von Rad describes Amaziah, the priest who opposed Amos, as "a keen-eyed observer with real insight into the force of Amos's words." He adds that the priest correctly recognized the prophetic message "as a real danger to the Israel of the day and to its religious and economic life to that date" (*Message of the Prophets*, 68).

16. John Bright described Jeremiah as the "prophet *contra mundum*" [against the world] and said that his "premonition of disaster" may have contributed to the fact that he never married. "Jeremiah felt that God had commanded him not to marry and that, in taking this course, he was to serve, proleptically, as a memorial to the death of his country. In his loneliness and childlessness he was to be a living symbol of the bereavement of his people" (*Covenant and Promise: The Prophetic Understanding of the Future in Pre-exilic Israel* [Philadelphia: Westminster, 1976], 149). Kathleen O'Connor interprets Jeremiah in the light of modern studies concerning trauma and disaster and says that this led her to the discovery that the book not only gave voice to the afflicted, but proved to be "a most effective instrument of survival and healing" for students who encountered the prophet's confessions (*Jeremiah: Pain and Promise* [Minneapolis: Fortress, 2011], 5).

what would now be described as "religious" was thoroughly integrated with every other aspect of culture. That being the case, the function and content of faith and worship mattered a great deal, since it either underpinned a society characterized by justice and mercy, or it functioned ideologically to grant an aura of sacredness to systems in which the exercise of power and privilege was exploitative and oppressive. The tragedy of biblical Israel was that, having been gifted a radical faith designed to bring into being the first kind of society, it progressively lost its way and degenerated into the second type. How did this come about?

With the capture of the old Canaanite city of Jebus by King David and its development as the new capital of Israel, Jerusalem ushered in a new phase in the nation's history. Earlier we noticed the emergence of cities throughout the Fertile Crescent and the iconic buildings – palaces, temples and granaries – which dotted their skylines, reflecting their religious, social and economic character. This same complex of structures appeared in Jerusalem during the reigns of David and his son Solomon, so that the very skyline of Israel's new capital eventually displayed visible evidence of the fusion of the covenantal tradition received from Moses with beliefs, values and practices imported from other peoples. As long as David ruled, the covenantal traditions retained their influence within the new urban culture which gained increasing significance in the nation, but once his son Solomon took the throne change was rapid, extensive and radical. Every single aspect of the negative developments which the aged Samuel had predicted and feared now became realities and, as we have already noticed, Solomon asserted his freedom to reshape the society according to royal fiats, reducing the role of religion to providing celebratory praise for his reforms and the uncritical adulation of his glory. Jerusalem was to become "exactly the kind of city to which Joshua had so vigorously and negatively responded."[17]

Turning back to Amos, we note how he exposes the drift of public acts of worship in Samaria towards loud and ecstatic songs of praise with no

---

17. Walter Brueggemann, *Mandate to Difference: An Invitation to the Contemporary Church* (Louisville: Westminster John Knox, 2007), 17. Elsewhere Brueggemann describes Solomon's reign as a model of a society "that smacks of *privilege, entitlement,* and *exploitation,* all in the name of the God of the three-chambered temple, the three chambers that partition social life and social resources into *the qualified, the partially qualified,* and the *disqualified*" (*Journey to the Common Good,* 54).

connection to the realities of social injustice and private greed which marked the lives of worshippers. Amos announced God's verdict on such religion: "I hate, I despise your religious festivals; your assemblies are a stench to me" (Amos 5:21). Over time the situation was to grow much worse as what has been called the "Royal Temple Ideology" in Jerusalem hardened into a fervent nationalism in which the very existence of the temple was interpreted as a guarantee that Israel would be inviolate, irrespective of its moral condition. By the time of Jeremiah, which we may describe as one minute to midnight, the covenant with David and the choice of Mount Zion as God's abode "had hardened into the national dogma which the people clutched to their hearts: *this* nation and *this* dynasty will always endure, for so God has promised!"[18]

In what may be the greatest example of prophetic preaching in all of this literature we catch clear echoes of this nationalist ideology in the mass chanting of the phrase, "This is the temple of the LORD, the temple of the LORD, the temple of the LORD!" (Jer 7:4). Jeremiah quoted this liturgical statement in a prophetic utterance delivered at the entrance to the temple, and then had the temerity to denounce such language as "deceptive words." The divorce between public devotion and private behaviour is immediately clear in what follows: "If you really *change your ways and your actions* and deal with each other justly . . . then I will let you live in this place" (7:5–8). As if attacking the liturgy was not bold enough, the preacher proceeded to engage in a wholesale repudiation of the Royal Temple Ideology and ended by stripping away the veneer of sanctity, describing the temple as a "den of robbers" (vv. 9–11)! In the uproar which followed the prophet barely escaped with his life.

If the prophetic critique of religion focused attention on the divorce between worship and ethical behaviour and its reduction to a form of ideology which justified a narrow nationalism, it was also prompted by the passionate conviction that Yahweh was being reduced to a cultic deity in this process. In other words, the prophets were concerned for the glory of Israel's God as the Creator and Lord of the whole earth and all its peoples. As we shall see, this theme was to move centre stage after the destruction of Jerusalem and the exile in Babylon, but it is present from the very beginning, as can be seen in a remarkable passage towards the end of the book of Amos:

---

18. John Bright, *Covenant and Promise*, 165.

> Are not you Israelites
> > the same to me as the Cushites?
> > > declares the LORD.
> > Did I not bring Israel up from Egypt,
> > > the Philistines from Caphtor
> > > and the Arameans from Kir? (Amos 9:7)

This astonishing text articulates a theology which is the antithesis of religion deployed as ideological support for a narrow nationalism; it insists on God's equal concern for all peoples and, in a rebuttal of a reading of the exodus as an unparalleled event, declares the divine involvement in the key historical moments of other nations. As James Luther Mays has said, Amos knows Yahweh "pre-eminently as the God of the world and his relation to Israel is viewed as an aspect of his total sovereignty."[19]

It will be remembered that Max Weber was concerned with the nature of the relationship between the Protestant Reformation and the emergence of the modern capitalist system, which compels us to ask: is there an analogy between the critique of religion by the Hebrew prophets six hundred years before Christ, and the context in which Christianity exists in the contemporary world? This is not to suggest that the nature of the relationship between religion and Weber's iron cage is straightforward, or that we can make a direct connection between this situation and the prophetic critique of pre-exilic Israel. We shall return to this subject later in this book, but here we suggest that any emergence of prophecy in the twenty-first century is bound to take seriously the criticism of religion in relation to the universal dominance of Mammon in a globalized world. We are not arguing that religion might act as the *basis* for such criticism, but rather that religion itself must be the *object* of criticism to the extent that it has functioned ideologically in support of this

---

19. James Luther Mays, *Amos*, The Old Testament Library (Philadelphia: Westminster, 1969), 6. Elsewhere he says: "Yahweh is exalted over against Israel, exalted in such a way that their existence as the people of Yahweh is stripped of all self-assertion and self-security that protects and hides them from the reality of Yahweh" (158). See too Walter Brueggemann's discussion "Exodus in the Plural (Amos 9:7)," in *Texts That Linger, Words That Explode: Listening to Prophetic Voices* (Minneapolis: Fortress, 2000), 89–103. He concludes that as the cry of Israel had risen up to God, "so we may imagine that the cry of these restive neighbors 'rose up to God,' for this God is oddly and characteristically attentive to the cry of the bondaged who find enough voice for self-announcement, that is, who become agents of their own history" (97).

development. As we saw in chapter 1, there is clear evidence that Christianity has succumbed to the attractive power of this all-embracing idolatry.[20]

We turn to the *third* theme common to pre-exilic prophecy, namely *the concern with the ecological consequences of the broken covenant and the link between human sin and selfishness and the threat posed to the whole of creation*. Once again it is important to notice that we are dealing here with pre-modern worldviews in which human activity has an integral relationship both to the rest of creation and to an unseen realm populated by spiritual powers. Evolutionary views of the history of religion and concepts such as "development" and "civilization" have conditioned us to regard such holistic worldviews with a patronizing sense of our own superiority, but as the extinction of species accelerates and the planet burns we need to hear the ancient prophetic perspective concerning the relationship between human sin and environmental degradation.[21]

While, as we have seen, the primary concern of the prophets was with Israel and its relationship with Yahweh, they were also deeply conscious of other nations, especially the successive imperial powers which cast long shadows across the ancient world. Walter Brueggemann has shown how the prophets struggled to maintain Israel's distinct identity and to "protect space for its liberated imagination," *always in the shadow of empire*.[22] The reality of the imperial powers of Egypt, Assyria, Babylon and Persia, of their vast armies spreading across the Fertile Crescent and clashing in pitched battles, and of new forms of military technology wreaking destruction and death on a scale previously unimagined, is reflected in the prophetic texts.[23] Consider the words of Isaiah which depict the impact on the created world of both

---

20. Karl Marx, who was the son of a Jewish convert to Christianity, was familiar with the Hebrew prophets, said that the criticism of religion "is the premise of all criticism." Christians have paid little attention to Marx's discussion of this subject, yet his insight into the ideological function of much religion during the modern period is deeply challenging. See David Smith, *Marx and Jesus in a Post-Communist World* (Leicester: Religious and Theological Studies Fellowship, 1992). Available online at https://biblicalstudies.org.uk/pdf/rtsf/marx_smith.pdf.

21. I have discussed this subject in *Seeking a City with Foundations: Theology for an Urban World* (Carlisle: Langham Global Library, 2019), 177–85.

22. Brueggemann, *Texts That Linger*, 74.

23. Max Weber's description of the broad context of the pre-exilic prophets is graphic: "Syria became a theatre of hitherto unprecedented military events. Never before had the world experienced warfare of such frightfulness and magnitude as that practiced by the Assyrian kings. Blood fairly drips from the cuneiform inscriptions.... As impending gloom beclouded the political horizon, classical prophecy acquired its characteristic form" (*Ancient Judaism*, 267).

urban economies built on greed and heartless accumulation, and military conflicts which left the earth barren and exhausted, destroyed beneath the weight of the insatiable appetites and loveless conquests of its inhabitants:

> The earth dries up and withers,
> > the world languishes and withers,
> > the heavens languish with the earth.
> The earth is defiled by its people;
> > they have disobeyed the laws,
> violated the statutes
> > and broken the everlasting covenant.
> Therefore a curse consumes the earth;
> > its people must bear their guilt. (Isa 24:4–6)

There is clearly an international, even universal, dimension to this text, as though the prophetic lens has widened to embrace the consequences of human sin and folly on a scale much vaster than the local, national concerns which are more often in view. It is the *world*, the whole earth and all its peoples, facing ecological disaster as the consequence of the breaking of the "everlasting covenant."

A number of times in this discussion we have used the phrase the "Fertile Crescent" to refer to the great arc of land which stretched from the Euphrates and Tigris valleys, round to Lebanon and Palestine, and down to the River Nile and Egypt. The name given to this entire region reflected its lush vegetation and a climate conducive to an abundance of fruitful fields and prosperous vineyards. And yet, as the urbanist scholar Jane Jacobs pointed out, a region once covered in forests suffered a devastating ecological collapse from which it has never recovered.

> To obtain more farmland and more timber, and to satisfy the plaster industry's relentless demands for wood fuel, the forests were cut faster than they could regenerate. Denuded valleys silted up, and intensified irrigation led to salt accumulations in the soil. Overgrazing by goats, allowing new growth no start in life, sealed the destruction.[24]

---

24. Jane Jacobs, *Dark Age Ahead* (New York: Vintage, 1993), 15.

Jacobs believed that the loss of the Fertile Crescent was a sobering warning to the modern world which, as it continues to urbanize at an unprecedented rate, paying lip service to crucial issues concerning sustainability, is "rushing headlong into a new Dark Age." Suddenly the words of Isaiah leap from the page, crossing the gap of more than two thousand years to address the existential crisis of the urban world of today. The same may be said of the prophet Hosea who described a society in which there was "no faithfulness, no love, no acknowledgment of God in the land," with negative consequences for the rest of creation:

> *Because of this* the land dries up,
>   and all who live in it waste away;
> the beasts of the field, the birds in the sky
>   and the fish in the sea are swept away. (Hos 4:1, 3)

The theme of creation, and of Yahweh as creator, becomes very significant after the loss of Jerusalem and during the exile, but it is important to stress that the concern of the pre-exilic prophets with the impact of human sin on the created world already indicates that the redemptive work of God in the election of Israel was understood to be related to the original divine purposes in creation.[25] Yahweh's vision of redemption extended beyond the chosen people to the nations and, ultimately, beyond humankind to the entire created world. There is theological significance in the fact that the Genesis creation narratives precede the story of the exodus; the latter describes the commencement of God's redemptive work which reaches towards its ultimate horizon *in the restoration and perfection of the former.* As Terence Fretheim says, God as creator has a purpose that spans the world, and his "redemptive activity on Israel's behalf must be understood to serve this universal intention."[26] He points out that many aspects of the Mosaic laws concerning social organization

---

25. Note the comment of Claus Westermann that the fact that God is creator means that "he continues to work in the world and in mankind even outside the people of God and without visible connection to his action in salvation history. God remains the Lord of mankind, the Lord of history, the Lord of the cosmos; the history of believers is not identical with the history of God with his creation" ("Creation and History in the Old Testament," in *The Gospel and Human Destiny*, ed. Vilmos Vajta [Minneapolis: Augsburg, 1971], 17).

26. Terence E. Fretheim, "The Reclamation of Creation: Redemption and Law in Exodus," *Interpretation* 45, no. 4 (Oct. 1991): 356.

have parallels among other peoples in the ancient Near East, and this fact is testimony "to God's work as creator among these peoples."

It is now made clear to the redeemed people what their responsibilities are in God's reclaimed world. The law is given to be of service in the ongoing divine task of the reclamation of creation. In the obedience of the law, Israel in effect becomes a *created co-reclaimer* of God's intentions for creation.[27]

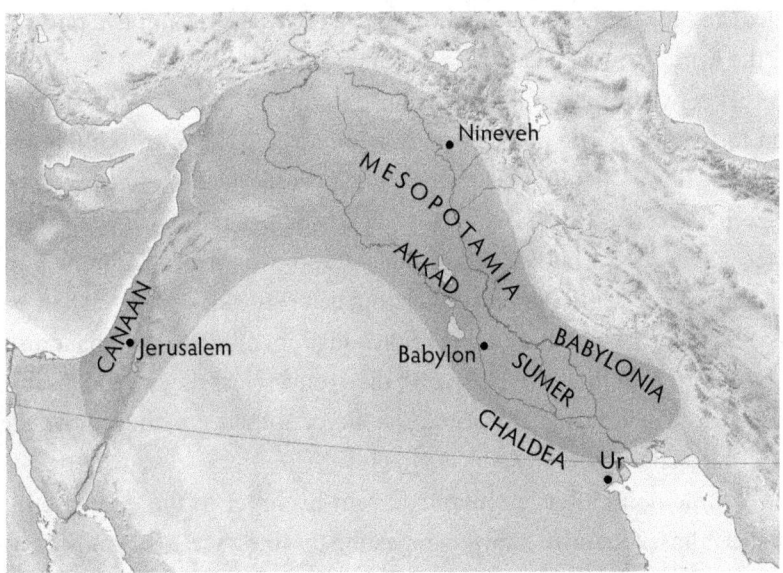

Figure 1: The Fertile Crescent in the Ancient Near East[28]

---

27. Fretheim, "Reclamation of Creation," 365. In a fascinating discussion of the ecology of Galilee, Sean Freyne comments, "For both parts of the Hebrew Bible – the Law and the Prophets – human life and the life of animals and plants are inextricably bound together for good or ill." He adds that in the biblical perspective as a whole, "human redemption can only be considered in conjunction with the redemption of the earth itself" (*Jesus, a Jewish Galilean: A New Reading of the Jesus-Story* [London: T&T Clark, 2004], 34).

28. Adapted from: Sémhur, https://commons.m.wikimedia.org/wiki/File:Fertile_Crescent.png. CC BY-SA 3.0, https://creativecommons.org/licenses/by-sa/3.0/deed.en

Coming to Terms with Endings

We have seen how the cataclysmic event of the destruction of the city of Jerusalem and the exile in Babylon divided Hebrew prophecy into two distinct phases. In the first of these, as is evident from the previous discussion, it was the difficult and costly task of the prophets to expose the corruption and apostasy of their own people and to announce that the historical trajectory of their society was moving inexorably towards tragedy, death and the collapse of the existing religious and sociopolitical arrangements. The mood of these prophets darkened as all hope of repentance and genuine transformation faded, and it became disturbingly clear that Yahweh's redemptive purposes for the world necessitated a truly radical, fresh beginning.

This conviction is dramatically illustrated in the letter which Jeremiah sent to the first group of exiles in Babylon, urging them to "build houses and settle down" and to "seek the peace and prosperity of the city" to which Yahweh had carried them (Jer 29:5–7). He encouraged the Jewish expatriates to recognize that the outworking of God's purpose for them and for the world would become clear in the land of exile, but before that could happen they had to come to terms with the ending of the kingdom of Judah and abandon all hope of a "return to normal." Beyond the agony of loss they would discover a newness which would transcend the limits of their previous knowledge and understanding.

At some point after Jeremiah had sent his letter to the exiles we find Ezekiel, himself living in Babylon, repeating this message: "The *end*! The *end* has come upon the four corners of the land! The *end* is now upon you" (Ezek 7:1–14). The radical transformation that was needed would be painful and it would be many years before the fresh vision emerged to be embraced by a new generation capable of moving beyond the darkness which found such moving expression in the book of Lamentations. However, only by accepting the ending of the old, familiar world could the exiles come to embrace the divine comfort and healing and the extraordinary gift of fresh hope.

We pause here to ask in what ways might the character and message of the pre-exilic Hebrew prophets suggest the nature of the challenges which would confront people possessing prophetic insight into the crisis of the modern world in the twenty-first century? In 1947, in the immediate aftermath of the Second World War, with the images of the Holocaust and the mushroom clouds over Hiroshima and Nagasaki seared into the consciousness of the post-war generation, Paul Tillich published a series of sermons preached in the USA with the title *The Shaking of the Foundations*. One of these studies was based on Isaiah 43:18–19: "Forget the former things; do not dwell on the past. See, I am doing a new thing!" I quote at some length from this exposition since it illustrates so well the analogy between the crisis of ancient Israel and that which increasingly envelops the modern world.

> At the beginning of our period we decided for *freedom*. It was a right decision; it created something new and great in history. But in that decision we excluded the security, social and spiritual, without which man cannot live and grow. And now, in the old age of our period, the quest to sacrifice freedom for security splits every nation and the whole world with really demonic power. We have decided for *means* to control nature and society. We have created them and we have brought about something great and new in the history of all mankind. But we have excluded ends. We have never been ready to answer the question, "For What?" And now, when we approach old age, the means claim to be the ends; our tools have become our masters, and the most powerful of them have become a threat to our very existence. We have decided for *reason* against outgrown traditions and honoured superstitions. That was a great and courageous decision and it gave a new dignity to man. But we have, in that decision, excluded the soul, the ground and power of life. We have cut off our mind from our soul; we have suppressed and mistreated the soul within us, in other men, and in nature. And now when we are old, the forces of the soul break destructively into our minds, driving us to mental disease and insanity, and effecting the disintegration of the souls of uncounted millions, especially in this country, but also all over the world.[29]

The analogy between the message of the pre-exilic prophets as we have discussed this above and the context of the contemporary world can be seen in this prescient analysis of modern culture and its crisis. Tillich went on to say that the new in history always comes when people least believe in it, but it

---

29. Paul Tillich, *The Shaking of the Foundations* (Harmondsworth: Penguin, 1962), 179–80.

appears "only in the moment when the old becomes visible *as* old and tragic and dying, and when no way out is seen. We live in such a moment; such a moment is *our* situation."[30]

Beyond the Abyss

What then of the "new beginning" for ancient Israel? If the message of the pre-exilic prophets was fundamentally *critical* and counterculturual, beyond the catastrophe and following years of anguish and lament the need was for the recovery of hope and for a fresh vision of God and his purposes for the world. Genuine movements of prophecy can never be only critical and resistant but must also offer an alternative vision and a credible hope for humankind and for the world. The repeated complaint of the author of Lamentations was that "there is no one to comfort me" – the phrase echoes like a mournful, clanging bell throughout the poems, and the charge is levelled not only at people who lacked the ability to express empathy, but also at God, who is said to have covered himself with a cloud "so that no prayer can get through."[31]

It is precisely that complaint which receives an extraordinary response from the great "prophet of the exile," identified by modern scholarship as "Second Isaiah" (or "Deutero-Isaiah"). The first words of his "book of comfort" pick up the complaint of Lamentations and offer a pastoral assurance to the wounded heart: "Comfort, comfort my people" (Isa 40:1). The chapters which follow demonstrate that this is no empty theological platitude, nor do they simply attempt to rework the old theology which has been found wanting, but display instead an astonishing newness and break completely fresh ground in the unfolding of a glorious vision which extends not only to the healing of Israel, but to the nations and the whole created world. What is announced in these chapters amounts to a second exodus, although the reminder of the deliverance which had brought the nation into being, when Yahweh had "made a way through the sea, a path through the mighty waters," is immediately followed by the instruction to *forget the former things* and no longer *dwell on the past* (Isa 43:16–19). The word of comfort to the exiles is genuinely transformative precisely because God is about to do an utterly "new

---

30. Tillich, *Shaking of the Foundations*, 183.
31. See Lam 1:16–17, 21; 3:8, 44, 49–50.

thing" which will surpass the events which had provided the foundation for Israel's existence and faith to this point.

Gerhard von Rad believed that Second Isaiah's description of the new exodus put "a question mark against Israel's original confession" and encouraged his contemporaries to "look away from that event which so far had been the basis of their faith, and to put their faith in the new and greater one."

> By the "new" event he means the saving act about to come after a long pause in the saving history, and which he as a prophet can foresee from the course of secular history.... And because the task Yahweh is now undertaking is so marvellous and will so eclipse his previous ones, Deutero-Isaiah believed that his contemporaries should concentrate all their thought upon it and turn away from the events which had previously given their faith its content.[32]

We may question whether the prophet's theology is as "supersessionist" as von Rad suggests, not least because elsewhere Yahweh *reminds* Israel that they are "descendants of Abraham my friend" and that he had taken them "from the ends of the earth" to be his servants (41:8–9). Claus Westermann observes that Second Isaiah appeals to tradition *more than any other prophet*, so that the intention in this text is not the displacement of the exodus tradition, but rather the urging of the exiles to "stop mournfully looking back and clinging to the past" and to open their minds to the fact "that a new, miraculous act of God lies ahead of you."

> Israel requires to be shaken out of a faith that has nothing to learn about God's activity, and therefore nothing to learn about what is possible with him, the great danger which threatens any

---

32. Von Rad, *Message of the Prophets*, 214–15. Daniel Smith-Christopher goes even further to suggest that the exodus event does not provide a helpful model for theology today. "Exodus is the road to nationalism and power. But there is another biblical paradigm. It is a warning against Exodus theology. In the place of Joshua the revolutionary conqueror, it points to Jeremiah the prophet of subversive righteousness and Ezra the priest of a radically alternative community. In the place of David the emperor, it points to Daniel the wise. In the place of Solomon's great Temple, it points to the perseverance of singing the Lord's song in a foreign land. It is a religion of the landless, the faith of those who dwell in Babylon" (Daniel L. Smith-Christopher, *The Religion of the Landless: The Social Context of the Babylonian Exile* [Eugene: Wipf & Stock, 1989], 205).

faith that is hidebound in dogmatism, faith that has ceased to be able to expect anything really new from him.[33]

While Second Isaiah spoke to a generation still traumatized by the loss of Jerusalem and the memory of the death and devastation which had accompanied it, there were other, more insidious sources of doubt concerning the faith of Israel. Jeremiah's earlier instruction to the exiles to "build houses . . . settle down . . . marry and have sons and daughters" had doubtless been acted upon for some time, and with that settlement came the possibility of assimilation to the religion and culture of Babylon. The architectural splendour of the city of Babylon and its hanging gardens is well known, and the brute fact of the empire's proven superiority as a world power must have presented a temptation to people who had been informed by their prophets that their own traditions had reached a terminal point. Indeed, Second Isaiah's devastating parody of the idols of Babylon must have been prompted to some degree by the knowledge that some exiles were attracted to the local cults, not least because assimilation to the conqueror's religion could result in material benefits.[34]

In fact, we do not need to speculate about this because the prophet Jeremiah, taken to Egypt after the fall of Jerusalem, reported his discovery of Jewish exiles "burning incense to other gods" (Jer 44:6–8). Faithful to the last, Jeremiah challenged this syncretism, only to be met with unambiguous rejection: "We will not listen to the message you have spoken to us in the name of the LORD! . . . We will burn incense to the Queen of Heaven." The exiles justified their worship of "the Queen of Heaven" on the grounds that, first, they were merely following a pattern of syncretic religion long practised by "our kings and our officials . . . in the streets of Jerusalem," and second, that at that time "we had plenty of food and were well off and suffered no harm" (44:16–18)![35]

---

33. Claus Westermann, *Isaiah 40-66: A Commentary* (Philadelphia: Westminster, 1969), 127–29.

34. Isa 44:6–22. See also Ezek 20:32. Peter Ackroyd comments: "It seems right to see here the despairing outlook of those who see no hope for the future, and look only to an assimilation to the ways of the nations" (*Exile and Restoration: A Study of Hebrew Thought in the Sixth Century BC* [Philadelphia: Westminster, 1968], 42).

35. John Bright comments that the goddess mentioned here was probably the Assyrian-Babylonian deity Ishtar whose cult may have been fused with that of a Canaanite goddess named Shapash (*Jeremiah*, The Anchor Bible [New York: Doubleday, 1965], 56).

Crucially for this study, there were *economic* factors at work here since the exiled peoples who had lost everything in their homeland were liable to be lured by material inducements to reach an accommodation with the dominant culture and its religion. Indeed, we may suggest that Jeremiah experienced this pressure himself when, bound in chains and about to be transported to Babylon, he was released and offered safe passage by the commander of the imperial guard, with the promise, "if you like . . . I will look after you" (40:1–4). To his credit, the prophet declined the offer of a sinecure provided by the empire, but references elsewhere to exiles who "have no money," and to others who were tempted to "spend money on what is not bread, and your labour on what does not satisfy" (Isa 55:1–2) suggest the significance of the economic dimension of the exile. Moreover, this was precisely the period in which money and coinage began to reshape the economic and social life of the ancient Near East.

It is against this background that Second Isaiah's extraordinary vision stands at the pinnacle of the history of Hebrew prophecy. The great visions contained in chapters 40–55 lifted the prophetic tradition to a new plane, extending the theology of creation beyond concerns with origins, or with the sustaining of the natural world, to embrace the belief that the God who had subdued the primal chaos in the beginning was now able to control the historical forces which threatened the social world with ethical and existential chaos. Yahweh, who had been reduced to the level of a cultic deity in Jerusalem, is now revealed as the God of the whole earth, the Lord, "the Maker of all things, who stretches out the heavens" (44:24), and who now calls the Persian king, Cyrus, his anointed servant to subdue the nations and bring deliverance to the exiles.[36] What is predicted in these extraordinary chapters is an event by which Yahweh will bring "my sons from afar and my daughters from the ends of the earth" (43:6) as the prelude to the universal salvation implied in the breathtaking invitation:

---

36. The enlargement of the doctrine of creation and its application to the unfolding of world history is evident again and again in these chapters. See 40:12–17, 25–28; 42:5–9; 43:15–21; 45:5–13, 18–25. Claus Westermann says that the emergence of Cyrus and the Persian Empire marked the point at which the close link "between a god's lordship and the political power possessed by his sphere of influence began gradually to be severed, until finally it broke altogether." He adds the significant comment: "The political power wielded by the Christian Church in the Middle Ages represents a serious decline from this insight of Deutero-Isaiah" (*Isaiah 40–66*, 16).

> Turn to me and be saved,
>> all you ends of the earth;
>> for I am God, and there is no other.
> By myself I have sworn,
>> my mouth has uttered in all integrity
>> a word that will not be revoked:
> before me every knee will bow;
>> by me every tongue will swear.
> They will say of me, "In the LORD alone
>> are deliverance and strength." (45:22–24)

Gerhard von Rad stresses the originality of this vision both in its universal reach and in the unveiling of the *pathos* of God. "Never before had Yahweh spoken in such a way by the lips of a prophet. Never before had he come so close to his people . . . laying aside anything that might alarm them in case he should terrify one of those who had lost heart."[37]

We noticed earlier that this prophet discerned the redemptive purposes of Yahweh from his reading of the meaning of secular history, specifically from the rise of the Persian Empire and the policies of Cyrus, now identified as God's anointed servant. The actions of Cyrus would set in motion the sequence of events which would ultimately result in the fulfilment of God's dream of shalom. The pre-exilic prophets had occasionally glimpsed "the last days" when the nations would "beat their swords into ploughshares," abandon even training for war, and when a highway would be constructed to link the great powers of the Fertile Crescent in an alliance which would lead the Lord Almighty to declare: "Blessed be Egypt *my people*, Assyria *my handiwork*, and Israel *my inheritance*" (Isa 19:25). This great vision was precisely the "new thing" which Second Isaiah now announced as being set in motion by the historical events he observed occurring in his time.

However, if Cyrus was the initial agent of the great transformation, its fulfilment in a universal redemption extending to all nations would require another, very different, servant of Yahweh. We cannot discuss the famous "Servant Songs" here except to notice, first, that the terminology they employ to describe Israel's renewal, predicting that the servant of the Lord will "restore *the tribes of Jacob*" (Isa 49:6), reaches back behind the history of the kings

---

37. Von Rad, *Message of the Prophets*, 217.

to the earliest period of the tribal confederation. Elsewhere in the prophetic books Yahweh is depicted as recalling this primal period in language which might be described as "wistful," identifying it as the time when "Israel was a child" and "I led them with cords of human kindness, with ties of love" (Hos 11:1–4). The same prophet anticipated Israel recognizing that the period of the monarchy had resulted in a distortion of the nation's true identity:

> We have no king
>   because we did not revere the LORD.
> But even if we had a king,
>   what could he do for us? (10:3–4)

Thus, in relation to Israel the work of the Servant will be to recover and renew a society shaped by the Mosaic concern for justice, creating a countercultural model of human community in the sight of all peoples, since the ultimate goal of the Servant's mission is to "bring justice to the nations," a task in which he would not falter until "he establishes justice on earth" (Isa 42:1–4).[38]

Which leads us to the second feature of these wonderful poems, namely the fact that since the Servant's task is to initiate a new exodus, transcending the scope and nature of that which brought Israel into being, this person will be a figure of importance to the world, to all nations, recalling the role of Moses at the beginning of Israel's history, but achieving nothing less than the redemption of humankind from slavery and the vanquishing of every hostile power through his obedience to the will of Yahweh. Von Rad describes the "universal sweep" of the prediction in these poems as going far beyond all previous prophecy in their anticipation of "the prophetic mediator for the world."[39]

Counterpoint: The Voice of Wisdom

To move from Second Isaiah to the book of Ecclesiastes is to pass from the sublime to the most down-to-earth, ambivalent and controversial piece of literature within the Hebrew Bible. It has been described as the strangest book

---

38. The Servant Songs are found in Isa 42:1–4; 49:1–6; 50:4–9; 52:13 – 53:12.

39. Von Rad, *Message of the Prophets*, 228. Elsewhere he says that once Yahweh has completed his work for Israel, "there will be a universal 'twilight of the gods' among the nations, for the heathen will realize the impotence of their idols" (216).

to gain recognition as Holy Scripture, and as diverging so radically from the teaching of the Law and the Prophets as to defy all attempts to harmonize its message with the "tone and teaching of the rest of the Bible."[40] If this were to be the case then perhaps we should have identified the shift as one from the sublime to the ridiculous!

Fortunately, it is not true. Ecclesiastes is recognized as belonging to the tradition of Hebrew thought and teaching known as wisdom literature. This already places it at a distance from the prophets since the "wise" in Israel, in common with parallel traditions among other peoples of the ancient Near East, confronted the hard realities of life and human experience, reflecting on the challenges posed by suffering, the persistence of inequalities, and the threat that death posed to the meaning of human existence. This is theology done at the coalface of real life, unwilling to take refuge in dogmatic certainties when they involve the suppression of the hard questions arising from life in the world, and determined to give voice to the pain and struggle of people crushed by injustice and unable to celebrate the visions of the prophets.

What makes this book of particular interest to us is that, like Second Isaiah, it is post-exilic and seems to have come from the Persian period following the reign of Cyrus.[41] The precise dating of Ecclesiastes has been much debated but

---

40. These are the words of R. B. Y. Scott whose original Anchor Bible commentary on this book covers little more than 150 pages. He suggests that the God described by this biblical writer "is not Yahweh, the covenant God of Israel," but a "mysterious, inscrutable Being whose existence must be presupposed as that which determines the life and fate of man" (*Proverbs and Ecclesiastes: A New Translation with Introduction and Commentary*, Anchor Bible [New York: Doubleday, 1965], 191). Contrast this approach with that of Jacques Ellul who, writing near the end of his life, said he had explored Ecclesiastes more than any other book in the Bible: "It has perhaps given me more, spoken to me more, than any other" (*Reason for Being: A Meditation on Ecclesiastes* [Grand Rapids: Eerdmans, 1990], 1).

41. Choon-Leong Seow says that our knowledge of the socio-economic environment of this period "has been significantly enriched in recent decades by a wealth of epigraphic finds" which reveal "the socioeconomic world in which Qohelet lived and taught" (*Ecclesiastes: A New Translation with Introduction and Commentary* [New Haven: Yale University Press, 1997], 21). Michael Welker notes that many scholars argue for a later date for Ecclesiastes, placing it in the Hellenistic period, but either way the emphasis upon "the unending effort to make money and hoard wealth" and "the dangers of dependence upon the arbitrariness of the powerful, which increases in a standardized, monetary system," remains a central concern of the author ("Kohelet and the Co-evolution of a Monetary Economy and Religion," in *Money as God? The Monetization of the Market and Its Impact on Religion, Politics, Law and Ethics*, eds. Jürgen von Hagen and Michael Welker [Cambridge: Cambridge University Press, 2014], 100–101). Elsewhere in that important book note Andreas Schüle, "'Do Not Sell Your Soul for Money': Economy and Eschatology in Biblical and Intertestamental Traditions," *Money as God?*, 365–78.

both internal linguistic evidence and the correspondence between the leading themes of the book and what is now known concerning this period of Persian dominance suggest that it may well have emerged at some point between the second half of the fifth century and the first half of the fourth century BCE.

Two features of the context of this book are particularly important. *First*, not only is Ecclesiastes post-exilic, but it comes from *the final phase of the history of biblical Israel* as this is recorded in the Hebrew Bible. Groups of exiles had returned to the ruins of Jerusalem under the leadership of Ezra and Nehemiah and the initial response to these events found expression in the ecstatic celebration of the psalms written in this period. The returning captives confessed to being "like those who dreamed," whose "mouths were filled with laughter, our tongues with songs of joy" (Ps 126:1–3). As Second Isaiah had predicted, Yahweh had indeed used his servant, Cyrus, to make possible the return to Palestine in order to rebuild Jerusalem, and in the process had healed the broken-hearted and bound up their wounds (Ps 147:1–3).

However, this initial euphoria was to fade as the full extent of the task of rebuilding became clear, and both the reality of the strength of opposition and internal divisions within the community became evident. The return from exile had not triggered the spread of the glory of the Lord throughout the earth as the prophets had seemed to promise, and discouragement now gave birth to doubts concerning the reliability of the prophetic words. We have evidence of this in the closing chapters of the book of Isaiah which appear to be the work of a disciple of the great prophet of the exile who, using language similar to that of his teacher, addressed the disappointment of the returnees at the seeming failure of prophecy:

> So justice is far from us,
>   and righteousness does not reach us.
> We look for light, but all is darkness;
>   for brightness, but we walk in deep shadows.
> Like the blind we grope along the wall,
>   feeling our way like people without eyes.
> At midday we stumble as if it were twilight,
>   among the strong, we are like the dead. (Isa 59:9–10)[42]

---

42. Sentiments like these are scattered in various places within the prophetic books. Note for example Ezek 12:21: "The word of the LORD came to me: 'Son of man, what is this proverb

Thus, while Third Isaiah reaffirmed, and even expanded, the great vision of his predecessor, he was also compelled to return to the *critical* perspective of the pre-exilic prophets, because social injustice and a religion devoid of transformative power had once again appeared in Jerusalem.

This is the context of Ecclesiastes, and it provides us with an explanation for the author's view of the relationship between God and human beings. Where the prophets speak of the divine pathos this writer stresses God's transcendence and separateness. Second Isaiah's core message was the announcement that the God who seemed to have gone missing from history during the Babylonian onslaught was present and active in the redemption of the world. Now, in a later context, the author of Ecclesiastes feels the necessity of insisting upon the *hiddenness* of God: "God is in heaven and you are on earth, so let your words be few" (5:2). While the exiles in Babylon needed to receive the "book of comfort," Ecclesiastes reflects a society drifting towards an easy, casual spirituality marked by an over familiarity with God which required a bracing challenge. Choon-Leong Seow comments that for this writer, "God and mortals do not belong in the same realms, and so one ought not to rush to bring forth every inane matter, as if the deity is an earthly agent available to respond to every human whim and fancy."[43]

Using the name Qohelet, which is a transliteration of the Hebrew, Seow points out that the repeated emphasis upon divine transcendence, and on the imperative need for humility and restraint in prayer, has many parallels in wisdom literature elsewhere in the ancient world, and is echoed in the warning of Jesus not to "keep on babbling like pagans," who think they will be "heard because of their many words" (Matt 6:7–8).

Which brings us to the second aspect of the context of Ecclesiastes. Under the rule of Persia there were changes in economic structures, including the growth in the influence of money, the increasing importance of commerce,

---

you have in the land of Israel: "The days go by *and every vision comes to nothing*"?'" And again: "Son of man, the Israelites are saying, 'The vision he sees is for many years from now, and he prophesies about *the distant future*'" (v. 27).

43. Seow, *Ecclesiastes*, 199. The hymn writer Isaac Watts expresses this same sense of divine transcendence: "God is in Heaven, and men below; / Be short, our tunes; our words be few; / A sacred reverence checks our songs, / And praise sits silent on our tongues" ("Eternal Power, Whose High Abode"). Rudolf Otto cited this hymn in *The Idea of the Holy* as a classic example of what he called the experience of the *numinous* (London: Oxford University Press, 1958), 221–22.

accompanied by the spread of insecurity, dissatisfaction and scepticism concerning the meaning of life. The vocabulary used by Qohelet reflects a deep concern with economic issues and includes significant references to the power and influence of money.[44] He lived through a period of history which witnessed a major transition from a non-monetary economy to one in which, with the growing influence of coinage and other structural changes, money began to play a significant role in commerce and trade. The discovery of government records at the imperial city of Persepolis has revealed the growing influence of money and its attractive power as a commodity which was increasingly hoarded and valued for its own sake. International trade gained unprecedented importance and penetrated beyond the port cities into the hinterlands, so that by the end of the fifth century BCE commerce was no longer confined to royal elites but was democratized and opened up to a new merchant class. Seow comments that the introduction of coinage by the Persians "radically transformed the economy of the Levant":

> Contemporaneous inscriptions are replete with references to money, most frequently mentioned in connection with taxes, wages, rent, loans, fines, inheritance, and the prices of goods and services. Money was used in everyday business transactions both large and small, given as gifts and bribes, and hoarded. Money had become not just a convenient medium of exchange; it had become a commodity.[45]

In fact, Nehemiah has left us with a vivid description of the spread and influence of this new commercial culture in his account of merchants who aggressively pursued trade on seven days a week within the walls of Jerusalem, "bringing in fish and all kinds of merchandise and selling them in Jerusalem on the Sabbath to the people of Judah." When, as appointed governor, he ordered the gates of the city to be closed until the Sabbath was over, "the merchants and sellers of all kinds of goods spent the night outside Jerusalem," waiting for the first light of day to resume their trading activity (Neh 13:15–22)! Elsewhere the increasing harshness engendered by this new economy is evident in the poverty of the vulnerable population of Jerusalem, compelled

---

44. See Eccl 4:4–6; 5:8–19; 11:1–2.
45. Seow, *Ecclesiastes*, 21.

to mortgage "our fields, our vineyards and our homes to get grain during the famine." In addition, the poor had to "pay the king's tax on our fields and vineyards" (5:1–8). Nehemiah's response was to denounce the exacting of usury and to decline "the food allotted to the governor" and other privileges, because "out of reverence for God I did not act like that" (5:14–16).

Choon-Leong Seow reports that economic texts from Mesopotamia, Egypt and Palestine all indicate the growing influence of "eager entrepreneurs more than willing to extend credit and supply cash. Indeed, the evidence points to an environment of investment and overall economic growth throughout the empire." However, this growth resulted in deepening socio-economic divisions as the farming of traditional family plots became unsustainable and they were taken over by absentee landlords. Members of the new elite lived in the growing cities and charged exorbitant rents to peasants who had been reduced to waged labour on what for centuries had been their ancestral land.

> It was a time for heady optimism about hitherto unimaginable opportunities. Yet, that optimism was offset by socio-political and economic realities on the ground, for there were no fail-safe rules that worked every time. It was a perplexing new world of rapid political, social and economic innovations, many of which were initiated in the seats of power that ordinary citizens of the vast empire could hardly comprehend.[46]

This situation is clearly reflected in the philosophy which permeates Ecclesiastes, signified by the Hebrew term *hebel*, variously translated as "vanity," "useless," "incomprehensible," "enigmatic" – and even "absurd." This wide variety of translations indicates the range of meanings of the word and the difficulty of conveying all its nuances in English, but it clearly carries negative connotations concerning human existence, especially as this was experienced in the kind of society known to the author. This is to underline the fact that Qohelet's conclusions and philosophy are highly contextual, arising within the specific historical and cultural experience we have just

---

46. Choon-Leong Seow, "The Social World of Ecclesiastes," in von Hagen and Welker, *Money as God?*, 158. Tom Holland describes Cyrus's rise to power as resulting in "the largest agglomeration of territories that the world had ever seen – and on a scale, certainly, that far exceeded the wildest fantasies of any Assyrian or Babylonian monarch" (*Dominion: The Making of the Western Mind* [London: Little, Brown, 2019], 7).

described. In the world "under the sun," human beings struggle to make sense of their existence and so create ways to supress troubling existential questions, attempting to evade reality in the endless quest for money, pleasure, wisdom and honour.

> They toil. They fret. They are never content with what they have. They accumulate wealth and hoard it. They long for more wisdom and understanding. . . . They strive to gain an immortality of sorts through fame, through their wealth, or their accomplishments. They try to be without offense whatsoever. In short, they try everything conceivable to take hold of the situation and gain some control. But nothing really works, since all is *hebel*.[47]

The Emerging Culture of Mammon

In the previous chapter we suggested that the roots of what Jesus would later identify as "Mammon" are to be discovered in the urban societies of the ancient world and that in precisely this context the alternative vision of a community shaped by "justice and justice alone" had come into being. We have now tracked the history of that community as it made its own fateful transition from tribal confederation to monarchic state and wrestled with the pressures to compromise its distinctive way of life and worship in a world in which successive imperial powers gained ever-widening control of vast swathes of territory. We have considered the emergence of the Hebrew prophets and their roles, both as passionate and courageous critics of their fellow countrymen prior to the loss of Jerusalem, and as visionaries bearing a message of comfort and hope as Babylonian power gave way before the rise of the Persian Empire.

The author of Ecclesiastes is a faithful witness to the far-reaching changes which he observed occurring within an imperial society as the seeds of the urban culture which had been planted in the ancient Near East centuries earlier now produced fresh growth in the form of imperial powers whose influence became more widespread than ever before. Throughout the vast

---

47. Seow, *Ecclesiastes*, 57.

area controlled by Persia, money began to reshape both social relationships and individual perceptions of the purpose of life in the ways described above.

The importance of Ecclesiastes arises, first, from its testimony concerning the broad historical situation within which the prophets had declared good news. We noticed above the economic dimensions of the experience of exile, and when Second Isaiah exposes the failure of money to meet the real and deepest needs of human beings (55:1–2) he is referring to a cultural context which was to progress towards the acquisitive and unhappy society which Qohelet so movingly describes. The fact is that prophecy never emerges in a historical vacuum, abstracted from the hard realities of the lives of those to whom it is addressed. This is precisely why we can be so thankful that Holy Scripture includes *both* the visions of the prophets and the honest reporting of the wise men. In fact, we may suggest that what we discern taking shape beneath these two strands of tradition are the contrasting lines of development which will reach their full expression, on the one side, in the imperious power of Mammon, and on the other, in the announcement of the Servant of Yahweh that the "kingdom of God" has broken into the present to bring down "rulers from their thrones," to lift up the humble and to fill "the hungry with good things" (Luke 1:52–53).

However, Ecclesiastes is important not only because it portrays such a realist picture of the cultural context of the ancient world during the Persian Empire, but, second, because that description has so many points of contact with the situation confronting people of faith in the globalized world of the twenty-first century. Many commentators have noticed this, including Robert Gordis who devotes an entire chapter to "Koheleth and Modern Existentialism." He points out that the modern world "has been marked by massive chaos and mass brutality unexampled in history" and that this has left "tremendous numbers of men and women" convinced "of the meaninglessness of life and the lack of purpose in the universe." This is reflected especially in the arts where modern painters, poets and musicians have depicted "the broken misshapen character of existence." Contemporary composers write atonal music, not to "shock the sensibilities of the traditional listener," but because they feel compelled to reflect "the disordered and chaotic pattern of our urbanized, technological lives, disaster-ridden and death-laden."[48]

---

48. Robert Gordis, *Koheleth: The Man and His World* (New York: Schocken, 1967), 113–14. William Brown makes a similar comment, suggesting that the "harmonic desecration" of modern

Even more to the point, the fact that *hebel* may be translated as "absurd" will remind readers of the reference to Albert Camus in chapter 1, and his use of this very word to describe the dilemmas facing contemporary people in a world where God seemed to have died. Writing in 1940, as Europe began yet again to tear itself apart, Camus said that the certainty of a God giving meaning to life "far surpasses in attractiveness the ability to behave badly with impunity. The choice would not be hard to make. *But there is no choice and that is where the bitterness comes in.*"[49]

These points of contact between Qohelet and the modern world are significant because in both cases the sense of a world gone amiss, of *hebel*, or the unbearable lightness of being, arise from particular cultural contexts in which money and possessions, material or academic success, become part and parcel of an idolatrous system which creates division, isolation and despair. Qohelet describes, or exposes, this condition; he does not advocate it. As Gordis says, there is a fundamental difference between this biblical author and the nihilism of the modern world:

> It is true that Koheleth is deeply pained by the realization that he cannot understand the purpose of the universe, a theme to which he returns again and again. But because he is a Hebrew living within the Jewish tradition, a world without God is impossible for him, because the existence of this world testifies to its Creator.[50]

The wise men of ancient Israel thus await with the prophets the coming of the Servant of Yahweh who will present the whole race descended from Adam with the critical decision between God and Mammon.

---

music is analogous to Qohelet's jarring description of his world (*Ecclesiastes*, Interpretation: A Bible Commentary for Teaching and Preaching [Louisville: John Knox, 2000], 13). Note Theodor Adorno's description of the music of Gustav Mahler as the explosive expression "of the pain felt by the individual subject imprisoned in an alienated society" (*Quasi una Fantasia: Essays on Modern Music* [London: Verso, 1998], 84).

49. Albert Camus, *The Myth of Sisyphus* (Harmondsworth: Penguin, 1975), 65. The term *hebel* also finds an echo in Zygmunt Bauman's description of a *liquid* culture characterized by "a new individualism, the fading of human bonds and the wilting of solidarity." See his *Liquid Times: Living in an Age of Uncertainty* (Cambridge: Polity, 2007), 24. He also discusses this concept in *Liquid Love: On the Frailty of Human Bonds* (Cambridge: Polity, 2003) and *Liquid Fear* (Cambridge: Polity, 2006).

50. Gordis, *Koheleth*, 115–16.

Pause for Reflection: The Lament of Isaiah

We have now surveyed the story of ancient Israel from the liberation of the slaves in Egypt to the covenant made with Yahweh and the formation of the tribal confederacy in the land of Canaan. We noticed how the liberated people were confronted with a momentous choice by Joshua, to "fear the LORD and serve him with all faithfulness." This required of them a decision which involved the total rejection of "the gods your ancestors worshipped beyond the River Euphrates" (Josh 24:14–16). When the people, perhaps far too hastily, confessed their loyalty to Yahweh who "himself... brought us and our parents up out of Egypt, from that land of slavery," Joshua rejected what we may call their "easy decisionism" and reminded them that the Lord is "a holy God; he is a jealous God" who demands absolute loyalty. Only in this way would the Mosaic vision of individual and community life become a reality. When they insisted that they would serve the Lord, Joshua set a stone in place as testimony to the fateful choice made on that day, as "a witness against you if you are untrue to your God" (Josh 24:17–27).

We now know the outcome and its terrible consequences. We have tracked the history of decline and fall, of the attractive power of the gods "beyond the River" whose worship seemed so much less demanding than Yahweh's insistence on "justice and justice alone." The growth of an urban culture and the demand for a king, so "we shall be like all the other nations" (1 Sam 8:10), accelerated the slide towards compromise and the forgetfulness of the liberating vision received through Moses. This was the context in which the great Hebrew prophets emerged, mounting a powerful critique of apostasy, yet articulating fresh and expanded hope of a messianic future in which

Yahweh would yet bring to pass his purpose of grace and mercy for Israel and the nations.

We should not move too easily from the tragedy of the failure of the covenant made with Moses as though this is of purely historical interest and contains little of significance for us. Before we move to the next phase in this story, in which we consider the life and death of Jesus and the emergence of the new community of Jews and Gentiles committed to following his way, we do well to reflect on an extraordinary statement of Isaiah concerning the tragedy of ancient Israel. Here is the lament he articulated as the darkness closed in and the catastrophe of the loss of Jerusalem drew ever closer:

> LORD, they came to you in their distress;
> > when you disciplined them,
> > they could barely whisper a prayer.
> As a pregnant woman about to give birth
> > writhes and cries out in her pain,
> > so were we in your presence, LORD.
> We were with child, we writhed in labour,
> > but we gave birth to wind.
> *We have not brought salvation to the earth,*
> > *and the people of the world have not come to life.*
> > (Isa 26:16–18)

The extent of the tragedy is measured by the immensity of the promise: "salvation to the earth" and life in its fullness and abundance for "the people of the world." This is to say that Israel's failure was not just some local difficulty of which we may take passing notice before assuring ourselves that our loyalty to the new covenant can never be in question. On the contrary, Isaiah grasped the world-historical, international dimensions of what was at stake and lamented the unspeakable tragedy of a missed opportunity to bring healing and shalom to the whole created world. In the chapter preceding the one from which this quotation is taken the prophet had glimpsed the vast extent of the salvation which God intended when "the shroud that enfolds all peoples, the sheet that covers all nations" was removed and God would "swallow up death for ever" and "remove his people's disgrace from all the earth" (25:7–8). Israel's failure, her capitulation to the values of the urban cultures of the imperial powers which bestrode the ancient world, resulted in that mysterious shroud remaining in place, blinding the nations to reality and preventing them from recognizing the true source of their liberation, freedom and unity.

Consequently, before we pass over this remarkable lament, treating it as a historical curiosity, we need to reflect whether this text might confront us with a challenge of enormous significance. On the final pages of his *Theology of the Old Testament* Walter Brueggemann refers to Joshua's demand for a decision between Yahweh and the "gods beyond the River" and relates this to the renewed summons to post-exilic Israel to testify as witnesses for Yahweh before an assembly of "all the nations . . . and the peoples" (Isa 43:8–13). In the first case the decision concerned "the internal ordering of Israel's life vis-à-vis competing religious alternatives," but in the second, beyond the tragedy of exile in Babylon, the issues had become much wider and now concerned "Yahweh versus the gods of Babylon and a decision about the truth of world governance." These texts, together with Isaiah's lament to which attention has been drawn, are "paradigmatic in every generation," since which witnesses are believed "concerning Yahweh or the gods of the empire . . . will determine the shape of the world."[1]

We are about to move this discussion into the New Testament, to the context of the first century of the Common Era and the story of Jesus and his community at a point in history which witnessed the emergence of the greatest imperial power the world had ever seen. The claims which the Roman Empire made for itself expanded to an unprecedented level of magnitude and involved a form of political religion which brooked no rivals.[2] This is the context in which Jesus renewed the centuries-old summons for a critical decision, now defined as the choice between God or Mammon. We shall explore the articulation of this crucial choice in what follows, but the important issue here is that two thousand years later, the challenge originally presented to Israel, then reformulated by Jesus, now reappears in the twenty-first century

---

1. Walter Brueggemann, *Theology of the Old Testament: Testimony, Dispute, Advocacy* (Minneapolis: Fortress, 1997), 747–50.

2. Gerardo Zampaglione describes the Pax Romana as embodying "the idea of external relations based on the great power achieved by the Roman Empire." The Romans believed that they had been "vested with the mission of imposing their laws and way of life on the rest of the world" and that "spreading peace among mankind meant subjecting other peoples to Roman dominion" (*The Idea of Peace in Antiquity*, trans. Richard Dunn [London: University of Notre Dame Press, 1973], 135).

"as the primary alternative to the deathly ideology of technological, military consumerism." That alternative, no longer simply verbalized but incarnated in the life and death of Jesus of Nazareth, presents a globalized world, still seemingly enshrouded by "the sheet that covers all nations," with the option of "Yahweh's passion for justice, passion for the well-being of the human community, and passion for the *shalom* of the earth." This testimony cannot "come to terms with the power of death, no matter its particular public form or its ideological garb."[3] In precisely this situation, an emergent world Christian movement must discover ways to engage in deep, critical examination of its relationship to the culture of Mammon if it is to avoid a situation in which it will have to repeat Isaiah's lament.

---

3. Brueggemann, *Theology of the Old Testament*, 741.

CHAPTER 4

God or Mammon: The Ultimate Decision

> The kingdom of God has come "near" in Christ: the great day of the Lord is about to come. . . . All those shattering, destructive, depressing, and disruptive forces now dominating the universe fly away in despair and anguish as soon as the king appears. . . . In the realm of secular relationships . . . the kingdom represents an unworldly abnormality, sheer foolishness, something that cannot be. (J. H. Bavinck)[1]

As we have seen, the successive imperial powers of Egypt, Assyria, Babylon and Persia impacted the public life of the Jewish people from the foundational story of Moses to the return from exile and the building of the second temple in Jerusalem. This is not to suggest that the experience of imperial power was uniform; the perceptions and policies of the ruling powers varied over time, from the enslavement in Egypt, to the hubris and violence of Assyria and Babylon, the latter described by the prophets as a brutal empire responsible for the destruction of "the whole earth" (Jer 51:25). In contrast, the more tolerant approach of Persia towards enslaved peoples reflected what has been called the "remarkably cosmopolitan vision" of Cyrus who "envisioned a multinational empire where foreign cultures were to be respected and preserved."[2] The empire of Cyrus not only permitted the return of exiled

---

1. J. H. Bavinck, *Between the Beginning and the End: A Radical Kingdom Vision* (Grand Rapids: Eerdmans, 2014), 45–46.
2. Joel Kotkin, *The City: A Global History* (New York: Modern Library, 2006), 23.

peoples to the lands of their ancestors, but actually funded such resettlements. Consequently, the interaction between the Persian Empire and the Jewish exiles was not antagonistic since the post-exilic leaders, Ezra and Nehemiah, were "authorized and funded by Persia."[3]

Having said this, the struggle of the Jewish people to maintain their distinct identity and to protect space for their "liberated imagination" remained intense and urgent whatever particular form imperialism took. As we noticed at the conclusion of the previous chapter, however humane the policies of King Cyrus might have been towards the Jewish captives, the massive expansion of Persian power and economic developments which gave a new licence to human desires for wealth, pleasure and status posed a different kind of threat to Israel's covenant faith, as can be seen in the reaffirmation of the Mosaic values which took place under the leadership of Ezra and Nehemiah. Their insistence that the communal life of the post-exilic Jewish people be reformed under the reign of Yahweh was a consciously countercultural move in the world which Qohelet had described as pervaded by the spirit of *hebel*.

We cannot discuss here the period of history which witnessed the end of the Persian Empire, the extraordinary impact of the rise of Alexander the Great, and the spread of Hellenistic culture, all of which prepared the way for the emergence of what was to prove to be the most influential of all the ancient political powers in the shape of the Roman imperium. However, two aspects of this period are of crucial importance since they provided the foundations for the worldview which Jesus later associated with "Mammon."

The first of these developments concerns a fresh stage in urban history in which the city took new forms and became increasingly significant for political, economic and social life. The founding of Alexandria in Egypt created a carefully planned metropolis which was to become "the symbol of the Hellenistic city for the whole Mediterranean world." It grew to a size which far outstripped the previous ideals of the Greek *polis* and constituted the model for other emerging urban settlements designed to promote the spread of Hellenistic ideas and values.[4] Helmut Koester has described how these new

---

3. Walter Brueggemann, *Texts That Linger, Words That Explode: Listening to Prophetic Voices* (Minneapolis: Fortress, 2000), 85.

4. Anthony Pagden says that the founding of empires has "always been closely associated with the creation of cities." Alexander the Great founded dozens of cities, including the building of six new urban settlements north of the River Oxus in a single year (*Peoples and Empires:*

cities "reflected the changed social and economic situation," creating urban spaces for the growth of new forms of communal life, including "trade and relaxation, entertainment and talk, private or public debates."[5]

The second development during the Hellenist era relates to the expansion of trade routes, the further growth in the significance of money, and innovations with regard to banking and systems of financial transactions. The conquests of Alexander opened up new vistas of the world beyond the Mediterranean, creating a vast trading area and resulting in an unprecedented mobility for large numbers of Greeks who traversed the trade routes in the quest for new wealth. Mason Hammond describes the prosperity which accompanied the spread of Hellenism:

> Travel, commerce, and finance flowed freely throughout the Hellenistic world and well beyond its frontiers: . . . to southern India and down the east coast of Africa in the track of the Egyptians; across the desert to hither Asia, northern India, and central Asia; through Marseilles into Gaul; across the Rhine and Danube into central Europe.[6]

The extraordinary achievements of Alexander the Great were to have a significant impact on European history, both in the immediate aftermath of his death at the age of thirty-two and in the longer term, up to and including the emergence of modern imperial powers in the shadows of which we continue to live in the twenty-first century. The story of Alexander, embellished with the myths which become associated with such figures, appeared to possess a supernatural quality which resulted in the ascription of divinity to him. In fact, Alexander had claimed that the god Ammon, recognized as Zeus by the Greeks, had addressed him *as his son*. Thus, the tradition of the divinity of kings, which we have seen was part of the context for the emergence of the Yahwistic faith of early Israel, reappeared and was to play

---

Europeans and the Rest of the World – From Antiquity to the Present [London: Weidenfeld & Nicolson, 2001], 4).

    5. Helmut Koester, *Introduction to the New Testament*, vol. 1, *History, Culture and Religion of the Hellenistic Age* (Berlin: de Gruyter, 1982), 72.

    6. Mason Hammond, *The City in the Ancient World* (Cambridge: Harvard University Press, 1972), 218.

an even greater role with the rise of Roman emperors who demanded not merely obedience, but worship.

Equally significant was Alexander's vision of an empire which would unite East and West, overcoming the prejudices of his Greek contemporaries, including his teacher Aristotle, that civilization was the prerogative of the Greeks alone, and all other peoples were barbarians. Alexander's dream of an ecumenical unity, which might be traced back to the Persian tolerance of other races, led the philosopher Plutarch to praise him as "one sent by the gods to be the conciliator and arbitrator of the Universe."[7]

However, the story of kings and generals is only one side of history, and there is another dimension which emerges from the underside of human societies in the experiences of the majority population whose voices frequently go unheard. Lewis Mumford comments that the narratives of the emergence of the Hellenistic cities reveal nothing of what was happening below the surface of urban life. There, from at least the sixth century BCE, "a countermovement of the spirit" had been gathering headway among groups who counted for nothing, including women, slaves and aliens. Precisely among such people new life was appearing as "axial ideologies revealed profound disillusion with the fundamental premises of civilization: its over-emphasis on power and material goods."[8]

This is an important observation as we move to consider the era of Roman power and discover how the celebration of empire in propaganda which went far beyond the claims of Alexander concealed the different reality in the urban slums and in the countryside where issues of landlessness, debt, and desperate struggles to live at, or often below, subsistence were the experience of the majority population. Mumford's description of the new religious movements which flourished before and during the Hellenist era applies equally to the world in which Jesus of Nazareth was born:

---

7. Quoted in Pagden, *Peoples and Empires*, 24.

8. Lewis Mumford, *The City in History* (Harmondsworth: Penguin, 1966), 236. The reference to "axial ideologies" recalls the view of Karl Jaspers that the sixth century before Christ witnessed a remarkable flowering of Asian religious traditions associated with the Buddha, Zoroaster, Mahavira, Confucius, and the emergence of Taoism and the Upanishads. See David Graeber's discussion of the Axial Age in his *Debt: The First 5,000 Years* (Brooklyn: Melville House, 2011), 223–50. I discovered Robert Bellah's *Religion in Human Evolution: From the Paleolithic to the Axial Age* (Cambridge: Belknap Press, 2011) too late to reference in this discussion, but it is a key text on the subject.

The movement . . . must be interpreted, I submit, as a profound revolt against civilization itself: against its lust for power and wealth, its materialistic expansion and repletion, its degradation of life to the servitude of the body, its destruction of spontaneity by vacant routine, and the misappropriation of the higher goods of life by a dominant minority.[9]

Israel in the Time of Herod the Great

This book is being written in a small town to the north of the city of Glasgow in Scotland. The main street of Kirkintilloch contains inscriptions embedded on the pavements to indicate the precise point at which the Antonine Wall once passed through this area.[10] Not far away there is a hill on which are traces of one of the many Roman forts which housed the legions sent to patrol the wall and defend this northern extremity of the empire. I have often stood on this hill looking north towards the mountains beyond and marvelled both at the vast extent of the empire and at the plight of the soldiers sent from places such as Syria and North Africa to man this remote barricade in the midst of a Scottish winter.

The mention of Syria draws our attention to the eastern boundary of the Roman Empire including, of course, Palestine and the Galilee of Jesus. Richard Fenn notes that Josephus's history of his people in the first century of the Common Era contains "an overwhelming account of death: carnage, piracy, massacres, and the wholesale crucifixion or burning of insurgents." Fenn concludes that any attempt to understand the social context of the New Testament and the early movement inspired by Jesus without "coming to grips with such terror and suffering" is bound to result in a "grievous

---

9. Mumford, *City in History*, 237.

10. The Antonine Wall was built in 142 CE and ran from the River Clyde to the Firth of Forth. Less well known than Hadrian's Wall to the south, it consisted of earthworks creating a ditch enclosed on either side by ramparts, with forts at strategic points along the way. The labour required to construct this barrier must have been phenomenal, and only twenty years after its completion it was abandoned!

misunderstanding of the world in which Jews and the Jewish Christians of the period were living."[11]

The destiny of the Jewish people to be incorporated within the Roman imperium, and to be ruled by monarchs appointed by Rome and serving the interests of the Caesars, was sealed when Herod the Great hastened to plead his case for kingship with the victorious Octavian following the defeat of Antony and Cleopatra at the Battle of Actium in 31 BCE. Octavian, who became the undisputed ruler of the empire and accepted the title Augustus, overlooked the fact that Herod had sent troops to support Antony and recognized his claim, even extending the sphere of his rule to Greek cities adjacent to his kingdom in Judea and Galilee. The historian Maurice Sartre summarizes the reign of Herod as follows:

> King by grace of Rome and detested by the Jews, Herod depended upon barbarian mercenaries and built a system of fortresses designed to protect him from his subjects rather than his neighbors.... The king's brutality in dealing with unrest as well as with his own relatives..., his many marriages (he had ten wives, many of them apparently at the same time), the real or imaginary depravities that transpired in those closed and often remote palaces – all these factors combined to lend credibility to the image of Herod as a bloody tyrant that was handed down without qualification by the Evangelists.[12]

If politically Herod and his dynasty expressed unquestioning loyalty to Rome, at the cultural level they were shaped by the Hellenist legacy, as is evident in the building of new cities, or the refurbishment of old ones, on models supplied by the Greeks. The planning of these towns, the prominent buildings within them, and their architectural styles, all reflected the influence of Hellenism. Perhaps to atone for his support of Antony, Herod sponsored the Actium Games in 28 BCE, which consisted of gymnastics and wrestling contests by naked men, chariot races and gladiatorial fights, and even the dreaded *venationes*, in which human beings fought to the death with wild animals. Herod commissioned the building of a theatre and an amphitheatre

---

11. Richard Fenn, *The Death of Herod: An Essay in the Sociology of Religion* (Cambridge: Cambridge University Press, 1992), 171.

12. Maurice Sartre, *The Middle East under Rome* (Cambridge: Belknap Press, 2007), 93.

in Jerusalem so that no expense was spared in celebration of the triumph and reign of Augustus. Elsewhere Herod's building projects were on a vast scale and at huge expense; in Samaria he created a new capital and called it Sebaste, the Greek equivalent of "Augustus," erecting a temple honouring Rome and its emperor, and commissioning a statue of Caesar resembling the god Zeus. Six thousand veterans from the Roman legions were settled in this area and given land to farm.[13] He then began work on Caesarea Maritima, which became an impressive port city and a key part of the vision for commercial and economic expansion. Michael Grant describes Herod as "a financier and speculator on a monumental scale." While he profited from the banking facility of the Jerusalem temple, he also founded royal banks throughout the country and possessed business contacts across the Greek world. He even secured a highly lucrative deal with Augustus, paying the emperor a capital sum in return for half the revenue of copper mines in Cyprus, "mines that were so extensive and productive" that they supplied the Indian market.[14] The climax of Herod's building projects involved the transformation of the city of Jerusalem, including the building of a spectacular royal palace and the recreation of the temple, a project which involved "a fusion of Jewish and Greek architectural styles, the very symbol of his efforts to link east and west."[15]

The death of Herod the Great occurred in 5 BCE, or possibly in the spring of the next year, and proved to be a pivotal event which "accelerated the forces which ultimately destroyed Israel in a disastrous rebellion, revolution and civil war."[16] A crisis of succession involving three of Herod's sons resulted in rival claims being referred to Augustus in Rome, and the eventual partitioning of ruling authority between Archelaus in Judea, Philip in the north of Syria, and Antipas in Galilee. Herod Antipas, whose rule forms a crucial aspect of the context of the life and ministry of Jesus, created a scandal by divorcing his wife in order to marry the wife of his half-brother, thus committing incest in the eyes of devout Jews. Uprisings, rebellions and violent repression were constant features of life in Palestine throughout most of the first century. A shepherd who possessed charismatic gifts declared himself to be the rightful

---

13. Justo L. González, *Faith and Wealth: A History of Early Christian Ideas on the Origin, Significance and Use of Money* (Eugene: Wipf & Stock, 2002), 72.
14. Michael Grant, *The Jews in the Roman World* (London: Phoenix Giant, 1999), 74–75.
15. Grant, *Jews in the Roman World*, 72.
16. Fenn, *Death of Herod*, 5.

king of the Jews and harried both royal and Roman troops, while a man known as "Judas the Galilean" took control of the royal arsenal in the city of Sepphoris, within sight of the village of Nazareth. The Roman governor of Syria responded with a reign of terror and razed Sepphoris to the ground before crucifying two thousand Jews. In 26 CE a fresh outbreak of rebellion resulted from the appearance of a whole procession of preachers and agitators who fed popular outrage at both the injustices of the Herodian rulers and the perceived sacrilege of Roman actions. Later in the century Emperor Caligula was to insist that he not only enter the Jerusalem temple, but erect a statue of himself within its precincts. Josephus reports the appearance of yet another charismatic rebel in 45 CE, who performed miracles before a vast throng and called for a new exodus. The violence of the repression which inevitably followed reached new levels of terror and, according to Josephus, resulted in the mass slaughter of twenty thousand Jews. The culminating point of this almost century-long series of revolts was reached in 66 CE with the rebellion that marked the commencement of the full-scale Jewish-Roman War, a desperate conflict which reached its terrible climax four years later with the catastrophe of the destruction of Jerusalem and its temple.[17]

It is important to remember at this point that Palestine was part of the Fertile Crescent and both Hellenist and Talmudic sources describe it as an area where soil and climate promised fruitful harvests of wheat, grapes and olive oil. Fruit was abundant and the waters of both the Mediterranean and the Lake of Galilee teemed with fish. At the very dawn of the history of biblical Israel this land had been described as "flowing with milk and honey," providing an ideal location for the social experiment of a community whose life together was to be shaped by their covenant with Yahweh. The prosperity of the area was therefore not in doubt, but a combination of the introduction of an alien system of land ownership and the imposition of new and multiple forms of taxation on an increasingly impoverished rural population created an ever-widening gulf between a wealthy elite and a frustrated and angry

---

17. Maurice Sartre says that this tragic history "underlined the desperation of minorities to obtain by terror what they could not win by persuasion" (*Middle East under Rome*, 118). Richard A. Horsley has described what he calls the "spiral of violence" in this period and suggests that the most fundamental cause "was the economic pressure brought on the peasantry for taxes and tribute and participation in an increasingly monetized economic life" (*Jesus and the Spiral of Violence: Popular Jewish Resistance in Roman Palestine* [Minneapolis: Fortress, 1993], 11).

people. "Slowly the villages of the land of Israel – once duly and solemnly distributed by God to the families, clans, and tribes of Israel – were passing into the hands of aristocratic families, who happened to have influence in royal or priestly circles or large reserves of disposable wealth."[18]

This then is the context of the life, teaching and death of Jesus of Nazareth, a situation of social tension and distress which is reflected in the narratives and parables of the gospels. Indeed, the paranoia and brutality of the aged King Herod is present on the opening pages of the gospels in the story of the "slaughter of the innocents" (Matt 2:16–18). As Kenneth Bailey has observed, there seems to be a contemporary conspiracy of silence in relation to a narrative which stubbornly refuses to conform to the sentimental retelling of the Christmas story which has become routine in the modern world.[19] Unfortunately, the New Testament as a whole has too often been read, interpreted and taught as though it were a context-less story, and the distorting lenses of modern, Western culture have blinded both scholars and preachers to the realities of the world we have briefly described. Once the context of first-century Palestine, and especially of Galilee, is allowed to contribute to our understanding of the gospel, it is as though an old picture in black and white is suddenly transformed into a blaze of colour and we see things we had never previously noticed. Critically for this book, that includes the central thrust of the Sermon on the Mount and the saying concerning "God and Mammon." *The definition of Mammon must take into account the historical, sociopolitical and spiritual context we have described and upon which we shall now attempt to sharpen the focus.*

---

18. Richard A. Horsley and Neil Asher Silberman, *The Message and the Kingdom: How Jesus and Paul Ignited a Revolution and Transformed the Ancient World* (Minneapolis: Fortress, 1997), 29.

19. See Matt 2:18. Bailey comments that Christians in the Middle East have faced endless conflicts and violence so that for them this text provides a lifeline since it, and the account of the crucifixion of Jesus at the other end of the gospels, are vital to the retention of faith amid mindless violence. "This story heightens the reader's awareness of the willingness on the part of God *to expose himself to the total vulnerability which is at the heart of the incarnation*" (Kenneth Bailey, *Jesus Through Middle Eastern Eyes: Cultural Studies in the Gospels* [London: SPCK, 2008], 58). Italics added.

The Galilee of Jesus

The building projects of Herod the Great, especially the developments at Jerusalem and Caesarea, reflected his determination to create a new cultural climate in Palestine involving international alliances, the introduction of new technologies, and the growing monetization of economic life. As was the case throughout the Roman Empire, new roads were built to facilitate international trading connections and the swift movement of armed forces. Herod concentrated his attention on the south, while levying heavy taxes on the population of Galilee to fund his expensive projects. It was in the troubled years after Herod's death, and during the reign of Antipas, "that the full effects of the Romanization of the Augustan age were felt directly in Galilee."[20] In other words, those changes coincided exactly with the life and ministry of Jesus of Nazareth. In the words of Sean Freyne:

> The values of a market economy with all the attendant signs of exploitation of the weak and ostentatious living of the wealthy are easily documented; specialisations in terms of more intensive harvesting of produce both from the land and lake, as well as production of goods for inter-regional trade in addition to domestic use were occurring; and there are clear signs of the extension of monetisation as a means of exchange. . . . It seems possible to link these developments with Antipas' foundations of Sepphoris and Tiberias, as symptomatic of the more complex changes occurring within the whole region.[21]

The mention of the rebuilding of the city of Sepphoris, modelling Greco-Roman values at the heart of Galilee, and the founding of Antipas's new capital of Tiberias on the western shore of the Lake of Galilee underlines the extent to which the urbanization characteristic of the Roman Empire was now impacting the lives of rural populations in traditional societies. Freyne describes the building of these cities as aggressive acts of Romanization by Antipas whose reign marked "the rapid development of the Galilean economy along

---

20. Sean Freyne, *Galilee and the Gospel* (Boston: Brill Academic, 2002), 95. I am greatly indebted to Freyne's scholarship which has massively increased my own understanding of the Galilean context of the life and death of Jesus. A full list of his relevant works can be found in the bibliography.

21. Freyne, *Galilee and the Gospel*, 113.

lines that were directly opposed to the Jewish patrimonial ideal, as this had been enshrined in the Pentateuch, upheld by the prophets and re-enacted by reformers such as Nehemiah."[22] The new cities thus formed the epicentre of a social, economic and religious revolution which posed a direct and powerful challenge to the traditions of Israel derived from Moses and the prophets.[23]

The city of Tiberias, named to honour the new Caesar, was begun in 18 or 19 CE and was the most visible and powerful expression of the far-reaching changes occurring across Galilee. The entire region around the lake experienced dramatic and rapid change as the centuries-old practice of fishing as a seasonal occupation of farmers in the period between sowing and harvest was superseded by industrial-scale developments. Harbours and jetties sprang up around the lake and towns like Magdala became centres for fish processing and the production of fish-related products. A fish sauce called *garum* was exported to cities across the eastern Roman Empire and Magdala came to be called Taricheae, or "Town of Salt-Fish."

> This was an industry that apparently brought great wealth to some and great misery to others: the Magdala excavations have revealed a complex pattern of narrow urban streets, reservoirs, and buildings where the town's putrid business was conducted – and at least one spacious private villa, whose owner proudly announced the source of his fortune with a mosaic depiction of a boat and a large fish installed on the floor of his entrance courtyard.[24]

---

22. Freyne, 191.

23. Note the comment of Alison Futrell that the Roman concept of the city was "infused with religious significance." The founding of a new city "was essentially the imposition of a cosmic structure on the landscape . . . intended to transfer the divinely ordered pattern of the universe into the physical setting of the new settlement. Not only the building of civic structures, but also the alignment of the roads, the placement of sanctuaries, and the division of cultivatable fields were determined according to the Roman understanding of the pattern of creation. The adoption of the urban model, therefore, was more than simply the adoption of Roman technical standards . . . it demanded a fundamental acceptance of, quite literally, a new world order, based on the Roman ability to control and manipulate the environment. *The spread of Roman urban forms was the spread of the Roman Imperium*" (Alison Futrell, *Blood in the Arena: The Spectacle of Roman Power* [Austin: University of Texas Press, 1997], 53–54; emphasis added).

24. Horsley and Silberman, *Message and the Kingdom*, 25. The importance of fishing within the new economy of Roman Palestine is discussed by K. C. Hanson and Douglas E.

If the produce of land and sea crossed Galilee en route to markets in the cities of the eastern empire, it has been suggested that Antipas's new palace on a cliff overlooking the lake was designed to divert the flow of diaspora pilgrims from the East, offering them an alternative to the established route to Jerusalem down the east bank of the River Jordan, by enticing them to cross the lake and take rest in the shining new capital. Marianne Sawicki suggests that Antipas intended to be the first to greet elite pilgrims to the land of Israel, "and the last to bid them farewell as they returned home." The new city of Tiberias thus represented the Galilean extension of Herodian ambitions to Romanize Palestine and to embed the local economy within the imperial system which increasingly dominated the entire Mediterranean world. In this way Antipas hoped to gain prestige beyond his borders, while at the same time opening up opportunities for business contacts, "not just for Herodians, but for any local agricultural or food-producing interests astute enough to get a piece of the action."[25]

If Herod the Great appears in the birth narratives of Jesus, his son Antipas plays an even more prominent role in the gospel stories concerning John the Baptist.[26] John's ministry, his rural location, striking appearance and prophetic language, must all be understood within the context of the cultural clash which we have described. His arrest and notorious execution by beheading is unsurprising given the ubiquity of uprisings and rebellion across Palestine and the violence with which perceived challenges to the ruling powers were invariably met.[27] Unlike his cousin, who seems to have engaged directly with the royal court in Tiberias, Jesus avoided the city, but John's fate must have confirmed to him the conviction that the path he was treading would eventually cost him his own life.

Oakman in *Palestine in the Time of Jesus: Social Structures and Social Conflicts* (Minneapolis: Fortress, 1998), 106–10.

25. Marianne Sawicki, *Crossing Galilee: Architectures of Contact in the Occupied Land of Jesus* (Harrisburg: Trinity Press International, 2000), 146.

26. See Matt 3:1–17; 11:1–19; 14:1–12; Mark 6:14–29; Luke 3:1–19; 7:18–35.

27. According to Josephus, the execution of John resulted from the fear of the royal elite that his popularity among the masses might foment yet another Jewish uprising.

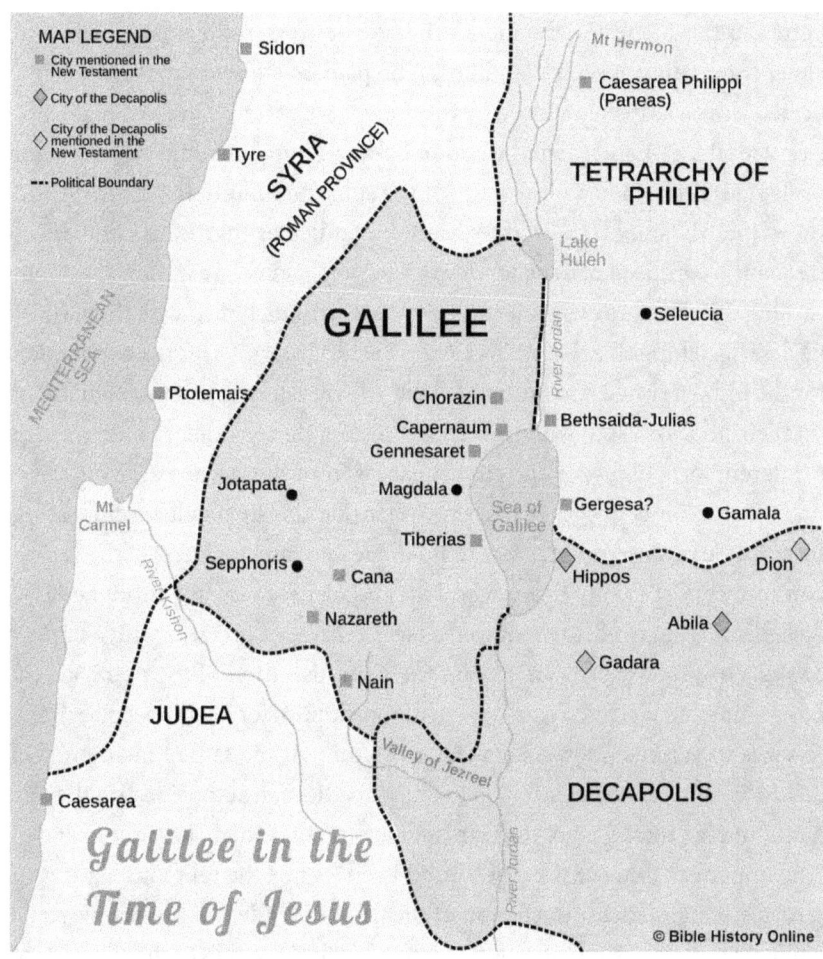

Figure 2: The Galilee of Jesus – note especially Tiberius and Sepphoris[28]

The term "Mammon" occurs only four times in the gospels, once in a passage concerning material possessions at the conclusion of Matthew's account of the Sermon on the Mount (Matt 6:24), and three times in the Lukan parable of the shrewd manager (Luke 16:9, 11, 13). However, the theme of money and possessions, and the way of life of which they are powerful agents and symbols, is pervasive in the actions and teaching of Jesus. The growth of the market economy and the culture which accompanied it is reflected at many

---

28. Bible History Online, "Galilee in the Time of Jesus," bible-history.com. Used with permission.

points in the gospels in the focus on day-labourers, problems of debt, and anger concerning absentee landlords who paid no attention to their tenants' needs. Jesus was deeply moved by the crowds who were "harassed and helpless" (Matt 9:36) and invited them to come to him and "find rest for your souls" (11:29). In a beautiful study of the subject of humility, Klaus Wengst notes that the language used by Matthew indicates that Jesus's audiences frequently consisted of dependent workers who had to "wear themselves out earning their meagre daily wage." Moreover, Christ identified with them when he described himself as being "meek and lowly of heart." "This is a designation for the impoverished and humiliated who deliberately accept their situation, set their hope on God, withdraw from the complex of violence and practise a different form of justice and righteousness from those who rule by force."[29]

Of course, it is important to remember that the alien culture emanating from Rome possessed the power to fascinate and lure members of the Jewish community, especially those who had already been deeply influenced by Hellenism. The royal elite required a large retinue of servants with a variety of skills to support its lifestyle, and the administration of the political and economic system created employment opportunities for Jewish people willing to serve in various roles, such as tax collectors. At the same time there was collusion between the Herodian kings and the Roman authorities, on the one hand, and "an increasingly venal aristocracy" on the other. The latter included "the upper echelons of the priesthood itself" since the religious leaders in Jerusalem maintained "the fiction of the theocratic ideal of the temple state, while themselves being thoroughly imbued with the values of the elite rich of the Greco-Roman world."[30] They attempted to serve both God and Mammon!

---

29. Klaus Wengst, *Humility: Solidarity of the Humiliated* (London: SCM, 1988), 39. Wengst points out that in Greek and Latin texts ordinary people are "looked down on from above" and are regarded as "common, mean, subservient and humble," whereas the Hebrew Bible "speaks from the perspective of these insignificant people" and identifies with those who are "exposed to being downtrodden and to humiliation" (16).

30. Freyne, *Galilee and the Gospel*, 198. For detailed studies of the social history of the Jesus movement, see Ekkehard W. Stegemann and Wolfgang Stegemann, *The Jesus Movement: A Social History of Its First Century* (Minneapolis: Fortress, 1999) and Jacob Neusner et al., eds., *The Social World of Formative Christianity and Judaism* (Philadelphia: Fortress, 1988).

The Elite Evangelist

I want to sharpen the focus of this discussion further by concentrating attention on a single account of the life and teaching of Jesus, namely the gospel attributed to Luke. There are a number of reasons for this choice. First, the theological significance of this writer's contribution to our understanding of the Jesus story is frequently overlooked. As Joel Green observes, the two volumes of Luke-Acts amount to 28 percent of the literature making up the New Testament as a whole, significantly more than the epistles of Paul, yet Luke has not received anything like the attention that his colleague and sometime companion has been given by biblical theologians.[31] Second, Luke is important for this study because more than any other writer, he places the story of Jesus and his community within the larger framework of the Greco-Roman world which we have described above. As Ulrich Mauser says,

> Luke wants to bind the life on earth of Jesus of Nazareth and the life of his growing community . . . into Greco-Roman society and Roman law and justice, because it is God's will that the purpose of Israel now be historically realized in the mission to the ends of the earth of a community in which both Jew and Gentile have the right to live together in peace.[32]

Third, Luke's gospel, together with the book of Acts, is particularly significant for us in the light of Karl Allen Kuhn's suggestion that he can be described as the *elite evangelist*.[33] The addressee of Luke's two volumes is a person of high status and the author's intention is, therefore, to communicate the gospel in a manner that is both contextually relevant and uncompromisingly faithful for hearers like the "most excellent Theophilus" (Luke 1:3 and Acts 1:1). However, not only were the first receptors of Luke's message members of the privileged elite, but the author himself possessed a high degree of education and significant literary skills, *which suggests that this was his background as well.* In the ancient world literacy did not exceed 10 percent of the population of the Roman Empire and among Jews in Palestine it has been estimated

---

31. Joel B. Green, *The Theology of the Gospel of Luke*, New Testament Theology (Cambridge: Cambridge University Press, 1995), 2.

32. Ulrich Mauser, *The Gospel of Peace: A Scriptural Message for Today's World* (Louisville: Westminster John Knox, 1992), 84–85.

33. Karl Allen Kuhn, *Luke: The Elite Evangelist* (Collegeville: Liturgical Press, 2010).

to have been as low as 3 percent.[34] That being so, Luke's obvious abilities as both a researcher and an author mark him out as "among the social elite of his day."[35] He writes, Kuhn says, for high-status searchers after truth whose privileged lifestyles he had himself shared, and invites them "to join him in leaving behind the kingdom of Rome, with all its privileges, trappings and inequities, to seek another, radically different realm" and a greater Lord.[36]

If this analysis of Luke's purpose and character is accepted, not only does his work provide us with a vital case study in Christian testimony to the elite strata of society towards the end of the first century, but by analogy it becomes hugely significant for Christian mission in the globalized world of the twenty-first century, where the gulf between a super-rich elite and huge numbers of people facing poverty, homelessness and marginalization grows ever wider. When Theophilus and his companions read, or listened to, Luke's "orderly account" they must have been immediately struck by the radical nature of the demands of conversion and discipleship. The Song of Mary (1:46–55) reveals from the very beginning the revolutionary nature of the gospel and the challenge it posed to the dominant order. There is no attempt to conceal the reversal of elite values and practices which will result from the in-breaking of the kingdom of God. Even when heard apart from its immediate historical context, the Magnificat can take the reader's breath away, but to listen to it within the setting we have described is to hear it in a completely new way. We recall the statement of Richard Fenn that to read the gospels without recognizing the background of terror and suffering is to risk complete misunderstanding, a warning which applies especially to Mary's Song if it is only ever heard in a tranquil setting such as choral evensong in a cathedral.

The poem we know as the Magnificat is the cry of a pregnant, unmarried young woman living amid the violence and chaos resulting from the

---

34. See Antoinette Clark Wire, *The Case for Mark Composed in Performance* (Eugene: Cascade, 2011), 3. This book reflects a growing focus on oral communication in New Testament scholarship. See also Richard A. Horsley, *Jesus in Context: Power, People, and Performance* (Minneapolis: Fortress, 2008).

35. Kuhn, *Luke*, 73.

36. Kuhn, 75. Justo González suggests that Luke's gospel could be called the "Gospel of the prosperous" because "its purpose is precisely to call to repentance an audience that was almost totally absent from the earliest preaching of the Jesus movement" (*Faith and Wealth*, 78).

Roman devastation of the city of Sepphoris and the surrounding villages.[37] It is inconceivable that Nazareth was spared the trauma which must have impacted all who dwelled within the hinterland of the ruined city. The campaign of the Roman general Varus by which Sepphoris was destroyed involved extreme violence and resulted in the surrounding countryside being littered with crosses erected to impale those who had survived the assault but were suspected of insurrection. As a consequence, the male population of this part of Galilee was significantly depleted, leaving many women widowed and young girls deprived of the possibility of marriage.[38] In any society this would be a tragedy, but in a traditional, village community it represented a catastrophe on many levels.

Consequently the pregnant Mary sings her prophetic song amid the trauma caused by imperial violence, and in the darkness of such a time she recognizes the coming of God into the brokenness of the world in a manner which will prove to be the turning point of all the ages. Mary is not inhibited by imperial violence and sings of the dethroning of kings, the reversal of the reigning values as the rich are sent away empty, and the raising up of the humble who are to be "filled . . . with good things." Her vision expresses the hope which flows from the action of Israel's God whose "mercy extends to those who fear him" and will result in radical social transformation. This remarkable young woman celebrates God's actions in history and expresses a miraculous confidence that he is about to enact the salvation long predicted by the Hebrew prophets. As Joel Green says, the story of Jesus is placed "in the midst of the political turmoil of the Roman occupation of Palestine" and it moves towards "a *Roman* act of execution, the crucifixion of Jesus as a pretender to the throne," avoiding any suggestion that the Roman political world "is a mere 'backdrop' to Luke's narrative."[39]

Mary's Song forms a remarkable parallel with Yahweh's response to the distress of the slaves in Egypt at the commencement of Israel's history, when

---

37. Richard Horsley comments: "In Galilee the movement led by Judas, son of the famous brigand-chief Hezekias, was suppressed within a few months, with great slaughter and destruction in the general area around Nazareth – shortly before Jesus came to live and grow up there" (Richard A. Horsley, ed., *A People's History of Christianity*, vol. 1, *Christian Origins* [Minneapolis: Fortress, 2005], 27).

38. Freyne, *Galilee and the Gospel*, 284–85.

39. Green, *Theology of the Gospel of Luke*, 8.

God had assured Moses that he had "seen the misery of my people in Egypt" and was "concerned about their suffering" (Exod 3:7–8). The Magnificat occupies a similar position at the commencement of the New Testament and in a new context of imperial violence it celebrates the knowledge that such suffering and oppression is known to heaven and draws the intervention of God. Mary is herself the personification of "the humble" who are to be "lifted up" by the messianic calling and ministry of the child she carries within her womb. "The one who utters the Magnificat cannot be a person of high standing. The birth of the messiah Jesus from a lowly maiden, who as a result has been exalted, already includes the eschatological elevation of the humbled and the fall from power of the rich man."[40]

The prominent role played by Mary at the start of this gospel draws our attention to the significant place occupied by women and children in Luke's version of the Jesus story. Kenneth Bailey comments that "Jesus was raised by an extraordinary mother who must have had an enormous influence on his attitudes toward women."[41] Those attitudes are among the most countercultural and world-transformative features of the gospel as Luke repeatedly describes the crucial role which women play in the unfolding drama.[42] We cannot examine this theme in detail, but notice the revelation that Jesus was accompanied on the road (that is, in public ministry) by two groups: the twelve apostles *and* "some women who had been cured of evil spirits and diseases" (8:1–3). Carmen Bernabé Ubieta comments:

> This is notable, since first-century Eastern Mediterranean society divided space by gender, ascribing the public realm to men and the private to women. This division was accompanied by the corresponding judgements as to the lack of honour (called shame in the case of women) of those who did not follow such rules, and did not stay within gender boundaries.[43]

---

40. Wengst, *Humility*, 42.

41. Bailey, *Jesus Through Middle Eastern Eyes*, 192.

42. See 7:11–17, 36–50; 8:1–3; 10:38–42; 13:10–17.

43. Carmen Bernabé Ubieta, "Mary Magdalene and the Seven Demons in Social-Scientific Perspective," in *Transformative Encounters: Jesus and Women Re-viewed*, ed. Ingrid Rosa Kitzberger (Atlanta: Society of Biblical Literature, 2000), 217. Note, however, the qualification expressed by Carolyn Osiek: "In the Roman world, status was always more important than gender; that is, higher social status took pre-eminence over the sex of the person involved" ("Family Matters," in Horsley, *People's History*, 212).

This transgression of existing social conventions, including Jesus's radical views regarding both the position of children and the significance of kinship structures and loyalties, must have created a scandal as he and his followers moved from village to village. Yet, as Ubieta says, the combination of the two groups, male and female, constituted a living demonstration of his mission "to announce the arrival of God's kingdom as good news to the poor." The twelve apostles were a highly visible symbol of Israel's role in "the end of time when God will realize his salvation," while the women who had been healed were "living proof of the beginning of that liberation which is announced for the oppressed" as the good news.[44]

Three of the women in this group are named as Mary from Magdala, "from whom seven demons had come out," Joanna, who is identified as the wife of "the manager of Herod's household," and Susanna. These details must not be passed over as merely secondary information because they point towards crucial elements of the gospel story. Take the case of Mary whose home town was, as we have seen earlier, at the epicentre of the social, economic and cultural changes impacting the communities on the shore of the Lake of Galilee. While all the women in this group are said to have been healed by Jesus, the case of Mary is exceptional in that she is described as having experienced multiple forms of demonic possession.

We are compelled to ask whether women were affected disproportionately by the pressures and turmoil known to the general population in a period of massive and threatening change under imperial rule. However we explain the phenomenon of demon possession, the frequency of its appearance during this particular period must be related to causes arising within that specific context. This suspicion is strengthened when, later in this chapter, Luke describes an encounter between Jesus and a demon-possessed young man in Gadara, a profoundly tragic figure expelled from human society and living naked in a burial ground. Responding to Jesus's question concerning his name, he identifies himself as "Legion," a term laden with military significance

---

44. Ubieta, "Mary Magdalene," 216. Joachim Jeremias comments, "Jesus accepts women into the group of disciples because he expects his disciples to control their desires. The old age is dominated by desires.... In the new age, purity rules, and disciplines even a man's gaze.... Nowhere in the social sphere does the new life make so striking an incursion into everyday affairs as here" (*New Testament Theology*, vol. 1, *The Proclamation of Jesus* [London: SCM, 1971], 227).

and suggesting that his tragic condition was related to the violence of the Roman forces in supressing resistance to imperial rule in this district.[45] As we have seen in relation to the destruction of Sepphoris, the military violence directed against the male population of Galilee, and the sexual violence against women which tragically accompanied such actions, resulted in terrible distress and trauma for the female population. Ubieta comments that the multiplicity of demons said to have possessed Mary Magdalene indicates the "special seriousness of the case" and implies that her symptoms covered "a whole set of acts which were an outward proof of an unconscious protest against the situation that the woman found herself in, calling (indirectly) for more attention and consideration."[46] In precisely the experience of women like Mary Magdalene the promise of the Magnificat was being fulfilled as she was delivered from the powers that enslaved her, while her unspoken protest was validated and her life assumed a new meaning. "Her life was no longer governed by strange dehumanizing forces that were contrary to God's will. Her body was no longer a burden, nor a barrier. God had begun to act, changing the boundaries that shaped society, and the criteria that were used to establish them."[47]

Even more remarkable is the case of Joanna, "the wife of Chuza, the manager of Herod's household." This seemingly minor detail is an astounding piece of information since it suggests that the impact of the Jesus movement had penetrated within the very heart of the royal establishment and begun its transformative work among the urban elite of Galilean society. At the same time it indicates that distress among women in Galilee was not confined to an underclass but was experienced by people whose external appearance might suggest that they lacked nothing. We have no way of knowing how Joanna had encountered Jesus, although Luke has earlier recorded John the Baptist's

---

45. Ched Myers comments that the term "legion" had only one meaning in the gospel writers' world: "a division of Roman soldiers." He cites Josephus's description of later Roman action in Gerasa in which the legions "killed a thousand young men . . . set fire to the houses and marched against the surrounding villages. Those who were able-bodied fled, the weak perished, and all that was left went up in flames" (*Binding the Strong Man: A Political Reading of Mark's Story of Jesus* [New York: Orbis, 1988], 191). I have discussed the story of the "Gadarene demoniac" in *Seeking a City with Foundations: Theology for an Urban World* (Carlisle: Langham Global Library, 2019), 195–97.

46. Ubieta, "Mary Magdalene," 220.

47. Ubieta, 223.

public denunciation of the evils practised in the court at Tiberias, an action which resulted in Herod Antipas confining him in prison (3:19–20). Since the whole thrust of the Baptist's message pointed forward to the one who would "baptise . . . with the Holy Spirit and fire" (3:16) it is highly likely that Joanna had heard John's prophetic announcement of the coming of Messiah.

The presence of Joanna within this group of female disciples triggers questions to which we have no answers: how did she manage to combine life in the city with life on the road? And what was the reaction of her husband, a high-ranking official at the court of Antipas? What we do know is that these women, drawn from different ends of the social spectrum, were attracted to Jesus, found deliverance and healing in him, and together played a crucial role in his mission both in Galilee and later during his passion in Jerusalem (23:49; 23:55 – 24:12). In other words, while marginalization occurred in obvious and visible ways among the poor and impoverished, the stories of women like Joanna alert us to a different form of alienation among the privileged and prosperous, a reality which might be especially painful since it lay concealed beneath the external trappings of honour and success. Carmen Ubieta points out that sickness relates not only to physical dysfunction, "but also to something more comprehensive, pointing to a breakdown in the meaning of life as a whole, a breach in the activities and relations that make life full and meaningful."[48]

I pause here to comment on this remarkable text. First, the presence of these women travelling on the road with Jesus and the apostles clearly subverted the dominant values concerning sexual roles in both Jewish and Roman cultures and signalled the radical nature of the new community to which Theophilus and his friends were attracted. At the same time, the singling out of Joanna is significant since she demonstrated the appeal of Jesus at every level of society, including among those close to power and privilege. However, her conversion and discipleship had economic consequences since Luke informs us that these women "were helping to support [the mission] out of their own means" (8:3). Joanna, and the other named women within the wider group, may have had independent resources which were now redirected towards the work of the kingdom of God. The idolatrous power of Mammon was broken and a new way of life was in the making.

---

48. Ubieta, 218.

If this text must have resonated powerfully within the culture of the ancient world, it has enormous relevance for Christianity in the globalized context of the twenty-first century. We shall say more about this later in the book, but these three named women offer a significant testimony to the liberating power of Christ both for the humble poor, and for people whose poverty of spirit and loss of meaning and purpose lie buried beneath an external facade of prosperity, public honour and success. In the first century this elite sector consisted of a small minority of the population, whereas in the Western world today the middle class which emerged with the development of modern capitalism is peopled with huge numbers of individuals whose external prosperity is accompanied by a hollowing out of existence and the suppression of the reality of human mortality. In such a context the message of the gospel may initially sound like bad news since it exposes the cruel idolatry of Mammon which must be renounced if Jesus is to be confessed and followed as Lord.

The Manifesto of the Kingdom

If an understanding of the context of Mary's Song sheds fresh light on the significance of that wonderful poem, the same thing must be said concerning the account of the commencement of her son's public ministry in the synagogue in Nazareth thirty years later. Luke reports what has come to be called the "Nazareth Manifesto" in which Jesus read from the scroll of the prophet Isaiah during the synagogue service in his native village and electrified his audience by declaring that the promise of the coming of "the year of the Lord's favour" was even then being fulfilled in their hearing (4:14–30). The memory of the carnage which had accompanied the destruction of Sepphoris would have remained powerful among Jesus's hearers and their longing for liberation must have deepened as they witnessed the growing Roman control resulting from the rebuilding of the city in a form designed to advance the geopolitical ambitions of Herod Antipas. In such a situation the mere reading of Isaiah's prophecy, announcing "freedom for the prisoners" and the release of "the oppressed," was bound to heighten tension, but in an oral culture the *manner* of the reading (or performance) and Jesus's dramatic claim that its central prediction was transitioning from prophecy to historical reality roused the audience to a fever pitch of excitement. Yet, despite this initial euphoria, something in that reading and in the subsequent commentary by

Jesus sparked a dramatic change of mood as the initial enthusiasm gave way to the fury of a mob bent on the elimination of Mary's son.

To understand this extraordinary change we must refer again to the history of Galilee. When the Assyrian invaders had destroyed the northern kingdom, they left the area depopulated until non-Jewish people gradually infiltrated Samaria. Eventually peoples from other nations settled in Galilee as well, a situation reflected in Isaiah's reference to "Galilee of the Gentiles" and the prediction that the time would come when the people of Israel, then "walking in darkness," would "[see] a great light" (Isa 9:1–2). At the point at which Jesus began his ministry this prehistory had "inspired Judeans to settle in Galilee and in some instances at least to see their presence there as a sign that the messianic times were imminent."[49] The village of Nazareth was itself known to be just such a Jewish settler community, which explains the initial euphoria of the synagogue audience as Jesus read one of their favoured texts and announced it to be "fulfilled in your hearing."

However, with his rabbinic authority strengthened by the reputation which his activity had created "through the whole countryside," Jesus interpreted Isaiah's statement in a manner which ran counter to the way the text was understood by his audience. He emphasized "good news to the poor" and the release of "the oppressed" but, crucially, chose to omit Isaiah's reference to "the day of vengeance of our God" (Isa 61:1–2). It was precisely phrases like this one, and the subsequent promise that the returning exiles would "feed on the wealth of nations" (61:6), which were used by Jewish settler communities to justify their claim to the land and the use of force in pursuit of its repossession. Jesus's opposition to this form of ethnic nationalism became even clearer when, in response to the rising tide of anger among his hearers, he cited the examples of Elijah and Elisha (key figures in the folk narratives of Jewish history) as enacting Yahweh's *compassion and mercy towards Gentiles!* Freyne comments that from the very beginning of his ministry Jesus had in view not just his own people, but Gentiles as well.

> It is not that, like Paul, Jesus was forced to change the focus of his mission from Israel to the nations. His familiarity with the biblical stories and characters ensures that he could never have

---

49. Sean Freyne, *The Jesus Movement and Its Expansion: Meaning and Mission* (Grand Rapids: Eerdmans, 2014), 21.

entertained a purely ethnocentric view of God's care, which was directed to the whole of creation.... Perhaps the single most remarkable saying in his teaching is the injunction to "love your enemies" (Matt. 5:44–45), where "enemy" should not be construed merely in terms of individuals but rather to include neighboring nations as well, who were traditionally viewed as hostile and enemies of Israel.[50]

The incident in the synagogue in Nazareth, which contains disturbing parallels with the situation in our world more than two thousand years later, suggests that the spirit of Mammon, manifested in ways that were highly visible among the privileged and powerful, was also at work at the opposite end of society as Jewish villagers, suffering trauma after decades of oppression, fell prey to nationalist demagogues promising a literal reversal of fortunes. In such a situation, Jesus walked a tightrope between the imperial power of Rome, on the one hand, and the ideology of a growing ethnic nationalism (so resonant of political populism in the globalized world today) on the other.[51] In precisely such a situation he offered his hearers a vision of the world which lay completely beyond the possibilities of the existing worldviews, but this promise of a different world was conditional on willingness to allow his prophetic words to transform minds, desires and wills and so open up undreamed-of imaginative possibilities.

The Sermon on the Plain

The shape and extent of those new possibilities are to be seen most clearly in the instruction which Jesus reserved for those who had committed themselves to discipleship. This teaching is recorded in the famous Sermon on the Mount at the beginning of Matthew's gospel and is paralleled in Luke by similar instructions scattered at different points in the Third Gospel. The teaching of Jesus in these texts is generally recognized to be the expression of the very core of his message concerning life within the kingdom of God,

---

50. Freyne, *Jesus Movement*, 145.

51. "Only the permanent following of Jesus could provide the incentive to remake the world in ways that were different to anything that either Rome or Jerusalem might have to offer" (Freyne, *Galilee and the Gospel*, 286).

yet throughout the subsequent history of Christianity it has been repeatedly treated as an "ideal," a transcendent model to which Christians should aspire, while claiming that the actual praxis demanded by Christ is simply impossible in the "real world." As a result, that "real world," the existing society structured by the ideology of Mammon, takes precedence over Jesus's articulation of God's dream of a new and transformed society in which the ancient vision of shalom is fulfilled.

In fact, the first disciples struggled with the challenges posed to their assumptions and behaviour by what has been called the "values revolution" which Jesus proposed. Freyne comments that even the briefest perusal of the gospels shows how much Christ's teaching "has to do with the dangers of wealth, the blessedness of the poor, and the need to follow his example in the renunciation of home, property and wealth."[52] When the disciples heard Jesus's requirement that a wealthy member of the elite, a genuine enquirer not unlike Theophilus, was required to sell everything, give to the poor and *then* "come, follow me," they responded with the astonished question: "Who then can be saved?" (18:18–29). Towards the end of his ministry, the request of James and John for pre-eminence indicated the degree to which existing cultural values continued to shape their desires, showing just "how domesticated even they, the Galilean fishermen, had become with the reign of Caesar." "Jesus was not about to replace one kingdom with another, as they expected. It would take the 'failure' that was about to be accomplished in Jerusalem to open their eyes to appreciate just how radically different his vision was, and the consequent urgency of the present moment."[53]

We limit consideration of the Sermon on the Plain to two passages unique to Luke which take us to the radical core of the Jesus movement. Where Matthew locates Jesus ascending "a mountainside" and then seated to instruct his disciples, Luke's setting is a "level place" where Jesus stands to teach (Luke 6:17). The differences in such details may simply suggest that this core message was repeated on various occasions in "oral performances" which were never identical to previous such pronouncements.[54] The first of our texts

---

52. Freyne, *Jesus Movement*, 92.

53. Freyne, 175.

54. James A. Maxey describes how his work as a translator among a tribal people in Cameroon opened his eyes to the similarities between the cultural patterns of oral communication in Africa and the context in which the New Testament emerged. "Could one

follows the Beatitudes which pronounce a series of blessings on disciples, but Luke then adds the following *woes* on the rich and privileged:

> But woe to you who are rich,
>   for you have already received your comfort.
> Woe to you who are well fed now,
>   for you will go hungry.
> Woe to you who laugh now,
>   for you will mourn and weep.
> Woe to you when everyone speaks well of you,
>   for that is how their ancestors treated the false
>   prophets. (6:24–26)

The unambiguous nature of this language cannot be avoided or diluted, not least because it is entirely consistent with the themes we have already noticed in Mary's Song and in the first public announcement of the coming of the kingdom of God in the Nazareth sermon. The warnings are directed to the upper stratum of an imperial society in which the division of power split the population into "a small power elite on one side and masses of the powerless on the other."[55] In contrast to the modern world, there was no "middle class" but a very small, mainly urban, upper stratum, and an enormous lower stratum straddling either side of the crucial divide above or below subsistence. Above that line it was possible to exist with some degree of economic security, but circumstances beyond an individual's control might swiftly transform a person's prospects, creating deep anxiety at finding oneself in peril. At the lowest level of all were the totally destitute, the "absolutely poor," of whom it has been said "they have only rags for clothes, and are without lodging or hope." Jesus's description of the opulence of the rich, both here and especially in the parable of the rich man and Lazarus (16:19–31), must be heard in relation to this deeply divided society. For example, his references to food

---

imagine the biblical text being performed in a like manner as a folk tale? These are the same biblical texts that were at one point in history oral compositions, performed in public, in interaction with the audience. The biblical message presented with the power of the spoken word, addressing a specific occasion and an audience, had been instrumental in the transformation of the hearers in early Christianity" (*From Orality to Orality: A New Paradigm for Contextual Translation of the Bible* [Eugene: Cascade, 2009], 11).

55. These are the words of Stegemann and Stegemann in *Jesus Movement*, 67. This classic study contains an extended discussion of the socio-economic structure of the ancient world in relation to the story of the Jesus movement.

and clothing are illuminated by the following description of the lavish way of life of the elite:

> A special mark of wealth was the convivial banquet, to which rich friends, neighbors, and relatives were invited. They were then offered the most select morsels from all over the Empire. Yet even beyond these banquets the lives of the rich were distinguished by their choices of nourishment. . . . The wealthy stood out from the rest of the population not only through their opulent eating habits but also through their clothing.[56]

The woes pronounced on the rich are thus directed to the elite who, like the rich man in the parable, lived in luxury, physically and socially sealed off from the rest of the world as the beneficiaries of a system in which the wealth of God's creation was syphoned off to maintain their privileges and to reward fawning acolytes incapable of speaking truth to absolute power. Within this system the plight of huge numbers of people locked into the lower stratum, including rural day-labourers and the slaves on whose labour the economy depended, was the reverse side of a society structured to make possible the opulence of the elite minority. In addition, this glaring imbalance required the continuous use of war and violence, including the threat of death by crucifixion, to sustain it. We have referred earlier to the violence of the Roman legions in supressing outbreaks of rebellion and insurrection among the Jewish people, and the use of crucifixion as a very public form of terror was justified by the ruling elite as a necessity to maintain the much-lauded Pax Romana. The historian Tacitus acknowledged that enslaved peoples drawn from conquered nations across the known world were "in our households, practicing strange customs, and foreign cults, or none – and it is only by terror that we can coerce such scum."[57]

If Jesus's solemn warning of judgement on the super-rich sounded distinctly subversive in the social situation we have described, the second passage unique to Luke can seem equally shocking, but in this case it is would-be

---

56. Stegemann and Stegemann, 79.

57. Quoted in Tom Holland, *Dominion: The Making of the Western Mind* (London: Little, Brown, 2019), xiv. On the very day this paragraph was typed a rebellion by shareholders of the clothing company Boohoo was reported. It arose because of the organization's failure to provide Asian workers in factories in Leicester with proper protection and fair wages. At the same time fifteen key managers were about to share a £150 million bonus (*The Guardian*, 19 June 2021, 46).

disciples who are likely to find his words disturbing. Immediately after the pronouncement of woe upon the hoarders of wealth and possessions, the "little flock" are reminded that they are the vanguard of a revolution of love: "Love your enemies . . . bless those who curse you . . . give to everyone who asks you" (6:27–31). This summons to radical discipleship is later expanded when Jesus spells out the concrete actions required of disciples in regard to ownership and possessions:

> Do not be afraid, little flock, for your Father has been pleased to give you the kingdom. Sell your possessions and give to the poor. Provide purses for yourselves that will not wear out, a treasure in heaven that will never fail, where no thief comes near and no moth destroys. For where your treasure is, there your heart will be also. (12:32–34)

In a world in which the cultural value of "honour" was associated with wealth and possessions, and the absence of money led to the ascription of "shame" for an individual, Jesus demanded what would today be described as a form of "downward mobility" which was the antithesis of the values of the dominant culture. This constituted the most direct challenge to the beliefs and policies of the Romans and their Herodian partners, but it also stood in the sharpest contrast to the attitudes of Jewish groups such as the Pharisees, who Luke says "loved money" and dismissed the teaching of Jesus concerning the impossibility of serving God and Mammon with sneering contempt (16:13–15).

However, we should not be too quick to pass judgement on this rejection of Christ since, as we have seen, the behaviour he demanded of would-be disciples ran completely counter to the values governing society and appeared to be utterly absurd from that perspective. John V. Taylor comments that what Jesus began in Galilee was a movement which has continued ever since of women and men "whose stock in trade is a kind of defiant absurdity, the absurdity of behaving openly as though they are living in a different world from this, under a different regime, with quite different assumptions." The "little flock" constituted the foundation of a new community committed to following Jesus, and they had "the gall to live as though God's future were already reaching into the present." In both the gospel and the book of Acts, Luke follows the progress of this community, dubbed the "people of The

Way," as they offered a broken world "a sign of that future which continues to haunt even those who reject it as unrealistic."[58]

Which brings us to the crucial observation that the radical praxis demanded by Jesus was inseparable from, and completely impossible without, the earth-shattering assurance which precedes his instruction concerning possessions: "Do not be afraid, little flock, for your Father has been pleased to give you the kingdom" (12:32). If, when reflecting on the words of Jesus, we *begin* with questions concerning the rejection of possessions and the feeding of the poor, we are likely to end up in confusion and will seek ways to evade the real challenge of the text. The practice of discipleship does not, cannot, stand alone; it flows from the revolutionary news that the kingdom of God has come among us, that the Father has entrusted to the "little flock" the experience of a totally new way of life which is nothing less than the beginning of the renewal, restoration and redemption of *all things.*

According to the Bible, from the beginning of creation God's kingdom reached out far beyond human individuals, or even entire societies; it possessed a *cosmic* dimension, stretching to the farthest reaches of the Milky Way and reaching down to the smallest animals, to birds, plants and flowers, and to the soil which sustains all life. Which is why Jesus insisted that his disciples should "consider how the wild flowers grow" and how the birds of the air have no need of storerooms or barns! In a society increasingly obsessed with money and possessions the followers of Jesus were not only to care for creation, but to show the wisdom and humility to learn from it (12:22–31).

This "kingdom of God," having been subverted and overthrown by human rebellion and hubris, was replaced by the ever-widening empires which rose and fell throughout history, but the prophetic hope of messianic renewal was now becoming a reality, and was entrusted to the little flock! It came with no vast armies waving banners and carrying weapons of destruction, and was completely devoid of sophisticated propaganda and coercion, making its way in a broken world through a small group of rather ordinary people determined to follow Christ and imitate his way. It is this utterly new reality, the coming of God, addressed by Jesus as "Father," which underlies the

---

58. John V. Taylor, *Kingdom Come* (London: SCM, 1989), 92. Joachim Jeremias says that all disciples of Jesus "have been shaken out of the security of their possessions" and experience "a revision of all values." Having discovered the great treasure, "all other values have faded in the light of the supreme value" (*New Testament Theology*, 223).

critical choice now presented to the people of Israel, and later to be offered to the entire human family: the decision to follow God rather than Mammon. The all-encompassing power of the latter was already obvious, but with the coming of Christ the radical alternative became visible as God initiated the "last days" and offered humankind the prospect of a world made new.

In 1946 the Dutch theologian Johan Bavinck published a remarkable book from which the quotation at the head of this chapter is taken. He had written *Between the Beginning and the End* during the German occupation of his country and at about the same time that Albert Camus was describing the "absurdity" of the culture of post-war Europe. As the horrors of the Holocaust came to be known and the first nuclear weapons were unleashed on the Japanese cities of Hiroshima and Nagasaki, Bavinck suggested that humankind was being confronted as never before with the choice between God and Mammon. Surveying the immediate post-war wreckage of Europe, he lamented that although the heavens continued to declare God's glory, "we alone have refused to be included in that act of worship," and human life was being reduced "into a flight to the bomb shelters." The culture which increasingly came to dominate the Western world had left human beings with no purpose other than "to safeguard ourselves from the calamities that threaten us from all sides." A generation which had witnessed horror and death on an unimaginable scale now had to choose whether to continue on the path of metaphysical rebellion, or to listen afresh to the invitation of Jesus and receive the gift of the kingdom of God. I quote at some length from Bavinck's comment on that kingdom because it describes so well the gift which the Father had granted to the "little flock."

> Christ's suffering and death – indeed the entire order of redemption – has no other purpose than the realization of the kingdom. Grace itself is not there for its own sake. The central point of the gospel is not us poor humans and our pain and suffering; rather, its entire focus is aimed at the unique and powerful reality that God wants to reinstate his kingdom.
>
> It is God's intention to unite all fractured parts of his creation into one overarching harmony. There is no such thing as individual salvation. All salvation is of necessity universal. The goal of our life can never be that we personally may enjoy God and

be saved in him. The goal of our life can only be that we again become part of the wider context of the kingdom of God, where all things are again unified under the one and only all-wise will of him who lives and rules for ever.[59]

Two Lukan Parables

According to Joachim Jeremias, the parables of Jesus "belong to the bedrock of the tradition about him" and are without any parallel in the literature of the intertestamental period or in contemporary rabbinic teaching. They occupy a particularly important place in Luke's gospel and we will briefly notice two of them which, taken together, lead us to the heart of Jesus's message. In approaching these narratives we must abandon any idea that what we are dealing with here are simple stories designed to communicate ethical values to unsophisticated, rural people. That the parables are artistically beautiful and, in Jeremias's phrase, take us "into the midst of everyday throbbing life" is indeed the case, but they emerge in contexts of fierce debate and controversy and concern issues of absolutely fundamental importance.[60] To downgrade them to simple tales intended to inculcate ethical principles is to ignore the profound nature of the teaching of Jesus and to miss the importance of his parables as perfect models of narrative, poetic theology of a kind that is desperately needed when "the western world is dying for want of a story."[61]

These comments apply especially to the (over)familiar parable of the good Samaritan (10:25–37). The context of debate and hostile questioning is immediately evident in the description of "an expert in the law [who] stood up to test Jesus." The question he presented concerned the conditions required to

---

59. Bavinck, *Between the Beginning and the End*, 34–35.

60. Jeremias, *New Testament Theology, Volume One* (London: SCM Press, 1971), 30. See also his *The Parables of Jesus*, 3rd ed. (London: SCM Press, 1972).

61. See John Carroll, *The Western Dreaming: The Western World Is Dying for Want of a Story* (Sydney: HarperCollins, 2001). He writes: "The spirit cannot breathe without story. It sinks to a whimper, deflating its housing characters, and condemning them to psychopathology – literally, disease of the soul. So it is for the young in the contemporary West – teenagers, those in their twenties, the hope and pride of their societies – and with them, swathes of their seemingly more assured elders. A malaise holds them in thrall, struggling to live in the present without vision of any future, or connection to even the organic tissue of being, their own personal past" (6).

attain "eternal life," but the debate shifts to the issue of neighbourly love – and it turns on the text in Leviticus 19:18 which, readers may recall, we discussed in chapter 3.[62] In the parable, as in the Hebrew Bible, the question is, how to define the neighbour? Where is the line to be drawn? In particular, how far does the obligation *to love* the neighbour extend? By raising this issue the questioner intended to draw Jesus into a topic of regular theological discussion among the rabbis. They all agreed that the commandment embraced fellow Jews, but some excluded proselytes, and they were certain that the duty of love should not be extended to Gentiles. The story with which Jesus responds to the lawyer's self-justifying question is completely authentic in its geographical and social details and drops a bombshell into this discussion. His description of a lonely traveller who suffers a grievous assault on the notorious road from Jerusalem to Jericho and is left unconscious and naked, and is thus bereft of both visible and verbal means by which his ethnic identity might be established, presents listeners with nothing other than a human being in desperate need. In Bailey's words, "He belonged to no man's ethnic or religious community! It is such a person that the robbers leave wounded beside the road. Who will turn aside to render aid?"[63]

The failure of a priest and a Levite to respond to this man's perilous situation sets a scene in which Jesus's audience probably anticipated that a good Jewish layman would now appear! The sequence priest–Levite–layman was a familiar one and would satisfy the anti-clerical attitudes of many of the listeners. No one could possibly have anticipated the unthinkable introduction of a hated Samaritan, a traditional enemy belonging to a people routinely cursed in the synagogue with a daily petition that Samaritans might not be partakers of eternal life!

Kenneth Bailey, who spent decades living and working in Palestinian villages, comments that while a story about a noble Jew who helped a wounded Samaritan might have been absorbed by Jesus's hearers, the parable's introduction of a Samaritan who fulfils the deepest intention of the law of God was unthinkable. Bailey himself confesses that he had never felt able to tell a

---

62. See note 11 on page 33 which concerns the translation of the Hebrew of this critically important text.

63. Kenneth Bailey, *Through Peasant Eyes: More Lucan Parables* (Grand Rapids: Eerdmans, 1980), 43. This wonderful book is an indispensable guide to the Lucan parables.

story to modern Palestinians about a noble Jew, or one concerning a noble Turk to Armenians:

> Only one who has lived as part of a community with a bitterly hated traditional enemy can understand fully the courage of Jesus in making the despised Samaritan appear as morally superior to the religious leadership of the audience. Thus Jesus speaks to one of the audience's deepest hatreds and painfully exposes it.[64]

The tables have been well and truly turned. But more is to follow: having exposed himself to the grave risk of assault by the bandits responsible for the original attack, the Samaritan places his life in even greater danger by transporting the wounded stranger to an inn and making costly provision for his care. The marvellous construction of this parable is evident in the way in which the central figure, having compensated for the failures of the priest and the Levite, ends up doing the same thing in relation to the actions of the robbers, caring for the victim they had assaulted and promising to "return," in contrast to their abandonment of the anonymous traveller.

The theological implications here are multiple and profound: the story exposes the sheer ugliness of religion without grace, while at the same time indicating that grace-filled living may be discovered where it is least expected. As Bailey points out, the religious professionals who ignored the needs of the stranger were constantly engaged in ritual practices of worship and sacrifice in the Jerusalem temple, but it is the outsider, the hated enemy, who "pours out the libation on the altar of this man's wounds."[65] We might describe the parable as a wonderful exposition of Leviticus 19:18, and as it reaches its conclusion Jesus asks who was neighbour "to the man who fell into the hands of robbers?" The lawyer is unable to utter the word "Samaritan," but cannot avoid the conclusion: "The one who had mercy on him." The instruction of Jesus to "go and do likewise" was surely intended to convince his questioner of the sheer impossibility of such a way of life apart from grace, while for the disciples it amounted to a summons to practise the love and compassion for all needy people which was to be one of the distinguishing marks of life within the kingdom of God. Finally, such compassion demanded a new attitude

---

64. Bailey, *Through Peasant Eyes*, 48.
65. Bailey, 50.

towards money and possessions: the Samaritan *paid* the innkeeper for both accommodation and care of the anonymous victim and committed himself to the reimbursement of unknown additional expenses "when I return"!

If the parable of the good Samaritan concerns the second great commandment, to "love your neighbour as yourself," we must ask where we find such a poetic description of the prior duty, to "love the Lord your God with all your heart and with all your soul and with all your strength and with all your mind"? The threefold parable in Luke 15 occurs in a similar context of hostility and controversy, sparked in this case by the actions of Jesus in welcoming "sinners" and eating with them (15:1–2). The climax is reached with the story often called "the prodigal son" (15:11–32) which is concerned not so much with the practice of discipleship as with its deepest *theological foundations*.

Once again, the narrative is completely true to the social and cultural context, both in the suggestion of tensions between the generations, and in the description of the urban flight taken by many younger people. The phenomenon of urbanization, then as now, created huge pressures on traditional, rural societies, and the city, with its different cultural values, acted as a magnet for the young who sought an escape from patriarchal structures.

It has frequently been said that anyone who attempts to wrestle seriously with this text will end up astonished at its richness and depth of meaning. While it arose from, and clearly reflects, the first-century context which we have described, it speaks in a remarkable way concerning the ambiguities and distress of human societies in every age, including the era in which we find ourselves today. During the Second World War the great German preacher Helmut Thielicke delivered a remarkable series of sermons on this parable in Stuttgart and Hamburg at a time when those cities were being reduced to rubble by Allied bombing. He called the series, which was attended by thousands of people facing a desperate plight, "The Waiting Father," and repeatedly discovered direct analogies between the ancient text and contemporary reality:

> Again this text catches at us and we feel that we are hearing a part of our own biography. But it also grasps at our whole generation. Is not Europe, is not the Christian Western world

on this same road of separation from its origin and the source of its blessings?[66]

We must limit comment here to a single question: how does this matchless text describe Yahweh, the God whom Jesus addressed as "Father" and taught his followers to do the same? There are three elements to the answer: first, *the father in the parable permits his son the freedom to reject him*. The action of the younger son in requesting the division of his father's estate when the older man was alive and in good health amounted to a scandalous wish for the father's death. Bailey reports asking many people across the Middle East what this request for inheritance while one's father was alive would mean in their cultures, and everywhere the answer was the same: the boy wished his father dead!

> In the Middle Eastern milieu the father is expected to explode and discipline the boy for the cruel implications of his demand. It is difficult to imagine a more dramatic illustration of the quality of love, which grants freedom even to reject the lover, than that given in the opening scene.[67]

Later in this present book we shall discuss the "death of God" in modern culture and this image of a wounded father, deeply pained by his beloved son's rejection and disdain, will become directly relevant. The father's pathos stems not only from the pain of personal rejection and public humiliation, but also (and perhaps much more) from his knowledge of the consequences of the beloved son's decision to migrate to the "distant country" and the perils of life in the city which would confront him there.

Which brings us, second, to the *father's unquenchable love, demonstrated in his waiting, yearning and embrace of the chastened rebel*. The turning point in the narrative is reached with the phrase "When he came to his senses..." (15:17). In Christian terminology it is the moment at which a process of conversion commences as the father's love and mercy, seen now from the perspective of the heartlessness of a world in which "no one gave [the son] anything," become the source of hope and the motor of repentance. We cannot

---

66. Helmut Thielicke, *The Waiting Father: Sermons on the Parables of Jesus* (London: James Clarke, 1960), 23.

67. Kenneth Bailey, *Poet and Peasant and Through Peasant Eyes: A Literary-Cultural Approach to the Parables in Luke* (Grand Rapids: Eerdmans, 1983), 165.

dwell on the extraordinary depiction of the father except to notice that he not only waits and watches continually, but at the first glimpse of the returning prodigal runs to meet him outside the village, heedless of his own reputation among neighbours and determined to embrace the son, so protecting him from the wrath of a community angered at the violation of its deepest values. In Bailey's words, "The father makes reconciliation public at the edge of the village. Thus his son enters the village under the protective care of the father's acceptance."[68] In the immediate context of the parable, this is Jesus's vindication of his own joyful embrace of "tax collectors and sinners," demonstrating their entrance into the new community by "eating with them," and expressing God's boundless mercy and kindness to the despised and alienated people who were forcing their way into the kingdom.

We noticed above that the parable of the good Samaritan can be seen as a commentary on the Levitical law concerning the neighbour and there is, I suggest, a similar connection to the Hebrew Bible in the description of the pathos of the father in Luke 15. Sean Freyne has noted the importance of the experience of the prophet Jeremiah as a "well-remembered precedent" to the ministry of Jesus, especially with regard to the conflict with the Jerusalem temple authorities.[69] There is, however, an even more direct and remarkable connection between the young Jeremiah and this parable, specifically concerning the pathos of the father. When Jeremiah realized that King Josiah's attempted reformation was doomed to failure because the apostasy of "faithless Israel" was too far gone to be arrested, he gave voice to a poetic utterance which reveals Yahweh's pathos as a *wounded father*:

> I myself said,
>
> "How gladly would I treat you like my children [or "sons"]
>   and give you a pleasant land,
>   the most beautiful inheritance of any nation."
> I thought you would call me "Father"
>   and not turn away from following me. (Jer 3:19)

---

68. Bailey, *Poet and Peasant*, 182.

69. See Freyne's excellent discussion in *Jesus, a Jewish Galilean: A New Reading of the Jesus-Story* (London: T&T Clark, 2004), 163–65.

The same pathos of God as a father lamenting a lost son reappears later in the prophecy where, if anything, it is articulated in poetic language which depicts ever more clearly the vulnerability of God's suffering love:

> "Is not Ephraim my dear son,
> > the child in whom I delight?
> Though I often speak against him,
> > I still remember him.
> *Therefore my heart yearns for him;*
> > *I have great compassion for him."*
> > declares the LORD. (31:20)

If, as Freyne suggests, the prophecy of Jeremiah played a significant role in the self-understanding of Jesus concerning his own messianic calling, these texts disclose the very heart of Yahweh and must surely have contributed to the shaping of the unforgettable image of the father in this parable. This has massive implications for this book because it reveals the character of the God who has offered the world a radical alternative to the reign of Mammon, and now in the person of Jesus invites the whole human family to return home from the far country.

The final element in the parable's description of the father concerns *his grace towards the elder brother, described as resentful, sullen, and devoid of grace in his responses both to the returning prodigal and to their loving father.* There are indications from the beginning of the story that all was not well with this son's relationship with his father and the hidden resentments, carefully nurtured and allowed to fester over time, burst into the open with his defiance of the father's wish that he join the celebration at the prodigal's return. The Arab commentator Said Ibrahim observes helpfully:

> The younger brother was estranged and rebellious while absent from the house, but the older son was estranged and rebellious in his heart while he was in the house. The estrangement and rebellion of the younger son were evident in his surrender to his passions and in his request to leave his father's house. The estrangement and rebellion of the older son were evident in his anger and refusal to enter the house.[70]

---

70. Quoted in Bailey, *Poet and Peasant*, 197.

The description of the older son is clearly held up like a mirror to Jesus's critics, that they might see themselves as they were and be humbled by their lack of grace and the debilitating self-righteousness of their religion. It is a mirror which can enlighten, disturb and become the agent of transformation for people at other times and places. This wonderful story has spoken repeatedly to musicians, writers and artists who have been captivated by the power and beauty of the narrative. It was especially important for the Dutch painter Rembrandt whose unfinished canvas *The Return of the Prodigal Son* was discovered in his studio following his death. In its turn this great painting impacted the life of the Catholic writer Henri Nouwen, and we leave this text with his response after gazing on Rembrandt's wonderful canvas in St. Petersburg:

> I am the prodigal every time I search for unconditional love where it cannot be found. Why do I keep ignoring the place of true love and persist in looking for it elsewhere? Why do I keep leaving home where I am called a child of God, the Beloved of my Father? I am constantly surprised at how I keep taking the gifts God has given me – my health, my intellectual and emotional gifts – and keep using them to impress people, receive affirmation and praise, and compete for rewards, instead of developing them for the glory of God.... Beneath it all is the great rebellion, the radical "No" to the Father's love, the unspoken curse: "I wish you were dead." The prodigal son's "No" reflects Adam's original rebellion: his rejection of the God in whose love we are created and by whose love we are sustained.[71]

The Mystery of Golgotha

As we conclude this chapter we may wonder how the "most excellent Theophilus" reacted to the story which Luke related. We have necessarily been very selective in the texts we have examined, so that, for example, the devastating parable of the rich man and Lazarus (16:19–31), or Jesus's encounter

---

71. Henri Nouwen, *The Return of the Prodigal Son: A Story of Homecoming* (London: Darton, Longman & Todd, 1994), 43.

with the rich young ruler (18:18–30), and the story of the conversion of Zacchaeus, whose salvation was demonstrated by the reparations made to the poor and oppressed (19:1–9), would all have presented the gospel's dedicatee with formidable challenges, as indeed they were to do in the coming centuries when increasing numbers of wealthy Romans were attracted to the Jesus movement. We have no information concerning Theophilus's response, but the fact that Luke later addressed a second volume to him suggests that the gospel had deepened his interest and curiosity and that his hunger for knowledge of Christ was undiminished.[72]

If the life and teaching of Jesus posed an enormous challenge to people belonging to the elite and privileged stratum of society in the ancient world, an even greater obstacle to faith and discipleship was to come in the gospel's account of the tragic and disgraceful end to that life. Earlier in this chapter we described the manner in which the Roman authorities used crucifixion as a means of social control and as a highly visible deterrent to people perceived to be criminals or political rebels. By the time Luke was writing his gospel this most barbaric form of execution had been deployed to an unprecedented degree at the climax of the Jewish-Roman war during the fall of Jerusalem in 70 CE. Josephus was an eyewitness of these terrible events and reported how the Roman general Titus gave his soldiers free rein to torture their victims in ways that defy description. Josephus said that the number of Jewish men executed in this way "was so great that there was not enough room for the crosses and not enough crosses for the bodies."[73]

Not only was death by crucifixion excruciating for the victim, but because a large proportion of the population of the Roman Empire accepted the propaganda which celebrated the coming of a universal peace as the result of imperial conquests, individuals who suffered death in this way were "defamed both socially and ethically in popular awareness." In other words, there is little evidence from this period of sympathy, let alone compassion, for "the boundless suffering of countless victims of crucifixion."[74] Given that this was

---

72. It is worth noting that the reference to Theophilus in Acts no longer includes the title "most excellent." Might this suggest that Luke's correspondent had recognized the implications of discipleship in regard to the culture of honour and status?

73. Quoted in Martin Hengel, *Crucifixion in the Ancient World and the Folly of the Message of the Cross* (Philadelphia: Fortress, 1977), 26.

74. Hengel, *Crucifixion in the Ancient World*, 88.

the case, how would the "most excellent Theophilus" have reacted to the story of the passion of Jesus of Nazareth?

In one of the most moving narratives in his gospel, Luke describes the depth of trauma which the death of Jesus on Golgotha created among his own disciples when, in the terrible darkness of the Holy Saturday which stands between cross and resurrection, we overhear a conversation between two of them walking away from Jerusalem with downcast faces, confessing their loss of hope beneath the long, deep shadow of the cross on Calvary (24:13–34). Martin Hengel concludes that to claim that God had entered into death "in the form of a Jewish manual worker from Galilee" was to invite derision and contempt, and he adds that even now "any genuine theology will have to be measured against the test of this scandal."[75]

Why then, knowing very well the opprobrium which the message of the cross would attract, did Luke and his fellow evangelists, following the pioneering mission of the "apostle to the Gentiles," make "Christ and him crucified" the focal point of their narratives?

The question can be answered in different ways, but I want to draw attention to a theme which runs through the Third Gospel from beginning to end: the announcement that in the life and death of Jesus a *peace* had come into the world which fulfilled the age-old dreams of the prophets of a time of universal reconciliation. Ulrich Mauser, in a rich study of the subject of peace in Luke's gospel, says that the word itself comes close "to being a theological term which captures the whole meaning of the Christ event."[76] The entire story is framed by the opening angelic announcement to shepherds of the arrival of "peace on earth" and the closing greeting of the risen Lord to his astonished disciples, "Peace be with you."

> In the Lukan writings, the whole ministry of Jesus . . . can be summed up by calling it the good news of peace. From his birth on, he is designated from above to realize peace on earth, a peace seen and praised by the Christian community, but yet in grave jeopardy because of its rejection by powerful and influential groups who manage, in the end, to get rid of the troublesome

---

75. Hengel, 89.
76. Mauser, *Gospel of Peace*, 46.

intruder through whom God's peace threatened to break out all over the world.⁷⁷

The peace of Christ thus came into direct conflict with the peace of Rome. The latter "embodied the idea of external relations based on the great power achieved by the Roman Empire" and was inseparable from the conquest and subjection of the nations by military might.⁷⁸ The Pax Romana thus constituted one point of reference for the peace of Christ, but the other was the dream of the Hebrew prophets that a time would come when the nations would abandon training for war, beat their swords into ploughshares, and together "walk in the light of the LORD." In fact, the very language of "peace" in the Greek New Testament involves a translation of the crucial Hebrew term "shalom," which means that it is freighted with the centuries-long anticipation of the healing of the brokenness of the world in the messianic age.

This obviously has huge implications for our understanding of the gospel since the life and teaching of Jesus posed a challenge to imperial power, not in the manner of the Jewish rebels whose armed struggle ended so tragically, but at a far deeper level which called into question the very nature of the power of which the Romans boasted. The incarnation exposed such power, and the Roman claims based upon it, as fraudulent and idolatrous, while the life of Jesus and his little flock displayed the radically different way of life together within the kingdom of God.

Johan Bavinck said that to stand at the foot of the cross of Jesus is to be overwhelmed with the mystery of this event and to feel that we are "at the outermost edge of our knowing and understanding." How can we comprehend the fact that humankind here "takes God and discards him, plunging him into the infinite depth of death"? What we witness here is not simply the tragic death of yet another victim of human cruelty and arrogance, but the clash of two kingdoms in which the incarnate God "is forcibly removed from the worldly domain and hanged on a rough piece of wood and driven back to the realm of the dead. Imagine humanity being alive and God being dead!"⁷⁹

The death of Jesus at Golgotha thus defies human understanding and its meaning must forever transcend our attempts to grasp it, no matter how

---

77. Mauser, 49.
78. See Zampaglione, *Idea of Peace*, 135.
79. Bavinck, *Between the Beginning and the End*, 113.

many theories of atonement are to be devised across the following centuries. However, what the New Testament affirms is that in the person of Jesus of Nazareth nailed to a Roman cross, God was reconciling the world to himself, and in that confession the image of God is forever transformed. The pathos of God, which we have already seen had been recognized within the Hebrew Bible, is now revealed in the passion of Jesus, so that through all the coming ages the "knowledge of the cross brings a conflict of interest between God who has become man and man who wishes to become God."[80]

It would be impossible to overstate the importance of this revelation of the being of God with regard to our concern in this book with the choice between God and Mammon. We have yet to discuss Mammon in the form it has taken in modern times, but the injustice, social division and cruel violence so clearly evident under the imperial powers of the ancient world already anticipate the regime of death which will emerge once Mammon's reign becomes well-nigh universal. The God who offers us the alternative is the Father revealed by Jesus whose sacrificial love for the world has been displayed on the hill of Golgotha.

---

80. These are the words of Jürgen Moltmann in *The Crucified God: The Cross of Christ as the Foundation and Criticism of Christian Theology* (London: SCM, 1974), 71. William R. Burrows warns against what he calls the "over-objectifying" of the Christ event, and describes the symbol "of the death of the God-man" as the "focal-point in the New Testament's portrayal of Jesus as liberating humankind from sin and death and as revealing the heart of Godself." However, if Jesus's death is "seriously misconstrued and falsely objectified, it will necessarily lead to dangerous consequences" ("A Seventh Paradigm? Catholics and Radical Inculturation," in *Mission in Bold Humility: David Bosch's Work Reconsidered*, eds. Willem Saayman and Klippies Kritzinger [New York: Orbis, 1996], 125).

CHAPTER 5

The Original Revolution

> The "forgiveness of sins" was a huge, life-changing, world-changing reality, long promised and long awaited. It was the fulfilment of Israel's hopes for restoration, coupled with the sense that when Israel was restored, this would somehow generate a new day for the whole human race. It is startling to reflect on just how diminished the average modern Western Christian vision of "hope," of "inheritance," or indeed of "forgiveness" itself has become. . . . We have domesticated the revolution. (Tom Wright)[1]

We have reached an important point of transition in the story we are attempting to tell in this book. In the previous chapters we described the emergence of the distinctive faith of biblical Israel in the ancient world and traced the centuries-long struggle to confess that faith in the context of the successive imperial powers which deeply challenged it. The decision to worship and obey Yahweh involved a commitment to a way of social and economic life together in a covenantal community which stood in the sharpest contrast to the hierarchical structures characteristic of the empires. The temptation to conform to "the way of the world" was constant and became stronger over

---

1. Tom Wright, *The Day the Revolution Began: Rethinking the Meaning of Jesus' Crucifixion* (London: SPCK, 2016), 115. Keith Hopkins comments that "the worship of a crucified criminal as the son of God, the divine exaltation of a humble human, the crucifixion of God . . . constituted a radical break with pagan polytheism. . . . Christianity subverted the whole priestly calendar of civic rituals and public festivals upon which Roman rule in the provinces rested. Christianity was a revolutionary movement" (*A World Full of Gods: Pagans, Jews and Christians in the Roman Empire* [London: Phoenix, 1999], 78).

time, but the memory of the exodus and of the tribal confederation remained alive and gave birth to the prophetic vision of a messianic age when all the nations on earth would find freedom, justice and peace as the reign of Israel's liberating God became universal.

Luke's first volume provided "an account of the things that have been fulfilled among us" (1:1), of the creation of a new, messianic community in the context of the most powerful and extensive empire then to have existed within human history. The subject which pervades his second volume, the book of Acts, concerns the transition by which that movement, birthed in the context of rural Galilee and with its urban focal point on the city of Jerusalem, expanded across the eastern empire, spreading the message of the crucified Messiah in the very different cultural context of the Roman cities which dotted this landscape. The narrative reaches its climax in the city of Rome itself with Paul's bold claim that "God's salvation has been sent to the Gentiles, and they will listen!" (28:28).

However, we begin at the beginning: Acts opens with an address to Theophilus in which Luke draws attention to his "former book" in which he had written "about all that Jesus began to do and to teach" (1:1). This clearly indicates continuity between the two volumes, both in the sense that the addressee remains the same and, more importantly, because the previous account of the life, death and resurrection of Jesus is the foundation of the story now to be unfolded. This means that the book of Acts cannot be treated independently of the gospel because the story of the life and teaching of Jesus provides both the core message to be taken "to the ends of the earth," and the non-negotiable pattern of the individual and shared lives of those who will enter the new community, later to be described as "the followers of the Way." We shall return to that phrase, but here we note that it references the life of Jesus in the context we have described in the previous chapter and in so doing suggests the urgent significance of the *praxis* of the movement that will bear his name.

The point being made here is important in view of the tendency of many scholars and commentators to argue that Luke's account of the missionary expansion of the Jesus movement in the cities of the Roman Empire is politically innocuous. This is the claim, for example, of Seyoon Kim, who argues that Luke's two volumes demonstrate "the politically innocuous nature of both the gospel of Jesus and the gospel of Paul." He further claims that Paul's letters contain "no warning about the imperial cult and no message subversive to the Roman Empire."[2]

Surprisingly, it is not only conservative evangelicals who propose such readings of the book of Acts, but scholars from the opposite end of the theological spectrum who argue for a liberationist interpretation of the New Testament can be found making similar statements. Steven Friesen accuses Luke of "being silent on the issue of economic justice" and claims that no attempt is made in the book of Acts "to explain the huge gap between the wealthy imperial elites and everyone else." This seems an odd statement in the light of the fact that at the very commencement of his narrative Luke twice records the radical social experiment of the early disciples in Jerusalem who "shared everything they had" (2:42–27; 4:32–37). Friesen dismisses this as the portrayal of "a quaint artefact of an idealized past" which is presented in such a manner as to confine the redistribution of goods "to an earlier period of history that has ended."[3]

I want to argue that the placement of this description of economic solidarity at the commencement of the story of the believing community is dictated by a concern which is exactly the opposite of that proposed by Friesen: it both functions as the *foundation* for the practice of the followers of Jesus in the future, and it is placed at this point as a concrete example of obedience to the radical teaching of Jesus in the Gospel, and as the direct consequence of the coming of the Holy Spirit. This is the action of a group of disciples for whom the memory of the words and deeds of Jesus remained a powerful reality, creating a form of apostolic community intended to function as the model for the people of "the Way" throughout the subsequent story.[4] It has also

---

2. Seyoon Kim, *Christ and Caesar: The Gospel and the Roman Empire in the Writings of Paul and Luke* (Grand Rapids: Eerdmans, 2008), 66, 77. This reading of the New Testament correlates with an understanding of mission in the modern world in which individual conversion is of central importance and poses no challenge to existing political or social structures. Kim tells us that Paul "just concentrated on winning believers in Christ and forming alternative communities in preparation for the eschatological consummation" (52–53).

3. Steven J. Friesen, "Injustice or God's Will? Explanations of Poverty in Proto-Christian Communities," in *A People's History of Christianity*, vol. 1, *Christian Origins*, ed. Richard A. Horsley (Minneapolis: Fortress, 2005), 251.

4. Note the words of Walter Brueggemann: "The common good of the early church spoke deeply against such stratification that was embodied in the imperial pyramid, even as it speaks now against unregulated possessive individualism and accumulation." The positioning of the description of this common life so early in Acts makes it "the basis of all that follows

remained as an abiding and disturbing challenge for Christianity across the following centuries. As C. Kavin Rowe puts it, the book of Acts can no longer be treated as "a simple *apologia* that articulates Christianity's harmlessness vis-à-vis Rome": "Rather . . . Luke's second volume is a highly charged and theologically sophisticated political document that aims at nothing less than the construction of an alternative total way of life – a comprehensive pattern of being – one that runs counter to the life-patterns of the Graeco-Roman world."[5]

We also need to stress that the reference to Theophilus indicates that Luke's purpose in compiling this history is the same as that which motivated his writing of the gospel, so that he remains the *elite evangelist*, responding to enquirers from privileged backgrounds in a manner that continues to be both contextually relevant and uncompromisingly faithful. If, as Friesen claims, Acts describes Roman military officers as "sympathetic characters," this is not evidence that Luke ignores the realities of imperial oppression, but rather the outcome of the practice of mission in the way of Jesus Christ. Luke feels compelled to obey Jesus in loving those regarded as enemies, and this leads him to the discovery of a deep hunger for truth and grace concealed beneath a Roman centurion's military garb. As we shall see, a central aspect of this story is the crossing of the cultural barrier between Jew and Gentile, a process initiated almost accidentally by the apostle Peter, who was compelled to confess that his inbred prejudices concerning non-Jews had been exposed by the face-to-face encounter with a Roman centurion, an experience through which "God has shown me that I should not call anyone impure or unclean" (10:28).[6]

---

in the book" (*Money and Possessions*, Interpretation: Resources for the Use of Scripture in the Church [Louisville: Westminster John Knox, 2016], 211).

5. C. Kavin Rowe, *World Upside Down: Reading Acts in the Graeco-Roman Age* (Oxford: Oxford University Press, 2010), 4.

6. The story of the encounter between Peter and Cornelius in Acts 10–11 is a key moment in Luke's narrative. Justo L. González describes "the enormity of this episode" in which a massive racial, cultural and religious barrier is crossed by Peter's act of entering the house of a Gentile who represented the colonial power which had "conquered practically the entire known world and thanked their gods for it." If this bold action resulted in the conversion of the Roman centurion and his household, it also transformed Peter to such an extent that we might describe his experience as a "second conversion." González points out that contemporary Christians are now the ones "who have laws, rules, and principles that . . . run the risk of being obstacles to our mission" (*Acts: The Gospel of the Spirit* [New York: Orbis, 2001], 134–35).

From Galilee to the Roman Urban World

The story told in Acts concerns the expansion of the Jesus movement, geographically, numerically and cross-culturally. In the previous chapter we described the context of the ministry of Jesus in a Galilee marked by rapid and far-reaching changes. A primary factor in the disruption of traditional patterns of life was the phenomenon of urbanization, first in the shape of the building projects of Herod the Great, then in the rebuilding of Sepphoris on a Roman model in the very heart of Galilee, and the even more dramatic emergence of the new capital of Tiberias on the shores of the Lake of Galilee. Sean Freyne has discussed the attitude of Jesus towards this urban culture in great detail and concludes:

> The consistent criticism of wealth as well as the rejection of the Herodian court life-style point unmistakably to *a distancing from that world, both physically and emotionally.* Jesus is not critical of the city, just as he does not romanticize rural life, but I do believe that the silence about a visit to Sepphoris or Tiberias is not accidental. His opposition is not to places as such, but to certain values that are associated with city dwellers, especially among the elites who shaped and dominated their ethos, especially as this was viewed from the distance of the peasant.[7]

Luke's second volume describes an interlocking series of transitions by which the story of Jesus as the promised Messiah was spread far beyond its original, Palestinian context. In this process the awareness of the universal significance of Jesus increased and the challenge which his life and message originally presented to Galilee and Jerusalem was discovered to have a similar revolutionary significance in Roman urban settings across the eastern empire. While the primary urban focal point for the Galilean Jesus had been the city of Jerusalem, over which he uttered a moving lament, the narrative of the cross-cultural spread of the gospel in Acts has the urban world of the Roman Empire as its main focus. The period of history during which the events described in this book occurred was precisely the era in which that empire attained its greatest glory and influence throughout the Mediterranean world,

---

7. Sean Freyne, *Galilee and the Gospel* (Boston: Brill Academic, 2002), 71; emphasis added. Many of the chapters in this volume deal specifically with the response of Jesus to an urbanizing culture and to Herodian economics.

and the boast of the Romans was that their conquests enabled them to become the agents of civilization, understood to mean "the 'citification' of the world." This phrase comes from Justo González, who adds that for the Romans, "the greatest human creation was precisely the city, and their purpose in history was to promote city life throughout their empire."[8]

The book of Acts is consequently a history of urban mission and the story it relates moves from Jerusalem to Caesarea, then on to Antioch, and thence to Athens, Corinth and Ephesus, before reaching the imperial capital itself. Laura Nasrallah notes that there is "something peculiarly geographical" about Luke-Acts, and she describes the narrative of Luke's second volume as being "restless and urban"; it relates the story by which "Christianity is propelled from the margins of empire to its very heart in the imperial capital of Rome."[9]

The contrast between this urban context and that which we have described in the previous chapter can be seen in the language of the famous Roman orator Aelius Aristides, who said that the world had never previously witnessed urbanization on this scale. It was now possible to traverse the empire and pass through a different city on every day of one's itinerary. In fact, using the celebrated Roman roads which connected cities to each other, a traveller might actually pass through two or three cities on the same day![10] Writing in the second century, Aristides reserved his most lavish praise for the imperial capital, describing it in terms which suggest striking parallels with the urban world of today:

> Here is brought from every land and sea all the crops of the seasons and the produce of each land, river, lake, as well as the arts of the Greeks and barbarians, so that if someone should wish to see these things, he must either see them by travelling over the whole world, or be in this city. . . . So many merchants' ships arrive here, conveying every kind of goods from every people every hour and every day, so that the city is like a factory common to the whole earth. It is possible to see so many

---

8. González, *Acts*, 10.

9. Laura Nasrallah, "The Acts of the Apostles, Greek Cities, and Hadrian's Panhellion," *Journal of Biblical Literature* 127, no. 3 (2008): 533–66.

10. Note the language of the Letter of James: "Now listen, you who say, 'Today or tomorrow we will go to this or that city, spend a year there, carry on business and make money'" (Jas 4:13).

cargoes from India and even from Arabia . . . that one imagines that for the future the trees are left bare for the people there and that they must come here to beg for their own produce if they need anything.[11]

The story Luke tells in the book of Acts may be said to pivot on the account of the Damascus road experience of Saul of Tarsus in chapter 9. This encounter with the risen Christ was to bring into the expanding Jesus movement a devout Jew who was entirely familiar with the culture of the urban world. In a now-classic study, Wayne Meeks noted that the city breathes through the language of Paul and that the mission he led "was entirely urban." Meeks comments that "the mission of the Pauline circle was conceived from start to finish as an urban movement," with the result that within a decade of the crucifixion of Jesus, "the village culture of Palestine had been left behind, and the Greco-Roman city became the dominant environment of the Christian movement."[12]

As we have seen, the growing numbers of converts who joined this new community are identified throughout the book of Acts as those "who belonged to the Way" (9:2). The recurrence of this phrase, and the absence of the terminology of "Christianity" (except as a label invented by outsiders to mock the followers of the crucified Jesus), strongly suggests that it was a distinctive mode of life, shaped by the stories converts had been told concerning the person of Jesus, which defined his Jewish followers and the ever-growing circle of gentile enquirers.[13] The use of this term suggests belief in the redemptive significance of the death and resurrection of Jesus, while at the same time clearly referring to the impact of his teaching and the example of the life that was cruelly ended on the hill of Calvary. That teaching and life, recorded in Luke's first volume, was now to be reflected in the praxis of the new community, such that there is an inseparable relationship between

---

11. Quoted in Richard Bauckham, *The Climax of Prophecy: Studies on the Book of Revelation* (Edinburgh: T&T Clark, 1993), 375. Notice the important comment of Alison Futrell in note 23 on page 75 of this present book.

12. Wayne A. Meeks, *The First Urban Christians: The Social World of the Apostle Paul* (New Haven: Yale University Press, 1983), 10–11.

13. Note C. Kavin Rowe's comment: "'Christian' was from first to last a term of derision, a way in which pagan 'outsiders' – Roman administrative and otherwise – could specify with a single word the problematic contour of the followers of the man *Christus*" (*World Upside Down*, 154).

faith and practice in which the apostles' preaching of the resurrection of Jesus resulted in "God's grace ... powerfully at work in them all [and] ... there was no needy person among them" (4:33).

When Peter found himself standing before "a large gathering" of gentile enquirers, he declared that God's message to Israel was "good news of peace [shalom] through Jesus Christ, who is Lord of all," and he explicitly stressed the *life* of the Christ who "went around doing good and healing all who were under the power of the devil" (10:27–38). In a suggestive phrase, Rowe concludes that the early church's practice of mission was "the embodied pattern of Jesus's own life ... as narrated in the Gospel of Luke and retold in the speeches of Acts."

> Thus, the truth claim about Jesus's Lordship does not lead in Acts to ... the need to coerce others for their own good but to a form of mission that rejects violence as a way to ground peaceful community and instead witnesses to the Lord's life of rejection and crucifixion by living it in publicly perceivable communities derisively called Christians.[14]

The early chapters of the book of Acts contain repeated indications that the dramatic growth of the Jesus movement was related to the impact of the radical nature of the shared life of the first disciples who, in the eyes of the populace of an occupied and troubled Jerusalem, *actually looked like the promised messianic community within which the power of Mammon was being broken and the Mosaic dream of a society shaped by love and justice was becoming reality.* In modern times Luke's depiction of this new community led Johan Bavinck to conclude that "however costly and well-organized" Christian witness within a secular society today may be, if it "is not rooted in a church that has found the secret of mutual love," it will be powerless and in vain.[15]

However, the attractive power of the shared life of this new community was interpreted by religious and political leaders as a direct challenge to the established structures of government and economy! Crucial as the praxis of

---

14. Rowe, *World Upside Down*, 173. He adds: "Theologically said, ecclesiology is public Christology."

15. J. H. Bavinck, *An Introduction to the Science of Missions* (Philadelphia: Presbyterian and Reformed, 1960), 47. He goes on to say: "The success of the work of missions and the work of evangelism depends upon the ability to arouse envy."

the first believers unquestionably was with regard to the credibility of their witness in the urban culture of the Roman Empire, we must not romanticize this practice of discipleship, turning it into a painless technique, or a "missional strategy" designed to achieve evangelistic success. Luke leaves not the slightest doubt that this radical community was bound to provoke a strong reaction from the defenders of imperial power and order, and it was therefore destined, like its Lord, to experience suffering and martyrdom. We are not at the halfway point in the book of Acts before we have seen Peter and John arrested, imprisoned and beaten, Stephen stoned to death by a frenzied mob, James beheaded, and Peter incarcerated for the second time and facing the prospect of execution. As Richard Cassidy has pointed out, a key word with which Luke describes the disciples' lives and witness is the Greek term translated as "boldness." This characteristic was recognized by the authorities who were astonished by the courage of "unschooled, ordinary men" who, they realized, "had been with Jesus" (4:13). This theme runs through Luke's narrative from beginning to end, so that in the final scene Paul is discovered bound in chains in Rome, awaiting Nero's life-or-death verdict on his case, and yet *boldly* preaching "the kingdom of God" and teaching "about the Lord Jesus Christ" (28:31).[16]

Turning the World Upside Down

We have described the Damascus road experience of Saul of Tarsus as a pivotal moment in this story because the transformation which occurred in his life was truly profound and brought into the movement a person who was to play a crucial role in its future. In the move from Luke's gospel to the book of Acts we cross not only from Galilee to urban Rome, but from the Jewish world shaped by the biblical narratives of creation and fall, of the gift of Torah, the praise of the Psalms, and the dreams of the Hebrew prophets, into a culture created by Roman myths and conquests, including the imperial claim that the Augustan age had brought universal peace to the world. This ideology, presented as "good news" through images, inscriptions, public festivals and

---

16. See Richard J. Cassidy, *Christians and Roman Rule in the New Testament: New Perspectives* (New York: Crossroad, 2001), 51–67. I must acknowledge my debt to Cassidy's work and pay tribute to his scholarship which has so persistently and courageously drawn attention to the imperial context of the New Testament literature.

games, and on coins minted in celebration of military conquests, was visible on the streets of every Roman city. Davina Lopez has alerted us to the huge significance of visual imagery in the Roman world and she describes how buildings, monuments and altars dedicated to the imperial cult embedded Roman claims within the very fabric of the cities, legitimizing the Roman domination of the world. The rule of the divine Caesars came to be presented "as the logical culmination, fulfilment and purpose of the 'fundamental principles of the world.'"[17]

If the message of the crucified Christ was to penetrate this culture it required a process of *translation* which would eventually bring it into direct confrontation and conflict with the ideology and idolatry of the empire. Not without reason did God reveal that Saul of Tarsus was chosen "to proclaim my name to the Gentiles and their kings and to the people of Israel," and that this task would involve him in much suffering (9:15–16). The scope of Paul's ministry and the extent of his vision of the reign of Israel's liberating God is encapsulated in his closing greeting to the church in Rome where he expresses the hope "that all [nations] might come to the obedience that comes from faith" (Rom 16:26). Lopez summarizes this messianic vision as follows:

> Paul, as an apostle who goes down among the defeated nations, has had to come to terms with the ideological configuration designating all others as inferior to Roman rule. In the prophetic new creation Paul is struggling so hard in labor to usher into being, all of the nations must turn away from idolatry – civic worship of the one master of the world – and turn as children toward the God of Israel, the creator of the world, who will reconcile them with one another and end war forever.[18]

The question might be asked at this point whether the ideology of Mammon has now receded and been replaced by a different form of political religion on the world stage? The answer is that, while the term itself does not appear in Luke's second volume, *the reality to which it refers is present on almost every page in the depiction of the enslaving power of money and possessions and the consequent immiseration of the slaves whose labour sustained*

---

17. Davina C. Lopez, *Apostle to the Conquered: Reimagining Paul's Mission* (Minneapolis: Fortress, 2008), 96.

18. Lopez, *Apostle to the Conquered*, 150.

the imperial economic system, and the migrants who streamed into the slums of the Roman cities, abandoning ancestral lands which had been appropriated by the super-rich, urban elite.[19]

We mentioned above that imagery on coinage played a significant role in promoting the Roman worldview throughout the empire. Larry Kreitzer has shown the ways in which numismatics can shed a great deal of light on the context of the New Testament as a whole since "coinage served as one of the primary vehicles of the communication of news and policies, in much the same way that official press releases on radio or TV function in the modern world."[20] Roman coinage was far from being a neutral channel of information; it was a powerful tool of imperial propaganda, celebrating Roman conquests and triumphs, reminding defeated peoples of their new identity as subjects of the empire, and promoting the cult of the divinity of the Caesars. One of the most famous such coins fulfilled all of these roles when it depicted the victory of Vespasian and Titus over the Jewish rebels in Jerusalem in 70 CE. The *Judaea Capta* deployed striking images of a dejected, bound female figure, representing the vanquished Jewish people, while the obverse showed the laureated bust of the victorious emperor. The frequent references to money in the book of Acts need to be heard in relation to both the idolatry of Mammon and the function of coinage as a means of propagating the Pax Romana.[21]

---

19. "The wealth of the patrician landowners who sat in the Senate, the tribunals that represented the *plebs*, the military power, the official artists who were protected by their patrons . . . even the architecture and statues in the cities and the circulation of Roman coins *contributed to a concentration of power with the intention of leaving no space for any alternative*" (Nestor Miguez, Joerg Rieger and Jung Mo Sung, *Beyond the Spirit of Empire: Theology and Politics in a New Key* [London: SCM, 2009], 8).

20. Larry J. Kreitzer, *Striking New Images: Roman Imperial Coinage and the New Testament World* (Sheffield: Sheffield Academic, 1996), 22.

21. Edmundo F. Lupieri observes that in New Testament times the Roman Empire had created "a relatively larger diffusion of a standardized monetary system" which resulted in "a flourishing market economy" which allowed "quick fortunes to be built and destroyed, especially those based on shipments of durable goods." The scenario for the dominance of this new economy was the many new cities designed "to serve as harbors or commercial centres" ("'Businessmen and Merchants Will Not Enter the Places of My Father': Early Christianity and Market Mentality," in *Money as God? The Monetization of the Market and Its Impact on Religion, Politics, Law and Ethics*, eds. Jürgen von Hagen and Michael Welker [Cambridge: Cambridge University Press, 2014], 379–81).

Figure 3: *Judaea Capta* **coin: 69–70 CE with image of the victorious Vespasian on one side and symbolic figures representing defeated and enslaved Jewish rebels on the other**[22]

Consider Luke's report of the response of Peter to the lame beggar who had "asked them for money" at the gate of the Jerusalem temple: "*Silver or gold I do not have*, but what I do have I give you. In the name of Jesus Christ of Nazareth, walk" (3:1–6). This incident comes immediately after the account of the sharing of goods within the Jerusalem community, an action which had resulted from the disposal of private property and the support of "anyone who had need." Did Luke perhaps intend that Theophilus and other wealthy enquirers would make a connection between Peter's disavowal of money and the gospel story of Jesus who, questioned regarding Roman taxation, requested the *loan* of a denarius in order to point out the significance of the image it bore (Luke 20:23–25)? Was there an apostolic decision to live outside the Roman market economy and so to model an alternative practice of a common-wealth in obedience to the example and teaching of their Master and Lord?

What is beyond dispute is the fact that concern about the relationship between faith and money surfaces continually throughout Luke's narrative. The seductive power of money and its vice-like grip on human desire is dramatically illustrated in the story of Ananias and Sapphira (5:1–9), while the complicity of certain mantic practitioners with extortion and material gain is exposed in the account of Simon the sorcerer who, despite believing the gospel and being baptized, viewed the gift of the Holy Spirit as a potential money-spinner, provoking Peter's unambiguous response: "May your money

---

22. Classical Numismatic Group, Inc. http://www.cngcoins.com. CC BY-SA 3.0 https://creativecommons.org/licenses/by-sa/3.0/

perish with you, because you thought you could buy the gift of God with money!" (8:18–24).

If the story told in Acts frequently highlights the pervasive power of money and the threat it posed to the practice of radical discipleship, it also indicates that the early experiment of sharing resources within the disciple community became the model for a tradition which can be traced throughout this history. The "daily distribution of food" to widows in Jerusalem created tensions between different ethnic groups within the emerging movement, but rather than abandon the project it was placed on a firmer basis and given a status alongside "the ministry of the word," thus becoming a key component in what might be called "integral mission." This combination of faith-as-trust-in-Jesus and faith-as-praxis resulted in the number of disciples increasing "rapidly" and "a large number of priests" becoming "obedient to the faith" (6:1–7).

When the movement spread beyond Jerusalem and Judea and the city of Antioch became the new centre of missionary expansion into the gentile world, the distinctive economics of the kingdom of God continued to shape the lives of converts, so that when a "severe famine" threatened the Mediterranean world during the reign of Claudius, the Antiochean church demonstrated its solidarity with impoverished Jewish believers by providing "help for the brothers and sisters living in Judea" (11:27–30). This action, which involved Barnabas and Saul transporting the donated funds to Jerusalem, is especially significant because it suggests that the economic implications of discipleship had been made clear in the missionary proclamation, and it anticipates the crucial importance which economic solidarity was to have in the future ministry of Paul, when (as we shall see) it became a distinguishing mark of the empire-wide movement of the people of the Way.

However, before we look more closely at Paul's missionary practice, we must consider the manner in which the conflict between God and Mammon deepened and intensified as the missionary translation of the gospel in the Greco-Roman cities of the eastern empire created previously unknown pastoral and theological challenges. Andrew Walls traces the origin of this cross-cultural movement back to the actions of anonymous Jewish believers in Antioch who "began to talk to their Greek pagan friends about Jesus, whom they and all other Christians at that time thought of as the Jewish national saviour." They "risked a dangerous translation" by ascribing to Jesus "the title their pagan friends used for their cult divinities – that is *Kyrios*, Lord. *That event marked the beginning of the conversion of the Greek world.*"²³

By the time we reach Acts 15 the initial trickle of gentile converts begun in Antioch has become a constant stream so that Paul and Barnabas can claim that God had "opened a door of faith to the Gentiles" (14:27). The debate triggered by this momentous development centred on the question of whether these new converts were required to abandon their own heritage and adopt a new ethnic (Jewish) identity in order to follow Christ. The conclusion, following long and passionate discussion, is summarized in the words of James that "we should not make it difficult for the Gentiles who are turning to God" (15:19). Walls has pointed out that this decision involved the repudiation of the Jewish practice of proselytization, by means of which Gentiles attracted to the synagogue had abandoned their previous identity "and entered the nation of Israel." Paul and his colleagues realized that "the path of the proselyte was a blind alley for gentile disciples of Jesus."

> They had to bring Christ to bear on areas of life of which people who had been observant Jews all their life knew nothing; and if they became proselytes, became in effect imitators of Jewish Christians, they would be disabled from bringing Christ to bear on those areas. The faith of Christ had immediately to be applied to situations quite outside the experience of the devout people who formed the backbone of the early Church.²⁴

The crucial decision made in Jerusalem liberated Paul and his colleagues to engage in the first great cross-cultural transmission of the faith of Jesus Christ in the ancient world, a development that was to have enormous historical consequences. In the context of the story Luke tells in Acts, it meant that the summons for a decision between God and Mammon took on a new dimension with regard to the urban world of imperial Rome and sparked public

---

23. Andrew F. Walls, *The Missionary Movement in Christian History: Studies in the Transmission of Faith* (Edinburgh: T&T Clark, 1996), 52–53; emphasis added. Notice, however, that *Kyrios* was also used in relation to the Caesars, as Oscar Cullmann observed: "We can assume as true that the profession *Kyrios Iesous Christos* . . . represents a kind of controversial response to the same title *Kyrios* given to the Hellenic deities *and the Emperor*" (quoted in Nestor O. Míguez, *The Practice of Hope: Ideology and Intention in 1 Thessalonians* [Minneapolis: Fortress, 2012], 80; emphasis added).

24. Walls, *Missionary Movement*, 51–52.

controversy once local authorities came to suspect that it posed a serious challenge to the very foundations of Greco-Roman culture. In Philippi, Paul's act of exorcism which liberated a slave girl whose owners treated her mantic gift as a valuable economic asset, led to the arrest of the apostles and the accusation that they were "throwing our city into an uproar by advocating customs unlawful for us Romans to accept or practise" (16:16–21). Rowe comments that the exorcism created "a tear in the basic fabric of pagan popular religion" and that since "religious life was woven together with material gain" this inevitably resulted in "the unravelling of mantic-based economics as well."[25]

Clearly, Paul and his colleagues were *not* advocating riotous insurrection, and in that sense the accusation made against them was false, yet from the slave owners' perspective the deliverance of the poor girl "in the name of Jesus Christ" displayed the destabilizing power of the gospel for a form of religion which not only justified slavery, but made money from it. Those who are perceived "to pose a threat of economic and religious disaster rarely elicit affection. Given such a confrontational display of power, it is hardly surprising that after their beating and imprisonment, the missionaries are finally asked to leave the city."[26]

Luke makes only brief mention of Paul's stay in the city of Thessalonica, but indicates that a reputation for insurrection had preceded the apostle and his colleagues and resulted in a baying mob hauling the missionaries' hosts before the city officials with the charge: "These men who have caused trouble all over the world have now come here. . . . They are all defying Caesar's decrees, saying that *there is another king, one called Jesus*" (17:5–9).

The description of the ministry in Thessalonica in Acts needs to be complemented by the information contained in Paul's correspondence with the young church within that city. On the basis of texts such as 1 Thessalonians 2:9 and 4:11–12 it appears that the majority of converts "came from the manual-labor sectors and from urban commerce, along with some companions from the lowest sectors in society, that is, male and female slaves and free individuals, and men and women with no fixed jobs."[27] It is tempting to speculate that, if this conclusion is accepted, some of those whom Luke described as

---

25. Rowe, *World Upside Down*, 26–27.
26. Rowe, 26–27.
27. Miguez, *Practice of Hope*, 39.

"bad characters from the market-place" (Acts 17:5), people without employment, reduced to loitering in public space in the hope of whatever casual day-labour might be available, could have been among these converts. Does Luke's designation of them betray his lingering elitist presuppositions about a class of people described as the "absolute poor," driven to the very margins of imperial society and generally classified as "the scum of the earth"?[28]

Whether or not this was the case, Paul's pastoral concern for his converts necessarily included the need for both guidance and example in relation to economic necessities in a society which excluded the majority of its inhabitants from either personal security or meaningful existence. The *guidance* is evident in the exhortation to "work with your hands . . . so that your daily life may win the respect of outsiders and so that you will not be dependent on anybody" (1 Thess 4:11–12); the *example* is set by Paul's own behaviour in refusing to place a burden of hospitality upon his converts, so that he recalls, "we were gentle among you, like a nursing mother taking care of her own children" (2:7 ESV). His testimony that the depth of his love for the poor in this city compelled him to share his life in companionship and solidarity by working "night and day" in "toil and hardship" (2:9) suggests that the artisan's workshop was the primary context within which the concrete reality of the kingdom of God became visible in the city of Thessalonica. As Miguez concludes, "Paul comes to love them with such intensity that he is willing to give them his own breath . . . and he has come to share with them in their efforts and sufferings his own servile labor."[29]

The proclamation of the reign of "another king," the appearance of a new community which embraced Jews, Greeks, "quite a few prominent women" (Acts 17:4), and slaves and labourers from the lowest stratum of society, and the challenge to the cultural values of shame, honour and patronage by a social vision in which converts would "not be dependent on anybody,"

---

28. Note Neil Elliot's comment: "The urban slums teemed with semiskilled or unskilled workers, scrapping for occasional work to keep them just above the level of beggary and destitution" ("The Apostle Paul and Empire," in *Hidden Transcripts and the Arts of Resistance: Applying the Work of James C. Scott to Jesus and Paul*, ed. Richard A. Horsley [Atlanta: Society of Biblical Literature, 2004], 98).

29. Miguez, *Practice of Hope*, 71. Miguez observes: "Evidently, Paul does not see in his work as an artisan . . . happiness or the fulfilment of the human condition. The work through which he supported himself during his stay in Thessalonica was heavy and tiring and would take his best hours" (65). See also 1 Cor 4:10–12; 9:18–19; 2 Cor 11:7, 27.

combined to present the ideology of imperial Rome with a challenge that could not be ignored.

There are many texts in the New Testament in which scholars have detected the presence of what have been called "hidden transcripts," articulations of the radical political implications of the message of the crucified Christ which would have been recognized within the community, but veiled from the eyes of imperial censors.[30] However, when Paul tells his Thessalonian converts that the people who "are saying 'Peace and safety'" will face sudden destruction "and will not escape" (1 Thess 5:3), it is difficult to avoid the conclusion that he makes a direct assault on Roman propaganda. The widely used phrase *pax et securitas* expressed the central boast of the imperial conquerors that they had established an unassailable power over the world. The "peace and security" which the Romans celebrated did indeed seem to be based on an "indestructible political unity and military strength," and the apostolic response to this was to say, "We cannot have an army that would refute it, *but we can have a hope that would relativize it.*" "Christians did not respond with another force that would oppress, persecute, and kill the agents of Roman domination, but responded with a negation of the order as a whole, with an invitation to adopt a differentiated practice in the light of a shortening present time."[31]

We return to Luke's narrative in the book of Acts and pick up the story in the city of Ephesus. The events described in Acts 19 make the reading of this book bear comparison with hearing a great symphony in which the gradual increase of tension finally results in a massive crescendo as the pressures which have been building up burst into an explosion prior to the triumphant resolution and conclusion. In fact, Luke records a double explosion, one which relates to the multiple practices of magic within Ephesus and results in an extraordinary "bonfire of the vanities" (19:18–20), and the other which impacted the great temple at the heart of the metropolis and triggered an uproar which spread through "the whole city" (vv. 23–41).

---

30. See for example N. T. Wright's discussion of what he calls "Paul's coded challenge to Empire in Philippians 3." The statement in 3:20 that believers' citizenship is in heaven, "and from it we await the Saviour, the Lord Jesus, the Messiah," contains titles routinely used of Caesar. "The whole verse says: Jesus is Lord, and Caesar isn't. Caesar's empire, of which Philippi is a colonial outpost, is the parody; Jesus' empire, of which the Philippian church is a colonial outpost, is the reality" ("Paul's Gospel and Caesar's Empire," in *Paul and Politics*, ed. Richard A. Horsley [Harrisburg: Trinity Press International, 2000], 173).

31. Wright, "Paul's Gospel," 178; emphasis added.

It is almost impossible for modern, Western people to appreciate the all-pervasive presence of magical practitioners in the ancient world, or to recognize the worldview which created the demand for such people. Moyer Hubbard speaks of a "thunderous collision" between the disenchanted universe of the post-industrial Western world, in which the cosmos has become empty and silent, and the unseen realm of the first century which was populated by a vast array of spiritual powers which were believed to impact human life in all kinds of ways.[32] Diviners, sorcerers and an army of priests offered access to supernatural help and protection related to difficulties in human relationships, including the affairs of the heart, protection from illness, whether physical or mental, and safety through the crucial turning points in life, especially pregnancy and childbirth, together with what has been called "imprecatory magic" by which spiritual powers might be invoked to cause harm or death for another human being.

In this context the proclamation of the lordship of the crucified Jesus was in the most profound sense *revolutionary*. It did not involve the denial of the reality of the spiritual realm, but declared that the lordship of the risen Jesus extended into every nook and cranny of that world, as well as to the spheres of creation and history. Consequently, the announcement of Jesus as *Kyrios* in Ephesus sounded like very good news to poor people since it not only challenged the political hegemony of the Caesars, but also exposed the perversion of popular religious cults, many of whose practitioners preyed on the vulnerability of the poor for their own material enrichment.[33]

What we witness taking place here is precisely the act of *translation* to which reference was made earlier, but this involved more than a merely linguistic process since the story of Jesus was retold in a manner that demonstrated the coming of the kingdom of God in the particular contexts of the

---

32. Hubbard's statement merits quotation: "The thunderous collision of our largely disenchanted universe (in the post-industrial West, at least) with the thoroughly enchanted universe of the first century is nowhere more earsplitting than when contemplating popular religiosity in its seemingly infinite permutations." *Christianity in the Greco-Roman World*, 26.

33. Peter Brown, discussing the Roman world centuries *after* Christ, comments: "Of all the collective representations that had to move, through the slow redrawing of the map of the divine world at the behest of Christian theologians and preachers, the ancient representation of the *mundus* was the one which shifted with the slowness of a glacier" (*Authority and the Sacred: Aspects of the Christianisation of the Roman World* [Cambridge: Cambridge University Press, 1997], 9).

Roman cities. The gospel was related not only as the means of atonement for sin, but as the despoiling of the unseen realm of the powers, so that the Christ who had "died for our sins" and was "buried" and "raised on the third day" (1 Cor 15:3–4) had *entered into the realm of the dead* and extended the victory won on Calvary within that sphere. Elsewhere in the New Testament, John of Patmos was to preface his Apocalypse with a vision of Jesus declaring: "I am the Living One; *I was dead*, and now look, I am alive for ever and ever! *And I hold the keys of death and Hades*" (Rev 1:18). Not only the world of the living, but also the realm of the dead is brought under the rule of the Prince of Peace, with the result that "neither angels nor demons . . . nor any powers, neither height nor depth," could separate believers "from the love of God" in "Christ Jesus our *Kyrios*" (Rom 8:37–39).

The truly extraordinary thing about Luke's description of the response to this message is that it was received and embraced not only by those who were the victims of perverted magical beliefs and practices, but also by a large number of *practitioners* who came to recognize what we may call their "professional lives" as having involved deeds which they now recognized as being "evil." They demonstrated the sincerity of their conversion through an extremely costly, public action which testified to their repudiation of the past and a complete severance from it! As Rowe says, the public burning of the scrolls which contained the secrets of their trade, and were valued at fifty thousand drachmas, displayed the irreversibility of the practitioners' confession:

> Books once burned can never be retrieved. The termination of magical practice and the burning of the books that make such practice possible thus visibly mark and publicly proclaim the end of a way of life. The life that supports and is supported by magic has gone up in flames.[34]

---

34. Rowe, *World Upside Down*, 43. Notice, though, that the decision to destroy the scrolls was freely made by the converts, not imposed by the apostles. Had this action been dictated by outsiders (as happened frequently when missionaries in the modern era required such acts as evidence of conversion), the outcomes could have included the loss of elements in local culture which were vital to the identity of the converts. They were given liberty to determine, under the guidance of the Spirit, those components of the past life which *they now identified* as "evil," and those which might be redeemed and placed at the feet of the crucified *Kyrios*.

What then of the second explosion? Luke moves to this incident by informing his readers that "there arose a great disturbance about the Way" (19:23). The focus shifts to the great temple of the goddess Artemis which enjoyed an international reputation and drew huge numbers of visitors. It was an ancient equivalent of a major tourist attraction and pilgrimage site, with its multi-breasted goddess the focus of devotion, especially for pregnant women who sought her protection during the perilous time of childbirth. Yet again, the inseparable relationship between religion and money is given prominence in the focus on Demetrius the silversmith, "who made silver shrines of Artemis" which "brought in a lot of business for the craftsmen."

The great temples of the ancient world not only created environments within which such "service industries" came into existence and flourished, but also functioned as banks, providing facilities for loans and the exchange of currency, thus supporting commerce throughout the empire and making possible the international trading activity of merchants, sailors and elite landowners.[35] Hubbard points out that in the shift from the sorcerers and practitioners of magic arts to the silversmiths whose industry depended upon the temple complex, the narrative underlines the connection which Luke repeatedly draws between spiritual and economic power structures, "and in this respect it portrays a single, isolated scene of a much larger cultural drama slowly beginning to unfold throughout the Greco-Roman world. What was the crucial issue that prompted the uproar? Money."[36]

Once again, the dramatic portrayal of the impact of the gospel in the book of Acts needs to be read alongside the letters addressed to the communities which sprang from the apostolic mission. The letter we know as that addressed to the Ephesians is almost certainly a circular epistle intended for a number of congregations, but what it says concerning the transformative power of the gospel, and the great vision of the universal extent of God's redemptive purpose in Christ, would have had a particular resonance in the city of

---

35. See the discussion of the economic function of temples in Dieter Georgi, *Remembering the Poor: The History of Paul's Collection for Jerusalem* (Nashville: Abingdon, 1992), 141–65. Luke has previously described Jesus's encounter with money-changers in the Jerusalem temple and his anger that the "house of prayer" had been turned into "a den of robbers," a phrase which clearly echoes the language of Jeremiah centuries earlier (Luke 19:45–46).

36. Moyer V. Hubbard, *Christianity in the Greco-Roman World: A Narrative Introduction* (Peabody: Hendrickson, 2010), 49.

Ephesus. Imagine, for example, the dynamic relevance of the description of the transforming power of grace for those practitioners of occult powers who had abandoned everything to follow Christ. Surely their experience is mirrored in the dramatic contrast between, on the one hand, a past life marked by "separation," "exclusion," being "without hope and without God in the world," and, on the other, the new life in Christ by which "the cravings of our flesh . . . its desires and thoughts" have been renounced by those who "have been brought near by the blood of Christ" (Eph 2:1–13). It is difficult to read these statements and not be reminded of the "double explosion" which had taken place in Ephesus and shaken that city to its religious and economic core. In that process "the mystery of Christ" had again been displayed, that "through the gospel the Gentiles are heirs together with Israel." Whereas the victories of the Roman legions had resulted in the suppression of local identities and had compelled the nations to accept their enforced incorporation within the empire, the people of the Way consisted of Jews and Gentiles who became "members *together* of one body, and sharers *together* in the promise of Jesus Christ" (3:2–6).

Andrew Walls described this event as "the Ephesian moment," a brief period in the first century in which a unity was achieved through the cross of Jesus that, rather than eliminating cultural differences, celebrated them as the means by which the richness and glory of grace might be displayed.

> The church must be diverse because humanity is diverse; it must be one because Christ is one. Christ is human, and open to humanity in all its diversity; the fullness of his humanity takes in all its diverse cultural forms. The Ephesian letter is not about cultural homogeneity; cultural diversity had already been built into the church by the decision not to enforce the Torah. It is a celebration of the union of irreconcilable entities, the breaking down of the wall of partition, brought about by Christ's death . . . (Eph 2:19–22).[37]

This underlines once more that the experience of conversion can never be an end in itself, but is the means to the far greater purpose of God in the

---

37. Andrew F. Walls, *The Cross-Cultural Process in Christian History: Studies in the Transmission and Appropriation of Faith* (Edinburgh: T&T Clark, 2022), 77.

creation of a new social body that transcends the ethnic and racial divisions of the old world and reconciles former enemies. Christ himself becomes "*our peace*," having "made the two groups one and . . . destroyed the barrier, the dividing wall of hostility" (2:14).

Is it any wonder that this messianic vision of a new, reconciled humanity should create alarm for the agents and defenders of imperialism? What happened in Ephesus was the first great tremor of an earthquake which was to shake the foundations of the ancient world since, notwithstanding the military might of the Roman Empire, the disturbance in this city pointed towards an alternative future to that embodied in the Pax Romana. Moreover, it strengthened the conviction of the people of the Way that, while still a marginal and vulnerable community, they were witnesses to the reign of Israel's God breaking into the present, justifying their hope that a different kind of human family was in the making and would result in the healing and restoration of the whole created world.[38] As Klaus Wengst says:

> The believers who participate in this peace therefore stand as it were in the breach which the resurrection of Jesus has made in the old world by marking the appearance of a new world; they hold fast to the interruption of an apparently closed course of history which has taken place in it and so represent the dawn of the new world.[39]

The final mention of the Ephesian church in the book of Acts is found in the description of Paul's later journey back to Jerusalem, when he invited the leaders of this community to meet him en route and addressed them in a moving farewell (20:13–38). At the conclusion of this valedictory message he drew attention to his own modelling of discipleship in relation to money and possessions. In a statement which must have stirred memories of the economic impact of the gospel in Ephesus, he testified that he had not "coveted anyone's silver or gold or clothing." Paul's personal praxis in relation

---

38. Nestor Miguez relates this situation to the role of Christianity in the twenty-first century when he writes that theology must "recover the place of the transcendent, of something that is *always beyond what Empire contains and what it wants to enclose*. Only when we are in this space of the transcendent, which Empire cannot contain, can we fashion a radical critique, which can never be carried out if we begin with the postulates that Empire consecrates in its immanence" ("Introduction," in Miguez, Rieger and Sung, *Spirit of Empire*, xii; emphasis added).

39. Klaus Wengst, *Pax Romana and the Peace of Jesus Christ* (London: SCM, 1987), 86.

to money clearly stood in the most striking contrast to the behaviour of the practitioners of magic who had enriched themselves by preying on the spiritual fears of poor people. By contrast, Paul expected *nothing* by way of financial support from his converts; neither here nor in Thessalonica had he received recompense for his teaching and pastoral care, but had worked with his own hands to supply "my own needs and the needs of my companions." Now he offers his practice as a model to be followed, so that "by this kind of hard work *we must help the weak*" (vv. 33–35).[40]

Here again we discover continuity with the economic practice of the first Jesus community in Jerusalem, reflecting the continuing struggle to create a commonwealth, but now on an international scale and as an alternative to the economics of the empire. The motivation for work and its rewards is transformed from the desire for personal advantage and material gain, into a social force involving the sharing of resources and an equality of status. The purpose of work and its rewards is not that of personal enrichment but the ability to "help the weak," so that the emergence of the people of the Way not only challenged the political myths of the empire but offered an alternative to its economic structure.

Finally, in a dramatic move, Paul takes the argument back beyond his own example, tracing it to its original source in the words of Jesus: "It is more blessed to give than to receive" (20:35). In that memorable phrase, which is recorded nowhere else, the economic assumptions of the empire are further undermined, as indeed are those of the economistic culture which now dominates the modern world in the twenty-first century.[41]

---

40. Peter Brown, in a fascinating discussion on money and ministry in the early church, says that Paul lived under the shadow of a negative stereotype of the religious huckster which became widespread in the ancient world, and that his words to the Ephesian elders showed "how important it was to steer clear of the accusation that he had lived off the toil of his followers." In all future centuries, "Christians looked back to it as the exemplary self-portrait of a man who had not taken the easy way out. Paul had gone out of his way to combine his missionary activities with hard work, shown by his hard hands" (*Treasure in Heaven: The Holy Poor in Early Christianity* [Charlottesville: University of Virginia Press, 2016], 10–11).

41. After this section had been written I discovered the following passage written by Richard A. Horsley. The initial sharing of possessions "was a key step in what began as a local movement among one people subjected to the Empire that then expanded steadily outwards among other subject peoples." He adds that only when Acts is read as the sequel to the Lukan gospel can we "get a sense of how it fits into the deeply conflictual politics and political economy of Roman Palestine and how the local Jesus-movement and its first expansion began to have implications for the Roman imperial order and the subsequent history of the Roman Empire"

The Collection

Earlier in this chapter I suggested that the followers of Messiah Jesus in Jerusalem appeared to have determined to live as a community outside the imperial market system, pioneering a commonwealth shaped by both the ethical and moral values of the Mosaic law and, more particularly, by the specific teaching and example of Jesus. Despite the increasing spread and influence of monetization, traditional patterns of economic life involving gift-exchange and barter continued to function, especially in rural and village life, and the rejection of private property – including the marketization of land – by the Jewish disciples of Jesus suggests a determination to model a radically alternative way of life together in the context of Jerusalem.

As we have seen, Paul's background and upbringing was that of a diaspora Jew, familiar from childhood with urban life, as his repeated expressions of pride in Tarsus, "no ordinary city" (Acts 21:39; 22:3), make clear. Our discussion of Paul's mission in the cities of the eastern empire has shown that his allegiance to the lordship of Jesus Christ was as absolute and passionate as that demonstrated by the first believers in Jerusalem, but the challenges he faced in cities like Ephesus, Athens and Corinth were of a different order from those confronting believers in Palestine. This meant that fresh initiatives were required if the distinctive ethic of the kingdom of God was to shape the economic practice of the new communities of the people of the Way in Roman cities.[42] This is an important point since Paul's practice – especially in relation to what we are identifying as "the collection" – has relevance to the challenges Christians face today in striving to be faithful to Jesus in a world dominated by global capitalism.

Luke makes only the most cursory mention of the project of the collection, reporting how, when on trial before the governor Felix, Paul testified that he had returned to Jerusalem "to bring my people gifts for the poor" (24:17). We may wonder why the author of Acts made no further reference to what was,

---

(*You Shall Not Bow Down and Serve Them: The Political and Economic Projects of Jesus and Paul* [Eugene: Cascade, 2021], 201–2).

42. "Paul's writings presuppose a monetary economy of worldwide proportions with a common (Roman) currency and an easy exchange of other currencies. This means that he was familiar with an urban society with a universal market-structure. He must have taken for granted industry, division of labor, trade, and a labor market that included slave labor" (Georgi, *Remembering the Poor*, 144).

according to the frequent mentions of this project in Paul's letters, a central feature of his practice of mission and a key component of his vision of what the gospel was destined to achieve. Paul's own account of a difficult meeting between himself and the leaders of the church in Jerusalem, including James, Peter and John, records an agreement that, as he fulfilled his God-given calling to preach Christ among the Gentiles, he would "continue to remember the poor" (Gal 2:10). The reference to "the poor" is pregnant with meaning, referring back to the significance of the phrase throughout the Hebrew Bible, but here specifically related to the believing Jewish community in Jerusalem which faced growing hostility and marginalization within that city. Prior to his encounter with Christ on the Damascus road, Paul had himself been a zealous agent of violent opposition to the Jesus people, but now, as his gentile mission bore ever more fruit, he regarded the unity of Jew and Gentile within the body of Christ as crucial to the credibility of the gospel. Which is why, perhaps with some irritation, he responded to the request of Peter and his colleagues that he "remember the poor" by insisting that it was "the very thing I had been eager to do all along" (Gal 2:10)! Brigitte Kahl concludes that "the collection" was "the emblematic trademark" of Paul's gentile mission in almost all his major epistles and it became "the social embodiment of the 'handshake of community' between Paul and the Jerusalem leaders." "The economy, politics and spirituality of the collection . . . in manifold ways subverts and contradicts the imperial order. What happens to the poor becomes a vital sign of the well-being or suffering of the collective body of Christ."[43]

It is not possible here to explore this theme in the detail which it merits, but two texts in particular will demonstrate the importance it had for Paul's concept of mission and the manner in which he understood this act of Christian solidarity to constitute a direct challenge to the reign of Mammon. First, the letters to the believers in the great city of Corinth reflect very clearly the extent of the struggle to establish the church in a context in which the local culture posed serious challenges to new converts. The disorders at the Lord's Table referred to in 1 Corinthians reflect the fact that the socio-economic divisions characteristic of the Roman Empire were resurfacing at the Corinthian church's communion love-feasts with the result that "one person

---

43. Brigitte Kahl, *Galatians Re-imagined: Reading with the Eyes of the Vanquished* (Minneapolis: Fortress, 2010), 279.

remains hungry and another gets drunk," and those "who have nothing" are left humiliated (1 Cor 11:21–22). Using the metaphor of the body, the apostle stresses that baptism is the portal by which converts pass from a corrupt and deeply divided world into the *one* body – "whether Jews or Gentiles, slave or free" – and are now to share equally in the life of one Spirit (12:12–13). In fact, he insists that within the *ecclesia* of Christ the values of status and honour embedded within the imperial social world are turned upside down; no one can disregard or despise another because God has given "greater honour to the parts that lacked it, so that there should be no division in the body" (12:24–25). What matters is not the esteem or status of individuals but the "common good" (12:7), and this new, countercultural community becomes a reality only when the mutual love so wonderfully described in chapter 13 flows freely between and beyond the people of the Way.

It is in 2 Corinthians that Paul turns to the specific issue of the collection and in doing so provides us with the most extended treatment of the economics of the kingdom of God in the New Testament. By the time this letter was written the collection among the gentile churches for the support of believers in Jerusalem was well advanced, as the opening reference to "the Macedonian churches" whose members had "urgently pleaded with us for the privilege of sharing in this service to the Lord's people" makes clear (2 Cor 8:1–5). In urging the Corinthian believers to fulfil their own previous promise to make their contribution to the collection, we notice two aspects of Paul's argument.

First, it is rooted in the example of the incarnate Jesus Christ who, "though he was rich, yet for your sake . . . became poor, so that you through his poverty might become rich" (8:9). In other words, the collection far transcends a simple act of charity and is, in fact, the expression of a totally new way of life shaped by the grace of God revealed in the Christ event. To drive this home Paul underlines the christological basis of such transformed values and behaviour at the conclusion of the chapter: "Thanks be to God for his *indescribable gift!*" (9:15). Dieter Georgi concludes:

> Paul argues emphatically for a God engaged in the human demise and impoverishment; Paul fights against a distant and unengaged deity. The deficiency of the pagan deities in his eyes would not be that they were too human, but that they were too little involved in the human dilemma. Justification is not

important merely between God and the individual, but it comes about and manifests itself in the interrelatedness of God, the world, and all humanity.[44]

The second aspect in Paul's argument in 2 Corinthians is that the collection is not a one-off, single event, but the beginning of a permanent way of life through which the people of the Way would become the harbingers of the transformation and renewal of the world. This becomes clear when Paul anticipates an ongoing cycle of the sharing of economic resources within the empire-wide body of Christ, so that the comparative "plenty" which enabled the gentile churches to relieve the poverty of their Jewish brothers and sisters in Jerusalem would likely be reversed in a new context in which "their plenty will supply what you need" (8:13–15). Twice in this text Paul indicates that the ultimate goal of such economic solidarity in obedience to the Rich One who became poor is that *"there might be equality."* He cites the biblical example of the exodus experience of the provision of manna in the wilderness when everyone was provided with *enough*!

I suggest that what is happening here is that the example of the shared life of the earliest community of Jesus-followers in Jerusalem is being transposed in the wider context of the Roman Empire in a manner that presages the spread of the revolution which had commenced on the hill of Golgotha until it reaches to the very ends of the earth. Dieter Georgi concludes that "the collection was meant to show that the Jesus-believing community represented a new creation with its roots in the resurrection of Christ, and to stress that this community was neither a prolongation of nor an addition to the old world order."[45]

Having looked at the discussion of the collection in the Corinthian correspondence, we note, second, the significant reference to it at the conclusion of the Letter to the Romans. In the penultimate chapter of this great epistle, Paul describes his burning ambition to reach the furthest western edge of the known world in order to make Christ known to the peoples of Spain. He expresses the conviction that his mission to the Gentiles in the cities of the eastern empire is completed since he had "fully proclaimed the gospel of Christ" across that vast region (Rom 15:19). Obviously, this does not mean

---

44. Georgi, *Remembering the Poor*, 159.
45. Georgi, 53.

that half of the Roman Empire was now evangelized, but rather that the seed of the gospel had been planted in major urban centres throughout that area, and the foundations were laid for the centuries-long task of translating the message in the Greco-Roman world.

Now the apostle's vision turns westwards to the peoples of the Iberian peninsula, regarded by the Romans as the ultimate barbarians, and still not completely pacified as they persisted in active resistance to incorporation into Caesar's empire. This is now the focal point of Paul's undiminished missionary ambition, so that he informs the disciples of Jesus in the imperial capital that he hopes to visit them "when I go to Spain" (15:24)! Then comes a great surprise: the ambition to pass through Rome on the way to preach "where Christ was not known" (15:20) will have to wait until a prior, urgently necessary obligation has been fulfilled, namely to deliver the now-completed collection to "the poor among the Lord's people in Jerusalem" (15:25–29). Having just announced that his missionary ambition is focused on the West, Paul says that he must first retrace his steps and go back East, notwithstanding his awareness that such a return to Jerusalem would involve great personal risk and danger (15:31).

I limit comment on this extraordinary passage to the following observation: Paul's delay in prosecuting his passionate missionary vision in Spain can be explained only by the recognition *that the delivery of the collection was itself an absolute theological and missiological priority of such importance that it took precedence over the desire to reach "the unreached."* Why was that? I suggest that since the delivery and acceptance of the collection would provide concrete evidence of cross-cultural solidarity within the Jesus movement, it would justify the claim that the kingdom of God had broken into the midst of human history. Paul's hope must have been that the reconciling power of the cross which had been displayed in Ephesus would be far more than a passing "moment," and that the collection would cement the visible unity of the body of Christ and so validate the truthfulness of the message he planned to take to Spain. As Dieter Georgi says:

> The collection of funds for Jerusalem in Paul's interpretation transforms the idea of an economy geared toward growth of production and profit as the Hellenistic economy already was. . . . Increase of wealth for him needs to be common wealth. The

money collected for Jerusalem grows also, but into a universal divine worship. The money involved becomes a social force, a gift from community to community. It is intended to forge the vitality of the community which it is given to. Here simple obedience and kindness are blended. In this process the subjugation of the universe under the Rich One who had become poor has begun, and the unification of humanity has been initiated.[46]

The fact that Luke remains completely silent in Acts concerning the fate of the collection in Jerusalem, despite knowing how crucially important this project was to Paul, may suggest that the apparent failure of this gift to result in the outcome Paul had so fervently hoped for was simply too crushing a blow to describe or attempt to explain.[47]

Today we have reason to wonder why modern biblical scholars and commentators so often seem to pass over this whole topic in silence, or even use its "failure" as evidence that it was a mistaken idea in the first place. For example, the British scholar C. H. Dodd, discussing the community of goods in the Jerusalem church, says that the first Christians "carried [the system of partial and voluntary communism] out in the economically disastrous way of realizing capital and distributing it as income." Dodd suggests that "no practical steps were taken to replace the capital thus dissipated; and when hard times came, the community had no reserves of any kind."[48] This surely amounts to passing judgement on the apostolic church and on the apostle Paul (and on Jesus himself, although Dodd never seems to realize this) from the perspective of modern economic theory. The people living the Way in the immediate aftermath of Pentecost, together with the apostle Paul and the radically countercultural project we have described, are dismissed as mistaken on the grounds that their praxis violated capitalist orthodoxy! Dodd's commentary on Romans was published in 1952, which perhaps absolves him to some extent of the charge of ignoring a central theme of the entire New

---

46. Georgi, 153.

47. See Tom Wright's discussion of this in *Paul: A Biography* (London: SPCK, 2018), 349–50.

48. From Dodd's commentary on Romans, quoted in Keith E. Nickle, *The Collection: A Study in Paul's Strategy* (Eugene: Wipf & Stock, 2009 [1966]), 24. Nickle himself says that there was "an effort at extensive common sharing realized in such a way that, although the practice was undoubtedly based on a definite element in the teaching of Jesus, *it was implemented in what proved to be an unrealistic, short-sighted manner*" (23–24; emphasis added).

Testament.[49] However, in the world of the twenty-first century such wilful blindness can no longer be excused, and as we seek to confront a networked, global culture increasingly in thrall to the idolatry of Mammon, the recovery of the economics of the kingdom of God must be an urgent priority for the world Christian movement.

The End of the Beginning

We recall here that when Saul of Tarsus first encountered the risen Christ on the Damascus road he was warned that the calling to take the gospel to the Gentiles, "and to the people of Israel," would involve a life of suffering for the name of Jesus (Acts 9:15–16). The failure of the collection project, resulting in Paul's arrest, trial and eventual execution under the reign of Nero, was the culminating point in that suffering. Paul's letters are replete with honest confessions concerning his personal struggles and disappointments, but the shattering of his hope that the collection would result in the public reconciliation of Jew and Gentile within the body of Christ must have been a very heavy blow. The generally accepted tradition concerning his execution in Rome suggests that this must have occurred between the years 62 and 64, so that Paul did not live to witness the Jewish-Roman war in Palestine and its terrible climax in the destruction of the city and its temple. For the people of the Way who did live through that time it must have seemed as though the Pauline hope of the spread of God's reign of universal justice and peace was rapidly disappearing over the horizon. The extreme violence of the Roman conquest, the loss of city and temple, and the scattering of the Jewish followers of Jesus as harder lines of ethnic distinctiveness were increasingly drawn on all sides, meant that doubts began to surface concerning the promise that all nations would flow into the city of God. These doubts are to be found in the New Testament literature from that period, together with evidence of growing pressures to compromise the radical nature of the gospel in order to seek some form of accommodation with the increasingly dominant ideology of the triumphant Roman Empire.

---

49. A growing chorus of voices can be heard within New Testament studies demanding that greater attention be given both to the imperial context of Jesus and Paul, and to the distinctive economics of the kingdom of God. See for example Justin J. Meggitt, *Paul, Poverty and Survival* (Edinburgh: T&T Clark, 1998).

Two texts stand out as examples of these trends. First is the Letter of James, often treated with suspicion in Protestant Christendom, partly because of the legacy of Martin Luther's view that James's teaching on the issue of faith and works lacks the doctrinal precision of the apostle Paul, but perhaps even more because James's clear prophetic denunciation of wealth and privilege, and the uncompromising declaration that "friendship with the world means enmity against God" (Jas 4:4), is uncongenial to modern Christians who have come to regard a culture of consumerism as normal. Which is to say that the reading and interpretation of this much-neglected book is inevitably shaped by the cultural and social context of the reader, a fact that the author himself seems to have realized when he warned of the peril of merely listening to the word and failing to act upon it (1:19–25).

The great Danish philosopher Søren Kierkegaard went against the stream of Christian orthodoxy in his time in many ways, not least in his very high estimation of the message of James. He described biblical scholarship as "the human race's prodigious invention to defend itself against the New Testament" and warned practitioners of this discipline of the perils of their craft:

> If you are a scholar, remember that if you do not read God's Word in another way, it will turn out that after a lifetime of reading God's Word many hours, every day, you nevertheless have never read – God's Word. Then make the distinction (in addition to scholarly reading), so that you will also really begin to read God's Word or at least will confess to yourself that you, despite daily scholarly reading of it, are not reading God's Word, that you do not want anything to do with it at all.[50]

What happens when we read James "in another way"? What if an alternative approach involves putting aside the assumption that there is a conflict between this writer and the apostle Paul? And what if the angle of approach we adopt becomes that of the poor and oppressed instead of the defence of our inherited socio-economic privileges? The snapshot of the congregations which James was dealing with in 2:1–7 immediately reminds us of the disorders at the Lord's Table in Corinth which we have noted earlier, and our

---

50. I owe both quotations to Richard Bauckham, whose excellent study of the book of James includes a fascinating description of Kierkegaard's understanding of it (*James: Wisdom of James, Disciple of Jesus the Sage* [London: Routledge, 1999], 5).

author's response closely parallels that of Paul. The rigid socio-economic segmentation of Roman society is clearly reflected in the special attention given to the man in "fine clothes," and this bias within the congregation suggests that the example of Jesus was being eclipsed by the influence of the imperial culture of honour and shame as the poor man is told to "Sit on the floor by my feet." We might almost suggest that the rich man and Lazarus in Jesus's parable in Luke 16 have suddenly reappeared in this passage, but the capitulation of the church to the dominant cultural values has resulted in the complete reversal of Christ's verdict on those two ways of life!

There are profoundly troubling issues here for Christianity in the modern world in which the gulf separating rich and poor has widened into a seemingly unbridgeable chasm, leaving many churches in Europe and North America serving people on the comfortable and prosperous side of that divide and unable to cope with James's "option for the poor." Elsa Tamez, writing from the underside of the global economy in Costa Rica, observes that many of the published commentaries on the Letter of James "are written in situations where there are many rich people in the churches," and she asks the pointed question: "How does one tell these members that according to James there is no room for them in the church?" (5:1–6).[51]

We cannot explore the text of James in detail, but one particular passage must be highlighted because it has such a direct bearing on the subject of this present book. In 4:13–17 people belonging to the merchant class are addressed directly and confronted with the critical decision between God and Mammon. The fact that such persons can be challenged in a letter addressed to a believing community highlights the extent to which the pressures to compromise the demands of discipleship were increasing, eroding the distinctiveness of "the Way." The language of the merchants quoted by James illustrates the manner in which Roman urban culture was shaping their life patterns, creating the self-confidence and arrogance with which they approached the future, and, above all, determining the objective which governed their motives and

---

51. Elsa Tamez, *The Scandalous Message of James* (New York: Crossroad, 1990), 21. Note Robert W. Wall's conclusion: "If James' brand of piety is taken seriously and at face value . . . a substantial portion of the North American church would become quite uncomfortable with the ease by which it has accommodated the upward economic mobility of liberal democracy while trying to follow after its downwardly mobile Lord" (*Community of the Wise: The Letter of James* [Valley Forge: Trinity Press International, 1997], 246).

movements: to "make money." James not only challenges the idolatry which drives these people, but exposes the futility of such a way of life since, when the superficial glamour is stripped away, the hollow nature of their lives is exposed: "What is your life? You are a mist that appears for a little while and then vanishes" (v. 14).

There is a striking connection between James's description of the emptiness of lives that are dedicated to the pursuit of personal wealth, and the similar judgement of the author of Ecclesiastes that life in such a culture reduces human existence to *absurdity*. We discussed the significance of Qohelet's use of the Hebrew term *hebel* at the close of chapter 3, but here we find his verdict repeated in the context of the Greco-Roman market system, so that in both Testaments human beings are warned that the idolatry of Mammon reduces their existence to a "mist," like the vapour trail of human breath, vanishing no sooner than it appears on a frosty morning. The word translated "mist" clearly recalls the language of Qohelet which "informs the merchant illustration in James."[52]

The tensions which are evident in the Letter of James are even more present in the final book of the Bible, the Revelation of John. It is tempting to suggest that in the crisis which confronts world Christianity in the era of globalization in the twenty-first century, no biblical book is more significant than this one. While we must recognize that the apocalyptic visions of this extraordinary work have given rise to perverse and dangerous misinterpretations, the fact remains that it emerged from a historical context which is analogous to our own. It is for this reason that it offers hope that the gift of prophetic imagination is capable of renewing hope for humankind and for the whole created world.

What then was that situation? All that we have said in this chapter concerning the imperial world which formed the context of the life and death of Jesus and the growth of the early church feeds into the answer to this question, but by the time John of Patmos was incarcerated on a remote island, the power and influence of the empire had increased and the condition of the churches in Asia Minor suggested that many of them were becoming the "people who had lost their Way." The letters to seven of these congregations in Revelation 2–3 reveal multiple problems of accommodation to the ideology and idolatry

---

52. Wall, *Community of the Wise*, 220.

of the Pax Romana, culminating in the near-terminal apostasy of the church at Laodicea, which boasted of its wealth while completely unaware of the reality that it had become "wretched, pitiful, poor, blind and naked" (Rev 3:17).

Adela Yarbro Collins has identified no less than five major causes of the crisis to which Revelation responds and she describes each of these as deeply traumatic experiences for the embattled believers. The terrible climax of the Jewish-Roman War and the destruction of Jerusalem in 70 CE has been likened to the Holocaust in the twentieth century, and those who witnessed this tragedy and lived through its aftermath had to wrestle with the resulting trauma and the unanswerable questions which arose from it.[53] In addition, the legacy of the violent persecution of believers, of the executions of Peter and Paul and the brutal orgy of violence inflicted on the followers of Christ after the great fire of Rome, remained traumatic three decades later for believers across this region. Revelation appears to make coded reference to Nero's propaganda and to the rumours which followed his death, depicting him as a forerunner of the Antichrist. By the turn of the century Christians found themselves in a world moving rapidly towards a situation in which the provincial governor, Pliny, could conclude that "it was his duty to execute any unrepentant adult male Christian who was properly accused."[54]

In addition, we have to recognize the personal challenge faced by the author of the book. We cannot be certain about the nature of the charge made against him by the Roman authorities, but it seems likely that their chronic suspicion of astrologers, diviners and prophets had resulted in the visionary author of Revelation being removed from the public sphere and sent into lonely exile. Not long after this book was written an imperial edict appeared which banned the reading of the Sibylline Oracles and the Hebrew prophets, suggesting that John and his churches existed in a precarious legal situation in which resistance to Roman ideology and their belief in an alternative future made them vulnerable to imperial surveillance and repression. John's

---

53. Jack Miles says that the horrors of the Roman assault on Jerusalem and the pogroms which took place elsewhere "bear comparison with the grisliest from the Nazi concentration camps." He adds that this "can scarcely fail to have raised many of the radical and desperate questions about God that, to some, seem to have arisen for the first time in the twentieth century" (*CHRIST: A Crisis in the Life of God* [London: Heinemann, 2001], 119).

54. Adela Yarbro Collins, *Crisis and Catharsis: The Power of the Apocalypse* (Philadelphia: Westminster, 1984), 100.

identification of himself as "your brother and companion in the suffering and kingdom and patient endurance that are ours in Jesus" reflects his lonely isolation from fellowship, to which was added the burden created by his knowledge of the condition of the congregations to which he was to write.

This then is the context in which the book of Revelation came to birth, and it suggests that this unique work was intended "to overcome the unbearable tension perceived by the author between what was and what ought to be." In Yarbro Collins's words:

> His purpose was to create that tension for readers unaware of it, to heighten it for those who felt it already, and then to overcome it by an act of literary imagination. In the literary creation which is the Apocalypse, the tension between what was and what ought to be is manifest in the opposition between the symbols of God's rule and the symbols of Satan's rule, between symbols of the authority and power of Christ and symbols of the authority and power of Caesar.[55]

The crucial turning point in John's book is the moment at which, having described both his own confinement on Patmos and the disheartening condition of the congregations he knew and loved, he glimpses "a door standing open in heaven" and hears a voice calling him to "Come up here . . ." (4:1). That door is the portal by which the harsh reality which he has just described can be *transcended*. There is another, greater reality than the one which is limited to the empirical world in which the privileged and powerful always appear to be victorious and dominant, while the hope of a new world fades as the church embraces a path of syncretism as the only realistic route to survival. It is in the act of passing through that door between earth and heaven that everything changes. The meaning of the crucifixion of Jesus, the Lamb "looking as if it had been slain" (5:6–14), is revealed in a new light, and his worthiness to open the sealed scroll which symbolizes the unfolding of history results in the assurance that he, not Caesar, holds the key to the future of the nations. He alone, who suffered death and desolation, is *worthy* to fulfil the divine purpose in history, so that the extraordinary visions and symbolism of this book begin to utterly transform the way the world is seen. Rome with

---

55. Collins, *Crisis and Catharsis*, 141.

its military might and economic dominance becomes the exact opposite of the civilizing power it boasted itself to be, and when the imperial propaganda is torn away it reveals imagery depicting the empire as both a beast arising from the sea and a prostitute seducing "the kings of the earth." As Richard Bauckham has said, a major function of this book is to "purge and refurbish the Christian imagination."

> It tackles people's imaginative response to the world, which is at least as deep and influential as their intellectual convictions. It recognises the way a dominant culture, with its images and ideals, constructs the world for us, so that we perceive and respond to the world on its terms. Moreover, it unmasks this dominant construction of the world as an ideology of the powerful which serves to maintain their power. In its place, Revelation offers a different way of perceiving the world which leads people to resist and to challenge the effects of the dominant ideology.[56]

This cleansing and refurbishment of the Christian imagination is closely related to the worship of God and of the Lamb "looking as if it had been slain." Ecstatic, joyful worship is a dominant feature of the book which is constantly erupting with outbursts of new songs, first sung by the redeemed from every tribe and nation, then joined by the whole creation, until every creature "in heaven and on earth and under the earth and on the sea" create a hallelujah chorus that reverberates throughout the cosmos. The empirical situation described in the first three chapters has not changed, but it has been transcended by an act of imaginative worship which opens up an entirely new dimension of reality and renews the Christian hope that the sacrifice of Calvary was not in vain. It is the slain Lamb who alone is worthy "to receive power and wealth and wisdom and strength and honour and glory and praise": all the qualities which had been so grotesquely misappropriated by the imperial powers are now ascribed to God and his Christ who are seated on the throne of heaven.

However, if Revelation celebrates the victory of Israel's God, it cannot do so without also describing the collapse of the world which crucified the Lord

---

56. Richard Bauckham, *The Theology of the Book of Revelation* (Cambridge: Cambridge University Press, 1993), 159.

of glory and enthroned Mammon in his place. The destruction of the new Babylon and its unjust economy is certain, resulting in the terrible laments of "the kings of the earth" and "the merchants" who "grew rich from her excessive luxuries." We are reminded of Aristides's description of Rome when Revelation predicts the judgement that will befall "every sea captain . . . and all who earn their living from the sea," transporting the endless cargoes of luxury goods, exotic food and the "bodies and souls of men" (18:1–24 NIV and NKJV)!

Finally comes the city with foundations in quest of which Father Abraham had set out from ancient Mesopotamia long ago, and into which the nations will now come, together with the kings of the earth who will "bring their splendour into it," discovering in this garden city the new tree of life whose leaves "are for the healing of the nations" (Rev 21–22).

I have referred to the analogy between the world of John of Patmos and that within which we find ourselves in the twenty-first century. We shall examine the contemporary context in detail in the second part of this book, but a crucial aspect of the analogy between these very different historical eras concerns the vital role played by a prophetic imagination both then and now. We are once again at this point touching on the subject with which we began, with Max Weber's question concerning the possibility of the reappearance of prophecy. That question arose precisely because of the loss of transcendence in modern culture, and it remains as a crucial issue for world Christianity at a time when the reach of Mammon has become global, and the Christian response looks not far removed from that of the churches of ancient Asia Minor. Which suggests that for us, as for John of Patmos, the "door standing open in heaven" is crucial, and the willingness to heed the call to "come up here," to engage in worship which opens new vistas, renews hope of deep transformation and strengthens a militant resistance to the ideology and cruelty of Mammon, will be fundamentally important to our response to the ultimate question of our times.

Pause for Reflection: Paul's Lament

We have suggested that the failure of the collection project and the subsequent arrest and imprisonment of the apostle Paul must have troubled and perplexed him and given rise to new questions concerning the outworking of the purposes of God within human history. The surprising silence of Luke concerning the fate of the collection in Jerusalem means that we are left to speculate concerning its reception by the Jewish followers of Jesus in that city. However, it is very clear that Paul's arrival in the city created considerable anxiety for the leadership of the Jerusalem community since, while they report to him that "many thousands of Jews have believed," this positive news is more than offset by the information that it was widely thought among those converts that "you teach all the Jews who live among the Gentiles to turn away from Moses" (Acts 21:20–22). What this and subsequent developments indicate is the existence of considerable hostility towards Paul on the part of believing Jews who continued to regard obedience to the law of Moses, including specifically the rite of circumcision, as a non-negotiable requirement for membership of the people of God. It is as though the decision of the council at Jerusalem had never been made and the fundamental principles of Christian identity had to be debated all over again! We must therefore conclude that in this febrile atmosphere, the gift from the gentile congregations was regarded as provocative, perhaps even as a kind of bribery, and was either received on terms which completely ignored the motivation of Paul's converts, or was actually rejected. Robert Jewett comments:

> Given the environment of violent, anti-Gentile hostility in Palestine, it seems likely that Paul's concern was that the offering

would either be refused or that it would be received under auspices that would not express the cross-cultural solidarity that he believed was central to the gospel. . . . It is very likely that Paul's fears about the acceptability of the offering to the Jerusalem church, under extreme pressure from nationalistic zealots, were fully justified.[1]

If the collection was rejected, not only would this have destroyed a project which had occupied a central role in Paul's life and work, it would have been a calculated insult to the apostle and his communities, and – worst of all – would have undermined his great vision of what the gospel was to achieve in uniting Jew and Gentile within the body of Christ. Furthermore, such rejection would contradict the apostle's claim that the message of the cross had brought healing and reconciliation between the peoples of the world, so eroding the credibility of his planned mission to Spain. Luke gives no indication that this experience in Jerusalem created a personal crisis for Paul, but the aftermath of the events he describes can be seen in the fact that, as a chained prisoner in Rome, Paul met with the Jewish leaders in that city and insisted that "it is because of *the hope of Israel* that I am bound with this chain" (Acts 28:20).

That pregnant phrase is a reminder that Paul had earlier written to the Jesus communities in Rome and discussed at length his own identity as a Jewish follower of Christ. In the great central section of the Letter to the Romans he wrestled with the *mystery* of the purposes of God in human history, especially as they concerned Jews and Gentiles. In Romans 9–11 Paul confesses that the failure of his own people to recognize and receive the crucified and risen Jesus as Messiah had caused him "great sorrow and unceasing anguish in my heart" (9:1–2). The language used echoes the classic Hebrew expressions of lament, and the connection with the Hebrew Bible becomes even clearer when, recalling the anguished request of Moses that he might be blotted out of the Book of Life as a substitute for his rebellious people, Paul wishes "that I myself were cursed and cut off from Christ for the sake of my people, those of my own race, the people of Israel" (9:3–4). The sincerity and depth of his love for his own people is very clear in this passage, even to

---

1. Robert Jewett, *Romans: A Commentary*, Hermeneia (Minneapolis: Fortress, 2007), 937.

the extent that he sounds like a person experiencing a serious identity crisis. His language is "neither superficial nor transitory" and this suggests that the struggle remained with him "as a chronic condition."[2]

How does Paul overcome this crisis and reconcile the painful reality of the "stumbling" of Israel with the redemptive purposes of God, especially since Israel's role in the drama of universal salvation had always been anticipated to be of central significance? Had the plan of God as it had been glimpsed by the prophets somehow miscarried, resulting in a totally unexpected turn of events? There is clear evidence in this passage that this was precisely the way in which some of Paul's Greco-Roman converts were inclined to interpret the situation, regarding the Jews as having "stumble[d] so as to fall beyond recovery" (11:11). This suggests that what we have earlier identified as the transcultural unity of the "Ephesian moment" had come under the most severe strain from Jewish nationalism on the one side, and gentile triumphalism on the other. Paul seeks to challenge both ideologies in order to preserve his vision of a catholic unity transcending cultural differences.

How does he do this? First, while Israel's refusal to recognize the messianic claims for Jesus created the pain and anguish we have described, Paul insists that this is not final and that God, whose gifts and call are irrevocable, is "able to graft them in again" (11:23). Second, he confronts the distressing appearance of pride and arrogance among gentile converts by warning them of the great peril they face if they regard their own status as unconditional, irrespective of their praxis. To assume the certainty of their election within the divine purpose even when they have clearly begun to compromise the Way would be to make precisely the same disastrous error which biblical Israel had done in the past, and so fall under the searing condemnation of the Hebrew prophets. In what might be claimed to be the most important statement in this entire discussion, Paul warns: "Do not be arrogant, but tremble. For if God did not spare the natural branches, he will not spare you either. Consider therefore the kindness and sternness of God: sternness to those who fell, but kindness to you, *provided that you continue in his kindness*" (11:20–23).

Readers may recall our earlier discussion of Isaiah's lament that the people of the covenant had "not brought salvation to the earth" and had failed to give birth to "the people of the world." It may come as a shock to discover the

---

2. Jewett, *Romans*, 559.

apostle Paul issuing a very similar warning to the new community of Jesus Christ, that they too must face the possibility of falling short of the calling they have received and so betraying the glorious hope of the reconciliation of humankind with God, and of the nations with each other. In his commentary on Romans, Robert Jewett quotes the extraordinary words of Frédéric Godet that provide a "haunting assessment" of the state of Western Christianity as long ago as 1883:

> It is but too clear to anyone who has eyes to see, that our Gentile Christendom has now reached the point here foreseen by St. Paul. In its pride it tramples under foot the very notion of that grace which has made it what it is. It moves on, therefore, to a judgement of rejection like that of Israel, but which shall not have to soften it a promise like that which accompanied the fall of the Jews.[3]

Those words were written at the very height of Western imperial power when Christian missionary organizations had seized the opportunity created by the global expansion of European political and economic influence to spread the message of Christ among all nations. From the perspective of the twenty-first century Godet's words have a prophetic quality since we have witnessed the subsequent collapse of Christendom and the emergence of the cultural vacuum described by Albert Camus on the opening pages of this book. Not for the first time, however, the decline and fall of Christianity in what had for centuries been its heartlands has been followed by the unexpected rise, or resurgence, of the religion across the southern hemisphere where it has taken root within a wide range of cultural contexts. Paul's warning to the Gentiles in the first century is now directed to this still-emerging world Christianity: will it *continue in the kindness of God*, offering a world increasingly in thrall to the hideous idolatry of Mammon the healing grace and liberating power which comes from God, whose judgements are "unsearchable" and whose "paths beyond tracing out" (Rom 11:33)? This question will hover over the remainder of the book as we turn to trace the ever-changing manifestations of Mammon and of Christianity's response to it across the past two thousand years.

---

3. Frédéric Godet, quoted by Jewett, 691. The source is Godet's 1883 *Commentary on St. Paul's Epistle to the Romans* (Grand Rapids: Kregel, 1977), 408.

Part 2

Historical Struggles

CHAPTER 6

Through the Eye of a Needle

> By the middle of the fourth century, Christianity had gone a long way towards assimilating the dominant culture of pagan Romans. An easy symbiosis had come into being between the cultivated pagan and the educated Christian. . . . Right across the social scale, religion made little perceptible difference to the outward shape of life. (Robert Markus)[1]

We have reached the point in this book at which we move from the biblical history of Israel and of the New Testament accounts of the earliest followers of Jesus and begin to track the progress of Christianity as it spread across the Roman world and engaged with the dominant imperial power and with the cultural and philosophical legacy of Greece. This story is both long and complex, and readers who wish to explore it at greater depth will need to turn to the sources to which reference will be made in what follows.[2] The apparent complexity and remoteness of this period of Christian history has discouraged many contemporary people from paying attention to it; "early church history" has seemed to be simply too daunting to justify the time and effort needed to grasp even its main outlines and significance. However, as Herbert Butterfield observed in the aftermath of the Second World War, European Christians were awakening to the discovery that they existed in a

---

1. Robert Markus, "From Rome to the Barbarian Kingdoms (330–700)," in *The Oxford Illustrated History of Christianity,* ed. John McManners (Oxford: Oxford University Press, 1992), 66–67.

2. See especially Peter Brown, *The Rise of Western Christendom: Triumph and Diversity, A.D. 200–1000,* 10th anniversary rev. ed. (Chichester: Wiley-Blackwell, 2013).

world in which nominal forms of faith were withering on the vine. The kind of religion which had resulted from compulsion, social conformity or as a passport to professional progress was rapidly disappearing. This situation, which came to be described as post-Christendom, was creating a new context which Butterfield believed to be "the most exhilarating period in the history of Christianity for fifteen hundred years." In other words, as Western Christians struggled to accept the loss of their position at the centre of European and North American culture, they had the opportunity to discover significant parallels between their emerging context and that of believers in the pre-Christendom era. They were increasingly discovering themselves to be living at a time "something like the earliest centuries of Christianity, and those early centuries afford some relevant clues to the kind of attitude to adopt."[3]

Before we explore what those "relevant clues" might be, we need to take note of a dimension of the growth of early Christianity which has often been overlooked but is of importance to the theme of this present book. While Luke's account of the spread of the message of the gospel traced its movement to the west, and in particular to the imperial capital of Rome, it nonetheless contains indications that the message of the Lamb of God "who takes away the sin of the world" (John 1:29) was spreading to areas beyond the boundaries of the empire, among peoples who spoke neither Greek nor Latin. The story of the Ethiopian eunuch (Acts 8:26–40) describes a convert who goes "on his way rejoicing," carrying the gospel into Africa, while the description of Saul of Tarsus's determination to root out any "who belonged to the Way" in the city of Damascus indicates the early eastward spread of the movement (9:1–2).

Recent studies of the growth of Christianity in a variety of geographical locations and cultural and linguistic contexts throughout the early centuries have led to the conclusion that what is today described as "world Christianity" is not an unprecedented phenomenon, but a *return* to the multicultural character of the original movement. Andrew Walls has described how the growth of churches in Europe during the early centuries was accompanied by what was "perhaps the most remarkable missionary movement that Christianity has ever known." That movement penetrated the Chinese kingdom, where it gained the ear of the emperor.

---

3. Quoted in Alan Kreider, *The Change of Conversion and the Origin of Christendom* (Eugene: Wipf & Stock, 2006), xvii.

In estimating the global reach of Christianity in the early centuries, it is worth remembering that the favourable response of the Chinese Emperor in 635 is almost exactly contemporary with the council in Northumbria described by Bede, which resulted in the conversion of King Edwin and the decision makers of that northern English kingdom. At this period, Christianity is a global faith, present, active, and growing from the Atlantic almost to the Pacific and with outposts from Siberia to Sri Lanka.[4]

Following Christ in a Hostile World

One of the stories in Luke's gospel which we did not examine in the previous chapters reports an encounter between Jesus and a man described simply as "a ruler" who was "very wealthy." This earnest seeker after "eternal life" had sincerely endeavoured to obey the demands of the law of God, but was told that he lacked one thing: "Sell everything you have and give to the poor, and you will have treasure in heaven. *Then* come, follow me" (Luke 18:18–29). The condition which Jesus insisted upon astonished his disciples who responded by confessing that their Master's demands appeared to have made salvation impossible! Surely, the narrow entrance to the kingdom of heaven was not now simply difficult to access, but had been slammed shut, bolted and barred. Jesus, who likened the access to salvation for the super-rich to a camel's ability to pass through the eye of a needle, acknowledged that the possibility of

---

4. Andrew F. Walls, *Crossing Cultural Frontiers: Studies in the History of World Christianity*, ed. Mark R. Gornik (New York: Orbis, 2017), 9. See also his "Eusebius Tries Again: The Task of Reconceiving and Revisioning the Study of Christian History," in *Enlarging the Story: Perspectives on Writing World Christian History*, ed. Wilbert R. Shenk (New York: Orbis, 2002), 1–21. Note Peter Brown's comment concerning "Christian regions that extended far beyond the Greco-Roman world on which conventional accounts of the rise and expansion of Christianity usually concentrate." He says that by 300 CE the world of the Mediterranean "was flanked by another Christianity, associated primarily with Egypt and with the wide spaces of Syria. We are dealing with a great third world of ancient Christianity that stretched far to the east of Antioch, as far as the Caucasus and Iranian plateau, and far to the south of Alexandria, as far as the Indian Ocean and the mountains of Ethiopia" (*Treasure in Heaven: The Holy Poor in Early Christianity* [Charlottesville: University of Virginia Press, 2016], xxii). I am deeply indebted to this book in what follows in this chapter.

such a conversion was absurd within the context of the world as it existed, but affirmed nonetheless that it was "possible with God."

This story, perhaps more than any other in the gospels, was to be discussed and debated throughout the early centuries of Christian history, both by the growing number of wealthy Roman pagans who naturally identified with the enquiring ruler, and by the leaders of Christian congregations who either insisted that the condition laid down by Jesus was non-negotiable, or suggested that the Roman rich might be permitted to discover an alternative route into the expanding movement. By the fourth century of the Common Era fierce debates had erupted between Christians across Europe on the meaning of "perfection," and they were triggered by a growing "uncertainty about what it meant to be a genuine Christian in a society of fashionable Christianity."[5]

Our primary focus here relates to the specific issues concerning wealth and possessions which are the subject of this book. Even with that limitation, this remains a vast topic since, as Peter Brown observes, wealth was a subject that "lay heavy on everybody's mind."

> The issue of wealth flowed like a great braided river through the churches and through Roman society as a whole. Wealth was not only about budgets and rent books; the stream of that great and diverse river touched many banks. . . . The yearly miracle of the harvest touched on the issue of the relation between man and the physical universe, and between God or the gods and the abundance of nature. The less welcome prodigy of administrative effort that brought the imperial tax collectors and the collectors of rents to the shops and villages all over the Roman world raised the issue of the legitimacy of wealth itself and of the empire that extracted it.[6]

What this means is that serious reflection on the issue of wealth and possessions cannot bypass the urgent questions which inevitably arise in relation to such a study. We have seen this in the New Testament where the

---

5. Markus, "From Rome to the Barbarian Kingdoms," 67.

6. Peter Brown, *Through the Eye of a Needle: Wealth, the Fall of Rome, and the Making of Christianity in the West, 350–550 AD* (Princeton: Princeton University Press, 2012), xxiv. After a study extending to 759 pages, Brown still warns: "In all our efforts, we are left peering over the edge of an abyss that drops into an unimaginably distant world" (xxix).

concern with poverty, injustice and oppression leads to reflection on wider issues concerning how the world came to be the way it is, and why it is so difficult to overcome the status quo in the interests of justice and peace. These issues will be unavoidable as we trace the transition from the Jewish phase of the Jesus movement, in which faith-as-*praxis* was so clearly reflected in the description of believers as the "people of the Way," into a Greco-Roman world shaped by Greek philosophy and Roman law and politics. In this context the message of Messiah Jesus had to be applied to urban cultures in which wealth and possessions were inseparably related to the legal underpinning of private ownership, especially of land, and to a system which resulted in obscene inequalities sustained by imperial violence. In other words, in dealing with this subject we are bound to notice the manner in which the early Christians were compelled to wrestle with a triad of fundamental issues concerning money, property and war.

Although Luke's designation of the Jesus movement as the "people of the Way" may not have survived long into the second century, the distinctive behaviour of the followers of Christ remained central to their identity and witness and was a crucial factor in the growth of the early churches.[7] Conversion involved turning towards Christ crucified and risen and a consequent transformation of values and behaviour in imitation of Jesus and obedience to his teaching. This required abandoning a previous manner of life, both with respect to social attitudes and practices and in relation to the realm of occult powers which, as we have seen, were ever-present realities in the ancient world. Justin Martyr's *First Apology*, written in the middle of the second century, refers to the struggle to be free from demonic powers and celebrates the liberty of those who, "having been persuaded by the Word," now follow "the only unbegotten God through his Son."

> Those who once rejoiced in fornication now delight in self-control alone; those who made use of magic arts have dedicated

---

7. On the terminology used to identify the followers of Jesus, note Arend Theodor van Leeuwen's comment: "Terms such as 'Christian' and 'Christianity' are foreign to the Gospel; for they reduce the eschatological acts of God in Jesus Christ to something which conditions and characterizes a particular religious group, dragging the Church, which is the people of God, down to the level of a sociological, cultural and religious phenomenon. To put it in the language of the New Testament: 'Christianity' is a word according to the flesh, not according to the Spirit" (*Christianity in World History: The Meeting of the Faiths of East and West* [Edinburgh: Edinburgh House, 1964], 145).

themselves to the good and unbegotten God; we who once took most pleasure in the means of increasing our wealth and property now bring what we have into a common fund and share with everyone in need; we who hated and killed one another and would not associate with men of different tribes because of [their different] customs, now after the manifestation of Christ live together and pray for our enemies and try to persuade those who unjustly hate us.[8]

The evidence of continuity with the apostolic communities described in the book of Acts is clear in the transformation of attitudes towards money, ownership, sex and power. Not that such a change occurred instantaneously or resulted from an isolated decision of the will; it involved an immense challenge which demanded the experience of the life-transforming power of the Holy Spirit. A century after Justin, an aristocratic Roman in North Africa who was used to a privileged life of wealth and luxury despaired of himself in the light of the apparent impossibility of radical personal change. How could a man such as he knew himself to be ever really change? How, asked Cyprian, "is such a conversion possible, that there should be a sudden and rapid divestment of all which, either innate in us has hardened into the corruption of our material nature, or acquired by us has become inveterate by long accustomed use?" Cyprian knew himself to be embedded within a culture of greed and selfishness: "When does he learn thrift who has been used to liberal banquets and sumptuous feasts? And he who has been glittering in gold and purple . . . when does he reduce himself to ordinary and simple clothing?" The answer to these existential questions came when, "by the help of the water of new birth, the stain of former years had been washed away, and a light from above, serene and pure, had been infused into my reconciled heart," so that "a second birth restored me to a new person."[9]

---

8. In Andrew Bradstock and Christopher Rowland, eds., *Radical Christian Writings: A Reader* (Oxford: Blackwell, 2002), 2.

9. Cyprian, *Epistle I to Donatus*, in Bradstock and Rowland, *Radical Christian Writings*, 2–3. Alan Kreider comments that Cyprian realized that the material possessions of his aristocratic class "possessed their possessors" and that his struggle "was not to believe what Christians believed; rather, it was to live as they taught – and as many of them seem to have lived" (*Change of Conversion*, 8).

Or consider the famous *Letter to Diognetus* in which the author insists that Christians do not use "a peculiar form of speech, nor lead a life which is marked out by any singularity." Their customs, clothing, food and general behaviour reflect their particular culture, and yet "they display to us their wonderful and confessedly striking method of life." Their distinctiveness was seen in the manner in which they reflected the character and being of the God whom they had come to worship through Jesus Christ:

> Do not wonder that man can become an imitator of God.... For it is not by ruling over his neighbour, or by seeking to hold the supremacy over those that are weaker, or by being rich, and showing violence to those who are inferior, that happiness is found; nor can anyone by these things become an imitator of God.... On the contrary, he who takes upon himself the burden of his neighbour... he who, whatsoever things he has received from God, by distributing these to the needy, becomes a god to those who receive (his benefits): he is an imitator of God.[10]

Alan Kreider describes conversion in early Christianity as "empowerment to do the impossible." The potential convert was required to *learn* the way of Jesus Christ, to *practise* that way by renouncing habits contrary to it, and, finally, to *confess* faith in the act of baptism which marked the decisive break between the old world and the new. Notice that the initiatory rite of baptism took place at the culmination of a process of instruction intended to inform enquirers of the teaching of the gospel and its ethical demands, much as we have seen Luke providing Theophilus with an account of the story of Jesus and the radically alternative way of life within the kingdom of God. However, given the all-pervasive presence of Roman ideology, a presence which took highly visible forms in public space in every city and was backed up by the threat of violence against nonconformists, the attractive power of the early Christian movement seems surprising and historians have puzzled over the reasons for the churches' growth within such a context.

In a study of what he called the "patient ferment" of the early church, Kreider drew on the work of the sociologist Pierre Bourdieu and his concept

---

10. Justo González, *Faith and Wealth: A History of Early Christian Ideas on the Origin, Significance and Use of Money* (Eugene: Wipf & Stock, 2002), 96. See also *Letter to Diognetus*, CCEL.org, accessed 11 April 2022, http://www.ccel.org/ccel/richardson/fathers.x.i.ii.html.

of a *habitus*: a form of knowledge deeply embedded within individuals and shaped by established social conventions, reinforced by shared narratives, including "the little stories of our family and community as well as the big stories that undergird our culture."[11] We may ask whether it was precisely something like this that Jesus had in mind when he spoke of the enormous power of Mammon. As we saw at the beginning of this book, the term signified an idolatrous *system* which gained control over the lives of those who succumbed to it and held them in a vice-like grip. Indeed, as we have just seen, this seems to have been precisely the understanding of an aristocratic seeker after truth like Cyprian who, even while asking himself deeply critical questions about his own way of life, simply could not envisage the possibility of his escape from this "iron cage." Kreider observes that the early Christian leaders understood perfectly well "the sheer difficulty of religious change" and for this reason were not content to regard conversion as merely involving new ideas, but recognized the need to work "to transform the habitus of those who were candidates for membership." The two crucial components of the process of conversion were, first, the practice of catechesis, by which enquirers' behaviour underwent radical transformation in response to their growing knowledge of Christ, and second, the sharing of the worship of Christ, through which "a new habitus was enacted and expressed with bodily eloquence."[12]

The enormous power of the Roman worldview and the continuing threat which it posed to Christian converts can be illustrated by considering the temptations posed by the notorious games which were a ubiquitous feature of life in urban areas. We discover Augustine confessing his profound sorrow over increasing numbers of Christians who "enter the church in their bodies but leave their hearts outside. . . . Why should the body, which is seen by men, be within, while that which is seen by God is left outside?"[13] It is to Augustine that we owe an account of the spiritual tragedy which befell a young Christian who was lured into the amphitheatre against his will. In his famous *Confessions* Augustine describes how one of his students named

---

11. Alan Kreider, *The Patient Ferment of the Early Church: The Improbable Rise of Christianity in the Roman Empire* (Grand Rapids: Baker Academic, 2016), 40.

12. Kreider, *Patient Ferment*, 41.

13. Quoted in Robert Markus, *The End of Ancient Christianity* (Cambridge: Cambridge University Press, 1990), 113.

Alypius happened to meet some friends who were on their way to the amphitheatre and persuaded him to accompany them. He was reluctant to be seen at "these cruel and bloody shows" but was confident that his revulsion at such spectacles would never be overcome. Augustine relates the incident:

> The whole place was seething with savage enthusiasm, but he shut the doors of his eyes and forbade his soul to go out into a scene of such evil. If only he could have blocked up his ears too! For in the course of the fight some man fell; there was a great roar . . . which fell upon his ears; he was overcome by curiosity and opened his eyes, feeling perfectly prepared to treat whatever he might see with scorn and to rise above it.

Augustine recounts the tragic conclusion: "His own fall was more wretched than that of the gladiator," since the uproar of the crowd "entered his ears and unlocked his eyes and made an opening for the thrust that was to overthrow his soul." Having exposed himself to the passions of the mob and the violence of the arena, "he drank in the madness, was delighted with the guilty contest, drunk with the lust of blood," and "took away with him a madness which would goad him to come back again."[14]

What makes this incident all the more tragic is the obvious fact that in the early centuries of the Common Era it had been Christians who had been victims of the obscene violence of the Roman "entertainments." Indeed, most of the early believers whose voices we have heard above were themselves to suffer martyrdom within Roman arenas. The testimonies of such converts reveal their sense that in the discovery of the message of Christ crucified and raised from the dead they had found a faith which not only gave new purpose to life, but was, quite literally, worth dying for!

Origen responded to those who were curious concerning the attractive power of the gospel by testifying that he had been drawn in response to Jesus's teaching and example. In particular, the command to "beat into plowshares the rational swords of conflict and arrogance and to change into pruning

---

14. In Alison Futrell, *The Roman Games: Historical Sources in Translation* (Oxford: Blackwell, 2006), 188. This book is invaluable as a source for understanding the role played by public games in Roman life. Tertullian frequently attacked the Roman bloodlust in passages like the following: "We renounce your public shows. . . . Our tongues, our eyes, our ears have nothing to do with the madness of the circus, the shamelessness of the theatre, the brutality of the arena" (from Futrell's section on "Christians and the Arena," 166).

hooks those spears that we used to fight with" offered the hope of genuine peace. In other words, in a society marred by cruelty and violence, where huge numbers of people were treated as the scum of the earth, Christianity brought a message of peace and justice and offered a profoundly counter-cultural vision of human society: "For we no longer take up sword against any nation, nor do we learn the art of war any more. Instead of following the traditions that made us "strangers to the covenants," we have become sons of peace through Jesus our founder."[15]

Clearly, as we have noted earlier, the Pax Christi stood in direct and stark contrast to the Pax Romana and so constituted a threat to a central plank of the imperial ideology.[16] But in the writings of the pre-Constantinian apologists of what has been called the "old catholic church," it was not only opposition to war and violence which drew the attention of the Roman authorities, but the nature of the Christian challenge to the underlying economic assumptions of the empire. This involved the questioning of fundamental aspects of Roman law, especially as it related to private ownership. It is striking how often the early Christian apologists mention the Sermon on the Mount and cite the sharing of material possessions in Acts 2 and 4 as providing the basis of their vision of life together. Charles Avila describes the work of Clement of Alexandria as representative of the position which the early Christians took on the matter of private property, insisting that it "is not properly human to regard property as something with which one may do as he likes simply because it is one's 'own.'" "The clear call is to cast aside the prevailing, absolutist, individualistic Roman law legitimation of property and embrace a new rationale of ownership, holding all things in such a way that they may be common to all."[17]

Despite variations in their approach and forms of argument, some basing their position on the practice of the apostolic community as described in the

---

15. *Against Celsus* 5.33, quoted in Louis J. Swift, *The Early Fathers on War and Military Service* (Wilmington: Michael Glazier, 1983), 57. By the third century the membership of the churches increasingly reflected the social composition of the world around them and numerical growth was accompanied by changed attitudes towards leisure and entertainment. Growing numbers of professing Christians now "flocked to the circus and the theatres . . . there to enjoy the spectacles along with their pagan neighbours" (Markus, *End of Ancient Christianity*, 101).

16. See Klaus Wengst's classic work *Pax Romana and the Peace of Jesus Christ* (London: SCM, 1987).

17. Charles Avila, *Ownership: Early Christian Teaching* (Eugene: Wipf & Stock, 2004), 41.

book of Acts, while others reach back to the biblical account of creation and discover there the foundational principles of human dignity and value, there is not a single voice to be heard in the early church arguing that such matters are "secular" concerns and therefore off-limits to theology and discipleship.

As we shall see, the conversion of the emperor Constantine, and the flood of converts which resulted from the changed social character of Christianity following that momentous event, created a situation in which "Christendom" came into being. However, the tradition of radical discipleship persisted and actually found one of its boldest and clearest expressions in the extraordinary ministry of John Chrysostom, the "golden-mouthed" preacher who became bishop of Constantinople in 398, just three years after Augustine had been consecrated as bishop of Hippo in North Africa. The social and economic divisions within the Byzantine capital were particularly acute, with a royal court filled with wealthy absentee landlords who drew vast resources from peasant labour on huge estates, while the city itself was flooded with poverty-stricken people living in squalid and unsafe tenement buildings.[18] A love for the poor and oppressed has been said to be a distinguishing characteristic of Byzantine monasticism and John Chrysostom's "burning zeal for social righteousness" is the classic example of this.[19] His preaching to the privileged and powerful was extraordinary and across the gap of the intervening centuries can still disturb the consciences of modern readers and challenge the fundamental nature of the world we see around us.

> Do not tell me that you cannot watch after others. If you are Christians, what is impossible for you is not to watch after them. Just as there are in nature things that cannot be denied, so it is in this case, for it has to do with the very nature of being a Christian. Do not insult God, as you would were you to say that the sun cannot shine. If you claim that a Christian is not able to be of service to another, you insult God and call God a liar.[20]

---

18. Peter Brown describes Chrysostom as constantly urging the rich to "look over the edge of a social precipice into a swirling and anonymous crowd of beggars, buffoons, and homeless immigrants gathered around them in a great city" (*Through the Eye of a Needle*, 235).

19. Kallistos Ware, "Eastern Christendom," in McManners, *History of Christianity*, 135.

20. Quoted in González, *Faith and Wealth*, 202. Shortly after typing this passage from Chrysostom I came across the following statement by Rowan Williams: "Love of neighbour, rather than being a chosen policy of personal behaviour, is grounded in the 'necessary' exposure

While Chrysostom appealed to the gospels and the example of the "people of the Way" in Acts, his critique of the Roman rich was based on a creational theology which enabled him to argue that the economic injustice he witnessed around him was a violation of God's purpose in creation and an abuse of the bounty of the natural world which was provided for the well-being of humankind. God has "filled the earth with goods, but gave each region its own peculiar products, so that, moved by need, we would communicate and share among ourselves." The very basis of human society is mutual need, "and God intended it to be so precisely in order that we may come together." We are made for communion, for fellowship and mutual support, so that the purpose of trade is not the enrichment of a privileged few, but the sustenance of all. Contrast this understanding of economic life with that which we discovered earlier in the language of the Roman orator Aristides, who celebrated the plunder of the riches of the world in the interests of the imperial elite.[21]

John Chrysostom asked his hearers to imagine two very different cities, one populated entirely by rich people, the other only by the poor. Put both communities on an equal footing: what would be the outcomes? The city of the rich will become paralysed since it lacks the skills of those people whose labour is taken for granted, but without which it cannot survive! "No field labourers, no carpenters, no builders, no bakers, no smiths." By contrast, the city of the poor will have no need of the things which the rich so value: gold, silver, jewels, silk! When the time comes to raise food, to bake or to build, which city will be able to do this? Chrysostom concludes with the remarkable verdict that the city of the poor would have no need of the rich, and that should the latter take up residence within it, they would bring about its destruction! "What are the rich for in the world, since they are useless?"

---

of the baptized believer to human pain; we are unavoidably 'co-sufferers'" (*Looking East in Winter: Contemporary Thought and the Eastern Christian Tradition* [London: Bloomsbury Continuum, 2021], 220).

21. See pp. 112–13. In his monumental study of Christianity in the late Roman Empire, Peter Brown concludes that it was "the redefinition of the Christian poor (derived from the Old Testament) that did most to secure the eventual triumph of Christianity in the cities in the course of the fifth century." It was language taken from the Hebrew prophets that "gave to the average inhabitant of the late Roman cities a new purchase on the powerful" and resulted in bishops such as Ambrose of Rome giving voice to the "cry of the poor" and demanding justice from the great and powerful (*Through the Eye of a Needle*, 80).

While this language may appear harsh, it was designed to awaken the privileged and wealthy to the reality of the consequences of their abuse of power, and to call them to repentance and conversion: "As long as you will not cease devouring and destroying the poor, I shall not cease accusing you of it.... Leave my sheep alone. Let my flock be. Do not destroy it; if you do, do not complain that I accuse you."[22]

The fact that, as we have seen, the early Christians questioned aspects of Roman law relating to property is of great significance, for a number of reasons. First, as the Filipino theologian Charles Avila has shown, the basic concept of private property which underlay Roman society has remained largely intact across the centuries and continues to operate within modern legal systems in much of the contemporary world. The right of private ownership remains an axiom in legal and economic theories, even being hailed as the "sacred" foundation of a free society. Avila, whose research into this issue was prompted by his discovery of the plunder of tribal peoples whose ancient lands in the Philippines were being appropriated and made subject to market forces, concludes that the issue of ownership which so preoccupied the early Christians "is as real today as ever, and just as urgently asked – only, this time, it is being asked by millions of people all over the world, and not just by a handful of great philosophers in the Mediterranean basin."[23]

The second reason concerns the biblical justification for the early Christian challenge to Roman law. The question to be asked here is whether, in addition to the teaching of Jesus and the example of the practice of his new community, we must also recognize that the apostle Paul articulates the message of the gospel in response to the imperial ideology, specifically to Roman *law*. We have already discussed the significance of Paul's collection for the poor of Jerusalem and seen this as an expression of the economics of the kingdom of God, but here the question arises whether his preaching of Christ more broadly constituted a direct challenge to the Roman legal system? In her groundbreaking study of Paul's correspondence with the Galatians, Brigitte Kahl has said that "the polarity of *law versus lawlessness* was firmly established in the Greek, then Roman rhetoric of civilized warfare against the barbarians, and especially against Gauls/Galatians." This enforcement of law in relation

---

22. Quoted in González, *Faith and Wealth*, 208.
23. Avila, *Ownership*, 12.

to the ownership of land, and the consequent sequestering of peasant smallholdings which had been passed down the generations, was the background to the work of the Christian thinkers we have discussed above, but as Kahl says, it "must not be ignored when we venture to evaluate the hermeneutical framework of Paul's passionate critique of the law." She poses the crucial question: "What if Paul were targeting Greco-Roman imperial *nomos* much more than Jewish Torah?"[24]

The Age of "Mediocrity"[25]

The conversion of the emperor Constantine in 312 was a huge turning point in the history of early Christianity. Robert Markus describes it as a "cataclysmic change" and suggests that to grasp its real significance we need to "have experienced something of the guilt and the shame for the Christian Church's willingness to accept, to enjoy and to exploit it and to carry the burden of its 'establishment' throughout so much of the history of Europe."[26] We have seen how, towards the end of the first century, the New Testament documents themselves contain evidence of the pressure to seek an accommodation with the imperial culture from critics who asked, "Where is this 'coming' he promised?" The world did not appear to have changed in any obvious sense, so that the claim that the turning point of the ages had arrived was dismissed as absurd![27] Over two hundred years later, the conversion of an emperor posed a completely new kind of challenge and, as the privileged and wealthy members of late Roman society began to stream into the church, the resultant transformation of Christianity created "a new divide in the seamless fabric" of the "last age."[28] Once again, the belief that the incarnation had

---

24. Brigitte Kahl, *Galatians Re-imagined: Reading with the Eyes of the Vanquished* (Minneapolis: Fortress, 2010), 6–7. She adds that this issue has a contemporary urgency and is not just of historical interest. "We live in a precarious time, when imperial globalization extends its grip ever more rigidly and destructively upon the planet, imposing a de facto martial law on whole populations, often under the aggressive auspices of a nominal Christianity. War and peace, competition or solidarity, poverty and wealth, consumption and pollution have become questions of the very survival of humanity."

25. I owe this terminology to Robert Markus who, in his excellent book *The End of Ancient Christianity*, has a chapter with the heading "Augustine: A Defence of Christian Mediocrity."

26. Markus, 25.

27. 2 Pet 3:4.

28. Markus, *End of Ancient Christianity*, 89.

inaugurated the "last days" could appear to be falsified, but this time it was the transformation of Christianity itself which posed the problem.

> As the respectability of Christianity and the advantages to be derived from adhering to it went on growing throughout the fourth century, the problem of what constituted real Christianity became more acute. It became truly pressing in the generation which grew up at the end of the fourth century, the first for which paganism had ceased to be a force still to be reckoned with, and at a loss to discern its identity in a society undergoing rapid mass-christianisation.[29]

Constantine's decision to adopt Christianity has been described as "a very 'Roman' conversion," in the sense that the emperor, no longer a young man but an experienced soldier and politician, had reflected on the growth of the new religion and the failure of attempts by his predecessors to suppress it. He concluded that "Christianity was a religion fit for a new empire,"[30] and within a year of becoming sole ruler he convened a gathering of Christian bishops to a council at Nicaea with the purpose of securing religious uniformity throughout his realm. This involved the attempt to define acceptable forms of belief for an empire-wide church and it reflected the Greek concept of orthodoxy which was subsequently to play a very significant role in European Christianity.[31] Faith came to be expressed in precise definitions of doctrine,

---

29. Markus, 32.

30. Brown, *Rise of Western Christendom*, 61. In 316, faced with growing tensions between Catholics and Donatists in North Africa, Constantine announced his intention to personally cross the Mediterranean to resolve the problem. "What more can be done by me," he asked, "than after expelling error and destroying rash opinions, to cause all men to agree together to follow true religion and simplicity of life, and to render to Almighty God the worship that is his due?" William Frend comments that Constantine was acting "as though he were on a higher plane than the religious powers on earth, rather as God's own Vicar than an ordinary mortal" (W. H. C. Frend, *The Donatist Church: A Movement of Protest in Roman North Africa* [Eugene: Wipf & Stock, 2020 (1951)], 146).

31. Andrew F. Walls, discussing the "Hellenistic-Roman Age" of Christianity, comments: "Of the new religious ideas which entered with the Christian penetration of Hellenistic culture, one of the most permeative for the future was that of orthodoxy, of a canon of right belief, capable of being stated in a series of propositions arrived at by a process of logical argument. Such a feature was not likely to mark Christianity in its Jewish period; Jewish identity has always been concerned either with what a person *is* or what he *does* rather than what he believes" (*The Missionary Movement in Christian History: Studies in the Transmission of Faith* [Edinburgh: T&T Clark, 1996], 18).

arrived at by logical debate, and binding on all Christians. The earlier focus on praxis, which had been a legacy from Judaism, began to be eclipsed by the demand for right belief, and those who questioned the dogmatic creedal formulations of an emerging Christendom risked being identified as heretics who posed a threat, not just to the Catholic Church, but to the unity and security of the state.

The dramatic growth of Christianity in the fifth century gave rise to fundamental questions concerning what was now distinctive about being a Christian, and how new converts related both to the earlier church of the martyrs and to the summons to "perfection" demanded by Jesus himself. This problem was compounded by the fact that the foundations of what came to be called Christendom were laid at precisely the same time that the Roman world was being flooded with gold. Ancient peoples had looked back to a supposed "moneyless utopia at the dawn of time," but the reign of Constantine witnessed "a frightening 'age of gold,' characterized by violence and a degree of social stratification that was unprecedented even by Roman standards."[32] Peter Brown comments that it cannot be a coincidence that Christian preaching on *treasure in heaven* took on "such a strong imaginative resonance in the cities of the Mediterranean and on the estates of Christian land-owners at this time."[33] The questions which arose in this context thus centred on the core issue of Christian distinctiveness when the dramatic growth of the churches and the transformation of their social character resulted in an increasing loss of the identity of the disciple community of earlier times.

It was in precisely this situation that Augustine, bishop of Hippo in North Africa, rose to prominence and developed a theology which was to have widespread and long-lasting influence, shaping faith and practice throughout the subsequent history of Western Christendom, both in its Catholic and later

---

32. Brown, *Through the Eye of a Needle*, 15. The French philosopher Chantal Delsol, discussing "economics as religion," notes that at the close of the Roman republic, "a race for wealth was underway and . . . this preoccupation permeated the city." She concludes that then, as now, when the acquisition of material goods "represents the only social 'ideal,' [it] builds nothing that can be shared: it instead establishes a collectivity of equals deprived of interrelationships and condemned always to want more. The wealthiest are ridden with jealousy and the poorest with envy" (*The Unlearned Lessons of the Twentieth Century: An Essay on Late Modernity* [Wilmington: ISI, 2006], 149).

33. Brown, 15.

in its Protestant expressions.³⁴ Augustine's account of his own conversion is widely regarded as a classic and his massive study *The City of God*, written as Rome came under increasing threat from the barbarian tribes of northern Europe, constitutes a key component of the theological legacy of the early church. Why then would a modern historian describe Augustine's theology as a justification for "Christian mediocrity"?

To answer that question we must consider the controversies in which Augustine was involved and the views of the people whose understanding of the threat which wealth and prosperity posed to authentic Christianity he persistently rejected. He was born in 354 in the town of Thagaste in modern Algeria, and after his conversion in his thirties under the influence of the preaching of Ambrose in Milan, returned to North Africa, becoming bishop of Hippo in 395. It has been said that Augustine was "first and foremost an African," and that he was influenced "by the Berber background of his upbringing."³⁵ There is a strange irony in the fact that his mother's name – "Monica" – displays his Berber roots since it was precisely among these people, scattered across the High Plains of the interior of North Africa, that the Donatist movement emerged and prospered, only to be relentlessly opposed by the Catholic bishop of Hippo!

Throughout the third century, Christianity in North Africa had flourished and was shaped by its particular geographical and cultural context in a manner which resulted in a strong and persistent countercultural stance. The leadership of Tertullian, who died ca. 220, and Cyprian, who suffered a martyr's death in ca. 258, had established the distinctive character of the African church, including the prominence given to suffering and especially to the role of the martyrs. The form taken by the Donatist movement had been presaged by Tertullian's well-known questions: "What has Athens to do with Jerusalem? What concord is there between the Academy and the Church?" The subsequent spread of the gospel within the hinterlands of Numidia and

---

34. Jürgen Moltmann says that after the Bible, Augustine's *Confessions* "is the most widely read book of the Western world." It is the primary source of the anthropology of the "restless heart," the "homelessness" of the Western – and now modern – soul. He adds: "Every cultural comparison shows that this is a Christian-Western-occidental anthropology, not in the least a universal anthropology" (*The Spirit of Hope: Theology for a World in Peril* [Louisville: Westminster John Knox, 2019], 96–98).

35. Frend, *Donatist Church*, 230. The discussion of Donatism here owes much to this brilliant book.

Mauritania, where it penetrated an indigenous population with a distinct, traditional culture and language, created a situation in which tensions were bound to arise with Latin-speaking Christians in the coastal, urban centres like Carthage. William Frend has described "two entirely different types of country in North Africa," with the Romanized cities of the Proconsular Province of the empire "able to sustain a large, urban population," while the High Plains of the interior, a land of densely populated villages, remained largely untouched by Roman civilization, and innately hostile to its incursions. Frend describes the latter region as follows:

> The Berber peasant used the same plough, dressed in the same type of hooded burnous, carried the same heavy club, and spoke the same Libyan language as he does today. Above all, the inhabitant of the High Plains was conservative, rooted in customs and beliefs originating in a remote past, deeply attached to his independence, and inwardly despising the outlook of his conquerors.[36]

Add the fact of the emergence of Christendom as we have described this above, and the consequent changing character of an imperial church, and the scene was set for the appearance of the countercultural movement known as Donatism. It arose as a response to a situation in which taxes levied on the poor increased, the oppression of the peasantry became ever more burdensome, while a minority of wealthy landlords were able to manipulate power, enabling them to avoid taxes and to live in ostentatious leisure. This was fertile ground for the appearance of prophetic resistance, and the movement led by Donatus was to fulfil precisely such a role, feeding off the anger and sense of outrage of his compatriots, and upholding and extending the tradition received from Cyprian and Tertullian.

A core aspect of that tradition involved honouring the sacrifice of the martyrs who had confessed Jesus at tremendous cost, including Christians such as the young married woman Perpetua, with a new baby on her breast, whose brutal execution at Carthage at the start of the third century had left an indelible memory of faithfulness unto death among the Berber people.[37]

---

36. Frend, 31.

37. Alison Futrell includes a long extract from *The Martyrdom of Saints Perpetua and Felicitas* and she comments that by rejecting the repeated pleading of her father that she "have

Thus, while the Catholic church of Constantine was struggling to find a point of connection to the age of the martyrs, the Donatists kept that tradition alive, not least because it mirrored their own experience.

As we have seen, the "spectacle" of violence in urban amphitheatres continued to be a feature of Roman urban life, and Donatism endorsed Tertullian's withering attacks on the idolatry which blinded the Romans to the depths of evil which they had rebranded as "entertainment."

> Certain it is that innocent men are sold as gladiators to serve as victims of public pleasure. Even in the case of those who are condemned to the games, what a preposterous idea is it that, in atonement for a smaller offense, they should be driven to the extreme of murder![38]

The question which inevitably arises here is: how did Augustine, often regarded as the greatest Christian thinker of the early centuries, come to adopt such an unrelentingly negative response to the Donatists, resorting to questionable methods in the attempt to compel them to abandon their heritage and unite with the Catholic Church? His campaign against Donatus and his followers involved the justification of state-sanctioned coercion on the basis of a reading of Luke's gospel which was to have disastrous consequences in the subsequent history of Christendom. Frend concludes that, notwithstanding his own Berber roots, the bishop of Hippo was conditioned by his social and intellectual environment in a manner that prevented him from ever really understanding the context and views of his Donatist opponents:

> Were social evils and injustices to be fought in the name of Christ, or were they to be tolerated for the sake of Christian unity? To all these questions Donatists and Catholics gave different answers. The issues were not those of "truth" versus "heresy," but of two opposed attitudes to society, attitudes which have persisted throughout the history of the Christian Church down to the present day.[39]

---

pity on your father's gray head," her conversion to Christ was "a rebellion more against the domestic power structure than the emperor; she has redirected her family loyalties toward the family of Christian believers" (*Roman Games*, 179).

38. Tertullian, *On the Spectacles*, in Futrell, 168.
39. Frend, *Donatist Church*, 332.

This conclusion suggests that the use of the language of "heresy" in relation to indigenous movements such as Donatism is, at best, misleading, and has much wider relevance with regard to a whole series of Christian encounters with peoples, cultures and languages which existed at the fringes of Greco-Roman dominance. Donatism was not an isolated case of resistance to the growth of a centralized, imperial church, but it was perhaps the most prominent example of such encounters with indigenous peoples across, and beyond, the empire. As Frend concludes:

> In Egypt, too, the centre of a similar tradition of dissent against the official religion of the Empire was in the Thebaid, in the villages of the Upper Nile, and its leaders . . . were Copts who knew of Greek civilization only in order to hate it. In Egypt and Asia Minor, as well as in North Africa, the "heretical" form of Christianity struck deepest root where native linguistic and cultural traditions were most vigorous.[40]

Hard on the heels of the Donatist controversy, Augustine found himself embroiled in another conflict concerning the nature of the church, only this time the teaching which he judged had to be refuted arose from within the mainstream of the Catholic tradition. The key figure here was the British monk Pelagius, whose teaching on the demands of genuine discipleship ran counter to the direction being taken by an emerging Christendom, yet attracted the interest of growing numbers of wealthy people in Rome. For such persons Christianity had brought with it distinct social advantages at a time when it had become the recognized state religion. They were able to combine their new faith with continued membership "of a ruling class committed to maintaining imperial laws by administering brutal punishments." As Peter Brown says, they "were prepared to fight tooth and nail to protect their vast properties," and could be heard "discussing at the dinner-table both the latest theological opinion . . . and the kind of judicial torture they had just inflicted on some poor wretch."[41]

The teaching of Pelagius, which might be seen as an attempt to return to the radical discipleship of the early centuries, came as a profound challenge

---

40. Frend, 59.
41. Peter Brown, *Augustine of Hippo: A Biography* (London: Faber & Faber, 1969), 346–47.

to the complacency of an increasingly dominant form of culture-Christianity and was welcomed by many wealthy and privileged people who experienced growing unease at the tension between their style of life and the words of Jesus which they heard read in worship. As Brown says, to such people the reforming message of Pelagius came as both a disturbing challenge and a welcome deliverance.

A key document from which we gain knowledge of the central beliefs of Pelagianism came from an anonymous writer and bore the title *De divitiis* – "On Riches." It contains an extended Christian response to the social divisions and economic injustices of the Roman "age of gold" and mounts a relentless critique of what are perceived to be the compromising views and actions of professing Christians in this situation. The defence of wealth on the basis that the division between rich and poor was ordained by God and formed part of the mystery of his will is repudiated with passion, and the writer insists that such extremes within society are in fact related to each other as cause and effect.

Whether they were aware of it or not, the rich had actively created the poor. For the rich had won the remorseless tug-of-war for limited resources which took place to the benefit of the rich. Every time someone overstepped the divinely ordained line of mere sufficiency by becoming rich, others were pulled down into poverty.[42] In *De divitiis* it is the combination of the author's perception of the *structural* nature of evil, and his identification of the sin of *avarice* – of craving for wealth – that makes his work so remarkable. The clarity of his insights and the passion with which he argues for justice for the poor can be seen in the following extended quotation.

> Does it seem just to you then that one man should have an abundance of riches over and above his needs, while another does not have enough even to supply his daily wants? That one man should relax in the enjoyment of his wealth, while another wastes away in poverty? That one man should be full to bursting point with expensive and sumptuous banquets far in excess of nature's habitual requirements, while another does not even have enough cheap food to satisfy him? That one man should

---

42. Brown, *Through the Eye of a Needle*, 315.

possess a vast number of splendid houses adorned with costly marble statues in keeping with the instincts of his vanity and pride, while another has not even a tiny hovel to call his own and to protect him from the cold and heat?[43]

This critical analysis of the structural injustices of the imperial world arose from a genuine sense of horror at the consequences of a society dominated by the rich and manipulated in their interests. However, it was accentuated "by the silent presence of Christ" who had "stepped down" to dwell among the poor in Rome! The Pelagians "focused with unusual power on the humility of Christ" and, like other writers at this time, including Jerome, they imagined Jesus "to linger quite literally among the poor who gathered at the steps of the great marble palaces."[44] In this respect the writer of *De divitiis* harked back to the Apologists of the second century in that his understanding of discipleship is clearly derived from the teaching and example of Jesus. To be a Christian is to follow the way of Jesus and to "imitate Christ in all things."

> *He* is a Christian who shows compassion to all, who is not at all provoked by wrong done to him, who does not allow the poor to be oppressed in his presence, who helps the wretched, who succours the needy, who mourns with the mourners, who feels another's pain as though it were his own, who is moved to tears by the tears of others, whose house is common to all, whose door is closed to no one, whose table no poor man does not know . . .[45]

When preachers demanding such radical discipleship appeared in North Africa, Augustine reacted against them on the grounds that their message ignored the struggle of believers with their besetting sins and envisioned a form of the church which was remote from reality in a still-fallen world. Markus describes Augustine's view of baptism as launching a believer "on a lifelong process of convalescence, rather than curing him once and for all and enabling him to make a clean break with his past." That unregenerate past would rear up again because it had existed in the form of "ingrained habit" and would never be wholly overcome in this life. Augustine recognized the

---

43. "On Riches," in Bradstock and Rowland, *Radical Christian Writings*, 17.
44. Brown, *Through the Eye of a Needle*, 315.
45. In Bradstock and Rowland, *Radical Christian Writings*, 14.

continuing existence of "dark layers" within himself and publicly confessed his personal struggle against sin: "Here I am, weep with me and weep for me, all you who do anything good within your inner selves." The *normal* Christian life involved casting oneself continually upon the mercy and grace of God: "O Lord my God, hear me, look upon me and see me; have mercy and heal me, You in whose sight I have become a question to myself."[46]

The petition in the Lord's Prayer by which Christians asked every day for the forgiveness of their sins became crucial for Augustine; it was "the touchstone of orthodoxy" and exposed what he believed to be the illusory nature of the Pelagian belief that baptized Christians might live without sin. Augustine's vision of the church of the future was the polar opposite of what he perceived to be Pelagian perfectionism; it consisted of "being able to hear the thunder of thousands of persons beating their chests, every day, as they recited the Lord's Prayer and remembered their sins." Brown concludes that the rich Christians of North Africa "heard this message with a certain relief"!"[47]

The Pursuit of Perfection

Augustine's response to both of the movements we have described has been seen as a significant stage in the process by which the Catholic Church came to embrace "the whole lay society of the Roman world, with its glaring inequalities of wealth and the depressing resilience of its pagan habits."[48] It is this which explains Markus's use of the word "mediocrity" to describe Augustine's view of the church in the world, a position which the bishop of Hippo justified on the basis that both "tares" and "wheat" must inevitably grow together

---

46. Quoted in Markus, *End of Ancient Christianity*, 54.

47. Brown, *Through the Eye of a Needle*, 362–63. It is worth mentioning here that Albert Camus, with whose work this book began, was profoundly influenced by the Christian philosophy of Augustine whom he referred to as "the other Algerian." Strangely, Camus's passionate defence of the poor and oppressed would seem to bring him much closer to Pelagius and compels us to wonder how different Christian history might have been had Augustine himself been ready to listen to his opponent's insistence on the life of Jesus as the model of discipleship. See Robert Emmet Meagher, *Albert Camus and the Human Crisis* (New York: Pegasus, 2021), 46–47.

48. Brown, *Augustine of Hippo*, 350. Elsewhere Brown says that Augustine's theology of grace "had room for acknowledged heroes *and for the average Christian.*" He recognized that "the Christian Church had come to contain a large number of distinctly *mediocre* persons" (*Rise of Western Christendom*, 89–90; emphasis added).

until the harvest, and only after the final judgement would the "perfection" envisaged by Donatists and Pelagians be realized.

However, if the influence of local, indigenous movements faded over time, another development *within* the Catholic tradition, inspired by a similar concern for faithfulness to the explicit teaching and example of Jesus, was destined not just to last, but to have an enormous influence on the future of Christendom. We refer, of course, to the rise of monasticism, which came to prominence at the very time that the church "was making its peace with the Roman Empire and with the world."[49]

It has been said that monasticism has been, after Christ's commission to his disciples, "the most important – and in many ways the most beneficial – institutional event in the history of Christianity."[50] In the thousand years and more between the conversion of Constantine and the Protestant Reformation, practically everything "that approached the highest, noblest, and truest ideals of the gospel" was done either by monks and nuns who had devoted their lives to the pursuit of "perfection," or by those who were influenced by their example.

Consider the distinctive form taken by the "holy men" of Syria in the fourth and fifth centuries as a striking example of how specific historical and cultural contexts can result in deeply challenging interpretations of biblical texts. At a time when, as we have seen, Christianity was being reshaped by its association with imperial power, radical forms of discipleship emerged which not only challenged the drift into mediocrity, but specifically took up once more the question posed by the choice between God and Mammon. We are concerned here with the spread of Christianity eastwards, at and beyond the limits of the Roman Empire and in linguistic and cultural settings which demanded the repeated translation of the biblical message. This is the region which Peter Brown has described as part of "a great third world of ancient Christianity which stretched far to the east of Antioch" where new traditions

---

49. Jaroslav Pelikan, *Jesus Through the Centuries: His Place in the History of Culture* (New York: Harper & Row, 1985), 113. The assertion that indigenous movements "faded" is, of course, open to challenge. For example, the suppression of Donatism was to be followed by the triumph of Islam in North Africa, and we are bound to ask whether Catholic opposition to a local movement demanding social justice on the basis of its reading of the Bible created fertile soil for an Arab prophet making similar demands on the basis of an alternative holy book?

50. These are the words of the historian Mark A. Noll in *Turning Points: Decisive Moments in the History of Christianity* (Leicester: Inter-Varsity Press, 1997), 84.

of Christian thought and devotion emerged "whose depths we have only begun to plumb."[51]

When we speak of "Syria" in this context we are referring to an area significantly larger than the modern state which bears that name. Maurice Sartre describes how the region's "coastal ports and its oases, or desert 'ports,' helped to place Syria and Arabia at the heart of a vast communications network" and gave this area "a fundamental place in the commercial history of the Roman Empire."[52] As has repeatedly happened, channels of commercial exchange – including in this case the great Silk Road – facilitated the spread of new religious ideas, and Christian "holy men" were to be found traversing these routes as bearers of the word of life. Syria may have acted as a frontier territory between Rome and Parthia, but it was "neither a cultural barrier nor a mere gateway and point of passage between East and West," but served "as an effective intermediary between two great civilizations which flourished on its borders."[53]

The remarkable spread of the message of Christ along the routes which criss-crossed the ancient world was due to an extraordinary band of apostolic messengers who "combined the missionary universalism of Saint Paul with the ideal of wandering poverty associated with the disciples of Jesus in the Gospels."[54] It has been suggested that these Aramaic-speaking messengers were socially and culturally closer to the Galilee of Jesus and his apostles than were the Latinized, urban churches of the Mediterranean world. Moreover, their response to the impact of Greco-Roman urbanization and commercial development was similar to that of the Jesus movement as described in the gospels. Syria had experienced the same kinds of tensions as those we have

---

51. Brown, *Treasure in Heaven*, xxii–xxiii. I must acknowledge here my deep appreciation of Brown's work. This book, along with his *Authority and the Sacred: Aspects of the Christianisation of the Roman World* (Cambridge: Cambridge University Press, 1997), are revealing of previously unknown dimensions of early Christian history, especially the fascinating story of the Syrian "holy men."

52. Maurice Sartre, *The Middle East under Rome* (Cambridge: Belknap Press, 2007), 241.

53. Brown, *Treasure in Heaven*, 40.

54. Brown, 40. R. M. Price traces the ascetic nature of Syrian monasticism "back to the presumed Syrian origin of the *Gospel According to Matthew*" with its description of discipleship as involving celibacy, poverty and homelessness (Matt 19:11–12, 21, 29). Many passages in the descriptions we have of the Syrian "holy men" clearly reflect the influence of the Gospel of Matthew and reveal "an essential continuity in Syrian asceticism going right back to the example of Christ." See Theodoret of Cyrrhus, *A History of the Monks of Syria*, trans. and with introduction by R. M. Price (Kalamazoo: Cistercian, 1985), xx–xxi.

earlier seen arising in Palestine in an age which witnessed the creation of more cities, spread across a vaster area, than at any previous time in human history.⁵⁵ Michael Decker concludes his detailed study of trade and economy in the antique East by concluding that rarely, if ever, prior to the industrial era, "have levels of agrarian development, intensity of settlement, and a combination of security, easy communications, and monetization, coalesced in the way that they did in the late antique East."⁵⁶

In precisely this context, a Syrian form of Christianity emerged, profoundly shaped by the Bible and its contextual interpretation in relation to local cultural situations. For example, the Syrian sources repeatedly focus on the issue of work, of the hard labour involved in tilling the land of the Fertile Crescent, and they discern a connection between this relentless toil and the Genesis account of creation and fall. The changes occurring across the ancient world at this time, including demographic growth, fuelled a quest for land which resulted in the opening up of new areas for agricultural production by wealthy people "who had the capital, the knowledge, and, above all, the interest to further enrich themselves."⁵⁷ The impact of this on traditional communities, living close to subsistence and facing growing indebtedness to the owners of large estates, is reflected in an inscription left by ploughmen who described their work as furrowing "*the hateful earth* beneath yokes [of oxen]." John Chrysostom, whose searching critique of injustice we noticed earlier, described the oppression of labourers on the estates close to Antioch, especially those involved in wine production, which was a primary source of wealth for rich landowners. Their workers received a pittance and were forbidden "to take any of the produce from the full wine vats."⁵⁸ Which suggests that the plight of such labourers had changed little from the time when John of Patmos had heard a voice crying out: "A kilogram of wheat for a day's wages, and three kilograms of barley for a day's wages, *and do not damage the oil and the wine!*" (Rev 6:5–6).

The response of Syrian Christians to this situation is illustrated in the pages of the remarkable *Book of Steps*, known as the Syriac *Liber Graduum*. This

---

55. Sartre, *Middle East under Rome*, 151.

56. Michael Decker, *Tilling the Hateful Earth: Agricultural Production and Trade in the Late Antique East* (Oxford: Oxford University Press, 2009), 258.

57. Decker, *Tilling the Hateful Earth*, 71.

58. Decker, 76.

is the work of an anonymous writer at some point in the second half of the fourth century and, according to its modern translator, its author lived "in a thought-world saturated by the Bible" and returned repeatedly to a theology of the cross. The fundamental call is to "renounce the world, empty oneself and become celibate, take up the cross and follow Christ." The repeated emphasis on humility, lowliness and self-emptying reflects a model of Christian community which stood in stark contrast to the emergence of Christendom in the Roman West, as indeed it does to contemporary Christianity today. As translator Robert Kitchen observes, "Particularly, in contrast to the public relations-conscious contemporary church intent upon 'church growth' the faith community of *Liber Graduum*, living in the not-too-friendly Persian Empire, offers a vision of simple reliance upon God's power and grace."[59]

It is impossible to convey here the spiritual richness of this work, but in order to provide a sample of its author's unusual insights into what it means to walk in the Way of Jesus Christ, we offer an extended quotation.

> But since the day our Lord dissolved enmity and reconciled with the blood of the cross what is on earth with what is in heaven, causing wars to cease from the ends of the earth, no longer when the Assyrian wakes up is it our Lord who awakens him; nor when the Roman descends to battle, is it our Lord who makes him descend . . . but [it is] evil rising up today in all of them.
>
> For our Lord made peace, but the sons of Adam do not wish to be peaceful and a person is not reconciled with his brother, as the apostle wrote, "if one has a disagreement with his neighbour, let him forgive, as Christ forgave all humanity." But if these had desired to turn away from evil things [they would have had peace]. Our Lord no longer makes wars today as in former times, but it is these people who fight today by their own desire. Whoever rises up against his neighbour, the Lord pulls him down. . . .
>
> Therefore in this world the two antagonists [i.e. the Persian and Roman empires] may raise their hands against one another with a sword and be slain, but in that [other world] to come,

---

59. Robert A. Kitchen, trans. and ed. (together with Martien F. G. Parmentier), *The Book of Steps: The Syriac* Liber Graduum (Kalamazoo: Cistercian, 2004), lxxxi.

they will be tormented, because they did not build upon the peace that our Lord Jesus had made on earth and in heaven, and because they raised up these wars that he had caused to cease from the ends of the earth. He said to them, look, my blood is yours: drink and live. But do not drink the blood of one another or you shall die. They killed him, drank his blood and were not ashamed, and see, here they are again, drinking the blood of their brothers, a thing that God hated and despised from the first day.[60]

Clearly, we have here a reading of the gospel which has striking parallels to the primitive Christian proclamation of the Pax Christi and the consequent opposition to war and bloodshed as a violation of the redemptive work of Jesus on the cross. However, this Syrian tradition goes further by tracing the relentless toil and labour which had become the common experience of human beings back to the biblical narratives of creation and fall. In a lengthy discussion of "The Tree of Adam" the writer describes how Adam and Eve "observed the earth and saw this thing on [the earth] *and loved it, evil had power over them and they knew it*." The Creator had warned them that the fruit of the tree of the knowledge of good and evil would "take you away from heavenly things and from the kindness of your Creator" and would "*bind you up in transitory things and in toil, anxiety and pride*." Over and over again this link between the fall and the human addiction to the earth – to land, possessions and wealth – is hammered home. Satan had cajoled Adam to look out over the earth, and he tempted Jesus in the same way, "*so that he might lust for the wealth of the earth and its transitory beauty as Adam and Eve had yearned for.*" In the wilderness the devil had confronted Jesus: "Look, see how the earth is attractive with its possessions and kingdoms." This unknown Syrian writer clearly believed that land as the source of wealth and prosperity awakens human desire and the spirit of covetousness. Eve was seduced and told Adam that "he might acquire wealth and become a king: 'Look, gold and silver are on earth and all sorts of pleasures. Possess and enjoy yourself; rule, increase, and multiply, the evil one counselled.'"[61] The contextual relevance

---

60. Kitchen and Parmentier, *Book of Steps*, 92–93.

61. These quotations come from Memra (chapter) 21 of *The Book of Steps*, pp. 231–49 of the edition cited. All emphasis is added.

of this exposition to the Middle Eastern world is remarkable and leads Peter Brown to conclude:

> Adam and Eve and their descendants had lost their first moment of sublime leisure. They had declined into the present careworn state of society. This was a society in which human beings were not only dominated by the need to work so as to eat, and thus to keep mortality at bay. They were also driven by a lust for land that was quite as fierce as any sexual drive. The lust for the land accounted for the brutal structures of present day society.[62]

It has been suggested that modern Western Christians have lost contact with the seriousness of such an understanding of the fall largely because of the influence of Augustine's view that what happened in Eden related to individual wills and was manifested in "unregulated sexual desire." By contrast, in the Syrian reading what mattered "was that Adam and Eve had rebelled against God by wishing to exercise God's power over the land." They had wished to be great landowners, "to *own* the lush earth of Eden, not simply to serve God *in* Eden."[63] The relevance of this to the modern world in which the economic system which has come to dominate the lives of millions of people has turned men and women into "willing slaves" is striking, and the unique testimony of ancient Syrian Christianity will be seen to be relevant when we come to confront contemporary challenges later in this book.

Before we leave the Syrian monastics we must note that, not content simply to interpret the Bible in ways that contextualized its message in relation to their times, they were actively engaged in challenging oppression and in the defence of the poor. There are accounts of a village priest cursing a landowner's cart which was overloaded and bearing more than his share of the peasant's harvest, while monks patrolled the banks of the Euphrates demanding that landowners destroy the records of debtors' bonds which were the means of the enslavement of labouring peasants. Not only the story of the fall, but the narrative of the gospels, and especially the sufferings and death of Christ, were understood in ways that exposed the injustices of the rich and powerful and comforted and relieved the distress and pain of the oppressed. Perhaps the

---

62. Brown, *Treasure in Heaven*, 57.
63. Brown, 59.

most extraordinary and moving example is found in the words of Ephrem the Syrian who said that "only the sweat of Christ that fell from the Cross could redeem an earth soaked, for millennia, in the sweat of Adam's brow."[64] The appearance and proliferation of monastic movements at the time at which Christianity was adapting its form and the content of its message to the new situation created by the conversion of the Roman emperor was to prove to be the beginning of a centuries-long tradition of radical discipleship which kept alive the memory of the teaching and example of Jesus. Eoin de Bhaldraithe comments that with the rise of monastic movements, the life of renunciation within such communities came to replace the original function of baptism as "the great divide of the human race," and in the following centuries it was the monastics who kept alive what had once been "features of the general church in the early period."[65] This verdict by a Catholic monk is paralleled by the conclusion of the Protestant historian Mark Noll who can say that, "almost by themselves, monks for more than a thousand years sustained what was most noble and most Christ-centered in the church." He affirms that the emergence of monasticism was both "a critical turning point in the history of Christianity" and "the very rescue of the church itself."[66]

Your Kingdom Come

We have seen that one particular petition in the Lord's Prayer became extremely important for Augustine. It may be suggested that across the following centuries, and perhaps more than ever in modern times, it has been another of those petitions which has repeatedly expressed the deepest longings of generations of Christians who have uttered this prayer, often with an urgency bordering on desperation: "*Your kingdom come, your will be done, on earth as it is in heaven*" (Matt 6:10).

The tension experienced by John of Patmos at the close of the New Testament period, a tension created by the contrast between the promise of the coming of the reign of God and the reality of the condition of the

---

64. Brown, 68.

65. Eoin de Bhaldraithe, OCist., "Early Christian Features Preserved in Western Monasticism," in *The Origins of Christendom in the West*, ed. Alan Kreider (Edinburgh: T&T Clark, 2001), 178.

66. Noll, *Turning Points*, 104.

churches known to the writer, has repeatedly surfaced across the centuries as Christianity seemed to fall far short of fulfilling all that the prophets and apostles had anticipated the gospel would achieve. The promise implicit within the Lord's Prayer, that the earth will be the context in which the glory of God is to be displayed, seemed to justify the hope that this great transformation would occur – or, at least, would commence – within history. As a result, whenever the state of the church and the strength of a resurgent Mammon has triggered renewed outbursts of pleading for divine visitations to bring life on earth into closer alignment with the will of God, these outpourings of intercession have been accompanied by actions consistent with such prayers. The cry to heaven for the kingdom to come has invariably resulted in new movements of radical discipleship, cross-cultural missionary initiatives, periods of spiritual and theological renewal, and the emergence of fresh prophetic visions of social transformation. As we shall see in the next chapter, the period often known as the Middle Ages, between the fall of the Roman Empire and the emergence of a new world in the "Age of Reform," was to witness the conflict between God and Mammon being played out in new ways following the recovery of Europe and the later extension of its economic and political power to previously unknown parts of the earth. Indeed, the spiritual conflict throughout the Age of Reform would eventually gain an unprecedented intensity and global reach, but before we confront that challenge we must consider what happened in the period we know as the Middle Ages, since it is precisely here that we discover the roots of the critical choice which now confronts world Christianity.

CHAPTER 7

The Age of Reform

> When in the tenth and eleventh centuries, the monasteries . . . launched their great movement of reform, the object was to bring monastic life more closely into line with the life of the first Christian community as described in *Acts*. . . . There were always some layfolk who noted, with bitterness, the gulf that separated the poverty and simplicity of the first Christians from the wealthy, hierarchically organized Church of their time. (Norman Cohn)[1]

In his groundbreaking studies of the history of Christian mission, Andrew Walls suggested that it was possible to identify six distinct phases in the period that stretches across two millennia, from the time of Christ to the postmodern, globalized world of today. In each of these phases the Christian message took root among particular peoples, creating a base from which it would eventually be transmitted cross-culturally into another context by means of a fresh translation. This process, elsewhere identified as "paradigm change," can be discerned within the New Testament itself, where the task of cross-cultural transmission is clearly evident in the story told in the book of Acts. The good news concerning Messiah Jesus is taken from its distinctively Jewish context into the gentile world, reaching the imperial capital of Rome and confronting the challenges posed by a Latin, urban culture across the

---

1. Norman Cohn, *The Pursuit of the Millennium: Revolutionary Millenarians and Mystical Anarchists of the Middle Ages* (London: Paladin, 1970), 38.

empire. Walls thus identifies the first age of Christianity as being "Jewish," while the second he describes as "Hellenistic-Roman."

The ground that we have covered thus far in this book correlates with these two phases, but we now make a big leap to explore Walls's third and fourth phases. These relate to the collapse of the western Roman Empire and the irruption of Islam in the Middle East, historical developments which could have signalled the end of Christianity but for the fact that it engaged in a further episode of missionary translation by means of which the tribal peoples who had swept across the old imperial borders were themselves converted to the faith of Jesus Christ. Walls identifies this as the *Barbarian Age* of Christianity, when the gospel was communicated among "peasant cultivators and their harsh, uncertain lives."[2] The conversion of the tribal peoples, in which Irish missionary monks played a crucial role, has been said to have resulted in a "Germanic folk-religious reinterpretation of Christianity" which, by the tenth and eleventh centuries, became normative throughout the Catholic Church and was to be "embodied in the European ideal of Christendom."[3]

That third phase came to end when Byzantium was overrun by Islamic forces and the faith of Muhammad, which had already spread along the coast of North Africa, advanced to the very gates of Europe. This precipitated the emergence of Walls's fourth phase, which he describes as the era of *Western Europe*, during which Christianity began its centuries-long identification with European Christendom, a phase which was to last until recent times.

---

2. Andrew F. Walls, *The Missionary Movement in Christian History: Studies in the Transmission of Faith* (Edinburgh: T&T Clark, 1996), 20.

3. James C. Russell, *The Germanization of Early Medieval Christianity: A Sociohistorical Approach to Religious Transformation* (Oxford: Oxford University Press, 1994), 209–10. See also Richard Fletcher, *The Barbarian Conversion: From Paganism to Christianity* (New York: Henry Holt, 1997). Russell comments that the missionaries who evangelized the Franks, Saxons and other tribal peoples employed a policy of *accommodation* with regard to local, tribal cultures on the assumption that a "more rigorous ethical and doctrinal formation would soon follow and *eliminate incompatible Germanic ideological elements*." However, this did not happen and "a Germanized form of Christianity [became] normative throughout Western Europe" (209, 211; emphasis added). By contrast, note Ronald Murphy's positive view of the ninth-century work known as the *Heliand*, in which an unknown evangelist to the Franks "remained faithful to the orthodox Christian teaching of the Gospel, and yet in his contemplation of that Gospel imagined an almost unthinkably new and different form of Christianity, thereby transforming the Gospel into the traditional religious imagery and values of his people" (G. Ronald Murphy, S.J., *The Saxon Savior: The Transformation of the Gospel in the Ninth-Century Heliand* [Oxford: Oxford University Press, 1989], ix).

The Resurgence of Mammon

Viewed from a broad historical perspective, Walls's third phase of Christian history took place during what we have come to know as the Middle Ages. The phrase suggests that this long period was a time between the classical era of Greece and Rome, on the one hand, and the emergence of the modern world with the Renaissance and Reformation, on the other. Understood in this way it may almost appear to be an interlude, an impression heightened when a value-judgement is made in classifying at least part of this era as the "Dark Ages." However, the manner in which we identify distinct historical phases, while legitimate and helpful, must not lead us to imagine that these are ever separate blocks of time, self-contained and divorced from the continuing flow of history. For example, we shall be considering the Protestant Reformation later in this chapter, but the roots of that movement have to be recognized as existing far back in the Middle Ages, as can be seen in the title of Steven Ozment's study *The Age of Reform 1250–1550*. The time frame here indicates that the Reformation cannot be understood apart from movements which occurred centuries earlier and demanded the reform of the papacy and a return to apostolic simplicity.[4]

The renewal movements we are concerned with here arose as a response to a particular context in which, after centuries of cultural and economic decline, Europe witnessed the revival of commercial activity and the rebuilding and expansion of cities.[5] Economic historians have described the High Middle Ages (ca. 950–1350) as a period during which a "commercial revolution" occurred. Lester Little observes that by the middle of the eleventh century, Europe was almost entirely free from "the pillaging attacks of outsiders," permitting a new economy to emerge as "countless local economies were amalgamated into a complex trade area that united the coasts of the English

---

4. According to Steven Ozment, the Protestant Reformers shared with earlier, medieval reform movements the conviction "that traditional church authority and piety no longer served the religious needs of large numbers of people and had become psychologically and financially oppressive" (*The Age of Reform 1250–1550: An Intellectual and Religious History of Late Medieval and Reformation Europe* [New Haven: Yale University Press, 1980], 222).

5. Fernand Braudel says that when the economic tide turned "with the boom of the eleventh to thirteenth centuries, the towns enjoyed a remarkable renaissance.... Modern, and ahead of their time, they signalled the future. Indeed, they were the future already" (*A History of Civilizations* [London: Penguin, 1995], 319).

Channel, the North and Baltic Seas, and the Atlantic Ocean as far south as Bordeaux and as far north and west as Iceland."[6]

This new economy was accompanied not only by the growth of urbanization, but also by the appearance of early forms of industry, especially the manufacture of woollen cloth which now became available across Europe for clothing, bed coverings and for decorative purposes. Flanders became the centre of this industry, with almost every town involved in textile manufacture, while the high quality of English wool created a thriving export market at the same time. This rapid expansion of trade and industry was accompanied by a significant growth in the importance of money and the invention of new methods by which funds might be transferred, thus anticipating the emergence of modern banking. The desire for stability and security "encouraged the formation of lasting – as against *ad hoc* – partnerships, i.e. companies," a development which facilitated the investment of accumulated funds for profit and created "an essential element of the capitalist economy."

> This turning point . . . marked the emergence of a wholly different attitude, one that calculated values to see whether any particular activity or transaction would be profitable. It marked the promotion of commerce and industry from their status as marginal activities to the level of key elements in European economic life.[7]

---

6. Lester K. Little, *Religious Poverty and the Profit Economy in Medieval Europe* (New York: Cornell University Press, 1983), 10.

7. Little, *Religious Poverty*, 18. See also Robert S. Lopez, *The Commercial Revolution of the Middle Ages, 950–1350* (Cambridge: Cambridge University Press, 1976). This work treats the new economy as an inevitable and almost problem-free development. The social impact of the "revolution" is largely ignored and Lopez writes that "organized religion is seldom revolutionary on earth, and practical ethics does not so much determine practical economics as it adjusts to it." With regard to the social injustice and economic divisions which were the consequences of this commercial revolution, Lopez can only ask "whether a more equally shared misery is better or worse than a diversified profile of riches and poverty. In economic terms, a low platform may serve for the launching of economic growth, but this cannot occur without the injection of some powerful driving force" (18). It is not difficult to detect here the influence of a modern, economistic ideology. When this present manuscript was almost completed, I discovered Janet L. Abu-Lughod's *Before European Hegemony: The World System A.D. 1250–1350* (Oxford: Oxford University Press, 1989). She discusses the rise of the cities of Bruges and Ghent in detail and argues that in the thirteenth century other "world powers" beyond Europe "had as promising a level of business acumen as, and an even more sophisticated set of economic institutions than the Europeans, who by the thirteenth century had entered their world system" (18).

It was in precisely this context that a movement of reform took place in which very large numbers of people were gripped by the desire for a return to apostolic simplicity and the way of life which Jesus had demanded of his first followers. The commercial revolution posed new and difficult questions to Christianity and the economic possibilities which this emerging urban culture opened up created a profoundly spiritual challenge to a hierarchically structured church. The temptation grew to seek an accommodation with the "profit economy" and in the later Middle Ages theology and piety were to be increasingly shaped by mercantile logic, so that in key areas, "the Church turned from a pact with the feudal social order to an alliance with the early capitalist economic way of the merchants and bankers."[8]

However, as the quotation from Norman Cohn at the head of this chapter suggests, significant numbers of lay Christians expressed the desire for reform and a return to the model of an alternative community which they found in the book of Acts. Perhaps the outstanding example is the emergence of the movement known as the *Humiliati* (the Humble Ones), which between 1170 and 1220 evolved from being an informal group of laypeople, initially suspected of presenting yet another heretical threat to the Catholic Church, to becoming an accepted and welcome expression of discipleship in a changing world. Pope Innocent III met a delegation of Humiliati leaders in 1198, approved of their description of their way of life, and recognized that their determination to follow Jesus within the new urban culture constituted a faithful and creative response to the contemporary context. Following this meeting, Innocent wrote to the leaders of the movement in nine cities across Italy, affirming the validity of their attempt to pioneer a new kind of community for laypeople who would continue to live and work in the secular world, yet be committed to the apostolic example of communal solidarity. The Humiliati had clearly heeded Jesus's call to act as "the salt of the earth" and "the light of the world," and to allow that light to "shine before others" that they might "see your good deeds and glorify your Father in heaven" (Matt 5:13–16). Pope Innocent urged them "to maintain peaceful relations with everyone, to return anything gained by usury or any other improper

---

8. Berndt Hamm, "'Buying Heaven': The Prospects of Commercialized Salvation in the Fourteenth to Sixteenth Centuries," in *Money as God? The Monetization of the Market and Its Impact on Religion, Politics, Law and Ethics*, eds. Jürgen von Hagen and Michael Welker (Cambridge: Cambridge University Press, 2014), 237.

means . . . not to lay up treasures on earth, not to love the world, and not to dissolve one's marriage except on grounds of fornication."⁹

Most extraordinary of all was Pope Innocent's approval of lay preaching, encouraging the Humiliati practice of weekly Sunday gatherings to listen to "one or more of their brothers known to be strong in faith, knowledgeable in religion, gifted in speech, and consistent in behaviour and speech."¹⁰ Witnesses of the social impact of this movement reported that the Humiliati "had converted many noble and powerful citizens," and indeed the emphasis in the papal letter on the restitution of ill-gotten gains suggests the presence of significant numbers of the new merchant class within their gatherings. At the same time, the evidence of the regular practice of mutual aid indicates that many Humiliati lived on the margins of urban society, "and that only the charity and solidarity of the Christian lay brotherhood to which they belonged kept them from slipping into a critical state of involuntary poverty."¹¹ Little concludes:

> The limits of Humiliati charity stretched beyond the order itself to embrace all the poor and downtrodden. They fed and clothed the poor and cared for the sick, giving special attention to lepers. The consciousness of their attempt to follow scriptural precepts seems assured by their constant readiness to hear readings from scripture and listen to sermons, as well as their requirement that a lay preacher be someone whose activity was consistent with what he preached.¹²

---

9. Little, *Religious Poverty*, 116. Hans Küng discusses Pope Innocent III at some length, describing him as "perhaps the most brilliant pope ever to rule." However, Küng concludes that it was precisely under this pope that "Romanization reached its climax," and he suggests that Pope Innocent "shrewdly domesticated the growing poverty movement in the church and approved those novel orders whose animating principle was the discipleship of the poor Jesus: the mendicant orders, the begging orders, of the Franciscans and Dominicans" (*The Catholic Church* [London: Phoenix, 2002], 100). By contrast, Innocent III's attitude towards the movement known as Catharism was very different. As a historian of the Cathar movement, Malcom Lambert, says, he "detested heresy, and especially Catharism. It was an enemy to be destroyed." Innocent "was not a gentle man: he rejoiced uninhibitedly over military triumphs" and argued that the death penalty and the Crusades were both appropriate means to deal with heretics (*The Cathars* [Oxford: Blackwell, 1998], 97–98).

10. Little, 117.
11. Little, 118.
12. Little.

One of the most important sources of our knowledge of the Humiliati is the much-travelled James of Vitry who, while waiting in Genoa for a ship to transport him to the Holy Land in 1216, reported to the pope his discovery of yet another new religious movement in the district of Liège. This group was marked by a similar depth of religious devotion among laypeople as was characteristic of the Humiliati, but uniquely it consisted of Christian women who chose to live together and encourage each other in the pursuit of simplicity and holiness. The women were known as Beguines and were numerous in what is now Belgium, but also present in France (where they translated the Bible into French and discussed its message in their meetings), the Netherlands and Germany. It was reported that two thousand members of this movement met in the city of Cologne, of whom almost 90 percent were from patrician families.[13] Many of these young women "scorned their parents' riches and rejected the noble and wealthy husbands offered them," finding in the movement a fellowship committed to chastity, and "preferring to live in poverty, having nothing except what they got by spinning and working with their hands, and being content with shabby clothes and simple food."[14] A contemporary observer concluded that the Beguines "surpassed in charity those who lived in cloisters, for in the midst of worldly people they were spiritual, in the midst of pleasure-seekers they were pure, and in the midst of noise and confusion, they led serene, eremitic lives."[15] Little concludes that these remarkable Christian women, like the Humiliati, "had shown a way of making the Christian life attainable by the laity, by women, by city-dwellers both rich and poor."[16]

Within the Catholic Church the enormous challenge posed by the profit economy thus resulted in a series of reform movements, including the attempt to close the gap between the clergy and the laity by encouraging the priesthood to model individual poverty and a shared life together. At the same time, entirely new monastic movements emerged, including the Carthusians, the Premonstratensians and the Cistercians. As this chapter was being written I happened to visit Dundee beside the great River Tay in north-east Scotland

---

13. Cohn, *Pursuit of the Millennium*, 160–61.
14. Little, *Religious Poverty*, 133.
15. Little, 134.
16. Little.

and while driving north I spotted a road sign pointing to the ruins of a monastery in the hills on the south bank of the river. I turned off to find this place, and discovered that it was the Cistercians, who were characterized by a desire for peace and solitude in order to establish "schools for Christ," who, many centuries earlier, had built this monastery looking down with a most glorious view of the wide Tay. I felt my spirit moved simply by standing on that holy ground.

We have not mentioned the most famous and widely influential of all the new communities which emerged at this time, namely the Dominicans and Franciscans. Both of these orders came into being in response to the challenges posed by the growth and influence of the urban culture we have described, and both sought to practise an entirely new type of monastic life in order to present a missionary challenge to the urban, profit economy.

> As for money, the Dominicans . . . decided that the brothers should never handle money nor receive alms in the form of cash. But the Franciscans had a more deep-seated hatred of money, which originated with Francis himself and was then projected by him to a remarkable degree on to the order as a whole. The stories told about Francis and money show an almost pathological fear of touching what to him was filthy and disgusting.[17]

The picture that emerges here is of a broad quest for faithful discipleship in which a wide spectrum of people, clerical and lay, sought to return to first principles. This meant offering a countercultural challenge to the direction that European society seemed to be taking, but it also brought the reformers into conflict with the upper echelons of the Catholic Church at a time when bishops and popes increasingly appeared to live in ways that conflicted with their own statements concerning the commercial revolution.[18]

---

17. Little, 164.

18. Note Andrew F. Walls's comment: "Monasticism was born of the desire for wholehearted discipleship, in repentance from a development in Christian history that had enabled affluent people to combine piety and self-indulgence. . . . All over Christendom, men and women covenanted to live under discipline, resigning personal rights and private property, avoiding relationships that would force them to put the interest of their own kin, or their feudal superior, before the welfare of the brethren or the poor" (*A History of the Expansion of Christianity Reconsidered: The Legacy of George E. Day* [New Haven: Yale Divinity School Library Occasional Publication No. 8, 1996], 16). However, he goes on to say: "Long a potential sign of the Kingdom, the monasteries over time became a counter-sign of the Kingdom. . . .

The tension which the reform movements created can be seen in the career of Arnold of Brescia (ca. 1100–55), who lectured on the Scriptures in Paris to students "who publicly begged their bread from door to door to support themselves and their master."[19] A witness of Arnold's ministry testified that he was relentlessly critical of the bishops "on account of their avarice and filthy lucre; most of all because of the stains on their personal lives, and their striving to build the church in blood." Eventually summoned to Rome to account for his preaching, Arnold was appalled by the luxury and wealth of the papal court where he discovered tables loaded with gold and silver plate. In 1147 he preached using language that takes us by surprise since it seems to anticipate Martin Luther centuries later:

> The Pope himself was not what he professed to be – an apostolic man and a shepherd of souls – but a man of blood who maintained his authority by fire and the sword, a tormentor of churches and oppressor of the innocent, who did nothing in the world save gratify his lust and empty other men's coffers to fill his own.[20]

It will come as little surprise that Arnold, who went on to demand a church reformed after the apostolic pattern of the book of Acts, and proposed a secular authority freed from ecclesiastical control, was eventually arrested, tried and hanged. His body was burned and the ashes scattered on the Tiber, "lest his remains be held in veneration by the mad populace."[21]

The Power of the Medieval Pulpit

The movement we have briefly described has been called "the evangelical awakening of the twelfth century" and it prepared the ground for what, during the following century, has been identified as "one of the great ages in the

---

Followers of the one who had nowhere to lay his head became over time collectively the major holders of real estate, the directors of the most profitable export business and a comfortable class of rentiers" (17).

19. Little, *Religious Poverty*, 109.
20. Little, 110.
21. Little.

history of preaching."[22] Indeed, as a remarkable study by G. R. Owst showed more than half a century ago, English preaching throughout the late Middle Ages mounted a persistent, often scathing, attack on the growing corruption of the church, and defended the cause of the poor and marginalized, not least by voicing their complaints and anguish.[23] Here is the Dominican John Bromyard, whose massive *Summa Predicantium* contains "the gathered fruits of mendicant preaching throughout the fourteenth century":

> O just God, mighty judge, the game was not fairly divided between them and us. Their satiety was our famine; their merriment was our wretchedness; their jousts and tournaments were our torments, because with our oats and at our expense they did these things. Their plenty was our scarcity. Their feasts, delectations, pomps, vanities, excesses and superfluities were our fastings, penalties, wants, calamities and spoliation. The love-ditties and laughter of their dances were our mockery, our groanings and remonstrations. They used to sing "Well enough! Well enough!" – and we groaned, saying "Woe to us! Woe to us!" O just Lord, the minstrels and the rich and shameful persons who received from them food and robes, cried "For largess! For largess!"; and we, the poor, their subjects and creditors, cried "Flee away! Flee away!" for such help themselves freely as often as they like, that is, they borrow and pay back unwillingly.[24]

Professor Owst's study is intended, as its title indicates, to demonstrate the importance of the language of the medieval pulpit with regard to the development of English language and literature, especially concerning the use

---

22. Little, 186, 196.

23. Readers who might not find the words "preaching" and "pulpit" set their pulses racing might reflect on the comment of Johan Huizinga: "The Franciscan friar Richard preached in Paris in 1429 during ten consecutive days. He began about five in the morning and spoke without a break until ten or eleven.... When at the close of his tenth sermon, he announced that it would be his last ... 'great and small wept as touchingly and as bitterly as if they were watching their last friends being buried; and so did he.' Thinking that he might preach once more ... on Sunday, the people flocked thither on Saturday evening, and passed the night in the open, to secure good seats" (*The Waning of the Middle Ages: A Study of the Forms of Life, Thought and Art in France and the Netherlands in the Fourteenth and Fifteenth Centuries* [Harmondsworth: Penguin, 1955], 12).

24. G. R. Owst, *Literature and Pulpit in Medieval England: A Neglected Chapter in the History of English Letters and of the English People* (Oxford: Basil Blackwell, 1961), 301.

of satire and humour. At the same time, it provides an unmatched history of preaching in the pre-Reformation church and demonstrates the existence of the unremitting and passionate opposition of the pulpit to the growing influence of Mammon. Here is Bromyard, contributing to what is described as a "great and bitter cry" from the pulpits of the land "against those . . . monsters of cruelty and extortion."

> If now the sheep and oxen, the fowls and capons and all the beasts which the rich eat and do not pay for . . . were to cry out in their bellies [as in St. Patrick's case], there would be a greater noise, perchance, in their bellies than in Noah's Ark where all the animals were together.[25]

Again and again the preacher exposes the heartlessness and rapacity of the rich and privileged, but his searching critique is no less severe with regard to the corruption of the church, beginning with the papacy. If those "who preside at that most Holy See knew how . . . the faithful . . . curse their pomp, which they judge to be a deviation from the path of Christ . . . they would cease from such things, for the sake of example."[26] On page after page of this extraordinary book we find such indictments, and it becomes clear that a veritable army of preachers perceived the root cause of the problem to be the growth of a hideous form of idolatry stemming from the worship of Mammon. "To such a degree are the people of to-day given up to avarice," says one of the preachers, "that they would sooner do things for gold than for God." Merchants and traders expose themselves to every peril on land and sea for gold, but not for God. A poor man is depicted as begging for help:

> "My Lord, for the love of Christ crucified and all the saints of God, help me." . . . Still there would be "neither voice nor hearing," although three or four words from that lord would probably expedite the whole business. But if that same poor man were to sell the few things he has and needs, or borrow gold . . . and offer it along with his request, then "the blind and deaf"

---

25. Owst, *Literature and Pulpit*, 320–21.
26. Owst, 251.

would straightway both hear and smile upon him. Lo! What great miracles gold works in such days as these![27]

The Dominican preacher John Bromyard concludes that to money "all hearts and deeds alike of evil men are obedient." In an extraordinary passage he concludes that the false god of money "works more miracles than the true God with his cross of wood." The God and Father of Jesus rectifies *some* who are lame and bent, *but not all*; Mammon, by contrast, "rectifies all cases in the court of the false, however 'tortuous' and 'curved' they may be."

> And if it [money] be had in plenty and with due reverence, it makes the lame walk and the captives go free. Deaf judges and lords and those in power, who – however unjust be your case – offer a deaf ear, it makes to hear. . . . Dumb advocates also it makes to speak.[28]

Commenting on the prophetic character of English preachers in the late Middle Ages, Owst describes how John Bromyard appeared to "catch fire," his sermon "shooting out its menacing sparks upon those sitting around" as the use of bitter satire aroused his hearers to protest at the injustices from which they suffered. Owst insists that Bromyard's intent was "nothing more than a powerful spiritual and moral corrective, wholly innocent of any revolutionary intent," but he adds that it is impossible to ignore the obvious fact that the preacher's words were capable of encouraging revolt "if they happened to fall upon 'the inflammable material' then lying about 'at the mercy of a spark.'"[29]

Professor Owst recognizes a clear connection between the passion for justice so evident in the medieval pulpit and the peasant revolts which erupted during the late Middle Ages. Citing Bromyard once again, he describes a sermon which displayed such an intensity of feeling that "it rivals even the masterpieces of later Revolutionary oratory." Here is a passage from the sermon in question:

> The poor man, indeed, if he steal the rich man's goods, is hung. The rich man is not punished at all for seizing the goods of the poor, even when he is worthy of the gallows. Wherefore says

---

27. Owst, 315–16.
28. Owst, 317.
29. Owst, 292.

Chrysostom . . . "If it were possible to give the rich their deserts, you would see the world's prisons everywhere full of them."[30]

Language of this kind, continually reiterated from the medieval pulpit, and heard in the open air in market squares and at traditional festivals, could hardly fail to stir an oppressed peasantry to action. As Owst acknowledges, "no society on earth could withstand forever the continuous shock of such Complaint, from within as well as without its borders." As the impassioned speech of recognized and responsible people within the church was taken up in popular rhyme and song, it became "the prelude to a revolt as in any of the other great revolutions of history."[31] Clearly, what we have uncovered here are the deep roots of both the later peasant revolts and the Protestant Reformation itself which, as we noted earlier, was the culmination of an "Age of Reform" begun centuries before. As Owst concludes:

> Finally, inasmuch as that type of preaching was not limited to England, but was to spread abroad throughout Christendom, it goes far to explain why "a wave of democratic agitation was sweeping over Europe" at the same period. In the Peasants' Revolt, as in that later Civil War between Puritan and Cavalier, it is still equally impossible to say, therefore, where the religious influences end and political influences begin.[32]

We do well to note Hans Küng's comment that "the history of the establishment of the church as an institution, as a political power, is one thing, and the history of the authentic life of Christians is another."[33]

Apocalyptic Spirituality

We need to consider the extent of the hardship and suffering experienced by Europe's population in this period. Between 1300 and 1500 the most severe

---

30. Owst, 303.
31. Owst, 285.
32. Owst, 306–7.
33. Küng, *Catholic Church*, 112. Note also the conclusion of Catherine Keller, who says that the story of the countercultural movements from the eleventh to the sixteenth centuries "has been virtually expunged from the standard accounts of church and state history, which figure them as mad, enthusiastic, or heretical if they could not be erased" (*Apocalypse Now and Then: A Feminist Guide to the End of the World* [Boston: Beacon, 1996], 110).

trials swept across the continent, bringing famine, disease – in the shape of bubonic plague – and the Hundred Years War between France and England which, with the invention of gunpowder and the development of heavy artillery, brought death and destruction on an unimaginable scale. Steven Ozment says that social structures and fundamental values were put to a terrible test in this period and that people across the continent found themselves walking through "the valley of the shadow of death."[34] Contexts like this have frequently given rise to the emergence of apocalyptic visions and dreams, promising an end to suffering and injustice through supernatural intervention, and anticipating the long-promised era of millennial peace and justice. Norman Cohn has provided a brilliant survey of such movements in his book *The Pursuit of the Millennium* and he concludes that such eschatological dreams proliferated among people "without land or with too little land even for subsistence; journeymen and unskilled workers living under the continuous threat of unemployment; beggars and vagabonds . . . who could find no assured and recognized place in society at all."[35]

However, although Cohn says that the greatest wave of millenarian excitement was precipitated by the Black Death, which removed two-fifths of Europe's population during the fourteenth century, the most significant and influential articulation of apocalyptic theology and spirituality came from a monk who was contemporary with Francis of Assisi, and whose reinterpretation of the book of Revelation was to play a major role in shaping the mission and history of the Franciscan movement. This was Joachim of Fiore, born around 1135 in Calabria, and becoming a celebrated figure, consulted by kings and popes, before his death in 1202. Joachim described a crucial experience at Easter 1184 when, having been frustrated that despite a lengthy struggle to understand the Apocalypse, he remained baffled by aspects of the text and retreated into a church to pray at midnight, pleading for the help of the Holy Spirit. "There came upon me an uncertainty concerning belief in the Trinity. . . . I prayed with all my might. I was very frightened and was

---

34. Ozment, *Age of Reform*, 8.
35. Cohn, *Pursuit of the Millennium*, 282.

moved to call on the Holy Spirit whose feast day it was to deign to show me the holy mystery of the Trinity."[36]

The system of interpretation which Joachim subsequently developed is too complex to be described here, but his statement points towards two central features of his teaching which were to have wide and long-lasting influence. Joachim's struggle with the Trinity resulted in the suggestion that the whole of human history might be understood as the unfolding of three distinct ages, each related to a different member of the Trinity. Put simply: the era of the Old Testament, of the law, pertained especially to the Father; the coming of the New Testament, of the gospel, to the Son; and the third age, which had in some sense begun, was related to the Holy Spirit, and was still to be revealed in all its fullness. Joachim's vision thus became a theology of *history* and it introduced the revolutionary belief that the full outworking of the blessings of the gospel was yet to come and was related, not to the hereafter, but to a historical transformation by which the Holy Spirit would indwell the whole human family. Here is Joachim writing to the abbot of Valdona:

> But when the time of wrath and the hour of temptation will have been completed, the Lord will gaze upon his people. His heart will rejoice, and no man shall take his joy from them. . . . When this little while is finished they will begin to see a time of peace on earth like nothing that has been since men began to exist on earth. No one will take their peace away from them.[37]

This expression of hope within history reflected the deep longing for the coming of the kingdom of God on earth to which we have earlier made reference, and it involved a revival of the kinds of millennial expectations which had once flourished in the ancient church. Such ideas had been eclipsed by the Augustinian insistence that "the only important climax in history had already occurred in the incarnation" and that the process of redemption in this world "was that of the individual soul," since a redeemed *society* must

---

36. "Joachim of Fiore," in *Apocalyptic Spirituality: Treatises and Letters of Lactantius, Adso of Montier-en-Der, Joachim of Fiore, the Franciscan Spirituals, Savonarola*, ed. Bernard McGinn (New York: Paulist, 1979), 99.

37. Joachim of Fiore, "Letter to the Abbot of Valdona," in McGinn, *Apocalyptic Spirituality*, 119. Valdona is thought to have been a Cistercian house in the diocese of Milan.

await "the blessedness of eternity."[38] By contrast, Joachim insisted that the prophetic anticipations of the coming of God's shalom in the Bible contained a fullness that had not yet been experienced, although he believed he had caught a glimpse of this future in the rise of the monastic movements which had come into existence during his lifetime. Thus, while the great spiritual ferment of the twelfth century, the longing for a return to the apostolic model of Christian community, had aroused hopes for a recovery of the purity of the church described in the book of Acts, Joachim anticipated something even greater, in the form of a historical era in which the healing, reconciling work of the Holy Spirit would flood the nations and renew the world, resulting in "a *renovatio* from the future rather than from the past."[39]

As we mentioned above, Joachim's apocalyptic spirituality was to influence the subsequent history of the Franciscan movement and it would later be shared by Spanish members of that order with a key player in the unfolding of world history, with consequences which would have horrified the devout monk of Calabria. In the thirteenth century, some of the followers of St. Francis, who became known as Franciscan Spirituals on account of their determination to follow to the letter their founder's example of extreme poverty, began to interpret Joachim's teaching as predicting their own central role in the eschatological drama. They came to believe that, together with the Dominicans, they were to be the forerunners of the third age of the Spirit, and that the extraordinary life of Francis himself had been foretold when John's Apocalypse described "the Angel of the Sixth Seal," whose advent would initiate "the critical period of history immediately preceding the coming of Antichrist."[40]

The "key player" to whom we referred above was none other than Christopher Columbus who had learned of Joachim's visions from the Franciscans he met in Spain. By this time the commercial revolution had spread its influence far and wide and, as progress in navigation opened up ever wider horizons for discovery, trade and conquest, the expansion of European political and economic power became increasingly fused with Catholic mission. Columbus believed that there was a connection between the victory of

---

38. Marjorie Reeves, "Preface," in McGinn, *Apocalyptic Spirituality*, xv.
39. McGinn, 108.
40. McGinn, 151.

the Spanish monarchs over the Muslims in Granada in 1492, the brutal expulsion of the Jews from Spain in the same year, and his own expedition, driven by an ambition in which commercial and religious motives were indivisible.[41] Thus, during his third voyage in 1498, he wrote to his royal patrons in Spain describing his certainty that his expedition fulfilled biblical prophecy since "it is from Spain that the spread of God's Holy Name will go forth." Yet in the very same letter he can celebrate the fact that it would be possible that "in the name of the Holy Trinity one could send as many slaves as one could sell, and also from Brazil." Two years later the influence of Joachite prophecy on Columbus's thinking is explicit: "I am making myself the messenger of the new heaven and earth of which our Lord speaks in the Apocalypse by the mouth of St. John." This belief in his destiny to fulfil biblical prophecy involved a perversion of Joachim's hope, as becomes even clearer when, on his fourth Atlantic crossing, Columbus writes: "Gold, what an excellent product! It is from gold that riches come. He who has gold can do whatever he pleases in this world. With gold one can even bring souls into Paradise."[42]

What the earlier preachers had condemned as a form of blasphemous idolatry, Columbus could celebrate as the sign of divine blessing. Catherine Keller concludes that the "discoverer" of new worlds had initiated the expansion of European colonial power in such a way that "those who followed immediately in his wake would so flood Europe with the gold and silver of America that a new economic system would arise." "Thus the global capitalist economy is directly indebted to the native peoples and the silver, gold, and resources their slave labor produced. The 'new Heaven and Earth' of which

---

41. James Reston Jr. describes how, when Columbus travelled from Granada to Seville, "and then onto Palos, from whence he departed for the New World, the roads must have been clogged with Jews departing Spain, scattering across sea and border in response to the Edict of Expulsion of Ferdinand and Isabella and their Inquisition" (*Dogs of God: Columbus, the Inquisition and the Defeat of the Moors* [London: Faber & Faber, 2006], xxiii). See, too, Kirkpatrick Sale, *The Conquest of Paradise: Christopher Columbus and the Columbian Legacy* (New York: Plume, 1991).

42. Jean Comby, *How to Understand the History of Christian Mission* (London: SCM, 1996), 56–60. Comby says, "Mediterranean Europe, in which prices were high, was involved in the mechanisms of a monetary economy. Portugal imported corn from the Maghreb and lacked labour. Gold was needed to buy luxury goods from the East, like silk and spices. In the fifteenth century the lack of gold led to a slow-down in trade; that is why the Mediterranean peoples launched out in passionate exploration. They sought the source of precious metal, first in Africa then in America. For Christopher Columbus, the word 'gold' had a magical and mythical resonance" (56).

Colon [Columbus] was the messenger would liberate Europeans not *from* private property but *for* its limitless pursuit."[43]

Joachim's visionary theology was to have a lasting and significant influence across the subsequent centuries, especially in central and eastern Europe. Cohn has tracked its underlying influence in later theories of historical evolution and suggests that it can be traced in the Marxist dialectic of three phases culminating in a communist society, and that even the language of the "Third Reich," lasting a thousand years, would have had little emotional significance if the Calabrian abbot's vision of "a third and most glorious dispensation had not, over the centuries, entered into the common stock of European social mythology."[44]

As late as 1913, as Europe moved towards the terrible conflict which was to tear the continent apart, the Czech composer Leoš Janáček set to music a poem with the title "The Eternal Gospel." The text imagines Joachim of Fiore reporting his discovery of the angel of the Apocalypse flying with the "eternal gospel" in his hand, announcing its message of an era "when affluence and worldly goods and riches / gold, jewels, all shall turn to dust."

> First came the Bible, then the joy of
> The Apostles' own testimony flooded the world.
> Now the Eternal Gospel's time has come.
> Now shall true freedom rule the human spirit,
> Which breaks all bonds that would enslave it.
> That Spirit kingdom: vision of the future!
> Love's kingdom summons us. The eternal kingdom.[45]

---

43. Keller, *Apocalypse Now and Then*, 162.

44. Cohn, *Pursuit of the Millennium*, 109. Keller describes the influence of Joachim's apocalyptic spirituality within the Enlightenment and the communist vision of a classless society, and concludes: "Cut loose in modernity from theistic moorings and textual accountability, the universal chronology of the apocalyptic vision came to subserve the manmade ends of the state, technology, and the market" (*Apocalypse Now and Then*, 20).

45. The poem was written by Jaroslav Vrchlicky. Janáček's musical setting has been recorded by Ilan Volkov and the BBC Scottish Symphony Orchestra on Hyperion 675517. The quotation is from the accompanying booklet note by Nigel Simeone.

The Protestant Reformation in Context

It will be recalled that in the first chapter of this book we introduced the work of the sociologist Max Weber who argued that there was a crucial connection between the Protestant Reformation and the later rise of industrial capitalism and the acquisitive society in which human existence eventually became like life in an "iron cage." This suggests that we have now arrived at a critically important stage in this discussion, but it is one fraught with difficulty on account of the complexity of the subject and the serious disagreements it has generated. We make absolutely no claim to be able to resolve such disputes, but the question of whether there were unintended consequences of the Protestant Reformation, and whether the fragmented Christianity which arose in Europe in the following centuries compromised the biblical vision of a reconciled humanity and weakened Christianity's resistance to the growing power and dominance of Mammon – these are issues we cannot avoid.[46]

As we have seen, the Reformation of the sixteenth century occurred at the end of a centuries-long "Age of Reform" which had witnessed repeated attempts to return to the apostolic models of discipleship found in the New Testament. Such movements demanding simpler lifestyles continued to emerge prior to the appearance of Martin Luther, including groups such as the Waldensians, Cathars, Lollards and the Bohemian Hussites. They all shared the fundamental conviction that the gospel demanded a Christianity which resulted in a "far greater moral excellence than traditional church piety had done."[47]

Our discussion of the Age of Reform would suggest that Protestantism can be viewed as the culmination of the era which had begun centuries earlier in

---

46. The conflicting reactions of historians to Max Weber's work can be seen in the contrast between A. G. Dickens's dismissive comment that "no one has a kind word for Weber's thesis," which he describes as a "specious theory," and Patrick Collinson's verdict that Weber possessed "one of the most powerful and open minds to apply itself to what has been called 'the miracle of the West.'" Collinson said that few theories "have been more widely misunderstood than the thesis advanced in Weber's *The Protestant Ethic and the Spirit of Capitalism*" and that Dickens had "little idea what Weber was going on about." See A. G. Dickens, *Reformation and Society in Sixteenth-Century Europe* (London: Thames & Hudson, 1966), 178–79, and Patrick Collinson, *The Reformation* (London: Phoenix, 2005), 174–77.

47. Ozment, *Age of Reform*, 208. The Czech Reformation led by Jan Huss is particularly relevant at this point. See Jan Milič Lochman, *Christ and Prometheus? A Quest for Theological Identity* (Geneva: WCC, 1988), especially his discussion "The Radical Heritage: Czechoslovak Roots," 1–12.

response to the commercial revolution.[48] Too often the crucial turning point identified with Luther has been treated as though it emerged from nowhere, and we have been presented with a before-and-after story in which a blaze of light suddenly bursts into the Dark Ages. However, as we have seen, the medieval world was far from being devoid of the light of Christ, and we have encountered only a sample of the many devoted followers of Jesus whose quests for radical obedience to the gospel lit up the medieval world. The urban historian Lewis Mumford could even state that no previous urban culture prior to the Christian cities in the thirteenth century had achieved "anything like the large-scale provision for the sick, the aged, the suffering, the poor" which characterized the medieval towns of Europe.[49]

Having said this, the immediate historical context for the Reformation was shaped by a number of specific factors which created a new and demanding challenge to Christianity. By 1500 the population of Europe, having been devastated in the previous century, was rising rapidly and has been estimated to have reached around 60 million. A growing number of these people were moving into expanding towns and cities, many of which had doubled in size, including Naples, London, Paris, Milan, Cologne and Strasbourg. While the majority of the general population of Europe remained rural, it was the expanding urban centres which increasingly became the sites of creative change and were crucial to the growth of the Reformation. In Ozment's words, "although the Protestant Reformation appealed to educated and uneducated alike, it presupposed for its success a literate urban culture and seems

---

48. As long ago as 1926, R. H. Tawney observed that the day "has long since passed when it could be suggested that only one-half of modern Christianity has its roots in medieval religion. There is a medieval Puritanism and rationalism as well as a medieval Catholicism. . . . The social theories of Luther and Latimer, of Bucer and Bullinger, of sixteenth-century Anabaptists and seventeenth-century Levellers . . . are all children of medieval parents" (*Religion and the Rise of Capitalism* [London: John Murray, 1926], 18).

49. Lewis Mumford, *The City in History* (Harmondsworth: Penguin, 1966), 365. Mumford describes Francis of Assisi as representative of "the effort to restore the original Christian spirit" by substituting "voluntary Christian service, a free exchange of gifts, for the ordinary arrangements of hiring and buying." His dream was of a new society which would replace "the power-driven, wealth-encrusted ego and dismantle, ultimately, the walled city, that ego's greatest collective expression" (366). Perhaps the outstanding example of monastic care for the sick and dying is to be seen in the Isenheim Altarpiece of Matthias Grünewald, an astonishing work of art created to support the ministry of Anthonite monks caring for victims of a particularly horrible disease in the hospital of their monastery in Alsace. See Andrée Hayum, *The Isenheim Altarpiece: God's Medicine and the Painter's Vision* (Princeton: Princeton University Press, 1989).

particularly to have attracted rising urban groups who had either experienced or were determined to come into a new political and economic importance."[50]

As we have seen, the last decade of the fifteenth century witnessed the opening up of the new worlds of the Americas through the expeditions of Christopher Columbus, but there had also been the eastward movement of European travellers such as Vasco da Gama, who reached the coast of India having sailed around the continent of Africa. These voyages resulted in a completely new perception of the world and its peoples, and they initiated a previously unimagined access to the wealth which was to become "a basic source of the period's social and ideological conflicts." R. H. Tawney captures the drama of this period in which economic power, "long at home in Italy, was leaking through a thousand creeks and inlets into western Europe for a century before, with climax of the great Discoveries, the flood came on breast-high."

> Heralded by an economic revolution not less profound than that of three centuries later, the new world of the sixteenth century took its character from the outburst of economic energy in which it had been born. Like the nineteenth century, it saw a swift increase in wealth and an impressive expansion of trade, a concentration of financial power on a scale unknown before, the rise, amid fierce social convulsions, of new classes and the depression of old, the triumph of a new culture and system of ideas amid struggles not less bitter.[51]

This was the immediate context of the rise of the Protestant Reformation, and that movement was itself driven both by the urgent need for a new Christian response to the momentous changes of the time, and by the perceived failures of the Catholic Church in precisely this situation. With regard to the first of these factors, the new economic revolution undermined the character of the medieval town as a community in which individuals played significant roles regardless of social status, and were mutually responsible for the common good. The new economy created and accelerated social divisions and tensions, creating class differences between merchants, who took

---

50. Ozment, *Age of Reform*, 192.
51. Tawney, *Religion and the Rise of Capitalism*, 69.

full advantage of the new opportunities for amassing personal wealth, and the growth of an urban proletariat angered by the injustice meted out to peasants. As Ozment says,

> The new economy raised social tensions to new levels within urban centers.... Capitalism and political centralization threatened the traditional urban ideal of society as a sacred corporation.... The ability of individuals and small groups to attain great wealth and political power at their own initiative changed this by giving rise to new political factions among both the successful and the oppressed.[52]

At the same time, the tragic failures of the Catholic Church to meet these challenges created a spiritual and moral vacuum which was to be filled by the new religious movements which together constituted the Protestant Reformation. Throughout the fourteenth century a long series of papal decrees had reversed the Vatican's earlier acceptance of the monastic reform movements, and now denounced the Franciscan ideal of poverty, even accusing those who had remained faithful to their founder's radical vision of the "Donatist heresy"! Pope John XXII struck the final blow to the monastic reform movement in a bull of 1323 in which he declared that Jesus and the apostles "had possessed goods both privately and in common and were not themselves practitioners of the abject poverty urged by observant Franciscans and Spirituals."[53] Five years later the same pope hammered the final nail into the coffin of the monastic reform movement by insisting that "evangelical perfection" was to be strictly defined as *spiritual* abnegation, "not the literal renunciation of physical possessions."

This reversal of the Church's previous endorsement of the monastic quest for radical obedience to the example and teaching of Jesus was the consequence of a change of attitude towards wealth and treasure. Berndt Hamm has described how, from the thirteenth century onwards – and in spite of the continuing resistance we have noted above – "those powers in the Church which developed a positive attitude to the acquisition of capital gained the upper hand, among them the influential Mendicant Orders and, of all people,

---

52. Ozment, *Age of Reform*, 197.
53. Ozment, 113.

even the Franciscans." "They opened for the rich merchants the possibility of liberating themselves from their notoriously bad consciences and their fears of Hell and Purgatory, of feeling at home in the Church and reaching Heaven without difficulty through trade."[54]

The consequences of this massive shift in Catholic teaching concerning wealth and possessions were many and went to the very heart of what it meant to be Christian. Commercial values and imagery now seeped into doctrine, pastoral practice, the notion of the afterlife and the realm of purgatory. As Hamm says, "The Church's treasure in the Hereafter functions like a colossal bank account from which particular sums can be debited in the form of the amount of indulgence."[55] The role played in the early Reformation by Martin Luther's polemic against the evils of the trade of indulgences is well known and reflects the widespread sense of spiritual oppression and despair which resulted from this practice. Furthermore, the Protestant articulation of the gospel took a form which challenged the Catholic compromise with the commercial culture head-on: Luther described the relationship between Christ and the believer as a "happy economy" involving an exchange made possible by pure grace between "the sins of the poor bride and the goods of her noble bridegroom" who blesses her "with his own wealth of righteousness." Luther's deliberate use of such imagery involves a kind of contextualization in the situation we are describing and it can be seen in one of his beautiful Christmas hymns of 1523: "He came in poverty to earth in order to have mercy upon us, and makes us rich in heaven and like his beloved angels. Lord have mercy!"[56]

In a detailed study of the impact of the early Protestant movement on the cities of Germany and Switzerland, Steven Ozment explored the nature of Catholic religious devotion at the level of daily life, describing this as the "burden of late medieval religion." He examined catechetical literature intended for priestly use at a child's first confession, and records the questions to be asked concerning *each* of the Ten Commandments. Here is the instruction to the priest for the examination of the fifth commandment:

---

54. Hamm, "Buying Heaven," 237.
55. Hamm, 240.
56. Hamm, 247.

Have you thrown snowballs or rocks at others? Have you had fights and hated those whom you fought (even your brother and sister)? Have you stoned chickens and ducks? Did you kill the emperor with a double-bladed axe? [This last question injected by the confessor to test alertness and truthfulness!][57]

Page after page of examples of this kind are cited, including instructions concerning the manner in which laypeople should wake from sleep each morning. They are told to examine themselves as follows: "O dear God, how I waste my precious time! . . . During the night all spiritual souls have sung God's praise [the vigils of the religious] and I have overslept. . . . There has been great lamentation in purgatory, and I have not prayed [for those who groan]." To this regulation of the waking moments of every day is added the demand that "you should spring from your bed, concentrate on making up for your neglect, and thank God for Christ's suffering for your sins."[58] In this context the appeal of the message of early Protestantism included the simplification of the practice of religious devotion that flowed from faith in Christ, and the transformation of values by which the service of one's neighbour became "the measure of value and importance within society." The Reformers' insistence on faith alone as the source of freedom and hope was accompanied by an equally strong assertion that that same faith was the dynamic source of service to others, and precisely one's contribution to the well-being of society would be the evidence of the authenticity of religion.

The Reformer Martin Bucer withdrew from the Dominican Order after conversations with Martin Luther and was later to spend considerable time with John Calvin during the Genevan leader's sojourn in Strasbourg. In 1523, frustrated by the relative absence of radical discipleship and the consequent lack of social reform, Bucer published a tract with the title *One Should Not Live for Oneself Alone but for Others, and How to Go about It*. The document was written in response to the urgent request of his congregation for a clear statement concerning the practical consequences of the adoption of the new faith. As the title clearly suggests, Bucer presented the reform movement as holding the promise of the transformation of ethics and social life, and

---

57. Steven Ozment, *The Reformation in the Cities: The Appeal of Protestantism to Sixteenth-Century Germany and Switzerland* (New Haven: Yale University Press, 1975), 23.

58. Ozment, *Reformation in the Cities*, 30.

he echoes the teaching of the early fathers in a creational theology which recognizes God's original design that all things should serve each other. In the beginning, Bucer says, "there was universal benevolence among all creatures," and this divine order, although frustrated by the fall, can be restored and renewed in Christ. He discourages parents from seeking unproductive vocations for their children, singling out the dangers of the role of merchants, "who, against God's command and Christian order, live without working and off the sweat of others – like the clergy!"[59]

> [Bucer] assures his new congregation that simple trust and faith in Christ mean freedom from the selfishness that prevents men from loving their neighbors as themselves, and he foresees the faithful becoming as selfless in their service to one another as Christ had been in his self-service of all men.[60]

We discover exactly the same concern with the *social* consequences of faith in the work of Guillaume Farel, who was to minister alongside Calvin in Geneva. His 1525 publication *Summary and Brief Description of All That Is Necessary for Every Christian to Have Confidence in God and Help His Neighbour* has exactly the same stress as Bucer on the double command to love God and one's neighbour. The *Summary* was the first French Protestant catechism designed for a popular, lay audience and it became widely read. We can perhaps understand why this should have been so when we read the following passage in which the new faith in Christ is described in almost mystical language:

> We must take care that Christ, by whose power alone all things are governed, appear radiant among us. We are confident that this will happen if in all things we are conformed to the evangelical rule, and if all dissension . . . is supressed by the peace of God . . . which dwells in our hearts.[61]

Calvin himself made it very clear on his return to Geneva in 1541 that the reforms he would pursue within the city would embrace both church and society, and that his exposition of the Bible would be committed to its

---

59. Ozment, 66.
60. Ozment, 66.
61. Ozment, 70.

application both to the renewal of the church and to the conduct of life within the city. Nowhere is this clearer than in the remarkable statement he made to the officials who had revoked his earlier sentence of exile:

> If you desire to have me for your pastor, correct the disorder of your lives. If you have with sincerity recalled me from my exile, banish the crimes and debaucheries which prevail among you. . . . I consider the principal enemies of the Gospel to be, not the pontiff of Rome, nor heretics, nor seducers, nor tyrants, but bad Christians. . . . I dread abundantly more those carnal covetousnesses, those debaucheries of the tavern, of the brothel, and of gambling. . . . Of what use is a dead faith without works? Of what importance is even truth itself, where a wicked life belies it and actions make words blush. . . . Re-establish there pure discipline.[62]

This distinctively Calvinist determination to apply the values of the gospel to the whole of life, to insist on both radical obedience to Christ in personal ethics and the reshaping of society so that it might reflect the righteousness of God, meant that the challenge posed by the emergence of capitalism was simply unavoidable. Tawney described Calvinism as "an active and radical force" which sought "not merely to purify the individual, but to reconstruct Church and State, and to renew society by penetrating every department of life, public as well as private, with the influence of religion."[63] A stance such as this demanded new and radical thought since it required a response to the context which we have described, and this could involve neither the simple repetition of the received position of outright rejection of commercial practices and values, on the one hand, nor capitulation to the power of money and wealth, on the other. Calvinism took a perilous path between the two extremes, recognizing "the necessity of capital, credit and banking, large-scale commerce and finance, and the other practical facts of business life."[64]

In treading this dangerous path, Calvin's treatment of capital has been described as a watershed. He assumed credit to be "a normal and inevitable

---

62. Ozment, *Age of Reform*, 366.
63. Tawney, *Religion and the Rise of Capitalism*, 102.
64. Tawney, 104.

incident in the life of society" and put to one side the frequently quoted passages in the Bible opposing usury, since they related to historical conditions that no longer existed. He therefore argued that "the payment of interest for capital is as reasonable as the payment of rent for land, and throws on the conscience of the individual the obligation of seeing that it does not exceed the amount dictated by natural justice and the golden rule."[65]

The phrase "throws on the conscience of the individual" is surely the Achilles heel here, for individual consciences are notoriously pliable, as the subsequent history of economics and society would sadly confirm. Nonetheless, it must be said that Calvin's own unwavering commitment to social righteousness is not in doubt as both his theology and his sermons make clear. Take, for example, the following passage from a sermon preached in Geneva:

> There would be those who would rather that the wheat spoil in the granary so that it will be eaten by vermin, so that it can be sold when there is want (for they only wish to starve the poor people). . . . See the wheat collected; how well our Lord has poured out his grace and his benediction so that the poor would be nourished. But the speculator will gather it in granaries and lock it up securely, till finally the cry of famine is heard. . . . What will happen? It will be spoiled and rotten. How true it is that our Lord is mocked by those who want to have much profit. . . . These people entomb the grace of God, as if they warred against his bounty and against the paternal love of God which he displays toward everyone.[66]

Fred Graham describes how Calvin, the pastor of housewives, labourers, the refugees who flooded into Geneva and members of the rising bourgeoisie, preached week by week with sermons in which he "explained carefully what he considered to be God's plan for mankind, and launched bitter attacks

---

65. Tawney, 107.
66. W. Fred Graham, *The Constructive Revolutionary: John Calvin and His Socio-Economic Impact* (Atlanta: John Knox, 1978), 56.

against those who trampled human love and perverted simple justice in their scramble through life."⁶⁷

This concern with social righteousness and the insistence of the Reformers we have referred to above, that justifying faith unites believers to Christ and motivates them to work together in the relief of human suffering, resistance to injustice and the creation of a holy commonwealth, shows remarkable likeness to the lives of those many people in the medieval period whose hopes and longings took very similar forms. Since those earlier movements ultimately failed to bring about the desired return of the Catholic Church to the purity and obedience of the apostolic people of the Way, we shall have to ask whether the Reformation was likewise unable to sustain its initial vision, and was overwhelmed by the advancing power and dominance of the ideology of capitalism. We close this chapter with the sobering conclusion of Berndt Hamm:

> On the whole, when considering the Middle Ages and the Early Modern Age, one can say that religion was never the decisive power behind a capital-oriented way of thinking, but again and again . . . it became the desired ally. The medieval Church and the denominations of the Modern Age received, internalized, promoted, moulded and domesticated the spirit and practice of capitalism; only rarely – and then for the most part from the position of outsiders and fringe groups – did they combat it. Theologically judged, the minority voices – Peter Waldes, Francis of Assisi, John Wyclif, or Thomas Muntzer, and their followers – have weight of evidence of a powerful biblical radicalism; yet in the history of Christianity, the symbiosis of capital and Church won through.⁶⁸

---

67. Graham, *Constructive Revolutionary*, 55. Kathryn Tanner, who has made a very significant contribution to the modern debate concerning Christianity and capitalism, describes Calvin's "robust account of grace" as being very important for the modern quest for an economy of grace or gift. Calvin was eager, she says, to emphasize divine grace in terms of "gift-giving from an ever-flowing fount of divine goodness accessible in Christ, God's fatherly beneficence to God's children, and human lives of gratitude for good gifts freely and liberally bestowed are arguably the dominant motif" ("Economies of Grace," in *Having: Property and Possession in Religious and Social Life*, eds. William Schweiker and Charles Mathewes [Grand Rapids: Eerdmans, 2004], 364).

68. Hamm, "Buying Heaven," 255.

CHAPTER 8

Expanding Europe

We have noted in the previous chapters the distinct ages, or eras, identified by Andrew Walls as periods in which Christianity was communicated in new cultural contexts and was reshaped by the process of translation within those host cultures. We have now reached the point at which we must consider Walls's crucial fifth stage, which he identified as *the age of expanding Europe.* Of this period, Walls writes: "The population of Europe was exported to other continents and the dominance of Europe extended, until by the twentieth century people of European origin occupied, possessed, or dominated the greater part of the globe."[1]

Clearly, we are dealing here with the centuries-long emergence of what we now call the modern world. This is a crucial period for this study because it is the point at which the capitalist economic system develops and expands in a way that will lay the foundation for the world which we now inhabit. Capitalism, restrained and widely viewed with ambivalence as long as medieval values continued to exert significant influence, now begins to break free from such restraints and commences its advance towards becoming the dominant world system.

At the same time, the fact that this period witnesses the commencement of the modern missionary spread of Christianity, first to the new worlds of the Americas, and eventually across the globe, demands that we reflect on the nature of the relationship between this phase of Christian history and the

---

1. Andrew F. Walls, *The Missionary Movement in Christian History: Studies in the Transmission of Faith* (Edinburgh: T&T Clark, 1996), 21. See also his "Toward a Theology of Migration," in his *Crossing Cultural Frontiers: Studies in the History of World Christianity*, ed. Mark R. Gornik (New York: Orbis, 2017), 49–61.

political and economic expansion of the European powers. We cannot ignore the fact that Andrew Walls twice uses the word "dominance," so highlighting the colonial and imperial realities which were to shape the modern world. As we have seen earlier in this book, Christianity came to birth in an imperial context as the radical faith of peoples who were the *subjects* of Roman power and dominance. It therefore moved from the social and geographical margins of power to the centre of political and military dominance in Rome, bringing with it a subversive vision of a new world of justice and love. The contrast with the European missions we are concerned with here is both striking and disturbing and we dare not evade the critical questions which it raises.

The Great Migration

The events of the 1490s opened up new worlds for Europeans and across the following centuries increasing numbers of them were to cross the oceans to settle in the Americas, on the coasts of Africa and in parts of Asia. A century after Columbus had first crossed the Atlantic, approximately one million Europeans had migrated to new territories overseas and the flow of migrants was to continue and increase. In the Americas and parts of Africa, new nations came into being using languages and following cultural models from Europe, while in the case of what became the United States, migration both overwhelmed an indigenous population and resulted in the emergence of a nation which would rival and eventually surpass European power.

From the very beginning of this movement, the encounter between Europeans and the indigenous peoples presented a series of fundamental questions to which previous experience provided no satisfying answers. How had these formerly unknown regions existed for so long without Europeans being aware of them? Where and how did the peoples who inhabited these lands fit into the history of humankind, and in particular, what was their relationship to the biblical narrative of creation? How questions like these were answered was of absolutely crucial importance since the view taken of the indigenous populations would determine the manner in which they would be treated.

The French writer Michel de Montaigne critiqued the widespread assumption that non-European, indigenous peoples were a subhuman species, and after talking at length with a captive tribal person who had been brought to France, he declared: "I find nothing barbarous or savage in this nation, except that we call barbarism whatever we ourselves do not do." He went further still and suggested that Europeans who recoiled from accounts of tribal cannibalism were hypocrites! Referring to the horrific violence which had swept across post-Reformation Europe, Montaigne declared: "I think it more barbaric to eat a man alive than dead; it is worse to tear a body apart on the rack while it still has feeling, or to burn a man alive, than to roast and eat him after he is dead."[2]

Such views anticipated the later critical approach towards European actions at this time, but those who crossed the oceans and encountered tribal peoples face to face were likely to be dazzled by the new worlds opened up by the maritime expeditions, and they were invariably confident of the superiority of the culture of Renaissance Europe at that time. They felt themselves to occupy a vantage point from which newly discovered peoples, whether in the extraordinary cities of Mexico or in the forests of the Americas, could be assumed to belong to inferior races. At the same time, the phenomenal riches discovered in the new territories, in regard to both the fecundity of nature and the seemingly infinite resources of precious metals, aroused fevered expectations of wealth and enrichment. The frustration of Portuguese sailors at their failure to locate expected treasures on the coasts of Africa was replaced by excitement at the discovery of real riches following the conquest of Mexico in the 1520s and of Peru a decade later. As Anthony Pagden says, the silver found in what was to become South America began to be mined and transported back to Europe and "until well into the eighteenth century, American silver poured unceasingly eastwards, first into the coffers of the Spanish crown and then outwards through German, Dutch and Italian bankers until it reached every part of the continent."[3]

---

2. Quoted in Theodore K. Rabb, *The Last Days of the Renaissance and the March to Modernity* (New York: Basic Books, 2006), 98–100.

3. Anthony Pagden, *Peoples and Empires: Europeans and the Rest of the World – From Antiquity to the Present* (London: Weidenfeld & Nicolson, 2001), 65. Mark Cocker describes the silver mines of Mexico as "sumps of misery" for the native people forced to labour in them. By 1600 the precious metals flowing into Spain's coffers created "a vast reservoir of wealth that for centuries served as a critical supply for the national economy and as a powerful stimulus for all European trade" (*Rivers of Blood, Rivers of Gold: Europe's Conflict with Tribal Peoples* [London: Pimlico, 1999], 20). The very word "Peru" became synonymous in European languages with fabulous wealth, while the image of "Potosi", "the 'rich mountain' whose veins [were] of silver, located by the Spanish in 1545, fulfilled their most extravagant hope of riches to be found in

As early as 1512 proposals had been discussed in Rome for Catholic missions to the recently discovered Americas, but when the Reformation burst upon Europe such ideas were put to one side as the challenge presented by Luther became the all-consuming priority. Three decades later the advance of Protestantism threatened the possibility of a permanently divided Christendom and, despite serious efforts to avert such an outcome, the Council of Trent, which opened in 1545, made that split a lasting reality. In this situation Catholics began to view mission to the newly discovered tribal peoples as a means of renewal and recovery from the losses they had suffered in Europe. It was suggested that the conquest of Mexico had opened the way for the proclamation of the gospel in the new world, creating "a counterbalance by the conversion of so many souls," and potentially resulting in the repair of "the great damage and loss which Luther provoked at that time in ancient Christendom."[4]

A key event for the Counter Reformation was the life-changing experience of Ignatius of Loyola (1491–1556) and the subsequent founding of the Society of Jesus. During convalescence, having been wounded in battle, Ignatius became absorbed by spiritual writings, including the famous *Imitation of Christ* by Thomas à Kempis. Poring over the works of the leaders of the monastic reform movements, he was profoundly moved by the examples of Dominic and Francis, convinced that "they had accomplished far greater feats than any knight on horseback and without the benefit of sword and armor."[5] In one of the strange ironies with which history seems to abound, Ignatius entered the Collège de Montaigu in Paris in the same year that John Calvin left it, a fact which illustrates the close intertwining of the events of this period.

The importance of the Society of Jesus in relation to Catholic missions overseas cannot be exaggerated, and while in Paris, Ignatius was joined by Francis Xavier (1506–52) who was to become a pioneering Catholic missionary in Asia. However, the missionary priests who accompanied the

---

the new colonies" (Olivia Harris, "The Earth and the State: The Sources and the Meanings of Money in Northern Potosi, Bolivia," in *Money and the Morality of Exchange*, eds. J. Parry and M. Bloch [Cambridge: Cambridge University Press, 1989], 235).

4. Jean Comby, *How to Understand the History of Christian Mission* (London: SCM, 1996), 58.

5. Steven Ozment, *The Age of Reform 1250–1550: An Intellectual and Religious History of Late Medieval and Reformation Europe* (New Haven: Yale University Press, 1980), 410.

conquistadores in the new world were to discover a fusion of violent military conquest with supposed evangelization that was to result in a difficult and painful legacy from the era of Christianity in the age of "expanding Europe." Mark Cocker, in a challenging history of European encounters with primal peoples, writes that the conquistadores "looked upon their American ventures as imbued with the religious spirit of their Old World conquests." "Like crusaders, Cortes' men were presented with papal bulls giving remission of sins committed during battle. At moments of intense fighting they would claim, as did their medieval forebears in the Holy Land, visions of the blessed apostles, St James and St Peter, riding out to assist them."[6]

There were, however, European Christians who, having read the Bible within the various reform traditions that we have explored, were appalled at the behaviour of their compatriots and articulated prophetic critiques of the violence and oppression visited upon the native populations. The best known of these critics was Bartolemé de las Casas (1484–1566), who arrived in Santo Domingo (now Haiti) in April 1502, having crossed the Atlantic on a ship that was part of the largest fleet ever to depart from Spain for the Americas. As he disembarked, the young priest was told that he had arrived at a propitious moment since a war was about to begin against the Indians and would result in many slaves becoming available. For some time Las Casas, shaped as he was by his own culture, remained passive and worked within the *encomienda* system, using native captives himself. However, on the Sunday before Christmas 1511, he heard a sermon which was to result in his "dramatic conversion from colonizing priest into Indian apostle."[7] The preacher was the Dominican Antonio Montesinos, whose bold language stunned an audience of slave owners who discovered themselves indicted of mortal sins and in urgent need of repentance:

> You are all in a state of mortal sin . . . by reason of the cruelty and the tyranny which you show to these innocent peoples. Say by

---

6. Cocker, *Rivers of Blood*, 77. He writes that the European faith "eventually became for tribal peoples worldwide both an important solace against, and a social bridge into, the alien world of their colonisers. Moreover, the army of genuinely humane missionaries who travelled out to the colonies to evangelise often served as important political champions for their indigenous flock" (15).

7. Anthony Pagden, "Introduction," in Bartolomé de las Casas, *A Short Account of the Destruction of the Indies*, ed. and trans. Nigel Griffin (London: Penguin, 1992), xiii–xli.

> what right and by virtue of what justice you hold these Indians in such cruel and horrible servitude. Who could authorize you to wage all these detestable wars on people who were living in peace and tranquillity in their country and to exterminate them in such vast numbers by murder and carnage unprecedented? . . . Are these people not human? Do they not have a soul, a reason? Are you not obliged to love them as yourselves?[8]

The sermon, and especially the final question, resulted in an agonized struggle with conscience until, three years later, Las Casas was himself preparing to preach on a text from Ecclesiasticus: "The bread of the needy is their life: he that defraudeth him thereof is a man of blood" (34:21–22 KJV). The young Spanish priest determined to spend his life in defence of the oppressed and in unrelenting resistance to the actions of his own countrymen. We cannot describe the work of this remarkable man in detail here, but an extract from his *Short Account* is sufficient to demonstrate the prophetic nature of his long life and ministry:

> God made all the peoples of this area . . . as open and innocent as can be imagined. The simplest people in the world – unassuming, long-suffering, unassertive, and submissive – they are without malice or guile. . . . They are also among the poorest people on the face of the earth; they own next to nothing and have no urge to acquire material possessions. As a result, they are neither ambitious nor greedy, and are totally uninterested in worldly power. Their diet is every bit as poor and monotonous . . . as that enjoyed by the Desert Fathers. . . . It was upon these gentle lambs . . . that from the very first day they clapped eyes upon them the Spanish fell like ravening wolves upon the fold, or like tigers and savage lions who have not eaten meat for days.[9]

The reference to the "Desert Fathers" is remarkable in that it suggests that the way of life of the indigenous peoples reflected a culture which Las Casas recognized as being close to the ideal recorded in the book of Acts and

---

8. In Comby, *History of Christian Mission*, 64.
9. Las Casas, *Short Account*, 9–11.

pursued within the medieval monastic movements, while the behaviour of the Spanish conquistadores was exactly the opposite.[10]

Fifty years after Las Casas had set foot on the soil of the new world, a young French Protestant pastor was to cross "that great and impetuous ocean sea," eventually making landfall in what is now Brazil, where he was to live for a relatively brief time among the Tupinamba people. This was Jean de Léry, whose account of his experiences was first published in French in 1580 as *Histoire d'un voyage*. This volume, which was not translated into English until 1990, provides an extraordinary description of Léry's life and work, and it should be recognized as a classic document in the history of Christian mission.[11] Like Las Casas, this Calvinist pastor was astounded by the way of life he discovered among tribal people and he recorded in great detail both the beauty of their social relationships and his own growing awareness of the contrasts between the culture of an indigenous people and that which he had left behind in post-Reformation Europe. Here he is describing the social solidarity of the Tupi:

> As for their natural fellow-feeling, every day they distribute to each the venison, fish, fruit, and other good things of their country, and not only would a savage die of shame (so to speak) if he saw his neighbour lacking what he has in his power to give, but also ... they practice the same liberality toward foreigners who are their allies.[12]

---

10. The French philosopher Chantal Delsol quotes Las Casas describing the Christians of the early centuries as living lives "in perfect accord with what they were teaching." She continues: "Las Casas thought that the abandonment of this consistency explained Christianity's deviation from its path in the sixteenth century. Where could the revolt of Hus or Luther have come from, *if not from the gaps that widened over the centuries between what the clerics said and how they lived?*" (*The Unlearned Lessons of the Twentieth Century: An Essay on Late Modernity* [Wilmington: ISI Books, 2006], 110–11; emphasis added). I have not been able to discover the original source in Las Casas.

11. I have discussed this work in "The Forgotten 'Grandfather' of Protestant Mission: Perspectives on Globalization from John de Léry," *Missiology: An International Review* 34, no. 3 (July 2006): 349–59.

12. Jean de Léry, *History of a Voyage to the Land of Brazil*, trans. and with an introduction by Janet Whatley (Berkeley: University of California Press, 1990), 168. Léry goes on to suggest, like Las Casas, that the behaviour of the native people had parallels with what can be found in the Bible: "In short, it is hard for me to express the hospitality that was offered us by those savages, who in truth acted toward us just as, according to Saint Luke in the Acts of the Apostles, the barbarians on the island of Malta treated Saint Paul and those who were with him after they had escaped the shipwreck" (168–69).

Léry's account of his new world experiences was written after his return to France and the resumption of ministry as a Reformed pastor in the town of Sancerre. In 1573 he found himself in a desperate situation as the wars of religion resulted in a terrible siege of his city, during which the starving population resorted to acts of cannibalism. He recalled his experiences in the jungles of Brazil and concluded that "one need not go beyond one's own country, nor as far as America, to see such monstrous and prodigious things."[13] As a horrified witness of the consequences of the St. Bartholomew's Day Massacre of Huguenots, the memory of the Brazilian forests and of the Tupi people continued to haunt him: "I often regret that I am not still among the savages."[14] Janet Whatley, who translated Léry's work into English, concludes that the primal cultures of the new world seemed to "resemble the old world in just those aspects that modernity – via the Reformation – would suppress in the name of a purer religion or a more efficient economic structure."[15]

The testimonies of men like these confirm the truth of Andrew Walls's statement that the cross-cultural missionary movement was to become "the learning experience" of European Christianity. We may ask precisely what were the lessons that people like Las Casas and Léry derived from their encounters with the peoples of the "new world"? First, both men express a sense of wonder and amazement at the discovery of the sheer beauty of the natural world, and at the relationship to it on the part of the indigenous peoples. It has been suggested that this exposure to a region untouched by the commercial and urban developments which had for centuries been transforming the landscape of Europe, and were even now accelerating as a direct consequence of the discoveries, explains the open-mouthed sense of wonder with which our missionaries described an unspoiled America. The world from which they came was one in which ancient forests were already under threat and land was everywhere being cultivated, reflecting a European attitude towards nature that increasingly appeared to be in sharp contrast to the

---

13. Léry, *History of a Voyage*, 133.

14. Léry, xxxvi. Readers may find the use of the term "savage" to be disturbing, but the whole tone of the discussion reveals Lery's respect, even admiration, for the native peoples and certain aspects of their way of life. The terminology hardened into a negative form of racial profiling at a later date with developments in the eighteenth and nineteenth centuries.

15. Whatley, in Léry.

reverence displayed towards it by the indigenous peoples. As a study of the Columbian legacy has suggested:

> It is but a short step from the fear of the wild to the love of the tamed and from there to the imperative of human domination and control of the natural world – hence the images of the subjection and mastery of the untamed landscape that are so frequent in late-fifteenth-century [European] culture.[16]

Second, as the quotations cited above indicate, both men became severely critical of their own cultures as a direct consequence of their experiences of the new world and its peoples. This is especially true of Léry who, in perhaps the most remarkable passage in his book, turns the dismissive comments of Frenchmen concerning "primitive" people back on themselves and the European culture of which they boasted. He urges them to "think more carefully about the things that go on every day over here, among us." He cites the terrible violence of the wars of religion, and then proceeds to draw attention to "what our big usurers do, sucking blood and marrow, and eating everyone alive – widows, orphans, and other poor people," so contrasting the economics of indigenous communities among whom he had lived in Brazil with the increasing greed and selfishness he now witnessed in contemporary France.[17]

Finally, while both men were utterly appalled by the behaviour of their compatriots and the tragic distortion of their faith which this involved, in their responses to such perversions they seemed to transcend the division between Catholic and Protestant which was tearing Europe apart. Indeed, the group with which the twenty-two-year-old Léry had crossed the Atlantic had included both Catholics and Huguenots at "almost the last moment when such collaboration was possible." Might it be that the insights these men gained as a direct consequence of their exposure to a new world may contain significant pointers for world Christianity today as it strives to discover new patterns of discipleship at a time when the whole of creation is under threat?

---

16. Kirkpatrick Sale, *The Conquest of Paradise: Christopher Columbus and the Columbian Legacy* (New York: Plume, 1991), 79. R. H. Tawney comments that for a thousand years "of unresting struggle with marsh and forest and moor, [Europe] had colonized her own waste places" and now "turned to the task of colonizing the world," entering a phase "of economic expansion which was to grow for the next four hundred years" (*Religion and the Rise of Capitalism* [London: John Murray, 1936], 71).

17. Léry, *History of a Voyage*, 131–32.

The Forgotten Holocaust

In 1992 the Chilean theologian Pablo Richard, contributing to a special issue of the journal *Concilium* marking the five hundredth anniversary of the arrival of Europeans in the Americas, wrote that in 1492, "*death came to this continent*: the deaths of human beings, the death of the environment, death of the spirit, of indigenous religion and culture."[18] The slaughter of indigenous populations by the actions of the conquistadores proved to be but the beginning of sorrows for the native peoples of the Americas. They suffered devastation not only from the cruelty and injustices of the invaders, but also from the spread of diseases to which they had no natural resistance. It is estimated that the indigenous population south of the Rio Grande was some 100 million souls when Columbus arrived; less than a century later it had been reduced to between 10 and 12 million, a catastrophe which has been described as "the greatest genocide in the history of humanity." The Brazilian anthropologist and writer Darcy Ribeiro describes the emergent new world as follows:

> In this way the earth and its innumerable peoples, a great part of the human race, were converted into a colonial possession and a profitable business, and acquired a new destiny. They were no longer to exist and be themselves, so doubling the potential of human activity, but to refashion themselves according to European dictates, defined by the profit motive.[19]

The collapse of the indigenous population resulted in the tragedy which had followed European expansion being extended and deepened as it embroiled the native peoples of the continent of Africa in the shape of the transatlantic slave trade. In the 1560s the Portuguese began transporting slaves from Africa to replace the lost labour force which had been provided by Indians, taking over half a million African people to work on

---

18. Pablo Richard, "1492: The Violence of God and the Future of Christianity," in *1492-1992: The Voice of the Victims*, eds. Leonardo Boff and Virgil Elizondo, *Concilium* Special (London: SCM, 1991), 59; emphasis added. It should be noted that Pablo Richard has himself contributed much to the service of indigenous people throughout Latin America, including biblical workshops with leaders from such communities which resulted in a remarkable exposition of John's Apocalypse. See Pablo Richard, *Apocalypse: A People's Commentary on the Book of Revelation* (Eugene: Wipf & Stock, 2008).

19. Darcy Ribeiro, "The Latin American People," in Boff and Elizondo, *Voice of the Victims*, 14.

plantations in South America. In the following century a further 1.7 million Africans were enslaved and transported, with the result that, as George Reid Andrews showed in a book with the title *Afro-Latin America*, the heart of the New World African diaspora "lies not north of the border, in the United States, but south." Ten times as many Africans were transported to Spanish and Portuguese America (5.7 million) as to the United States (560,000).[20] Holland, France and England joined in the trade and in 1672 the Company of Royal Adventurers was founded in London as the British came to play a major role in the triangular trade, with Liverpool becoming "the greatest port for shipping negroes in Europe."[21]

I pause here to reflect on personal experience in the light of what I have just written. In 1977 I and my family boarded a Nigerian cargo ship, the *Ahmadu Bello*, in London, bound for the coast of eastern Nigeria. Delays at ports en route extended this journey to more than five weeks, which meant that there were many opportunities to relate to the Nigerian crew and learn from their perspectives regarding contemporary Africa. I discovered considerable scepticism about my reasons for relocating to the rainforest of the Cross River State in the Niger Delta, but one conversation was especially significant and has remained with me ever since. We were invited to dine at the captain's table, and he turned out to be a large, affable Nigerian who, it transpired, had accommodation in Liverpool. I have never forgotten the passion, driven by a controlled but deep anger, with which he said to me: "I am not willing to watch my continent become a playground for rich Westerners!" We had called at the port of Banjul in the Gambia and seen exactly the kind of development he had in mind as wealthy Europeans lay on the beach beside a luxury hotel just out of sight of the poverty so evident within the city. At the time, I was shaken by the captain's anger, although subsequent experience in Nigeria provided the context within which I came to understand it, and while writing the previous paragraph that honest African voice has sounded in my ears once again across the years.

---

20. George Reid Andrews, *Afro-Latin America, 1800–2000* (Oxford: Oxford University Press, 2004), 3.

21. Laënnec Hurbon, "The Slave Trade and Black Slavery in America," in Boff and Elizondo, *Voice of the Victims*, 92.

The "expansion of Europe," including the Christian missionary movement which occurred in its wake, cannot be properly understood or evaluated apart from the knowledge of its consequences for millions of people whose lives and societies were disrupted or destroyed by it. George Reid Andrews reminds us of what this involved:

> Africans did not choose to come to the New World. These decisions were made for them, first by the African rulers and merchants who enslaved, bought, and sold them, then by the European and American merchants and ship owners who transported them to the New World, and finally by the slave owners who bought them. No Africans would ever have chosen the destination to which most of them were sent: the sugar, coffee, tobacco, cacao, and cotton plantations of the Caribbean, Atlantic and Pacific coasts.[22]

When economic historians write concerning the expansion of European power and influence their interest is focused, understandably, on what might be called the mechanics of the movement which was to result in the emergence of an economic and cultural system which would ultimately dominate the world. For example, Janet Abu-Lughod, in a brilliant study of the economic revolution which began in the thirteenth century, refers to the "geographic reorientation" that provided "the windfalls of wealth that eventually were spun into industrial gold."[23] There is no mention of the staggering cost of millions of human lives, or of the destruction of ancient cultures which were the bearers of a wisdom that the human family could ill afford to lose.[24]

---

22. Andrews, *Afro-Latin America*, 13. Note the verdict of Anthony Pagden: "Modern slavery was the creation of a new form of empire-building. It was developed to supply the manpower for a particular socio-economic unit – the sugar plantation – which had been unknown in the old world. It was sugar that was responsible for the massive growth in the slave trade, between the fifteenth and eighteenth centuries, and it was the value of sugar to the economies of the slaving nations which made the abolition of slavery at the end of the eighteenth century such a protracted and uncertain business" (*Peoples and Empires*, 109).

23. Janet L. Abu-Lughod, *Before European Hegemony: The World System A.D. 1250–1350* (Oxford: Oxford University Press, 1989), 362–63.

24. Theodore Von Laue, in a classic study of world history, asks: "How has it happened that scholars of human affairs, in history or the social sciences, have proceeded with so little awareness of the moral dimension?" To his great credit, his own work exemplifies a methodology which involves asking precisely such questions (*The World Revolution of Westernization: The Twentieth Century in Global Perspective* [Oxford: Oxford University Press, 1987], 371).

If this kind of economistic history fails to address the fundamental moral and ethical questions which arise from the story it is relating, what shall we say about the history and theology of Christian missions which is frequently presented with exactly the same lacunae? We have reached the point in this book at which Jesus's warning of the impossibility of serving both God and Mammon comes into its sharpest focus, simply because the emerging "world system" which the economic historians describe so clearly marks precisely the point at which the decision for God or Mammon takes on a universal, global significance. European Christians have justification to celebrate their nineteenth-century predecessors' role in the abolition of the slave trade, but they have no such warrant to evade the painful reality of the holocaust which was the consequence of the moral failure of European Christendom. Michael Stroope has said that the colonial legacy of mission "is difficult to overcome and cannot be casually dismissed."

> Mission language is firmly rooted in the spirit of conquest and colonization. Modernity does not inoculate mission from these problems but is instead inclined toward them with a spirit of its own. An attempt to reframe, redesign, or reform mission does not erase these memories, nor does it rescue mission from its legacy.[25]

Puritans and Capitalists

It may be remembered that in the first chapter of this book we discussed the work of Max Weber and his focus on the role played by the English Puritan movement at the critical point of the emergence and growth of the modern capitalist system. We have now arrived at precisely that juncture in history at which major changes and dislocations occurred as a consequence of the wealth which flooded into Europe following the incursions into the New World. That wealth was to trigger a commercial revolution on a scale which far exceeded the earlier surge in economic activity which we have discussed above. It constituted a new era in which "a seemingly limitless field

---

25. Michael Stroope, *Transcending Mission: The Eclipse of a Modern Tradition* (Leicester: Apollos, 2017), 348.

to economic enterprise" opened up and, in doing so, sharpened "the edge of every social problem."[26] This dramatic growth in commercial activity was accompanied by new forms of financial organization as "capital poured into the growing London money market" and commerce, industry and agriculture were transformed by what Tawney described as "a virus of hitherto unsuspected potency, at once a feverish enterprise and an acid dissolving all customary relationships."[27]

The century which divides the Reformation from the English Civil War witnessed vast changes in both economic life and Christian responses to this revolution. There were attempts to appeal to the traditional, medieval ethic, despite the fact that this obviously did not relate to the new developments which were transforming economic practice throughout Europe. Describing the situation in Britain, Tawney comments on the response of the Church of England to the challenges posed by the growth of early capitalism:

> Objective economic science was evolving in the hands of the experts who wrote on agriculture, trade, and, above all, currency and the foreign exchanges. But the divines . . . waved them on one side as the intrusion of Mammon into the fold of Christian morality, and by their obstinate obscurantism helped to prepare an intellectual nemesis, which was to discredit their fervent rhetoric as the voice of a musty superstition.[28]

This can be illustrated by the fate of an Act introduced in 1552 which was designed to prohibit all charging of interest, described at the time as "a vice most odious and detestable, as in divers places of the holy Scripture it is evident to be seen." This was clearly consistent with the centuries-long Christian resistance to usury, but by 1571 the Act had been repealed on the grounds that "the law should not impose on business a utopian morality."[29]

Given this context, Weber's focus on the Puritans was important since, as the followers of John Calvin, they moved beyond the static position received from the medieval era and developed a theology and pastoral practice which was intended to address the existential situation in the England of their time.

---

26. Tawney, *Religion and the Rise of Capitalism*, 85.
27. Tawney, 136–37.
28. Tawney, 158.
29. Tawney, 180.

Weber argued that the Puritan merchants of "the heroic age of capitalism" came to regard "intense worldly activity" as the means of overcoming "religious doubts" and providing the assurance of grace.[30] That is to say that, as inheritors of Calvin's theology – both his doctrine of election and predestination, and his profound social concern, including the acceptance of the charging of interest under specific conditions – the Puritans taught that faithfulness in a calling within the realm of business could provide tangible evidence of one's membership of the elect people of God. Christians could now find employment within the new world of commerce with a good conscience, provided that their work was done for the glory of God and in the service of his kingdom. Tawney recognized this acceptance of the realities of commercial practices to be of momentous importance:

> It meant that Calvinism and its offshoots took their stand on the side of the activities which were to be most characteristic of the future, and insisted that it was not by renouncing them, but by untiring concentration on the task of using for the glory of God the opportunities which they offered, that the Christian life could and must be lived.[31]

We cannot, however, overlook the fact that this transition involved immense struggles. The social and religious turmoil in Britain during the first half of the seventeenth century was such that this period has been described as "the most terrible years through which the country has ever passed."[32] In 1591 a report described the widening chasm between rich and poor as making "yeoman and artificers gentlemen, and of gentlemen knights, and of the poorest sort stark beggars." Leading Puritan ministers were to debate whether it was justified for the poor to steal food in order to keep their families alive, and some – including a figure as prominent as John Donne – argued that it was so. A document which circulated among the lords of England in 1607 described the nature of the transformation taking place as follows: "The poor man shall be satisfied in his end: Habitation; and the gentleman not hindered in his

---

30. Max Weber, *The Protestant Ethic and the Spirit of Capitalism* (London: Counterpoint, 1985), 111–12.

31. Tawney, *Religion and the Rise of Capitalism*, 108.

32. Peter Bowden, quoted in Christopher Hill, *A Turbulent, Seditious, and Factious People: John Bunyan and His Church, 1628–1688* (Oxford: Oxford University Press, 1989), 16.

desire: Improvement." The means by which that "improvement" was attained included the enclosure of common lands, which resulted in the poor being reduced to beggary, "doomed by the rich man's desire for public improvement which profits him privately." These are the words of Karl Polanyi in a landmark study to which we shall return. He continues:

> Enclosures have appropriately been called a revolution of the rich against the poor. The lords and nobles were upsetting the social order, breaking down ancient law and custom, sometimes by means of violence, often by pressure and intimidation. They were literally robbing the poor of their share in the common, tearing down the houses which, by the hitherto unbreakable force of custom, the poor had long regarded as theirs and their heirs'. The fabric of society was being disrupted; desolate villages and the ruins of human dwellings testified to the fierceness with which the revolution raged, endangering the defences of the country, wasting its towns, decimating its population, turning its overburdened soil into dust, harassing its people and turning them from decent husbandmen into a mob of beggars and thieves.[33]

This was the context within which the Puritan movement emerged and its leaders wrestled with the crucial ethical issues concerning work, wealth and money in what has been described as a "transitional stage" in which "capitalist production was struggling forward in a society whose institutions were still largely pre-capitalist."[34] Labourers were not yet divorced from the soil, and the creation of a large pool of wage-earning workers, which would become an essential precondition for the growth of industry on a large scale, was a development which still lay in the future.[35]

---

33. Karl Polanyi, *The Great Transformation: The Political and Economic Origins of Our Time* (Boston: Beacon, 1957), 37.

34. Christopher Hill, *Puritanism and Revolution* (London: Panther, 1968), 219.

35. Note Polanyi's comment: "Not before the last decade of the eighteenth century was . . . the establishment of a free labor market even discussed; and the idea of the self-regulation of economic life was utterly beyond the horizon of the age. . . . And just as the transition to a democratic system and representative politics involved a complete reversal of the trend of the age, the change from regulated to self-regulating markets at the end of the eighteenth century represented a complete transformation in the structure of society" (*Great Transformation*, 74).

What we are describing here will be familiar to millions of people belonging to indigenous societies today in South America, Africa and many parts of Asia. Their struggles resulting from the transition from traditional societies to nation states operating within a global capitalist economy closely parallel the European experience in the seventeenth century. Moreover, those struggles can enable us to understand the nature – the tragedy – of the period we are discussing. Tawney wrote that with the expansion of finance and international trade, questions concerning the duty to love one's neighbours became urgent, and although Christianity continued to insist that, according to Jesus, all people fell within that category,

> it did not occur to it to point out that, as a result of the new economic imperialism which was beginning to develop . . . the brethren of the English merchant were the Africans whom he kidnapped for slavery in America, or the American Indians whom he stripped of their lands, or the Indian craftsmen from whom he bought muslins and silks at starvation prices.[36]

The Puritan movement has been described as the most important religious phenomenon of the seventeenth century and as the "true English Reformation." It was built on the foundation laid by John Calvin's theology, and inspired by the example of his attempt to apply the gospel to social and economic life in an urban setting. That example had deeply impressed British exiles in Geneva, including John Knox, who was to give the Scottish Reformation its distinctive form.[37] While it is difficult to summarize the character of this movement, its essence is captured by Tawney when he writes that the Puritan "remakes, not only his own character and habits and way of life, but family and church, industry and city, political institutions and social order." Puritan religious experience had something in common with the medieval longing for the contemplation of God; indeed, seventeenth-century

---

36. Tawney, *Religion and the Rise of Capitalism*, 185.
37. Eric J. Hobsbawm suggested that Scotland "derived three things from its Calvinist revolution": first, its "remarkably democratic educational system"; second, the concern for the poor which remained the responsibility of local kirks; and third, "the Calvinist ideal of perfection through labour" which "contributed to that remarkable technical competence of the Lowland Scots which was to make Clydeside the great centre of shipbuilding and to fill the steamers of the world with Scots engineers" (*The Pelican Economic History of Britain*, vol. 3, *Industry and Empire: From 1750 to the Present Day* [Harmondsworth: Penguin, 1969], 304–5).

sermons dwelt often on the interior life of the human soul, but such mystical experience was never an end in itself, but the source and dynamic of a life in which Christian action sought to glorify God "in a world given over to the powers of darkness." Such a life was shaped by the individual's calling, by a vocation in which the Reformation insistence upon the priesthood of all believers came into its own.[38]

Here is the influential Cambridge preacher William Perkins in a publication of 1601 entitled *On the Vocations, or Callings of Men*: "Every person of every degree, state, sexe, or condition without exception, must have some peronall and particular calling to walke in."[39] Here is the emergence of the Protestant work ethic, embedded at this point in time within a Christian worldview which ensured that any suggestion that the Puritan might be "the friend of economic licence" would have been wide of the mark. Christopher Hill suggested, however, that over the course of the seventeenth century a trans-valuation of values took place by which human labour, which in the ancient world had involved hard physical toil and had been regarded as "the curse of fallen man," began to be transformed into a religious duty, "a means of glorifying God in our calling." At the same time, poverty "ceased to be a holy state" and was eventually to become "presumptive evidence of wickedness."[40] By the end of the seventeenth century we discover evidence of this shift in Richard Steele's book of 1684, *The Tradesman's Calling*. The author draws a damning contrast between the work of the humblest labourer and the life of prayer and contemplation:

> The begging friars and such monks as live only to themselves and to their formal devotion, but do employ themselves in no one thing to further their own subsistence or the good of mankind . . . yet have confidence to boast of this their course as a

---

38. William Temple said that Calvinism, "which began as a system of regimentation, where economic activity was subject to severe moral restraint, became ultimately the mainspring of unrestricted enterprise and competition." The Reformers "never intended to produce such a monster as the Economic Man of the last hundred and fifty years; the Puritans were austere in their demands for self-denial in respect of most things which money can buy. But their fundamental individualism . . . undermined the appreciation of wealth as essentially social and therefore subject at all points to control in the interest of society as a whole" (*Christianity and Social Order* [New York: Seabury, 1977], 55–56).

39. Hill, *Puritanism and Revolution*, 222.

40. Hill, 215.

state of perfection; which in very deed, as to the worthiness of it, falls short of the poorest cobbler, *for his is a calling of God, and theirs is none.*[41]

The seventeenth century trans-valuation of values is complete when Steele elsewhere addresses the urgent and growing problem of poverty by insisting that it would be good for "idle beggars" if "fewer people spent their foolish pity upon their bodies" and showed "some wise compassion upon their souls." There is a shift here by which the problem of poverty is being divorced from the consequences of structural changes in society, and is perceived to be the result of wilful idleness, so that the charitable response to the poor "is not to enervate them by relief, but so to reform their characters that relief may be unnecessary."[42] It is sobering to read these comments from the perspective of the twenty-first century and to realize once again the unintended consequences of what might have seemed at the time to be a simple adjustment in the theology of work.

We need at this point to listen to a different voice from this same period, that of the imprisoned tinker of Bedford, John Bunyan (1628–88). He lived through this tumultuous time in English history and witnessed the Civil War, the execution of Charles I, the Protectorate of Oliver Cromwell, the appearance of swarms of sectarian groups, including Quakers, Diggers and Ranters, and the eventual restoration of monarchy, lords and the episcopate. Bunyan served in the parliamentary army and spent almost one-third of his life in Bedford gaol, viewing the Puritan revolution from the underside of an increasingly fractured society within which a bewildering variety of dreams and visions of the future were articulated, debated and eventually suppressed. He was the pastor of a Baptist congregation which was viewed as "a turbulent, seditious, and factious people," and therefore subject to surveillance and the constant threat of repression. Bunyan was surprisingly honest about the depth of his own internal struggles while on pilgrimage to the Holy City:

---

41. Quoted in Tawney, *Religion and the Rise of Capitalism*, 241; emphasis added. He cites a work of 1656, *A Vindication of a Regulated Enclosure* by Joseph Lee, which anticipates the direction which economics was to take in the following centuries: "It is an undeniable maxim that everyone by the light of nature and reason will do that which makes for his greatest advantage.... The advancement of private persons will be the advancement of the public" (259).

42. Tawney, 267.

> How can you tell but that the Turks have as good Scriptures to prove their Mahomet the Saviour, as we have to prove our Jesus is? And could I think that so many tens thousands, in so many countries and kingdoms, should be without the knowledge of the right way to heaven; if there were indeed a heaven, and that we only, who live in a corner of the earth, should alone be blessed therewith?[43]

These anguished questions reflected the turbulence of the times through which Bunyan lived and his encounters, especially while in prison, with a bewildering array of views and questions. He also witnessed the reappearance of apocalyptic theologies, and the expression of radical social alternatives of the kind that were to be voiced during the "Putney Debates" of 1649, when it was asserted that "the poorest man in England is nott att all bound in a strict sence to that Government that hee hath not had a voice to putt himself under."[44] Those radical voices included a significant number of women, some demanding their right simply to be heard, while others, such as Anne Wentworth, protested at the injustice of the treatment meted out to them in a patriarchal society. Having been thrown out of hearth and home by her abusive husband, she refused to keep silent beneath a hail of false accusations of infidelity and blasphemy:

> And this is the thing, the only thing, that makes my Husband and hundreds more, to be wroth with me, and endeavour to take away my good Name, in spreading abroad that I keep Men company. . . . But as the Pharisees of old said of the Son of God, that he was a gluttonous man, a Wine-bibber, a friend of publicans and sinners, and one that hath a devil; and yet he bore it patiently: so shall I wait in patience, how the Lord Jesus doth love and like of their defaming me, which will be seen and known openly, for to be revealed to Generations to come.[45]

---

43. From *Grace Abounding to the Chief of Sinners*, quoted in Hill, *Turbulent, Seditious and Factious People*, 75.

44. Andrew Bradstock and Christopher Rowland, eds., *Radical Christian Writings: A Reader* (Oxford: Blackwell, 2002), 111.

45. Bradstock and Rowland, *Radical Christian Writings*, 156.

John Bunyan knew and understood this "underground" world, and the depths of despair and hopelessness which provided fertile ground for the flourishing of such longings and hopes. Christopher Hill concluded his study of Bunyan and his Bedford congregation by saying that it is difficult to identify "any great writer in seventeenth- or eighteenth-century England who was as passionately, fiercely, and theologically on the side of the poor as Bunyan."[46]

I suspect that the English composer Ralph Vaughan Williams would have agreed with that verdict, having spent much of his life writing music inspired by *The Pilgrim's Progress*. It was a labour of love that culminated in the opera with that title, first performed in 1951. To listen to (or better still to watch) that work, and especially the third-act depiction of the pilgrim's journey through Vanity Fair, is to realize the visionary nature of Bunyan's ministry and his acute perception of where the socio-economic innovations of the seventeenth century might eventually lead:

> Come and buy! Come and buy!
> Come and buy from our booths all the pleasures of man,
>   Come and buy, come and buy,
> Nothing endures so choose while you can, so choose while
>   You can, come and buy
> What is value but money? What's life but estate?
> Who wanders alone, leaves pleasure too late.
> Here is all that earth offers and all to be sold
> For the power and the glory are servants to gold.[47]

John Bunyan offers us a contrasting perspective on the Puritan revolution, one which viewed the changes of the seventeenth century from the underside of that society, and recognized the dangers that lay ahead if the gospel's promise of the kingdom of love and justice were to be lost amid the rising demands for individual liberty to be accorded to personal acquisitiveness. Bunyan was anxious, as Hill puts it, to emphasize "community, charity, the rights of the poor,"[48] and the longer he lived the more he realized that even the godly were succumbing to the values of the market.

---

46. Hill, *Turbulent, Seditious and Factious People*, 357.

47. From the libretto of Ralph and Ursula Vaughan Williams accompanying the recording of *The Pilgrim's Progress* by the Orchestra and Chorus of the Royal Opera House, conducted by Richard Hickox, Chandos CD 9625(2).

48. Hill, *Turbulent, Seditious and Factious People*, 22.

CHAPTER 9

Mission and Empire

The end of the Empire has been for us the most traumatic event to befall Britain after 1945 or even 1918 – literally so, for the patient is still traumatized, unable to recognize what has happened to him.... What we do not see is any appreciation of the profound influence of the Empire on *British* society for a good two hundred years, nor of the crisis which its end necessarily meant for *us*. (Nicholas Boyle)[1]

The two hundred years which followed the Puritan era were to witness rapidly accelerating social and political changes which would transform the lives of the European peoples in the most radical way. The tension which we have noticed above between "habitation" and "improvement," or between traditional, integrated communities and a new kind of restless, increasingly rootless society, was to increase to unbearable levels during the Industrial Revolution of the eighteenth century. Mechanization, rural depopulation, and the growth of new forms of urbanization resulted in "a catastrophic dislocation of the lives of the common people." Karl Polanyi discovered "the political and economic origins" of the modern world in precisely this period, when "improvement" became an ideology which swept all before it, with incalculable human costs.

Before the process had advanced very far, the labouring people had been crowded together, in new places of desolation, the

---

1. Nicholas Boyle, *Who Are We Now? Christian Humanism and the Global Market from Hegel to Heaney* (Edinburgh: T&T Clark, 1998), 23.

so-called industrial towns of England; the country folk had been dehumanized into slum dwellers; the family was on the road to perdition; and large parts of the country were rapidly disappearing under the slack and scrap heaps vomited forth from the "satanic mills."[2]

Polanyi's book *The Great Transformation* was written during the Second World War and it traced the origins of the economistic culture which was to sweep all before it and would eventually extend its dominance to a global scale. The relationship between "a vast movement of economic improvement," on the one hand, and a veritable avalanche of social dislocation, on the other, suggested that "an entirely new institutional mechanism was starting to act on Western society," and this development posed an enormous threat to human well-being. The Industrial Revolution was the beginning of a change which was "as extreme and radical as ever inflamed the minds of sectarians, but the new creed was utterly materialistic" and operated on the assumption that "all human problems could be resolved given an unlimited amount of material commodities."[3]

It is not possible here to explore Polanyi's remarkable work in detail, but his crucial argument concerns the nature of the relationship between social existence and the function of the economy. Using the findings of modern anthropological research, he demonstrated that human economies were historically embedded within social relationships. This was, as we have seen, the discovery of the earliest missionaries to the Americas, and Polanyi endorsed such findings and concluded that traditional peoples had never acted "to safeguard individual interests in the possession of material goods," but always behaved in ways that furthered *social* claims, and *social* assets. They valued material goods "only in so far as they serve this end." The evolution of a different kind of society in which the market came to dominate both the behaviour of individuals and the wider political culture involved a reversal of all previous social history in which economic life had been embedded within a social structure.

---

2. Karl Polanyi, *The Great Transformation: The Political and Economic Origins of Our Time* (Boston: Beacon, 1957), 41.

3. Polanyi, *Great Transformation*, 42.

> Ultimately, that is why the control of the economic system by the market is of overwhelming consequence for the whole of society: it means no less than the running of society as an adjunct to the market. Instead of economy being embedded within social relations, *social relations are embedded within the economic system*.⁴

Long before a looming ecological crisis alerted the general public to the severity of the catastrophe towards which unrestrained greed and acquisitiveness is leading the human race, Polanyi had recognized the impossibility of pursuing endless economic growth without threatening the destruction of the created world. A self-adjusting market could not exist beyond the stage at which its patent illusions were exposed by the hard reality of the limits imposed by the very nature of the world within which humanity exists. As long ago as 1944, Polanyi had predicted that the market ideology was simply unsustainable since it was bound to annihilate both "the human and natural substance of society," and would turn the created world "into a wilderness."⁵

The Great Century?

By the early years of the nineteenth century the conditions in which the millions of people who had migrated from the British countryside into the slums of expanding cities such as London, Manchester and Glasgow were truly terrible. Friedrich Engels famously reported on "the condition of the working class" in Manchester in 1844 and estimated that 350,000 labourers and their families were housed in "wretched, damp, filthy cottages" in streets that were in a most deplorable condition. He insisted that normal family life was made impossible in such circumstances and that "only a physically degenerate race, robbed of all humanity, degraded, reduced morally and physically to bestiality, could feel comfortable and at home." What made life in the early industrial city worse still was the "brutal indifference" and "unfeeling isolation of each

---

4. Polanyi, 60; emphasis added.
5. Polanyi, xxv. In a chapter titled "Market and Nature," Polanyi says of land: "It invests man's life with stability; it is the site of his habitation; it is a condition of his physical safety; it is the landscape and the seasons. We might as well imagine his being born without hands and feet as carrying on his life without land. And yet to separate land from man and organize society in such a way as to satisfy the requirements of a real-estate market was a vital part of the utopian concept of the market economy" (187).

in his private interest" in this situation. The urban culture which accompanied the Industrial Revolution appeared to encourage the narrow self-seeking which had become the "the fundamental principle of our society everywhere." People living in comfortable circumstances elsewhere in the city appeared to be completely ignorant of the conditions of the poor and had themselves degenerated into isolated "monads," driven by their own self-interest.[6]

Karl Polanyi regarded this "atomization" of society as the direct and predictable consequence of the ideology of market capitalism which had turned the individual quest for wealth and advancement into a positive virtue, with the result that social bonds were shattered and separate class interests hardened into something not unlike an urban apartheid.

> But if the workers were physically dehumanized, the owning classes were morally degraded. The traditional unity of a Christian society was giving place to a denial of responsibility on the part of the well-to-do for their fellows. The Two Nations were taking shape. To the bewilderment of thinking minds, unheard-of wealth turned out to be inseparable from unheard-of poverty. Scholars proclaimed in unison that a science had been discovered which put the laws governing man's world beyond any doubt. It was at the behest of these laws that compassion was removed from hearts, and a stoic determination to renounce human solidarity in the name of the greatest happiness of the greatest number gained the dignity of a secular religion.[7]

We shall return to the importance of the claim that a "secular religion" was now shaping what would become a post-Christian society since this obviously has significance in relation to our central concern with the choice between God and Mammon. However, before we reach that point we must ask what else was happening during these two centuries in which the modern world was taking its distinctive shape. There were features of this period which led many people at the time, and a significant section of the British population today, to regard the 1800s as the "great century." It was an era which witnessed the celebration of an advanced technological and industrial culture and of

---

6. Friedrich Engels, "The Great Towns," in *The City Reader*, eds. Richard LeGates and Frederic Stout, 4th ed. (London: Routledge, 2007), 52, 58.

7. Polanyi, *Great Transformation*, 106.

colonial expansion which resulted in the creation of a British Empire on which the sun never set. The expansion of British power had begun under the Stuarts and Cromwell when mercantile interests were awakened by the New World opened up by settler communities in North America, including the St. Lawrence Basin in Canada. By the beginning of the nineteenth century, European powers exerted control over an estimated 35 percent of the earth's land surface, but the extent of imperial acquisitions and dominance was to increase throughout this century. The use of the term *imperialism* to describe this phenomenon is justified since, as Giovanni Arrighi observes, no previous empire "had ever before incorporated within its domains so many, so populous, and so far-flung territories" as the British did in this period.

> Nor had any territorialist ruler ever before forcibly extracted in so short a time so much tribute – in labor-power, in natural resources, and in means of payments – as the British state and its clients did in the Indian sub-continent in the course of the nineteenth century. Part of this tribute was used to buttress and expand the coercive apparatus through which more and more non-Western subjects were added to the British territorial empire. But another, equally conspicuous part was siphoned off in one form or another to London, to be recycled in the circuits of wealth through which British power in the Western world was continually reproduced and expanded.[8]

What is of crucial importance here is the recognition that this unprecedented expansion of economic and political power was accompanied by the spread of the free market ideology which we have described above. Which is to say that the "great transformation" which Polanyi believed had undermined traditional social values within Britain was now being exported to the rest of the world and used to justify imperial power as the agent of global enlightenment. Arrighi reaches a conclusion that, despite using different terminology,

---

8. Giovanni Arrighi, *The Long Twentieth Century: Money, Power and the Origins of Our Times* (London: Verso, 2010), 55. The expansion of British imperial power is described by Harry Magdoff who says that by 1815, despite the loss of the American colonies, Britain had obtained an empire "that straddled the globe from Canada to the Caribbean in the Western Hemisphere around the Cape of Good Hope to India and Australia. This empire was sustained by . . . maritime power that far exceeded that of any of Britain's European rivals" (*Imperialism: From the Colonial Age to the Present* [New York: Monthly Review Press, 1978], 24).

has striking parallels with Polanyi's claim that a new kind of secular *religion* was involved in this global development:

> Free-trade imperialism ... established the principle that the laws operating within and between states *were subject to the higher authority of a new, metaphysical entity* – a world market ruled by its own "laws" – allegedly endowed with supernatural powers greater than anything pope and emperor had ever mastered in the medieval system of rule.[9]

The global spread of this ideology was thus justified by the claim that the growth of British imperial power was "the motor force of a general expansion of the wealth of nations."[10] Presented in this way, the empire was depicted as a global force for good, a claim intended to pacify resistance abroad, while at the same time creating acceptance, and even pride, at home. Nowhere was this celebration of empire more clearly on display than at the Great Exhibition at the Crystal Palace in Hyde Park in London in 1851 where the "exhibits" included peoples from every corner of the world, transported to Britain in order to be displayed as living examples of the benefits flowing to them from British imperial rule. As Anthony Pagden puts it: "They, the 'uncivilized,' the 'savage,' the 'barbarian,' would give the Europeans their labour and their raw materials, their 'surplus' as it comfortingly came to be called; the Europeans in compensation would bring them enlightenment, technology, Christianity, even cleanliness."[11]

The positive claims made for British imperial rule not only involved the suppression of the evidence of the corruption, greed and violence which

---

9. Arrighi, *Long Twentieth Century*, 56; emphasis added. Note M. Douglas Meeks's comment on "God concepts in market economics": "Although orthodox economics ... refuses to reflect 'God' in its domain, it cannot be doubted ... that economists make representations of another level of reality. They point to a 'netherwold,' a beyond of hidden forces, which is full of assumptions grounding the market mechanism.... The market may be considered free of God and thus all authoritarian influences. But the working of the market depends on coercive conceptions once applied to God but now given as presuppositions of the market human being" (*God the Economist: The Doctrine of God and Political Economy* [Minneapolis: Fortress, 1989], 64–65).

10. Arrighi, 57.

11. Anthony Pagden, *Peoples and Empires: Europeans and the Rest of the World – From Antiquity to the Present* (London: Weidenfeld & Nicolson, 2001), 145. He describes a poster promoting Pears' soap in 1887 depicting a partially naked African staring in wonder at a rock inscribed with the words "PEARS' SOAP IS BEST."

accompanied the spread of empire, they also ignored the reality of the tragedies resulting from the destruction of indigenous cultures in Africa and Asia, and the social and economic injustices which continued to disfigure British society itself. Andrew Mearns's 1884 book *The Bitter Cry of Outcast London* exposed the realities of the lives of thousands of people "trapped in fever dens" within a few miles of Hyde Park and the Crystal Palace! Overseas visitors to London at the time of the Great Exhibition were appalled by the contrast between the glamour and wealth flaunted in the city's West End and the squalor and destitution of the East End. The great Russian writer Fyodor Dostoevsky came away from the Crystal Palace profoundly shocked by what he discerned to be its spiritual implications, describing it as a kind of "Biblical illustration, some prophecy of the Apocalypse fulfilled before your eyes." "You feel that one must have perpetual spiritual resistance and negation so as not to surrender, not to submit to the impression, not to bow the knee before the fact and deify Baal, not to accept the existing as one's ideal."[12] Dostoevsky was even more disturbed by the stark contrast between the glittering celebration of what was paraded as British progress, and the dreadful conditions he discovered elsewhere in the city, where he witnessed "a pitiless wilderness of wild, half-naked, besotted proletarians, gloomily drowning their despair in debauchery and gin."[13]

If the advocates of British imperial rule could describe the 1800s as "the great century," that same phrase has also been used with regard to Christianity and its missionary expansion in this period. It will be remembered that Andrew Walls identified the growth of the political and economic power of Europe as being concurrent with his "fifth age" of Christianity and its mission. This raises a series of difficult, yet unavoidable, questions concerning the relationship between the Christian faith, mission and imperialism.

The beginnings of what has come to be called the modern missionary movement are widely assumed to be found in the work of the Baptist shoemaker William Carey and his *Enquiry into the Obligations of Christians to Use Means for the Conversion of the Heathens* of 1792. As we have seen, there had been a remarkable example of cross-cultural missionary effort at the time of

---

12. Joseph Frank, *Dostoevsky: The Stir of Liberation, 1860–1865* (London: Robson Books, 1986), 239.

13. Frank, 239.

the Protestant Reformation, and Carey himself made frequent reference to the inspiration he drew from the earlier work of German Moravians. Carey's colleague William Ward, writing while sailing to India in 1799, expressed gratitude to the Moravians for their example in language which suggests their importance for the history of mission: "Thank you Moravians! Ye have done me good. If ever I am a missionary worth a straw, *I shall owe it all to you, under our Saviour.*"[14]

Carey's distinctive and crucial role in laying the foundations of a movement that was to play a significant part in British society in the era of imperialism was in his proposal to "use means" to ensure that the good news of Jesus Christ be taken to the new worlds recently brought to the awareness of Europeans by the influential reports of Captain Cook. The proposal for the creation of a voluntary society for the purpose of mission was a genuine innovation and a concept which rang alarm bells among the governing elite who, in the wake of the loss of the American colonies in 1776, and especially after the French Revolution in 1789, were fearful of any political activity among "sectarian groups." The strong suspicion that radical ideas were festering beneath the surface of a deeply divided society made Carey's *Enquiry* suspect. The fact that it was published in London by Joseph Johnson, who had also printed Tom Paine's *Rights of Man* and Mary Wollstonecraft's *Vindication of the Rights of Woman*, and that it was in this man's house that William Blake had warned Paine to flee to Paris in 1792, would have done nothing to allay the suspicion that Carey's proposed "society" would be subversive of British colonial interests.

There was an additional reason for the establishment's suspicion of Baptist intentions, and this relates to what we might describe as the apocalyptic dimension of the theology which shaped Carey's vision. He shared with other evangelicals a spirit of expectation that the world was about to be transformed by the grace of God, a hope which was characteristic of the broader evangelical movement associated with the "Great Awakening." We cannot discuss this in detail here, but the imperative of mission arose at a time when the

---

14. My source concerning Carey and the early Baptist mission is the *Periodical Accounts* which began to be published in 1795 and contain all the correspondence between Carey and his colleagues in India and the supporting friends in Britain, represented especially by Andrew Fuller, Baptist pastor at Soham in Cambridgeshire. The statement from Ward is from the *Periodical Accounts* of 1801 and I reference it as PA II (1801), 2.

American theologian Jonathan Edwards had articulated a post-millennial theology which anticipated the imminent fulfilment of the Bible's prophetic visions of a glorious age when the whole earth would be filled with the knowledge of the love of God. Edwards anticipated

> a time of wonderful union, and the most universal love, peace and sweet harmony; wherein the nations shall "beat their swords into ploughshares" and God "will cause wars to cease to the ends of the earth." . . . A time wherein the whole earth shall be united as one holy city, one heavenly family, men of all nations shall, as it were, dwell together as brothers and children of the same family. . . . A time when the world shall be delivered from that multitude of sore calamities which before had prevailed and there shall be a universal blessing of God upon mankind, in soul and body, and in all their concerns, and all manner of tokens of God's presence and favour.[15]

We catch a clear echo of Edwards's theology in the title of the crucial sermon which Carey preached in Nottingham in 1792: "Expect Great Things from God; Attempt Great Things for God." The same confidence that the world stood on the brink of a great turning point, and that the promised kingdom of God was about to break into human history to an unprecedented degree, can be seen on the first page of the *Enquiry*. Carey affirms that God "repeatedly made known his intention to prevail finally over all the power of the Devil, and to destroy all his works, and set up his own kingdom and interest among men, and extend it as universally as Satan had extended his."[16] The crucial issue for us at this point concerns the relationship between this evangelical vision of a world transformed by grace, and the cultures of both imperial Britain, on the one hand, and the wider world which Carey was to encounter in India, on the other.

In respect of mission and imperialism, the reaction of the authorities to the prospect that Baptists belonging to the tradition of John Bunyan might take up residence in India speaks for itself. The essayist Sydney Smith warned

---

15. Jonathan Edwards, *The Works of Jonathan Edwards*, vol. 2 (London: Westley & Davis, 1834), 279.

16. William Carey, *An Enquiry into the Obligations of Christians to Use Means for the Conversion of the Heathens* (Didcot: Baptist Missionary Society, 1991 [1792]), 32.

that the upsurge of evangelical religion in the eighteenth century bore the same marks as the last "eruption of fanaticism" which, a century and a half before, had "destroyed both Church and Throne with its tremendous force." The thought that Baptist missions might operate in the colonies was horrifying to Smith and he warned that if the British were to "teach the natives a better religion, we must take care to do it in a manner that will not inspire them with a passion for political change."[17] The message was clear: Baptists in the colonies would be subversive of British imperial interests.

Which brings us to ask: how did the mission, once established with its base at Serampore, relate to that cultural context? With regard to the religious situation, shaped by ancient Hindu traditions, the correspondence between Carey and his supporters in Britain suggests that they demonstrated remarkable humility and sensitivity, and that the first priority was to *learn* – to master new languages, understand cultural traditions and priorities, and respect and serve local people. William Ward, whom we mentioned above, standing on the deck of his ship as it at last approached Calcutta, uttered a statement which reflected this determination to identify with an Asian people and their culture: "I have already longed to be a converted Hindoo. I feel pleased with the idea of spending my life with the gentle and placid Hindoo."[18]

Twenty years later, with the wealth of experience he had gained from immersion in the host culture and language, Ward responded to an enquirer from Britain that true understanding of another religion can only come about as the result of the respect and sincere friendship which allows the conversation partner to share his or her deeply held beliefs. "Statements made by

---

17. Sydney Smith, *The Works of the Rev. Sydney Smith* (London: Longmans, Green, Reader & Dyer, 1869), 112. It must be stressed that in the late seventeenth century, dissenting congregations were by their very nature radical organizations. The Duchess of Buckingham heard George Whitefield preach and declared that evangelical doctrine "was strongly tinctured with impertinence and disrespect towards superiors, in perpetually endeavouring to level all ranks and do away with all distinctions."

18. PA II (1801), 11. Ward uses the term "Hindoo" in a broad cultural sense to mean the non-Muslim population of Bengal. Brian Stanley has written the definitive history of the Baptist Missionary Society and concludes that, while the initial apologetic of Carey and his colleagues was "uncompromising and even confrontational," their approach was moderated by experience as they recognized "the wisdom of a more positive evangelistic approach." Stanley concludes that while "the Serampore pioneers were more prepared than many later missionaries to see good qualities in Hindu culture, their essential conviction remained that Hinduism was a religion of darkness waiting for the light of the Christian gospel to dawn" (*The History of the Baptist Missionary Society, 1792–1992* [Edinburgh: T&T Clark, 1992], 46–47).

themselves will be more correct than what you can find in books; and in gaining the relation from one on whom the system has made a strong impression, you will find matter for thought, for sermons, for prayer, which you could obtain by no other means."[19] This approach predates the much later development of the methodology which was to be used in anthropological research, and it takes us by surprise to discover in the early nineteenth century the practice which missiologists were much later to describe as "contextualization"!

Finally, there is one piece of evidence that, above all others, reveals the extent to which this remarkable group of early Baptist missionaries demonstrated the liberating power of the kingdom of God, first in the sight of the "humble poor" of India for whom they poured out their lives in service, but also in stark contrast to the behaviour of their British compatriots, whose motivation for being on the subcontinent was invariably that of personal enrichment. The "Form of Agreement" drawn up in 1805 and unanimously affirmed by all members of the Serampore missionary community contained the following commitment to a way of life which involved economic equality:

> Let us ever shut out the idea of laying up even a cowry for ourselves or our children. If we give up the resolution that was formed on the subject of private trade when we first united at Serampore, the mission is from that hour a lost cause. . . . Woe to that man who shall ever make the smallest movement toward such a measure! . . . No private family ever enjoyed a greater portion of happiness, even in the most prosperous gale of worldly prosperity, than we have done since we resolved to have all things in common, and that no one should pursue business for his own exclusive advantage.[20]

This radical commitment to what looks like a form of Christian communism, reflecting both the pattern of the primitive church in the book of Acts and the monastic communities of the medieval period, created tensions when critics from England voiced suspicions that the missionaries were "rolling in affluence." Joshua Marshman reacted to such criticisms with some bitterness:

---

19. PA II (1801), 15.
20. PA III (1806), 210–11.

> Think then, how I must feel, while engaged in these circumstances, to recollect that there are any *Christians* to be found in my country, who refuse to stir a finger towards this great work, and perhaps treat it with contempt.... Not that the Saviour needs the help of any; the cause will go on whether those around **** ever contribute to its support or not.[21]

Historian Brian Stanley has discussed this tragic controversy in detail, concluding that it arose from the fact that the apostolic practice at Serampore "was founded on fundamental principle, and not merely on economic necessity."[22]

From the perspective of the subject of this present book, the "Form of Agreement" of the Serampore community is evidence of a renewed commitment to take the example and teaching of Jesus seriously, and we must wonder whether the negative reaction to it from British Christians was the result of the profound challenge it posed to the way of life emerging there as the result of the "great transformation" which we have described as taking place in Europe. We may also add that the simplicity of life to which the Serampore group committed themselves was to leave its impress upon the modern missionary movement in the future, and this aspect of Christian praxis in the sphere of economics continued to be both a puzzle and a challenge in a culture increasingly in thrall to the idolatry of Mammon.

Resistance, Reform, Renewal

Between Carey's *Enquiry* of 1792 and the outbreak of the First World War in 1914, huge changes occurred, including within British Christianity. The nature of that change can be seen in the spirit of optimism which pervaded the World Missionary Conference in Edinburgh in 1910 where, according to Brian Stanley, the voice most audible in the public sessions "was one of boundless optimism and unsullied confidence in the ideological and financial power of western Christendom."[23] That confidence, and its relationship

---

21. PA III (1806), 120. The asterisks in this quotation are in the original, presumably inserted by Andrew Fuller to avoid offending supporters in the town that Marshman had named!

22. Stanley, *History of the Baptist Missionary Society*, 57.

23. Brian Stanley, *The World Missionary Conference, Edinburgh 1910* (Grand Rapids: Eerdmans, 2009), 16. As early as 1815 William Ward had lamented the changes he observed in British Christianity: "We hear incessant references made, with a degree of pride, to institutions

to what has been described as the imperial plunder of the 1880s, is revealed even more starkly in sermons preached at this time, including the following which was delivered at the annual meetings of the Baptist Missionary Society in 1896:

> The united energies, faith and wealth of Great Britain and the United States, if intelligently directed, should be able in a few years to conquer heathen darkness, and bring all earthly principalities into loyal and loving devotion to Christ. . . . As the flags of the two living nations blend together, let us bathe them in the splendour of the Cross of Christ; and as they move together about the globe, let us see to it that between them and over them ever gleams the Cross.[24]

This is not simply a case of mission becoming an accomplice to imperial power but, even more shockingly, *that power itself is identified as the agent of mission*, bathed "in the splendour of the Cross of Christ." Six years later J. A. Hobson was to publish a study of imperialism which became widely read and remains influential as a critique of the source and practice of Western colonialism. Hobson recognized that many people in Victorian Britain felt "a genuine desire to spread Christianity among the heathen," and that most British missionaries were "untainted with admixture of political and commercial motives." They did not desire "to push British trade or 'sanctify the spirit of imperialism,'" but no one should be surprised that "the selfish forces which direct Imperialism" would seek to "utilise the protective colours of these disinterested movements." Politicians, soldiers and company directors, Hobson said, "instinctively attach themselves to any strong, elevated feeling which is of service, fan it and feed it until it assumes fervour, and utilise it

---

without number for removing human ignorance and bringing in the millennium; but oh! how little reference to that agency without which all these mighty operations are doomed to terminate in a mere exhibition of human imbecility and derision from the powers of darkness." He deplored the spirit of the annual missionary gatherings in London which had become "a religious jubilee" celebrated with "the feelings of conquerors." (From a volume titled *Farewell Letters* published in London in 1821.)

24. G. C. Lorrimer, *Missionary Sermons, 1812–1924: A Selection from the Discourses Delivered on Behalf of the Baptist Missionary Society on Various Occasions* (London: Carey Kingsgate, 1924), 182.

for their ends."²⁵ Alas, in the case of the sermon quoted above, the use of the fan was scarcely required since in this instance imperial power had already been baptized in the service of mission!

The question which arises here is of momentous importance to the subject of this book: *how and why did British Christianity change in the course of the nineteenth century so that it not only used the spread of imperial power to facilitate its mission, but at times embraced colonialism as itself a component of that mission?*²⁶ The nineteenth century witnessed a long, often bitter, series of struggles between the forces driven by the ideology of improvement, which "pressed forward for boundless and unregulated change in society," and movements of resistance, both from those who suffered the social consequences of the "great transformation," and by social reformers and political activists who were appalled by the human costs paid among the expanding populations of the urban poor. Polanyi, looking back on the social history of this critical period, comments that "a deep-seated movement sprang into being to resist the pernicious effects of a market-controlled economy," and he argues that without such "protective counter-moves," human society "would have been annihilated."²⁷

Christian voices were prominent in that "deep-seated movement" and they arose from the conviction that resistance to the injustices which they observed arising from the application of the ideology of the self-regulating market was demanded of them as disciples of Jesus Christ. Their stance frequently met with opposition from congregations within the rising middle class within which new denominations emerged among people whose wealth and property was a consequence of their professional activity within the market system.

Let us consider a few examples, beginning in Scotland with Thomas Guthrie (1802–73). An outstanding preacher in a country that produced

---

25. J. A. Hobson, *Imperialism: A Study of the History, Politics and Economics of the Colonial Powers in Europe and America* ([N.p.]: Adansonia Press, 2018 [1902]), 124–27.

26. Lesslie Newbigin, himself a major player in the missionary movement, wrote that Christian missions shared in the global expansion of Western political, commercial and military power and "were, in fact, among the main carriers of the ideas of the Enlightenment into other countries. Through their schools, universities, hospitals, and training programs, they made widely available the new way of understanding the human situation. They were (in very many cases) quite happy to see their work as part of the civilizing mission of Europe" (*Proper Confidence: Faith, Doubt and Certainty in Christian Discipleship* [Grand Rapids: Eerdmans, 1995], 33).

27. Polanyi, *Great Transformation*, 79–80.

a galaxy of great preachers, he is remembered to this day by a statue to be found on Princes Street in Edinburgh, describing him as "The friend of the poor and oppressed." Around the midpoint of the nineteenth century Guthrie preached a series of sermons on Luke 19:41 with the title "The City: its sins and its sorrows." He made clear his view that urbanization should not be regarded as an evil, despite the fact that its present form resulted in terrible hardships for many of the city's inhabitants. The city streets may be places where "the most daring and active wickedness" takes place, but they are also the location of "diligent, zealous, warm-hearted and devoted" Christianity, and Guthrie praises God that urbanization holds enormous potential for human well-being. He extols the beauty of Edinburgh, where "two distant ages gaze at each other across the intervening valley," and where there "seems nothing here to weep for." However, the preacher had regularly walked the streets of Edinburgh after dark, entering areas that were completely unknown to his middle-class congregation, and he had undertaken meticulous research concerning the plight of the excluded and despairing sector of the population of Scotland's capital.

> As a man, as well as a minister of that blessed gospel that recognizes no distinction between rich and poor, I protest against the wrongs of a class that are to the full as unfortunate as they are guilty. They deserve succor rather than censure ... and I wish to know why the upper classes of society should enjoy from the legislature a protection denied to those who stand more in need of it? ... People wonder that there is so much crime. If they saw what some of us have seen ... they would still wonder, but wonder that there was so little crime. To expect from those who have been reared in darkest ignorance, and in a very hot bed of temptations, anything else but crime, is sheer folly.[28]

Guthrie was acutely aware of a *social* problem that was blighting the city of Edinburgh, and he believed that here, no less than in London and Glasgow, the yawning gulf between rich and poor was visibly eroding the very foundations of civilized existence. In his pulpit ministry Guthrie identified the urban

---

28. Thomas Guthrie, *The City: Its Sins and Sorrows; Being a Series of Sermons from Luke XIX.41*, Michigan Historical Reprint Series (New York: Robert Carter & Brothers, 1857), 112–13, 134.

crisis which sociologists were later to discuss at length, and he warned his middle-class congregants that without political action to address the erosion of societal values, the future appeared bleak.

> Let that continue – let this undermining process go on till *a convulsion come*, and no power on earth can prevent the pyramid from toppling over.... The upper classes should know – God grant that they may not learn the lesson when it is too late! – that whatever be the distance between them, no elevation separates their interests from the lowest people.... Those who neglect the interests of others shall themselves suffer in the end.[29]

Guthrie's bold preaching was backed up by action: the statue referred to above depicts a poor child sheltered within the minister's long cloak, a reference to his founding of "ragged schools" which provided a haven and a basic education for children from the slums.

In England at almost exactly the same period we find a preacher/activist who took some pleasure when he learned that a journalist had described him as a "strolling agitator." This is Edward Miall (1809–81) whose work seems to have gone largely unnoticed in studies of this period. I discovered his *The British Churches in Relation to the British People* (1849) almost by accident and realized that I had stumbled upon treasure![30] Miall was acutely aware of the ambiguities of church growth and sensitive to the currents running in the wider culture which posed serious questions concerning the depth and authenticity of an expanding evangelical movement. Guthrie and Miall approached the problems of their age from contrasting theological positions, yet at many points their analyses and critiques overlapped. Here is Miall describing the nature of the class structure which was hardening into a serious fracture of the social body, and was increasingly reflected in denominational divisions within British Christianity:

---

29. Guthrie, *The City*, 164; emphasis added.

30. I have discussed Miall in *Transforming the World? The Social Impact of British Evangelicalism* (Carlisle: Paternoster; 2nd ed., Milton Keynes: Paternoster Digital Library, 2005), 34–38, and in "A Victorian Prophet without Honour: Edward Miall and the Critique of Nineteenth-Century British Christianity," in *Tales of Two Cities: Christianity and Politics*, ed. Stephen Clark (Leicester: Inter-Varsity Press, 2005), 152–83.

A machinery deliberately put together with a view to the political ascendency of only one order, an external form that is meant to give expression to the will of one class as paramount to that of all others, a structure that practically excludes the influence of the poor, and which, consequently, leaves them unprotected from the oppressive habits and exactions of the rich, legislation that is sure of siding with property against labour – magistracy which must needs be partial to the wealthy – institutions and forms of rule which help the powerful to crush the weak, instead of shielding the weak from the aggressions of the powerful . . .[31]

It may be suggested that Miall's political perspective is sharper, one might say more explicitly prophetic, than that of his Scottish contemporary, but underlying both men's approaches is the deep conviction that the abuses and injustices they were challenging resulted from the inexorable growth of the worship of Mammon. Guthrie lamented "a system of trade which offers up our children in sacrifice to the Moloch of money," while Miall challenged the "national exaltation of pounds sterling" which, he said, would result in a stagnant political system from which escape would be possible only when the truth "prominent everywhere in the Gospel" was recognized and acted upon, that "human nature is to be honoured rather than wealth – *that man comes before property*."[32]

However, in the book mentioned above, Edward Miall alerted Victorian Christianity to both the increasing encroachment of the love of money and possessions, and the disturbing reality of the churches' declining influence on significant sectors of British society. The book was published in the wake of the Chartist movement through which working people had demanded that

---

31. Edward Miall, *The Politics of Christianity* (London: Arthur Miall, 1863), 63. Miall's comment on the class bias inherent within the British political system is confirmed in C. B. Macpherson's history of liberal democracy in which he observes that Jeremy Bentham conceded "manhood franchise" only when he "had become persuaded that the poor would not use their votes to level or destroy property." Thus, the "founding model of democracy" in no way viewed it as "a morally transformative force," but was based on the assumption "that man is an infinite consumer . . . and a national society is simply a collection of such individuals" (*The Life and Times of Liberal Democracy* [Oxford: Oxford University Press, 1977], 37, 43).

32. Miall, *Politics of Christianity*, 71; emphasis original. Guthrie's reference to "the Moloch of money" comes in a passage in which he asserts that the modern system of trade builds fortunes on "the ruins of public morality and domestic happiness." *The City: Its Sins and Sorrows*, 145.

the churches identify with their quest for basic justice, only to be rejected and humiliated by churchgoers who bemoaned the invasion of their pews by people lacking the respectability of appropriate clothing! The Chartist movement has been described as an attempt by poor people to articulate a counter-Christianity "which would deliver the religion of Jesus Christ from the disgrace brought upon it and ensure its continued credibility with working people."[33] The rejection of the Chartist demands in 1839, and the humiliation its advocates suffered when preachers in parish churches across the land delivered sermons thundering against their actions, resulted in the increased alienation of the poor from congregations which had confirmed by their deeds that they served the interests of the privileged segment of British society. Miall attempted to counter the damage done to Christianity by seeking conversations with Chartist leaders, and he directed his prophetic ire towards established religion:

> Religion as embodied in the written word of God, and in that more emphatic living Word which "was made flesh and dwelt among us," uniformly champions the cause of the weak, the friendless, the oppressed – religion, embodied in modern organizations, preaches up the rights of the powerful, and dwells mainly upon the obligations of the powerless. . . . Once, her favourite occupation was to move as an angel of love and mercy among outcasts, to breathe hope into the spirits of the desponding, to wipe away tears as they rolled down the cheeks of the neglected . . . and when her impulses or duties took her among the great, her theme of discourse was the vanity of perishable honours and possessions. . . . In our day . . . she is more at home with the comfortable, than with the wretched.[34]

Remarkable as Miall's critical analysis of the condition of Christianity in Victorian Britain was, even more unusual was his attitude towards colonialism. He wrote a series of articles in the 1840s which were later published

---

33. See Eileen Yeo, "Christianity in Chartist Struggle: 1838–1842," *Past and Present* 91 (May 1981): 109–39. I discuss the Chartist movement in *Transforming the World?*, 30–34.

34. Edward Miall, *The British Churches in Relation to the British People* (London: Arthur Hall, Virtue & Co., 1849), 203–4. In these paragraphs I have drawn upon my "A Victorian Prophet without Honour," Clark (ed), *Tales of Two Cities: Christianity and Politics* (Leicester: Inter-Varsity Press 2005): 1152–183.

as *The Politics of Christianity* in 1863. In the fevered atmosphere which followed the Great Exhibition, claimed by Prince Albert to point towards "the realization of the unity of mankind," Miall had the temerity to point out "the crimes" that had given the British control over a large part of the planet! The acquisition of the colonies had repeatedly involved "fraud, injustice, cruelty, and fiend-like atrocity such as few could read without mingled indignation and shame."[35] The same compassion which he showed towards the poor and oppressed in the slums of British cities was now directed towards the millions of "aboriginal peoples on the other side of the world." Miall insisted that they too were human beings, made in the image of God and requiring protection "from oppression by the colonists." In perhaps one of his most remarkable statements, Miall says that Christianity "nowhere gives countenance to the modern pretence that civilization may trample on barbarism, strength prey on weakness, or white-complexioned humanity play havoc with black." In an extraordinary conclusion, he muses on what the future might look like in the colonies and concludes that in the coming centuries there could be developments in those distant lands "that will provide a 'fresh start' for humanity." In remote regions of the world, untouched by the negative aspects of modern civilization, we might anticipate the emergence of new forms of society operating a different model of social life in preparation for "those glorious triumphs of the moral over the material which we are taught to expect will signalize the mature age of this our world."[36]

As a footnote to this brief summary of Miall's work it is worth pointing out that the material in *The British Churches in Relation to the British People* was originally intended as a series of lectures to be delivered in the Exeter Hall in London, the gathering place for the annual May meetings which drew thousands of evangelicals for celebrations of missionary work around the world. However, when the committee got sight of an outline of the content of the lectures, they took fright and withdrew permission for the premises to be used for this purpose. Does this tragic rejection of the prophetic voice we have just heard suggest the emergence of a form of Christianity which was to result in the kinds of views found in the sermon mentioned at the

---

35. Miall, *Politics of Christianity*, 147.
36. Miall, 143.

start of this section, bathing the flags of Western nations "in the splendour of the Cross of Christ"?

We have listened to two Christian voices within the "deep-seated movement" of resistance to the imposition of the ideology of the free market in the nineteenth century. If we broaden the focus on this movement, it is possible to identify three strands which interacted with each other, yet made distinctive contributions both in service to the deprived and in the development of the vision of an alternative form of industrial society. The first of these strands we may identify as *the growth of urban missions*. City Missions sprang up, first in Glasgow, then spreading to other cities, with the London City Mission developing significant work and, in the process, gaining detailed knowledge of actual conditions in the capital's East End. Andrew Mearns's *Bitter Cry of Outcast London*, which we mentioned above, brought to public attention a body of shocking information concerning the squalor in which huge numbers of Londoners lived and his sources included the agents of the London City Mission and the Baptist minister of the East London Tabernacle, Archibald Brown.

In its turn, the *Bitter Cry* played a significant role in the lives of William and Catherine Booth, founders of the Salvation Army, and its influence can be traced in Booth's own work, *In Darkest England and the Way Out* (1890). The title was clearly intended to be provocative, both by challenging negative presuppositions concerning Africa, and in puncturing imperialist arrogance regarding the state of Britain itself. Here is Booth, revealing the extent to which his own understanding of evangelism and mission had undergone change as a direct consequence of the encounter with the disabilities and tragedies resulting from multiple deprivation in London's East End:

> The bastard of a harlot, born in a brothel, suckled on gin, and familiar from earliest infancy with all the bestialities of debauch, violated before she is twelve, and driven out into the streets by her mother a year or two later, what chance is there for such a girl in this world – I say nothing about the next?[37]

---

37. William Booth, *In Darkest England and the Way Out* (London: Salvation Army, 1890), 13.

William Booth was aware of growing political demands for change (he had arrived in London in the same year that Karl Marx took up residence in the city), and he recognized the importance of political action to respond to the conditions he encountered. A social structure that had resulted in a "waste continent of humanity," three million enslaved people "from Plymouth to Peterhead," and a poor-law system which gave the unemployed a night's shelter in exchange for stone-breaking, was "an outrage which, if we read of it occurring in Russia or Siberia would find Exeter Hall crowded with an indignant audience."[38] Booth was explicit in his opposition to unbridled capitalism and declared his strong support for "the principle of co-operation," but his passionate commitment to activism made him suspicious of utopian visions of future social transformation.

> The individualist tells me that the free play of Natural Laws governing the struggle for existence will result in the Survival of the Fittest, and that in the course of a few ages . . . a much nobler type will be evolved. But meanwhile what is to become of John Jones? The Socialist tells me that the great Social Revolution is looming large on the horizon. In the good times coming . . . all stomachs will be filled. . . . It may be so, but in the meantime here is John Jones growing more impatient than ever because hungrier, who wonders if he is to wait for a dinner until the Social Revolution has arrived. What are we to do with John Jones?[39]

The second strand in the Christian response to the social impact of free market ideology may be described as *municipal regeneration*. This involved the development of a social gospel, or even a "municipal gospel," through which distinguished preachers with large, middle-class congregations urged upon their hearers active engagement in local politics to bring about substantial change in the very fabric and appearance of the city. Asa Briggs has told the story of what he describes as "the vast accumulation of social capital which the Victorians raised," resulting in "a huge development of public offices, hospitals, schools, sewage farms and water works." Preachers in cities such as Birmingham, Manchester and Glasgow developed a "municipal gospel"

---

38. Booth, *In Darkest England*, 70.
39. Booth, 77–78.

through which they urged their middle-class hearers to become involved in local politics and apply the message of Christ to the urgent practical issues of the times. Here is R. W. Dale, minister of Carrs Lane Church in Birmingham from 1854 to 1895:

> The gracious words of Christ, "Inasmuch as ye did it unto one of these my brethren, even the least, ye did it unto me," will be addressed not only to those who with their own hands fed the hungry, and clothed the naked, and cared for the sick, but to those who supported a municipal policy which lessened the miseries of the wretched and added brightness to the life of the desolate.[40]

Urged on by such ministers, middle-class Christians in Glasgow stood for election to the city council, took control of local politics, and raised taxes to fund the creation of a supply of safe drinking water to the city's population, so bringing to an end the frequent outbreaks of cholera which had decimated the slums. The fruits of such transformations resulting from the "municipalization" of local services and the creation of facilities providing efficient administration, care of the sick, education and access to the arts are still visible on urban skylines from Bristol to Aberdeen, with town halls, libraries, museums and hospitals prominent.

The third strand of resistance concerns the emergence and development of *new visions of what an industrial society might become when the relationship between politics and economics was re-envisaged by the demands of truth and justice*. This involved a move beyond the previously mentioned responses in that it required both a serious critical examination of the underlying causes of the divisions between rich and poor in a modern society, and a credible concept of an alternative social model, capable of providing the foundation for a new and transformative politics. The sources of such a vision came both from the rising movements of protest and rebellion from below, and from among Christian intellectuals in privileged positions who recognized that their confession of the truth of the gospel compelled them to resist the idolatry of Mammon and work towards a new kind of society shaped by

---

40. Quoted in Asa Briggs, *Victorian Cities* (London: Penguin, 1968), 201. See also Tristram Hunt, *Building Jerusalem: The Rise and Fall of the Victorian City* (London: Phoenix, 2004).

justice and love. It is not possible here to trace the history of this movement in detail, but I want to identify representative figures from contrasting social backgrounds who played key roles in the decades-long struggle to discover and enact an alternative vision of a modern society.

Keir Hardie was born in 1856 in a mining village in the west of Scotland and grew up in a home constantly overshadowed by illness, debt and suffering. As a boy he was sent out to earn money, becoming the only lifeline for a home in which repeated tragedies left his parents destitute and despairing. He found employment with a baker whom he later described as "a leading light in the religious life of the city of Glasgow." One morning, having been nursing his dying brother, Hardie arrived late for work and was summoned upstairs to the baker's family living room. He described being kept waiting outside the door while the owner said grace, and when admitted he found the master and his family seated around a large table "loaded with food and beautiful things."[41] In the presence of the family the boy was humiliated by a lecture on the "sin of sloth" and warned that any recurrence would result in instant dismissal. Two days later, his brother's condition worsening, he came late again and the threat was carried out with two weeks' outstanding wages withheld as a punishment. The young Hardie was overwhelmed by the harshness of his employer and considered committing suicide. In time he recovered from this experience but it contributed to the development of a burning passion for social justice, a deep loathing of religious hypocrisy, and an unrelenting search for an alternative understanding of both the Bible and the gospel from that which had driven the actions of his heartless employer.[42]

The subsequent life and work of Keir Hardie as a militant activist seeking justice for working people, his role as founder of the Independent Labour Party and his courage seen in his speeches as a Member of Parliament have led to him being described as "a prophet of a new social order."[43] Hardie

---

41. The description is from A. Fenner Brockway, "James Keir Hardie (1856–1915)," in *Christian Social Reformers of the Nineteenth Century*, ed. Hugh Martin (London: SCM, 1933), 229.

42. I have here drawn upon my *The Kindness of God: Christian Witness in a Troubled World* (Nottingham: Inter-Varsity Press 2013), 114–18.

43. This is the conclusion of his leading biographer, Kenneth O. Morgan, who goes on to claim that Hardie was "a secular prophet in an age of waning faith" (*Keir Hardie: Radical and Socialist* [London: Phoenix, 1977], 289). The description ignores the profound influence of Christ and his teaching on Hardie's life and work, and it overlooks the testimony of his friend

was as courageous in the clarity and consistency of his resistance to the prevailing orthodoxy of "political economy" as he was in constantly challenging the comfortable, middle-class churches whose emasculated gospel appeared to support this system. In 1892 he was present at an assembly of Congregational ministers in Bradford and heard a speaker claiming that he had said in Parliament that "Christianity was dead" and he was glad of this! Amid the uproar which followed, Hardie rose to defend himself:

> What he had said was that the Christianity of the schools was dead, and that the Christianity of Christ was coming to the front.... The reason the Labour Party had turned its back upon the Church was because the Church had turned its back on them [No, No]. They got respectable congregations on Sunday and preached to please respectability [Cries of No. No.] But they did [Cries of No. No. and "It is false."] They forgot the writhing and suffering mass of humanity outside the walls of their churches [Voices, No. No.] In the slums of the cities, men, women and children made in the image of God were being driven down to hell for all eternity, and they had no helping hand stretched out for them [Cries of "It is false" and interruption.]

The appeals of the chairman that the speaker be allowed a fair hearing were drowned out by a chorus of opposition and "amid some confusion Mr. Keir Hardie left the platform."[44] Hardie, although unconventional in many ways, was fiercely critical of formal Christianity and of the prevailing political culture, but his prophetic voice announced that the "hidden masses" would no longer accept servility and gross injustice, since they had begun to catch sight of a pathway to a better society of justice and equality.

The social and intellectual background of Richard Henry Tawney could hardly be more different from that of Hardie. Born in Calcutta in 1880, where his father was a Sanskrit scholar, he was educated at Balliol College, Oxford, where he established a close friendship with William Temple, later to become a much-respected archbishop of Canterbury. Tawney was to play a major role

---

Fenner Brockway, who said that, heartbroken by the tragedy of the First World War, Hardie confessed near the end of his life that, if he could live again, he would devote his life "to the advocacy of the Gospel of Christ" ("James Keir Hardie," 239).

44. "The Congregational Union at Bradford," *The British Weekly*, 13 October 1892, 401.

in the development of Christian Socialism, particularly at the level of the intellectual foundations of a serious critique of free market economics. He dared to imagine the values, structures and policy priorities of a new kind of social state in which economics would be reconciled with morality and would serve social ends.

Tawney loathed war, but news of German atrocities in France in 1914 led him to believe that he had a moral duty to enlist, a decision which nearly cost him his life as he was seriously wounded in the Battle of the Somme in 1916. The experience heightened his sense of the corruption and vulnerability of European culture, while at the same time strengthening his profound conviction of the urgency for radical sociopolitical change. Readers of this book will have recognized my debt to Tawney's work, especially with regard to his masterly *Religion and the Rise of Capitalism* (1926). He had previously published *The Acquisitive Society* (1920), and in 1931 completed *Equality*, the three titles together providing perhaps the most significant contribution to the interwar debates concerning the political future. They became much-studied texts within the growing Labour movement.

Tawney's Christianity was understated but nonetheless a pervasive influence on his thought and actions. It provided a spiritual depth to his analysis, both of the evil entailed in the false image of the human being as a purely economic creature, and of the destructive consequences of what amounted to a hideous form of idolatry. He was not only a brilliant scholar, but a fine teacher who devoted considerable time and energy to the Workers Educational Association (WEA), later confessing that he had himself learned much through interaction with working people. Keir Hardie would have been delighted to hear Tawney describe Labour socialism as "an ethically based working class phenomenon helped by intellectuals and officials, not the other way around."

> The impulse behind the movement has been obstinately and unashamedly ethical. The revolt of ordinary men against Capitalism has had its source neither in its obvious deficiencies as an economic engine, nor in the conviction that it represents a stage of social evolution now outgrown, but in the straightforward hatred of a system which stunts personality and corrupts

human relations by permitting the use of man by man as an instrument of pecuniary gain.[45]

The influence of Tawney's faith on the shaping of his distinctive understanding of socialism, and of the path to achieving it, can be seen most clearly in his conviction that "English society was too sick with economic egotism to make the transition smoothly." Since social transformation required limits on incomes, "ordinary people had to be weaned from the assiduously nurtured fantasy of becoming rich." Political action would be fruitless unless it was accompanied by the ability to *imagine* "a society not stoked by the corrupt luxury tastes of the rich." The building of a new and different kind of community demanded more than isolated political action and would require the elimination of "the poison of greed and insatiable acquisitiveness fuelling British capitalism."

> [Society] must rearrange its scale of values. It must regard economic interests as one element in life, not as the whole of life. It must persuade its members to renounce the opportunity of gains which accrue without any corresponding service, because the struggle for them keeps the whole community in a fever. It must so organize industry that the instrumental character of economic activity is emphasized by its subordination to the social purpose for which it is carried on.[46]

The language Tawney used to describe the radical nature of the change that would be required to reject the acquisitive society and replace it with a community in which wealth was redefined in terms of its social ends, and of the well-being of both the neighbour and the whole created world, would seem to demand a transformation very much like that which the Bible describes as *conversion*. Tawney does not use this language, perhaps because he wished to distance himself from the highly individualistic and narrowly spiritual manner in which Christians were inclined to present it in their evangelistic activity at the time. We may ask, however, whether Tawney was in fact far closer to a genuine understanding of the vision found within the New

---

45. Quoted by Gary Dorrien, *Social Democracy in the Making: Political and Religious Roots of European Socialism* (New Haven: Yale University Press, 2019), 437.

46. Quoted by Dorrien, *Social Democracy*, 362.

Testament itself than were those who made "conversion" central to their proclamation yet emptied the term of the profoundly challenging implications it contained in the book of Acts and the Pauline letters. Here is Tawney's challenging conclusion concerning the "acquisitive society":

> It assures men that there are no ends other than their ends, no law other than their desires, no limit other than that which they think advisable. Thus it makes the individual the centre of his own universe, and dissolves moral principles into a choice of expediencies.... Under the impulse of such ideas men do not become religious or wise or artistic; for religion and wisdom and art imply the acceptance of limitations. But they become powerful and rich. They inherit the earth and change the face of nature, if they do not possess their own souls; and they have that appearance of freedom which consists in the absence of obstacles between opportunities for self-advancement and those whom birth or wealth or talent or good fortune has placed in a position to seize them.[47]

Tawney lived to see the post-war Labour landslide electoral victory and the creation of a national social insurance system, a publicly funded National Health Service, and the building of a million new council houses. His own work had contributed to the intellectual underpinning of such programmes and until his death in 1962 he continued to plead that the true mission of Christian socialism was "to fight the idolatry of money and success." At his funeral in Highgate Cemetery, the then leader of the Labour Party, Hugh Gaitskell, praised him as "a believer in liberty and equality – *a man who loved his faith.*"[48]

---

47. R. H. Tawney, *The Acquisitive Society* (Lector House, 2022 [1920]), 16.

48. Dorrien, *Social Democracy*, 407; emphasis added. In a fine recent biography of Tawney, Lawrence Goldman discusses his Christianity and its relationship with his socialism at length. He also observes that in 1928 Tawney attended a crucial meeting of the International Missionary Council in Jerusalem and "found himself drawn towards delegations representing the younger Christian churches in colonized areas like India, China, Africa and the Philippines whose theology, politics and language interested him greatly." Tawney commented that Christians from "emerging nations" had discovered "a distinctive conception of Christianity" which contrasted strongly with European civilization, and that the established relations between Europe and non-European countries "are contrary to the nature of things *and are no longer tenable.*" While Christianity in the West appeared to be "soporific," in Africa and the East, "as in the Roman

The Cross and the Flag

Having surveyed the Christian contribution to the "deep-seated movement of resistance" to the acquisitive society, we must return to reflect on the language of those who regarded British imperialism as an ally in the task of world evangelization and talked, as we have seen, of bathing the flags of Britain and America "in the splendour of the Cross of Christ." Language of this kind reflected the significant cultural shifts which occurred during the closing decades of the nineteenth century, and it suggests that a change had taken place in the *social* character of the missionary movement in the course of that century.[49] The Great Exhibition, despite its critics, contributed to the growth of a fervent nationalism, while the conferring of the title "Empress of India" on Queen Victoria in 1877 further boosted the imperial ideology, and consolidated a new sense of British identity associated with a national mission to extend the blessings of civilization to the rest of the world.[50] The extraordinary journey of H. M. Stanley down the full length of the mighty River Congo disclosed the immense riches which lay at the heart of Africa and triggered the infamous "scramble" for colonies at the Berlin Conference of 1884. This vast continent was to be parcelled out among the European powers, with Britain and France claiming approximately four million square miles each, while Portugal, Spain and Italy all staked their claims to ensure their colonial presence in Africa. Within a quarter of a century, Western political control of Africa had expanded from one-tenth of its land mass, to a situation in which by 1900 virtually the entire continent fell under European governance.

The growth of the ideology of empire was further boosted by the impact of evolutionary thought, especially when this came to be applied to the history of

---

Empire, it appears to have some of the qualities of an explosive" (*The Life of R. H. Tawney: Socialism and History* [London: Bloomsbury Academic, 2014], 147).

49. In 1810 supporters of William Carey in England had composed a poem which began with these lines: "Whilst some the song to chiefs and patriots raise / With nobler theme I loftier spirits praise" (PA IV [1810], 257).

50. See Nicholas Boyle's comment: "As the modern sense of nationhood came to be established, Britain found its national identity and purpose not through internal constitutional conflict leading to revolution – the European norm – but through acquiring and running an overseas Empire" (*Who Are We Now?*, 23). In 1872 Benjamin Disraeli presented a choice to the British people, either "to be a comfortable England," or to become "a great country – an imperial country – a country where your sons, when they rise, rise to paramount positions, and obtain not merely the esteem of their countrymen, *but command the respect of the world*" (quoted in Theodore Von Laue, *The World Revolution of Westernization: The Twentieth Century in Global Perspective* [Oxford: Oxford University Press, 1987], 16).

peoples and religions. Darwinian theory influenced the understanding of the development of the nations and their belief systems, with the result that sharp distinctions were drawn between "higher" and "lower" forms of social and religious life. The recently discovered tribal peoples of Africa were classified as "primitive" and "savage," and even described as "living fossils" whose behaviour confirmed both their "childishness" and, by contrast, European maturity and superiority.[51] The missionary movement was certainly not immune from such thinking, the prejudicial language with which indigenous peoples were identified as "animists" lasting long into the twentieth century and lingering even yet in some circles.

The achievements of Stanley attracted the attention of rulers and politicians across Europe, including King Leopold II of Belgium who had been seeking some way by which his small nation might have a share in the riches expected to flow northwards from the opening up of Africa. Eight years prior to the Berlin Conference, he had convened a Geographical Conference in Brussels to which he invited a swathe of notable people, including politicians, explorers and missionaries. Sir Thomas Fowell Buxton, famous as an anti-slavery activist and a well-known evangelical, was there, as was the president of the Church Missionary Society. Leopold's welcoming speech has been described as a masterpiece of diplomacy, concealing his ambitions beneath noble rhetoric which disavowed self-interest and claimed to be solely concerned to promote civilization in regions "it has not yet penetrated." "Need I say that in bringing you to Brussels I was guided by no egotism? No,

---

51. Edmund Leach described how the new discipline of anthropology was led by scholars who "rejected the unity of mankind postulated in the Bible in favour of a theory that there are a variety of man-like species *of which only the white-skinned European is a fully rational human being.*" He adds that this new, "arrogant and ethnocentric science . . . fitted perfectly with the ethos of the era of European colonial expansion and the westward movement of the American frontier, for it rested on the basic premise that all non-Europeans are stupid, childish, barbarous and servile by their very nature" (*Social Anthropology* [Glasgow: Fontana, 1982], 15–16; emphasis added). See Andrew Walls's discussion "Carrying the White Man's Burden: Some British Views of National Vocation in the Imperial Era," in his *The Cross-Cultural Process in Christian History: Studies in the Transmission and Appropriation of Faith* (Edinburgh: T&T Clark, 2002a), 177–93. He notes the great influence of Rudyard Kipling and concludes that his poetry promoted the pervasive view "of the special chosenness of Britain, the vision of a beneficent, worldwide British Empire of free, consenting partners revealed as part of the emerging purpose of history" (182).

gentlemen, Belgium may be a small country, but she is happy and satisfied with her fate; I have no other ambition than to serve her well."[52]

Here is the classic example of what J. A. Hobson meant when he argued that the forces of imperialism "attach themselves to any strong, genuine elevated feeling which is of service," and "utilise it for their ends." Once Leopold had obtained what he wanted when the Berlin Conference recognized his claim to a vast area of Central Africa, the mask began to drop and his real intentions became clear. He recruited Stanley as his agent in the Congo, writing that he wanted to create "a federation of free negro republics." The reality was an insatiable appetite for land and the riches it held. Leopold instructed the explorer to "purchase as much land as you will be able to obtain, and place successively under suzerainty . . . as soon as possible and without losing one minute, all the chiefs from the mouth of the Congo to the Stanley Falls."[53] Perhaps in imitation of Queen Victoria, he considered taking the title "Emperor of the Congo," and in May 1885 named what was to become a privately controlled country as the État indépendant du Congo, even providing it with a national anthem: "Towards the Future."[54]

What that future involved was a tragedy of indescribable proportions, involving a degree of human suffering which defies description, and which was to set in train a seemingly unending catastrophe which would eventually engulf the whole of Central Africa, and continues until today.[55] What happened in Africa in the closing decades of the nineteenth century, despite the ending of the triangular slave trade earlier in that century, was the

---

52. Adam Hochschild, *King Leopold's Ghost: A Story of Greed, Terror and Heroism in Colonial Africa* (London: Pan Books, 2012), 44–45.

53. Hochschild, *King Leopold's Ghost*, 70. Note Kevin Grant's comment: "In a fundamental sense, all systems of imperial taxation were built on the arrogation of land by European regimes, generally under the classic colonialist principle of *terra nullius*, or vacant land. Since the fifteenth century, European explorers had claimed land that was, to their eyes, uncultivated, undeveloped, and, thus, unoccupied. In this tradition, the imperialists of the late nineteenth century claimed ostensibly vacant African lands, then imposed taxes on the indigenous communities as just compensation for the privilege of living on the land" (*A Civilised Savagery: Britain and the New Slaveries in Africa, 1884-1926* [London: Routledge, 2005], 23).

54. Hochschild, 87.

55. Adam Hochschild's book tells this story with clarity and sympathy, while Jason K. Stearns's *Dancing in the Glory of Monsters: The Collapse of the Congo and the Great War of Africa* (New York: Public Affairs, 2011) brings the tragedy up to date, and Gerard Prunier's *Africa's World War: Congo, the Rwandan Genocide, and the Making of a Continental Catastrophe* (Oxford: Oxford University Press, 2010) is a detailed study of the wider impact of the Congo crisis across the continent.

reappearance of slavery under the disguise of "contract, or indentured, labour." In 1906 an observer commented: "While we have been dreaming of progress and benevolence, there has grown up among us a strange product, born of the union between greed and science, suckled on cynicism and schooled in the subtleties of the law. It is nothing less than a civilised savagery."[56]

The tragic story which unfolded in the Congo, and its wider impact both then and now, cannot be related here, except to notice Gerard Prunier's comment on the devastation which European imperialism wrought on a continent populated with clans and tribes for whom *society* was of fundamental concern, and the state "was a construct many could live without."

> Colonial European logic played havoc with that delicate cobweb of relationships. New borders were drawn not so much in violation of preexisting ones but according to a different logic. African borders had been porous membranes through which proto-nations were breathing, and the colonial borders that superseded them were of the pre-1914 cast-iron variety.... African social and cultural ways of doing things were neither taken into account nor questioned; they were simply *made obsolete*.... The Europeans rationalized African cultures to death.[57]

What we cannot avoid is the involvement of Christian missions in this context. King Leopold was careful to recognize the desire of British missionary societies to establish a string of bases, enabling the expansion of their work along the entire course of the River Congo, and he went to considerable lengths to cultivate missionary leaders, including Sir Hugh Gilzean Reid, a prominent Baptist, who was hosted in Brussels on a number of occasions and awarded the Knight Commander of the Order of the Crown. In 1903, an official delegation from the Baptist Missionary Society crossed the Channel to present Leopold with a "Memorial of Thanks," expressing the hope that "the people of the Congo may ever have the advantage of just and upright rule." This was despite the fact that from the mid 1880s, Baptist missionaries on the ground in the Congo were reporting terrible atrocities being committed by members of Leopold's Force Publique. One such missionary, George Grenfell,

---

56. Harold Spender, "The Great Congo Iniquity," *The Contemporary Review*, July 1906, 45; quoted on the opening page of Kevin Grant's *Civilised Savagery*.

57. Prunier, *Africa's World War*, xxix; emphasis added.

had seen clear evidence in January 1886 of the state's racist brutality, and privately derided the images of "peace and plenty" which Belgian propaganda was attempting to spread in Europe. Four years later he reported witnessing slaves chained neck to neck and the abduction of their women as hostages to be held until the menfolk paid a ransom for their release. However, he chose not to make this knowledge public, warning that the information was "strictly private and confidential" and must not be used to "publicly question the action of the State." According to Kevin Grant,

> the missions tolerated [state-sanctioned slavery] due to their dependence upon the state for security, transportation services, and African labour, which they received in exchange for taxes. Although the British missions made occasional protests to the state, they generally declined to protest publicly in Europe for fear that the state would expel them from the river.[58]

There were other Christians who refused to remain silent, and were vociferous in public protest in the face of the imperialist propaganda which attempted to conceal the scandal of the systematic violence perpetrated against tribal peoples. E. V. Sjöblom, a Swedish Baptist missionary, wrote frequently concerning the atrocities he had witnessed and, in a public meeting in London in 1897, described how members of Leopold's army were rewarded according to the number of severed African hands and feet they had collected. When photographic images of piles of severed hands, or of children lacking hands or feet, started to circulate in Britain, the public began to see beyond the smokescreen of imperial propaganda and recoiled at the horror taking place in the Congo. Even more significant was the work of an Afro-American missionary, William Sheppard, sent to the Congo in 1890 by the General Assembly of the Southern Presbyterian Church in the USA. There

---

58. Kevin Grant, *Civilised Savagery*, 45. Grant concludes: "At no time did the Protestant missions on the Congo establish a closely united front in opposition to the state's policies, nor did the majority of the brethren in any mission participate actively in public protests against the regime. It was only after years of failed attempts to expand inland that the executive of the Congo Balolo Mission condemned the Congo Free State in the British press in April, 1903, with the Baptist Missionary Society following suit in October, 1905" (47). In his history of the Baptist Missionary Society (BMS), Brian Stanley concludes that Leopold's policy in the Congo involved the sacrifice of indigenous peoples "on the altar of the white man's profits" and that the BMS "continued to defend Leopold against the mounting volume of criticism until 1905" (*History of the Baptist Missionary Society*, 135).

is irony in the fact that it was the activity of the white supremacist senator John Tylor Morgan, who had advocated American recognition of Leopold's Congo in the hope that slaves liberated in America would emigrate there, which made possible Sheppard's enlistment for missionary service. He arrived in the Congo with his colleague Samuel Lapsley, staying initially in the small town of Matadi at the very point at which an Englishman had just come ashore there and was preparing to move upstream: his name was Joseph Conrad.

Sheppard was the first black American to serve in mission in the Congo, and his approach to his task was markedly different from that of his white co-religionists, not least because of his sense of what might be called a homecoming: "I always wanted to live in Africa. . . . I felt that I would be happy, and so I am." He speaks of being glad to be among "my people" in "the country of my forefathers."[59] However, this joy was to be tempered by grief at the discovery of the horrors he witnessed in the rainforests bordering the River Kasai, where he had settled among the Kuba people. They had repeatedly repulsed the attempts of Belgian traders to enter their kingdom and Sheppard was the first foreigner to reach the town of Ifuca, where he became proficient in the local vernacular and studied a society possessing "one of central Africa's most sophisticated political systems."

Sheppard's arrival in Africa coincided with the invention of the pneumatic tyre and an explosion in the market for rubber which was to have disastrous consequences for peoples across the continent. Nowhere did this boom result in greater suffering than in the equatorial rainforests of Central Africa, and Sheppard witnessed columns of exhausted men, carrying grey baskets of rubber on their heads, "sometimes walking twenty miles or more to assemble near the houses of European agents, who sat on their verandas and weighed loads of rubber." Sheppard found his mission station overwhelmed with desperate refugees and was to witness the devastation of a local culture which he greatly admired. In 1908, he described the tragedy which befell the Kuba people:

> These great stalwart men and women, who have from time immemorial been free, cultivating large farms of Indian corn, peas, tobacco, potatoes, trapping elephants for their ivory tusks

---

59. Hochschild, *King Leopold's Ghost*, 154–55.

> and leopards for their skins, who have always had their own king and a government not to be despised. . . . These magnificent people . . . have entered a new chapter in the history of their tribe. Only a few years ago, travellers through this country found them . . . one of the most prosperous and intelligent of all African tribes. . . . But within these last three years how changed they are! Why this change? . . . There are armed sentries of chartered companies who force the men and women to spend most of their days and nights in the forests making rubber, and the price they receive is so meagre that they cannot live upon it.[60]

This article and Sheppard's frequent descriptions of the grave injustices inflicted upon tribal peoples were widely circulated and drew a hostile response from Leopold. The Compagnie du Kasai sued Sheppard for libel, demanding 80,000 francs in compensation. The trial took place in Leopoldville, six hundred miles from the Kasai homeland, and in a strange, manipulated verdict, Sheppard was declared not guilty, while the Compagnie was also vindicated.

The trial of William Sheppard brought news of the horrors which accompanied imperialism in the Congo to growing public attention and contributed to a renewed campaign against slavery. Baptist missionaries who had previously remained silent concerning the abuses they had witnessed now came to play a major role in this movement. In particular, John and Alice Harris, who had sailed for the Congo four days after their wedding in 1896, devoted themselves to working in the African interior, "before returning to Britain to become the most influential leaders of British anti-slavery in the first half of the twentieth century."[61] Their pioneering use of photographic evidence of atrocities in lectures delivered in "lantern-slide" meetings across Britain thrust the issue of reform in the Congo to the centre of British politics in the run-up to the General Election of 1906.

However, criticism of the abuses which had disfigured the Belgian colonial project did not imply that imperial rule elsewhere now became suspect. On the contrary, it served to enhance the British perception that their national mission was based upon the union of commerce and Christianity, so that the

---

60. Hochschild, 261.
61. Kevin Grant, *Civilized Savagery*, 31.

horrors of the Congo threw into sharp relief what may be termed "British exceptionalism." This involved the belief that Protestant Christianity, reshaped by the evangelical movement of the late nineteenth century, could harness the power of an industrial, capitalist culture to serve moral ends and result in the positive transformation of Africa and the world. This belief in the providential role of British imperialism gained fresh impetus as Europe moved towards the First World War, when it came to be contrasted not only with the catastrophe of the Congo, but with what was now depicted as Germany's greed and violence. Evangelicals such as John Harris argued that British commerce could serve distinctly Christian objectives, supplanting and destroying immoral trades, including the slave trade. They also suggested that colonization would establish "a British material culture and thus facilitate cultural assimilation to a civilized model," creating consumer desire for British goods and a Protestant work ethic within wage-earning economies. Alice Harris toured British Army camps during the First World War lecturing the troops on subjects such as "Britain's Coloured Colonial Children" and "The Triumph of Christian Imperialism." She celebrated the benevolence of the British Empire and contrasted it with the dismal record of other European nations, insisting that the cardinal principle of British colonization was that of service, whereas the colonizing activities of other European powers had been "primarily and very largely, colonization in the material interests of the motherland."[62] In 1917 John Harris published *Germany's Lost Colonial Empire* in which he argued that, while Britain's expansion had been driven by "a genuine desire to seek the good of the inhabitants over which Britain's flag was hoisted," the motive of German imperial policy was blatantly selfish, and justified the claim that the rich resources of their colonies in Africa were "waiting to be tapped by a more effective and just British administration."[63]

---

62. Grant, *A Civilized Savagery*, 144. Note the comment of Vinoth Ramachandra that Protestantism was "profoundly changed" when co-opted into imperialist discourse. "For many Victorian Christians, British gunboats were the agents of the divine will. Massive blind spots paralyzed an evangelical challenge to the evils committed by colonial governments." He cites the use of indentured labour, often of *Indian* migrants, on plantations in British colonies ("Globalization, Nationalism, and Religious Resurgence," in *Globalizing Theology: Belief and Practice in an Era of World Christianity*, eds. Craig Ott and Harold Netland [Nottingham: Apollos, 2007], 226).

63. Grant, 147–48. I imagine that this whole discussion may cause raised eyebrows among my friends in Ireland. Anyone familiar with the British role in Ireland at this time will know that the claim regarding the benevolence of imperialism rings very hollow on the other

One may ask whether the seeds of the conflicts which were to devastate Europe later in the twentieth century were being sown here. In the 1930s Archbishop Temple, warning of the drift towards another world war, was to condemn attitudes which treated Germany as solely responsible for the First World War: "We have to ask not only who dropped the match but who strewed the ground with gunpowder."[64] Certainly, observers who viewed these events from a distance detected that the real sources of Europe's internecine conflicts were to be discovered in precisely the scramble for colonial power and pre-eminence. Here is W. E. B. Du Bois, writing in 1915:

> We speak of the Balkans as the storm-centre of Europe and the cause of war, but this is mere habit. The Balkans are convenient for occasions, but the ownership of materials and men in the darker world is the real prize that is setting the nations of Europe at each other's throats today.... The present world war is, then, the result of jealousies engendered by the recent rise of armed national associations of labor and capital, whose aim is the exploitation of the wealth of the world mainly outside the European circle of nations.[65]

The End of Christendom

It will be remembered that the era of Christian history we have been discussing was identified by Andrew Walls as the *fifth age* in the story of the spread of the faith concerning Jesus Christ, and he described this as the phase of *expanding Europe*. However, he also observed that this expansion was accompanied by, or gave birth to, a number of extremely significant developments. One of these was the beginning of what Walls called "Christian recession" in Europe, as evidence of the loss of faith, of a turning away from the religion which had defined European identity, began to accumulate. In fact,

---

side of the Irish Sea. There is in fact a significant overlap between the tragedy of the Congo and the Irish quest for freedom in the person of the tragic figure of Roger Casement. But that is another story!

64. Quoted in Dorrien, *Social Democracy*, 379.

65. W. E. B. Du Bois, "The African Roots of War," *The Atlantic Monthly* 15, no. 5 (May 1915): 707–14; WebDuBois.org, accessed 19 January 2023, http://www.webdubois.org/dbAfricanRWar.html.

the signs of this recession had been present much earlier in the nineteenth century since – as we have seen – Edward Miall was outspoken in the 1840s concerning the serious malaise he believed was affecting Christianity and undermining its credibility among thoughtful people. Miall challenged the widely held assumption that Britain was a "Christian country" and warned that a large and growing segment of the population regarded established religion as complicit in the oppression "which crushes them to the earth." He campaigned relentlessly for the disestablishment of the Church of England and argued that the privileged status of that organization had resulted in the most horrible distortion of Christianity, turning it into part of the state's apparatus "to mount guard over crowns, coronets, titles of distinction, exclusive privileges and sources of temporal wealth." As a result, oppressed people were moving from a mere distaste for the outward forms of Christianity to a "malignant hatred" of it.

> We pass through life under the influence of a dream.... We are a Christian people.... And generation succeeds generation without the churches being thoroughly awake to the fact that very much of this is but a pleasant fiction – and that the spiritual life which really exists among us, is extremely small.[66]

Later in the same century, as the connection between the Bible and the flag came to be affirmed with ever greater fervour, the voices of those who were repelled by what they regarded as a form of syncretism increased in number and grew louder. Among those voices was that of John Ruskin, who had abandoned the evangelicalism of his mother and eloquently expressed the reason for his doubts:

> I know of no previous instance of a nation's establishing a systematic disobedience to the first principles of its professed religion. The writings which we (verbally) esteem as divine, not only denounce the love of money as the source of all evil, and as an idolatry abhorred of the Deity, but declare mammon service to be the accurate and irreconcilable opposite of God's service: and, whenever they speak of riches absolute, and poverty absolute, declare woe to the rich, and blessing to the poor. Whereupon we

---

66. Miall, *British Churches*, 382–83.

forthwith investigate a science of becoming rich, as the shortest road to national prosperity.[67]

What we witness here are the first tremors presaging the collapse of Christendom! The claim that imperial Britain was the model of a Christian civilization was being falsified both by the widening gap between the message of the gospel and the political and economic forces reshaping society, and by colonialism itself which, in another historical irony, became the solvent of Christendom by undermining the identification of Christianity with Europe. Andrew Walls, writing of the missionary movement, concludes:

> A movement that arose in the heart of Christendom helped Christianity to survive the death of Christendom. A project that was soaked in the Enlightenment helped to produce a Christianity whose strength now lies in its independence of the Enlightenment. An expression of Christianity that arose from interaction with the deep currents in European culture has helped to foster a Christianity that will depend for its future on its critical interaction with the ancient cultures of Africa and Asia.[68]

A second development consequent on the cross-cultural communication of the Christian message made possible by European expansion concerns the *reception* of that message among the peoples on the receiving end of colonialism. If critics *within* European Christendom perceived the failure of the churches to inculcate the radical teaching and example of Jesus within their own constituencies, primal peoples *beyond* Christendom, discovering that teaching as the result of missionary translations, were even more likely to discern the mismatch between the narrative of the gospel and the material culture of the white people who had shared it with them. The message of the

---

67. John Ruskin, *Unto This Last and Other Writings* (London: Penguin, 1997), 203. Elsewhere in this book he sounds very much like Tawney: "We need examples of people who, leaving Heaven to decide whether they are to rise in the world, decide for themselves that they will be happy in it, and have resolved to seek – not greater wealth, but simpler pleasure; not higher fortune, but deeper felicity; making the first of possessions, self-possession; and honouring themselves in the harmless pride and calm pursuits of peace" (227). See also Elisabeth Jay, *Faith and Doubt in Victorian Britain* (London: Macmillan, 1986) and Hugh McLeod, *Class and Religion in the Late Victorian City* (London: Croom Helm, 1974).

68. Walls, *Cross-Cultural Process*, 235.

crucified God was recognized and welcomed as self-evidently liberating and political in the most radical sense, so that the missionaries who had prioritized language-learning and translation into vernacular tongues were repeatedly surprised when their receptors discovered previously unrecognized depths of meaning in familiar biblical narratives. Primal peoples discovered not only a Christ who "speaks our language," but a Saviour who clearly knew "our world," both at a cultural level, where there was little distance between the living and the dead, and in the political sphere in which Jesus clearly understood and shared the lives of oppressed people suffering under imperial power. Hearing the Bible in vernacular languages consequently empowered non-Western peoples to resist the racial profiling which humiliated them, and offered a new source of identity which enabled the recovery and purification of their own cultural values. Thus, the translation projects of missions, notwithstanding the mistakes of the missionaries, "helped to create an overarching series of cultural experiences, with hitherto obscure cultural systems being thrust into the general stream of universal history."[69]

We conclude this chapter with a concrete example of the processes we have identified, and appropriately our case study comes from the Congo. Simon Kimbangu was born in 1889 and raised by his paternal aunt, Kinzembo, who had converted to Christianity as the result of contact with Baptist missionaries. As he grew up, Simon was deeply influenced by his aunt's faith and drawn to the person of Jesus. He felt a call to preach, but when the charismatic, prophetic nature of his ministry began to attract large numbers of his people, he was opposed by missionaries and began to arouse the interest of nervous Belgian authorities. An official report on the rapidly growing movement recognized that Kimbangu's intention was "to create a religion that fits the native's mind-set," and it acknowledged that "our European religions . . . do not answer the needs of the African, who demands protection and solid facts." Nonetheless, when Kimbangu's meetings began to draw vast crowds of

---

69. Lamin Sanneh, *Translating the Message: The Missionary Impact on Culture* (New York: Orbis, 1989), 2. At the conclusion of a crucial chapter on "Vernacularization and Westernization" Sanneh writes: "In their vernacular work, Christian missions helped nurse the sentiments for the national cause, which mother tongues crystallized and incited. The dramatic effects of vernacular translation *thus prejudiced the colonial cause as much by historical coincidence as by ideological justification*" (125; emphasis added). See also Sanneh's *Encountering the West: Christianity and the Global Cultural Process – The African Dimension* (London: Marshall Pickering, 1993).

people, many abandoning their employment by white settlers, so that "boys serving in European homes were leaving the linen unwashed and sneaking away to Kimbangu's meetings" and European ladies "suddenly had to do the cooking themselves," the colonial powers determined to intervene.[70]

Simon Kimbangu was arrested in September 1921 and after a trial which interpreted his saying that "the White man will become Black and the Black man will become White" as evidence of insurrection, he was condemned to death. The outcry against this verdict resulted in it being commuted to life imprisonment and he remained behind bars for thirty years until his death in 1951. His son, Diangienda, explained that the prophetic statement which cost his father a life sentence in a colonial prison was clearly intended as a prophecy of the coming of independence for the African peoples, and he testified that Kimbangu had abhorred violence and prayed constantly for the peace of the world. Diangienda recorded many of his father's prayers, including the following which he was said to use every day throughout his imprisonment:

> I give Thee thanks, O God Almighty, who created the heaven and the earth. Heaven is Thy throne, and earth Thy footstool. Thy will be done on earth as it is in heaven. May Thou bless all races on earth – mighty ones and little ones, women and men, Whites and Blacks. May the blessings from above pour on the whole world, so that we may all enter Heaven. We ask all this in hopes of obtaining it in the name of Jesus Christ our savior. Amen.[71]

The story of Simon Kimbangu is remarkable and belongs within the centuries-long tradition of Christian suffering and martyrdom which we have discussed earlier in this book. But when it is seen within the context of Central Africa which we have examined above, it becomes even more extraordinary. Kimbangu, as Sanneh says, "summed up in his own person the destiny of his people and their age," and he sought to infuse in them "a dynamic sense of

---

70. Aurélien Mokoko Gampiot provides a detailed description of Kimbangu's early ministry and a transcript of his trial in *Kimbanguism: An African Understanding of the Bible* (University Park: Pennsylvania State University Press, 2017), 71–75.

71. Gampiot, *Kimbanguism*, 69.

purpose, a notion that they were appointed for greater ends than humiliation under foreign conquest."⁷²

---

72. Lamin Sanneh, *West African Christianity: The Religious Impact* (New York: Orbis, 1983), 207. Kimbangu's movement resulted in the creation of the Church of Jesus Christ of the Prophet Simon Kimbangu which by 1966 had half a million members and became affiliated to the World Council of Churches. In 2010 German film-makers Claus Wischmann and Martin Baer produced a DVD titled *Kinshasa Symphony* which depicts the extraordinary creation of the Orchestre Symphonique Kimbanguiste. The film follows the 200 African musicians preparing to perform Beethoven's Choral Symphony in Kinshasa, a city of ten million inhabitants. One may ask whether this achievement by Kimbanguist Christians was the fulfilment of the prophecy that "the Black man will become White." And what might it mean for the white man to become black?

CHAPTER 10

From Pillar to Post

We have reached the stage at which this study has completed a full circle and now returns to our starting point in the contemporary world. We began, it will be remembered, with Albert Camus's lament at the *absurdity* of a culture in which God appeared to be dead, so that the human longing for meaning, for justice, was frustrated and the rebel found him- or herself engaged in a "hopeless encounter between human questioning and the silence of the universe." In the immediate aftermath of the horrors of the European killing fields, the gas chambers, and the mushroom clouds over Japan, Camus concluded that the overthrow of the throne of God had left human beings to face alone the task of creating justice, order and unity, and in so doing, attempt to establish "the dominion of man." Far from celebrating this situation, Camus shuddered at the prospect of such a future and concluded that it "cannot come about without appalling consequences of which we are only, so far, aware of a few."[1]

Eighty years later we are in a position to discern those outcomes more clearly and have even greater reason to be apprehensive in a world in which "the sky is empty, the earth delivered into the hands of power without principles."[2] The formidable challenge before us in these final chapters is, first, to attempt to identify the major changes which have taken place since the 1950s and to reflect on the ways in which the capitalist system has mutated into new forms and extended its reach to a global scale. Second, we must ask

---

1. Albert Camus, *The Rebel* (Harmondsworth: Penguin, 1971), 31.

2. Camus, 117. According to Howard Mumma, Camus's quest for meaning brought him close to faith before his tragic death. See his *Albert Camus and the Minister* (Brewster: Paraclete Press, 2000).

how the biblical exposition in the first half of this book might be applied to the situation described in its second section.

Before we attempt to discuss our contemporary context, I want to caution that there can be no simple fusing of the horizon of the biblical literature with that of the modern world, and we will have to resist the temptation to seek for an easily won optimism concerning the future. Of course, there are grounds for hope that the message of the gospel can provide an alternative, liberating vision for the future of the human family, but this cannot result from a mere regurgitation from the past, since we are compelled to address the social, cultural and economic realities of a world transformed by industrialization, urbanization, and the technological developments which spawn ethical issues the likes of which we have never faced before.

One of those "technological developments" relates to the manufacture of weapons of mass destruction, and even as these lines were being typed my newspaper carried a story with the headline: "World's Nuclear Arms Stockpile Rises in 'One of the Most Dangerous Periods in History.'" Based on research done by the Stockholm International Peace Research Institute (SIPRI), the report indicates the existence of 12,512 nuclear warheads globally, with around two thousand of these kept "in a state of high operational alert, meaning they are fitted to missiles or are held at airbases hosting nuclear bombers."[3] The director of SIPRI warns that it is imperative that governments find ways to co-operate, "in order to calm geopolitical tensions, slow arms races and deal with the worsening consequences of environmental breakdown and rising world hunger." Yet the global arms race persists with little sign of public outrage, nor is there much evidence of churches recognizing this as a matter of significant concern for those who follow the Prince of Peace. It is as though the proliferation of nuclear weapons, like the global spread of market economics, has to be accepted as a fait accompli against which resistance is futile, if it is not actually seen as a distraction from the true concerns of the Christian mission. Here lies one source of my hesitation

---

3. Daniel Boffey, "World's Nuclear Arms Stockpile Rises in 'One of the Most Dangerous Periods of History,'" *The Guardian*, 12 June 2013. Russia and the United States between them possess more than eight thousand of these weapons; China is reported to have 410, France 290, UK 225, followed by Pakistan 170, India 164, Israel 90 and North Korea 30.

about expressing a facile confidence regarding Christianity's ability to be the agent of God's peace and reconciliation in our broken world.[4]

Mammon, Globalization and "The End of History"

In the decades following the Second World War the quest for social and economic recovery in a Europe devastated by the terrible conflicts of those years was to result in a social revolution of such magnitude as to lead a distinguished historian to describe it as "the greatest and most dramatic, rapid and universal social transformation in human history." The historian was Eric Hobsbawm and the transformation which he said had cut us off for ever from the world of the past was what he described as "the death of the peasantry."[5] From earliest known times the vast majority of the human race had lived from the land, or fished from the seas, and until the midpoint of the twentieth century most inhabitants on earth continued to pursue such traditional forms of life. As we have seen, the transformation to which Hobsbawm referred had been underway for well over a century in Britain, having accelerated dramatically with the Industrial Revolution. However, when the Second World War began in 1939, few people could have foreseen that within the coming decades the situation would change to such a degree that no country in Western Europe would have more than 10 percent of its population engaged in farming, except the Irish Republic, Spain and Portugal.

Beyond Europe the same period was to witness the rise of new nations across the southern hemisphere as colonized peoples demanded the withdrawal of imperial powers and established newly independent nations. In Asia, European colonial power diminished rapidly after 1950, and with the

---

4. Note Alan Lewis's warning: "There is about us a 'psychic numbness,' a generational and cultural pathology which refuses to face the reality of what we have done with our promethean nuclear fire, or to imagine the awfulness of what we could still do. Without such pathological suppression of the deadly truth would the populations of East and West have with such docility permitted their respective governments to devote immense resources to an escalating arms race, digging a superfluity of silos, amassing ever greater stockpiles, inventing still 'smarter' missiles, even after they had brought the world at least once to the precipice of cataclysm?" (*Between Cross and Resurrection: A Theology of Holy Saturday* [Grand Rapids: Eerdmans, 2001], 279).

5. E. J. Hobsbawm, *Age of Extremes: The Short Twentieth Century, 1914–1991* (London: Abacus, 1995), 288–89. Commenting on the speed and universality of this change, he writes: "For 80 per cent of humanity the Middle Ages ended suddenly in the 1950s, or perhaps better still, they were *felt* to end in the 1960s."

two most populous nations of India and China already independent states, it increasingly became a marginal political presence. The United States established an informal empire in Asia, as elsewhere across the globe, "constituted by military bases, economic pressures and political coups," but the West in general was to discover that "the Asian ability to assimilate modern ideas, techniques and institutions" had been underestimated, and was to be turned against the West itself.[6] As Hobsbawm observed, *when the land empties the cities fill up*, so that by the 1980s an astonishing 42 percent of the global population had become urban, with cities across Asia, including Seoul, Karachi, Manila, New Delhi and Bangkok, being flooded with migrants from the countryside and facing the immense social challenges posed by rapid urbanization. City populations were no longer to be measured in the hundreds of thousands but in the millions, and the rapidity and magnitude of urban growth was inevitably accompanied by the social pathologies which had afflicted British cities in the nineteenth century, only now on an unprecedented scale.

Meantime, in Europe the post-war period witnessed the descent of the "iron curtain," dividing the continent between a communist East and the capitalist West. The movement of resistance to the concept of the "free market" which we discussed in the previous chapter, having achieved progressive political outcomes in the immediate post-war period, was to falter as rival ideologies split both Europe and the wider world, and capitalism came to be increasingly identified with democracy and freedom.[7] Two aspects of the history of the second half of the twentieth century are of crucial importance to our study, and we will reflect on them before concluding with the nature of the challenge which confronts world Christianity today.

The first characteristic of the post-war, post-colonial world to notice concerns the manner in which the ideology of the free market became embedded as a form of sociopolitical orthodoxy across the Western world, and at the same time determined the nature of "development" for emerging nations and

---

6. Pankaj Mishra, *From the Ruins of Empire: The Intellectuals Who Remade Asia* (New York: Farrar, Straus & Giroux, 2012), 7.

7. David Coates discusses "The Slow Disintegration of the UK's Postwar Settlement" in his *Flawed Capitalism: The Anglo-American Condition and Its Resolution* (Newcastle-upon-Tyne: Agenda, 2018), 149–89. See also Manfred B. Steger, *Globalisms: The Great Ideological Struggle of the Twenty-First Century*, 3rd ed. (Lanham: Rowman & Littlefield, 2009).

peoples throughout the Global South.[8] The ideological conflict between the West – increasingly dominated by the economic and military power of the United States – and Eastern Europe, where what came to be called "really existing socialism" expanded from the Soviet bloc after 1949 to include China, continued until the collapse of the Soviet empire as the 1980s gave way to the 1990s. Even before that epochal turning point, Western ideas equated with modernity were presented as the only way forward to the new nations, despite the fact that they contrasted so sharply with traditional cultural values, and so made turmoil and resistance inevitable.

We have seen how this clash of worldviews impacted tribal peoples on the continent of Africa; in Asia opposition arose not only within indigenous cultural contexts, but from the ancient religious traditions of Buddhism and Hinduism. Mahatma Gandhi regarded modernization as posing a dangerous threat, especially because it exalted wealth and prosperity as the supreme goal of the good life, and elevated technology and machinery to an importance that, he feared, would lead to the eclipse of the life of the spirit.

The hope that Asian peoples might discover an alternative path forward based on the ancient traditions of the East has proved to be unfounded. Pankaj Mishra concludes that much of what was called the "third world" now seems likely to repeat, "on an ominously larger scale," the West's tragic experience of modern development. In the case of China not only has Confucianism been unable to provide the spiritual resources to resist modernization, but Chairman Mao was similarly powerless in the face of global market forces. As to modern India, Mishra concludes:

> India displays even more garishly than China the odd discontinuities induced by economic globalization: how by fostering rapid growth in some sectors of the economy it raises expectations everywhere, but by distributing its benefits narrowly, it expands the numbers of the disenchanted and the frustrated,

---

8. On "development" see Michael L. Budde's discussion "The Church after Development" in his *Foolishness to Gentiles: Essays on Empire, Nationalism, and Discipleship* (Eugene: Cascade, 2022), 94–112. He writes: "The buzzwords of the present day – 'sustainable development,' 'integral development,' 'local/participatory development' – seem on balance to be fresher fig leaves on the extractive and coercive practices of capitalism, in which the adjectives (sustainable, integral, local, participatory) provide ideological cover for the same old things that have created the worlds we inhabit today" (101–2).

often making them vulnerable to populist and ethnocentric politicians. At the same time the biggest beneficiaries of globalization find shelter in such aggressive ideologies as Hindu nationalism.[9]

This brings us to the second important aspect of the history of this period, which concerns the manner in which capitalism itself has evolved and reshaped political discourse and policy-making in the era of full-blown globalization. Paul Lakeland, discussing theology in the context of contemporary American culture, comments that the multiple crises that overshadow the world today can all be traced back to an insatiable lust for money and power, and that behind this materialistic ethos is an even more ominous crisis: "the degradation of the very notion of the human, brought on by the complex mechanism today called neoliberalism."[10]

This terminology has been widely used in discussions of modern politics, but it is important to stress that it signifies more than a simple modification of classic liberalism since it refers to a genuine mutation in economic theory, creating the intellectual foundations for a quite new cultural system. Eugene McCarraher explains that where classic liberal theory had regarded the market and the state as separate spheres, with the latter serving the interests of an entire community, and thus frequently resistant to market demands, a new generation of economists aimed to remake the state – and everything else – into the image and likeness of the market. "Aiming to refashion not only the state but also the moral and metaphysical imagination as well, neoliberals *elevated the market to a position of absolute ontological sovereignty.*"[11] "In the neoliberal theology of the market, the world is a business; money is the measure of all things; mercenary, professional, or technical talent is the existential equivalent of sanctity; and the successful entrepreneur is the autocratic icon of morality and beatitude."[12]

---

9. Mishra, *Ruins of Empire*, 308.

10. Paul Lakeland, "Spiritual Resistance: Theology in the Age of Neoliberalism," *Commonweal* 144, no. 6 (June 2020): 24. This was Lakeland's presidential address at the Catholic Theological Society of America Convention in 2019.

11. Eugene McCarraher, *The Enchantments of Mammon: How Capitalism Became the Religion of Modernity* (Cambridge: Belknap Press of Harvard University Press, 2019), 591; emphasis added.

12. McCarraher, *Enchantments of Mammon*, 591.

It is not possible here to discuss this subject in detail, but its importance for an understanding of the contemporary world cannot be overstated. The source of the ideas which resulted in this mutation is to be found among a group of economists who taught at the University of Chicago and the London School of Economics from the 1960s, chief among whom was Friedrich Hayek. His 1944 book *The Road to Serfdom* became a founding text of the movement and was widely influential – including among its avid readers Margaret Thatcher and Ronald Reagan. Contemptuous of religion when it hindered the absolute freedom of commerce and technology, Hayek nonetheless wrote about market forces in language which sounded strangely theological: he described the free market as the *cosmos* – a "higher, supraindividual wisdom" which transcends the knowledge of any single person, so that most decisions should be left "to a process we do not control."[13] *The market knows best!*

Readers may recall that in the 1940s Karl Polanyi had already discerned the emergence of "a secular religion" in the ideology of the free market, and Giovanni Arrighi likewise described the absolute trust in market forces as amounting to a belief in "a new metaphysical reality" endowed "with supernatural powers."[14] In the nineteenth century the implicitly religious character of the free market went largely unrecognized because Christianity remained a significant social force, but with the rise of neoliberalism the claim that unfettered market forces demand complete obedience and submission became much more explicit, and political and economic policies would be shaped by it. Christians who continued to believe in a transcendent deity discovered

---

13. McCarraher's discussion of Hayek, Ayn Rand and other leading advocates of neoliberalism is extremely helpful. See chapter 26, "The New Testament of Capitalism: The Resurgence of Evangelical Enchantment and the Theology of Neoliberalism," in *Enchantments of Mammon*, 580–610.

14. See Polanyi, *The Great Transformation*, 106–107, and Arrighi, *The Long Twentieth Century*, 56. On the same page Arrighi says that the economic laws "operating within and between states were subject to the higher authority of a new, metaphysical entity – a world market ruled by its own 'laws' – allegedly endowed with supernatural powers greater than anything pope and emperor had ever mastered in the medieval system of rule." Douglas Meeks discusses "God concepts in market assumptions" as follows: "Although orthodox economics, as a moral principle of its scientific character, refuses to reflect 'God' in its domain, it cannot be doubted on close inspection that economists make representations of another level of reality.... The market may be considered free of God and thus of all authoritarian influences. *But the working of the market depends upon coercive conceptions once applied to God but now given as the presuppositions of the market human being*" (M. Douglas Meeks, *God the Economist: The Doctrine of God and Political Economy* [Minneapolis: Fortress, 1989], 64–65; emphasis added).

themselves in a strange new world in which their faith had become somehow circumscribed and divorced from a whole range of professional activities in which the new beliefs became ever more pervasive.

The radical transformation resulting from the spread and dominance of the form of capitalism we have just described has been identified as a *culture of economism*. Rafael Esteban, a Catholic priest teaching at the Missionary Institute in London, and Jane Collier, a professional economist lecturing in Cambridge, describe "economism" as follows:

> It is the economic aspect of our lives that more than any other shapes our understanding, our evaluations, and our aspirations, and hence conditions our actions. It is the economic that generates our culture's rituals and defines our symbols. Our language conveys the depth of that influence; our cultural stories – our myths – are stories about wealth, success, power, progress, growth and prosperity. Our institutions, whether they be business corporations or hospitals or universities or charity foundations, are run on economic criteria.[15]

The social, cultural and religious consequences of this mutation in capitalism are many and are of profound significance. For example, with regard to the understanding of the human person, or the impact on anthropology, the market economy envisaged by neoliberalism requires, and itself *creates*, the human being as a *consumer*. The virtues of generosity, sharing and contentment, which were embedded within traditional cultures and shaped the practice of Christian discipleship, now become obstacles to the success of the market and are replaced by a different set of values and a new definition of happiness. Few scholars have explored this aspect with such insight as Zygmunt Bauman, and in his book *Consuming Life* he suggests that the crucial difference between traditional cultures and consumerism is to be found in *the reversal of the values attached respectively to duration and transience*.

> In the inherited hierarchy of recognized values, the consumerist syndrome has degraded duration and elevated transience. It lifts the value of novelty above that of lastingness. It has sharply

---

15. Jane Collier and Rafael Esteban, *From Complicity to Encounter: The Church and the Culture of Economism* (Harrisburg: Trinity Press International, 1998), 10.

shortened the timespan separating not just the want from its fulfilment . . . but also the birth moment of the want from the moment of its demise, as well as the realization of the usefulness and desirability of possessions from the perception of them as useless and in need of rejection.[16]

Bauman concludes that a consumer society "cannot but be a society of excess and profligacy – and so of redundancy and prodigal waste." Hence, the creation of such a culture has consequences that extend beyond changes in individual values and attitudes, and include the despoiling of the earth by the production of mountains of disposable consumer goods and their packaging. The contrast with the life of discipleship in obedience to the Christ who, having declared "You cannot serve God and Mammon," told his followers not to "worry about your life, what you will eat or drink; or about your body, what you will wear," is absolute![17] In the context of such a cultural clash, Christians are surely faced with some extremely difficult questions. Bauman writes that individuals "who settle for a finite assembly of needs" and avoid seeking new needs to arouse "a pleasurable yearning for satisfaction" are stigmatized as *flawed consumers* – "the variety of social outcast specific to the society of consumers."[18] Yet so powerful is the ideology of neoliberalism, so seductive its propaganda, and perhaps most of all, so appealing to misdirected human desire, that the lifestyle of consumption appears to have merged seamlessly with much contemporary Christianity. Here is the verdict of Brad Gregory, describing his own American context:

> Conflating prosperity with providence and opting for acquisitiveness as the lesser of two evils until greed was rechristened as benign self-interest, modern Christians have in effect been engaged in a centuries-long attempt to prove Jesus wrong. "You

---

16. Zygmunt Bauman, *Consuming Life* (Cambridge: Polity Press, 2007b), 86. Elsewhere Bauman writes that the story told by consumer culture "has no interest in waste." He notes that two kinds of lorries leave factory yards every day: one drives to warehouses and department stores, the other to rubbish tips. The consumerist story trains us to welcome the first lorry and ignore the second! "Waste is the dark, shameful secret of all production." Bauman concludes: "Rubbish collectors are the unsung heroes of modernity" (*Wasted Lives: Modernity and Its Outcasts* [Cambridge: Polity, 2004], 27–28).

17. Matt 6.

18. Bauman, *Consuming Life*, 99.

cannot serve both God and Mammon." *Yes we can.* Or so most participants in world history's most insatiably consumerist society, the United States, continue to claim through their actions, considering the number of self-identified American Christians in the early twenty-first century who seem bent on acquiring ever more and better stuff, including those who espouse the "prosperity Gospel" within American religious hyperpluralism.[19]

The rise of neoliberalism occurred at the very point at which the means of communication were being revolutionized by the invention of the World Wide Web, so shrinking the spaces between cities across the globe and making possible instant contact across national and regional boundaries. This provided the new market culture with the means to extend its reach to every corner of the world and stimulated the creation of new financial systems which promised hugely enlarged profits. Theologian Kathryn Tanner has described the new *spirit* which came to inhabit the economic system which, after the collapse of the Soviet Union, extended its reach to every part of the world. This resulted in claims that humankind had now arrived at "the end of history" since it was asserted that no alternative to the international market society was conceivable.[20] Tanner explains the multiple ways in which contemporary capitalism became finance dominated, with profits in banking, insurance, property and land markets vastly exceeding the amounts generated by industrial or service sectors. She concludes that the amount and frequency of transactions in finance "dwarf [those] of other economic activities" and that it is not uncommon "for the money changing hands on foreign currency exchanges in a single day to equal that of the whole of world trade in a year."[21]

---

19. Brad S. Gregory, *The Unintended Reformation: How a Religious Revolution Secularized Society* (Cambridge: Belknap Press, 2012), 288. Chapter 5 of his book, "Manufacturing the Goods Life," is directly relevant to our discussion, 235–97.

20. Francis Fukuyama published *The End of History and the Last Man* in 1992. Five years later, reflecting on the controversy which the book provoked, he wrote that God may indeed be the only source of belief in human dignity, and that "if God has indeed died, then we are in a lot of trouble and need desperately to find another source on which to base our belief that human beings have dignity. Enlightenment rationalism is not the solution, it is part of the problem" ("Reflections on *The End of History* Five Years Later," in *World History: Ideologies, Structures, and Identities*, eds. Philip Pomper, Richard Elphick and Richard Vann [Oxford: Blackwell, 1998], 213).

21. Kathryn Tanner, *Christianity and the New Spirit of Capitalism* (New Haven: Yale University Press, 2019), 11. See also her *Economy of Grace* (Minneapolis: Fortress, 2005). In

The human and social consequences of this mutation in capitalism, to say nothing of its global, ecological impact on our planetary home, have been catastrophic. The earlier creation of a market society resulted in a widening gulf between rich and poor, creating both millionaires and paupers, and the mutation of capitalism in a globalized world has had a similar result, only on a universal scale, and to an extent which is, frankly, terrifying.

Saskia Sassen has examined the consequences of the global dominance of the market economy in a series of penetrating studies which focus especially on the role played by cities in the world economy. She notes that while historically cities were "deeply embedded in the economies of their region," those that become strategic sites in the global economy (identified as "world cities") tend to be "disconnected from their region and even nation." As a result, large areas that are peripheral to the city are increasingly excluded from the major economic processes that fuel growth within the new system.

> The state itself has been transformed by its role in implementing the global economic system, a transformation captured in the ascendance of agencies linked to the domestic and international financial markets in most governments of highly developed countries and many governments of developing countries, *and the loss of power and prestige of agencies associated with issues of domestic equity.*[22]

In her book *Expulsions: Brutality and Complexity in the Global Economy*, Sassen broadens the scope of her research to examine in great detail what she describes as "the emergence of the new logics of *expulsion*": the growth in the numbers of people, enterprises and places "expelled from the core social and economic orders of our time."[23] Of particular interest, given our earlier discussion of the importance of land and the impossibility of regarding it as

---

the introduction to this book, Tanner describes her approach to the subject as follows: "There is no point in looking to theology for insight on economic questions if theology merely ratifies the economic principles that the wider society takes for granted anyway.... On the one side, there is theological economy, made up of the fundamental principles for the production and circulation of goods as those exhibited in the Christian story of God and the world; on the other side, there is the economy in the usual, narrow sense" (x).

22. Saskia Sassen, *Globalization and Its Discontents* (New York: Free Press, 1998), xxiii–ix; emphasis added. See also her *Cities in a World Economy*, 4th ed. (Los Angeles: Sage, 2012).

23. Saskia Sassen, *Expulsions: Brutality and Complexity in the Global Economy* (Cambridge: Belknap Press of Harvard University, 2014), 1.

a marketable product in traditional societies, is Sassen's chapter "The New Global Market for Land." She describes the large-scale acquisitions of land by foreign investors and governments taking place in many parts of the world, resulting in the forced expulsion of tribal peoples who have existed in such areas from time immemorial. Among the examples Sassen cites are the following: Saudi investors have spent $100 million to grow wheat, barley and rice on land leased by Ethiopia's government; China has obtained rights to grow palm oil for biofuels on 2.8 million hectares of Congo (*of Congo!*), and is negotiating a similar deal with Zambia; while in Pakistan 500,000 hectares were due to be leased to Gulf investors, "with the bonus of a security force of 100,000 to protect the land."[24] Sassen concludes:

> Lands acquired by foreigners include vast stretches of national territory populated by villages, smallholder agriculture, rural manufacturing districts, and the actors that make these economies and reproduce them. . . . Much of this politico-structural complexity is today being erased from its home territory as a result of these acquisitions. At the extreme, we might ask what citizenship is worth when national territory is being downgraded to foreign-owned land for plantations, leading to the eviction of everything else – flora, fauna, villages, smallholders, and the traditional rules that organized land ownership and use.[25]

How can anyone be surprised that in a world like this, growing numbers of displaced people, traumatized not just by the physical experience of expulsion from traditional lands but also by the shock of the brutal destruction of their entire way of life, the loss of the social, cultural and religious worlds they shared together, should seek refuge wherever they can hope to sustain their lives and those of their children? There are no political schemes that can "stop the boats" so long as the deep, underlying causes of migration in the global economic system remain in place. In addition, significant numbers of the people expelled from their traditional land on the continent of Africa will be Christians, since it was precisely among primal groups on that

---

24. Sassen, *Expulsions*, 107.

25. Sassen, 115. A subsequent chapter in the book has the title "Dead Land, Dead Water." It is a horrific catalogue of the extent of the forces threatening life on earth and should be required reading for us all (149–210).

continent that Christianity witnessed significant growth. This surely suggests that Christianity in the West is bound to be hospitable to migrant brothers and sisters, and that they frequently belong within the category of the "suffering church" which has until now been far too narrowly conceived.[26]

The Fall of Icarus

The forces we have described at work in the economic system have resulted in multiple problems, including the widening disparities of wealth and power, the ecological crises which threaten the very future of humankind, and the rise in forms of nationalist politics which contain too many reminders of the fascism which resulted in the destruction of Europe in the last century. Wolfgang Streek discusses a series of "systemic disorders" which have marred capitalism, including *oligarchic inequality* which results in a small elite "becoming unimaginably rich," making them "independent from the fates of the societies from which they extract their wealth." In the United States, the gulf between the incomes of the top 400 taxpayers and the bottom 90 percent has been calculated to correspond to "the difference in material power between a senator and a slave at the height of the Roman Empire."[27] Here, then, is a point at which the world described in the first half of this present book does indeed provide a parallel to our contemporary context, and this becomes even more significant when Streek (who repeatedly expresses his appreciation of Karl Polanyi's work) recognizes the possibility that a challenge to economism may come from religious sources. "Cultural definitions of the good life have always been highly malleable and might well be stretched further to match the onward march of commodification, *at least as long as radical and religious challenges to pro-capitalist re-education can be suppressed, ridiculed or otherwise marginalized.*"[28]

---

26. Sassen's work on "expulsions" is parallel in some respects to Zygmunt Bauman's *Wasted Lives* where he writes that protracted misery "makes millions desperate, and in an era of global frontier-land and globalized crime one can hardly expect a shortage of 'businesses' eager to make a fast buck or a few million bucks capitalizing on that desperation" (73).

27. Wolfgang Streek, *How Will Capitalism End? Essays on a Failing System* (London: Verso, 2016), 28–29.

28. Streek, *How Will Capitalism End?*, 60; emphasis added.

The marginal status of religious challenges to the culture of economism is due in part to the fact that those who propagate neoliberal ideas are perfectly aware that religions in general, and Christianity in particular, inculcate values which run completely counter to the patterns of behaviour which they regard as essential to a flourishing market economy. The Johannine instruction not to "love the world or anything in the world" does little to stimulate economic growth, and when this is followed by the announcement that everything in that world, "the *desires* of the flesh and the *desires* of the eyes, and *pride in possessions* – is not from the Father" (1 John 2:15–16 ESV), the last thing neoliberal entrepreneurs would wish to see is a revival of such religion! Ayn Rand, whose books have been very influential in the United States, attracting readers "spellbound by her tales and philosophical defenses of unbridled egoism," poured scorn on the concept of charity which, she argued, "threatened not only to sanction a massive redistribution of wealth but also to demolish the moral infrastructure of capitalist property relations."[29] Eugene McCarraher describes her work as follows: "Emboldening the piracies of finance capital, feeding the cyberculture's exhilarant ambitions of technological sublimity, and bracing a new plutocracy with a conviction of its own existential superiority, [Rand's] kitschy and melodramatic tributes to greed augured an epoch of spectacular pillage."[30]

However, if the neoliberal contempt for religious values is one factor in their marginalization, another is the dismal failure of professing Christians to resist the attractions of consumerism and so to fall into the very trap which the Letter of James and the Revelation of John had warned about! As long ago as 1961, the sociologist Peter Berger examined the values practised within American churches and concluded that modern religious institutions do not generate values differently from the wider society, but ratify and *sanctify* "the values prevalent in the general community." The most that could be said was that church members "hold the same values as everybody else, but with more emphatic solemnity." Church membership did not demand "adherence to a set of values at variance with those of the general society; rather, it means a

---

29. McCarraher, *Enchantments of Mammon*, 606.
30. McCarraher, 610.

stronger and more explicitly religious affirmation of the same values held by the community at large."³¹

At the same time, it has become increasingly clear that the values shaped by, and essential to, a culture of economism are incapable of satisfying the ineradicable human quest for meaning, for answers to the questions which arise from the tragic dimensions of human existence, and from the (repressed) awareness of death. We noticed at the beginning of this book how modern writers frequently discovered that ancient Greek myths can illuminate the condition of people today, and the French philosopher Chantel Delsol has proposed that the myth of the fall of Icarus, who crashed to earth having imagined he could transcend the human condition and fly to the sun, provides an enlightening image of the postmodern condition. Imagine, Delsol says, that instead of perishing after his fall, Icarus survived and, realizing that he was condemned to return to the old life on earth, struggled mightily to cope with his disappointment. That, she suggests, is precisely the position of people in the modern West:

> Western man at the beginning of the twenty-first century is the descendant of Icarus. He wonders into what world he has fallen. It is as if someone has thrown him into a game without giving him the rules. When he asks around for instructions, he is invariably told they have been lost. He is amazed that everyone is content to live in a world without meaning and without identity, where no one seems to know either why he lives or why he dies.³²

It is not possible here to do more than illustrate the richness of Delsol's work, but two aspects of her critical analysis of postmodern culture are especially important as we draw this book to its conclusion. First, she discusses what we have identified above as the culture of *economism*, and concludes

---

31. Peter Berger, *The Noise of Solemn Assemblies: Christian Commitment and the Religious Establishment in America* (New York: Doubleday, 1961), 41. In an influential book first published in 1899, Thorstein Veblen observed that "the spiritual attitude bred in men by the modern industrial life is unfavourable to a free development of the life of faith." In a culture increasingly dominated by "conspicuous consumption" (a phrase he invented), forms of religion that rise "appreciably above the average pitch of devoutness in the community – may safely be set down as in all cases atavistic." *The Theory of the Leisure Class* (Oxford: Oxford University Press, 2007), 198-99.

32. Chantel Delsol, *Icarus Fallen: The Search for Meaning in an Uncertain World* (Wilmington: ISI Books, 2003), xxiv.

that in the desert created by the loss of universal values "only one end is ultimately left standing – that of living well in the greatest comfort imaginable." The triumph of economism has already been guaranteed, since derision is cast upon any values that might be able to stand up against it or even to occupy part of its territory. "*With the devaluation of all things unmarketable, the market becomes the sole climate of existence.*"[33]

In the second place, Delsol offers insightful comments on the failure of traditional religions to respond credibly to the context which she has described. Religions seem incapable of providing what is needed in the modern age and in their attempts to engage with contemporary people, the dialogue (if it exists at all) has become *pathetic*. The churches speak of transcendence, but the modern person has been socialized in immanence; they glory in centuries-old tradition; the modernist lives in a society which is precarious. They speak of truth; their interlocutors do not know what truth means, so that "the two are so far apart . . . that it is a pitiful sight" to witness the efforts made by religions in such conversations. This leads into a passage which seems so powerfully relevant to Christian mission today that I quote it at length:

> Contemporary man, disillusioned and weary of everything, expresses his desire for the absolute with all the innocence and candor of the first man. And only the essential can take on meaning for him. Thus the details of religious truth or morality, refined over twenty centuries of history, seem to him to be no more than petty wrangling. Institutional religions, however, have . . . ultimately given the greatest importance to forms that obscure the essential and hide it from view. And so now if our contemporary wishes to sincerely meditate upon the enigmas of existence, he is instead presented with dogmas and traditions that . . . appear perfectly superfluous to him, at least in comparison to the questions he asks. For example, the existence of a triune God seems superfluous to a man who is only at the point of wondering what makes him different from other animals. This sincere individual who seeks God in his own way, cannot help thinking he is being made fun of when he is answered in such a

---

33. Chantel Delsol, *The Unlearned Lessons of the Twentieth Century: An Essay on Late Modernity* (Wilmington: ISI Books, 2006), 139.

way. . . . Curious and often hungry for the primordial questions, he finds himself faced with religions that rest on thousand-year-old doctrines and awkwardly try to enlighten him by beginning with the end.[34]

Living through a "Long Saturday"

In 1990, George Steiner delivered the Gifford Lectures in the University of Glasgow. He made no reference to the myth of Icarus, but suggested that the spirit at the end of the twentieth century was one of "core tiredness," a sense of "late afternoon in ways that are ontological – this is to say, of the essence, of the fabric of being." He described the nineteenth century as a time when, underwritten by "the exploitation of industrial labour at home and colonial rule abroad," Europeans had "experienced a privileged season, an armistice with history," which sustained a "reasonable hope."[35] Between us and the Victorians, however, stands another century, during which "for the whole of Europe and Russia" life became "a time out of hell." This was the century which witnessed a "collapse of humaneness" resulting, not from "riders on the distant steppe or barbarians at the gates," but from within the context "of the high places of civilization, of education, of scientific progress and humanizing deployment, be it Christian or Enlightened."[36] Steiner went on to draw the following conclusion which, while different to that of Delsol,

---

34. Delsol, *Icarus Fallen*, 200. In addition to Delsol's work, her fellow philosopher Jean-Luc Marion has written *A Brief Apology for a Catholic Moment* (Chicago: University of Chicago Press, 2021). His approach is broadly similar, arguing that the possibility of a "Catholic moment" arises in a secular France because in precisely that society "the possibility of a community that puts the *universal* into operation is in play." The universal is everywhere crumbling and revealing "that French society is mortal, that it can break down, that it does not possess the promises of eternity. Who can re-establish the universal among us?" (84). I must add that French Catholic theology during and after the Second World War, when the country had been overrun by the Nazis and a puppet state was established in the south, has rightly been viewed as a striking example of *resistance to tyranny and idolatry*. The story is told in Sarah Shortall's *Soldiers of God in a Secular World: Catholic Theology and Twentieth-Century French Politics* (Cambridge: Harvard University Press, 2021).

35. We recall here the "boundless optimism and unsullied confidence in the ideological and financial power of western Christendom" which, according to Brian Stanley, was dominant at the World Missionary Conference in Edinburgh in 1910 (Stanley, *The World Missionary Conference, Edinburgh 1910* [Grand Rapids: Eerdmans, 2009], 16).

36. George Steiner, *Grammars of Creation: Originating in the Gifford Lectures for 1990* (London: Faber & Faber, 2001), 2–3.

complements hers and adds an important dimension to the critical analysis of the culture we have inherited:

> We have not begun to gauge the damage to man – as a species, as one entitling himself *sapiens* – inflicted by events since 1914. We do not begin to grasp the coexistence in time and space . . . of western superfluity and the starvation, the destitution, the infant mortality which now batten on some three-fifths of mankind.[37]

Steiner concluded that the twentieth century had "given to despair a new warrant" and placed in doubt "the theological, the philosophical and the political-material insurance for hope." It had resulted in "the eclipse of the messianic," and had altered "life-expectancy" so that it was "no longer a messianic-utopian projection, but an actuarial statistic."[38]

Elsewhere, in another widely read book, Steiner argued that any coherent account of human speech's ability to communicate meaning and feeling is "underwritten by the assumption of God's presence."[39] It is impossible to summarize the complex argument which unfolds in this brilliant study, but its conclusion is important with regard to our subject: "What I affirm is that where God's presence is no longer a tenable supposition and where His absence is no longer a felt, indeed overwhelming weight, certain dimensions of thought and creativity *are no longer attainable.*"[40] In other words, the "death of God" has enormous cultural consequences, the extent of which we are perhaps only now discovering. On the closing pages of this book Steiner suggests that there is a particular day in Western history "about which neither historical record nor myth nor Scripture make report." That day is a Saturday which "has become the longest of days." The unspoken reference here is, of course, to the Easter story and the blank day between the cross and resurrection when it really did appear that God had died and that the hope of redemption was obliterated. The theological significance of that empty, hopeless, interminable day has been almost completely ignored by Christians, yet its importance in the cultural context we are discussing can hardly be

---

37. Steiner, *Grammars of Creation*, 4.
38. Steiner, 4.
39. George Steiner, *Real Presences: Is There Anything in What We Say?* (London: Faber & Faber, 1991), 3.
40. Steiner, *Real Presences*, 229.

overstressed, not least because it suggests that our experience of the loss of God is analogous to that which is to be discovered at the very heart of the Easter message. Steiner describes the experience of modern, Western people as "the long day's journey of the Saturday," between "suffering, aloneness, unutterable waste on the one hand, and the dream of liberation, of rebirth on the other."[41] What this implies, in the words of Alan Lewis, is that contemporary Christians are sent "by the Easter Saturday God into an Easter Saturday world, for the sake of that world's new Easter life and eschatological renewal."[42]

A final voice we need to hear as we draw this discussion to its close is that of Terry Eagleton who, in his *Culture and the Death of God*, examines the crisis occasioned by God's "apparent disappearance." This analysis of contemporary, Western culture reaches a conclusion that sets the scene for our own concluding comments. Few modern scholars display the depth of theological and biblical knowledge to be found in these pages, but even more unusual is the keen perceptiveness of Eagleton's discussion of the role of faith during the "long Saturday" through which we must live. He criticizes the claim that history has come to an end as nothing more than a triumphalism based on "the post-Cold-War West's increasingly high-handed political activities across the globe," one consequence of which was the unleashing of a radical Islamic backlash. The claim that history had arrived at its end "simply succeeded in prising it open again; the end of one grand narrative was the occasion for the birth of another, that of the so-called war on terror."

> Western capitalism, in short, has managed to help spawn not only secularism but also fundamentalism, a most creditable feat of dialectics. Having slain the deity, it has now had a hand in

---

41. Steiner, 232.

42. These are the words of Alan Lewis, whose *Between Cross and Resurrection* offers a unique and brilliant theological study of Easter Saturday (344). It so happened that in the very week that the two paragraphs above were written I heard a performance of Michael Tippet's oratorio *A Child of Our Time* at the Edinburgh Festival. I have rarely been so moved by a piece of music; the story it tells is quintessentially that of our "long Saturday," between the horrors described by Steiner when, as Tippet expresses it, "the world turn[ed] on its dark side," and the hope which he brilliantly discovers in the Negro spirituals which the chorus sing as the promise of the longed-for collapse of "the city of the usurers"!

restoring him to life, as a refuge and a strength for those who feel crushed by its own predatory politics.[43]

It is, however, Eagleton's concluding comments on the role of religious faith today which relate to our concern with the decision for God or Mammon and I quote them at some length:

> If religious faith were to be released from the burden of furnishing social orders with a set of rationales for their existence, it might be free to rediscover its true purpose as a critique of all such politics. In this sense, its superfluity might prove its salvation. The New Testament has little or nothing to say of responsible citizenship. It is not a "civilised" document at all. It shows no enthusiasm for social consensus. . . . What it adds to common-or-garden morality is not some supernatural support, but the grossly inconvenient news that our forms of life must undergo radical dissolution if they are to be reborn as just and compassionate communities. The sign of that dissolution is a solidarity with the poor and powerless. *It is here that a new configuration of faith, culture and politics might be born.*[44]

With that challenge in mind, we turn to reflect on how world Christianity, with its new heartlands located in a huge range of cultural contexts across the Global South, might respond to the world we have described.

---

43. Terry Eagleton, *Culture and the Death of God* (New Haven: Yale University Press, 2015), 197–98.

44. Eagleton, *Culture and the Death of God*, 207–8; emphasis added.

CHAPTER 11

World Christianity and the Great Unravelling

A truncated Gospel ... can only be the basis for unfaithful churches, for strongholds of racial and class discrimination, for religious clubs with a message that has no relevance to practical life in the social, the economic and the political spheres. (René Padilla)[1]

The cultural crisis of the modern, Western world, serious as it is, must not be allowed to overshadow and obscure the reality of different developments elsewhere on our planet. Terry Eagleton himself lamented the fact that almost all cultural theorists in Western academia pass over in silence "the most vital beliefs and activities of billions of ordinary men and women, simply because they happen not to be to their personal taste."[2] With regard to Christianity, Andrew Walls had long ago recognized that as Western Christendom entered a period of significant recession and decline, the liberating message of Jesus Christ was bearing unexpected, largely unnoticed, fruit in the phenomenal growth of indigenous movements across what came to be called the Global South. This was related to another theme in Walls's work concerning the "infinite translatability" of the message of the gospel, and the pattern of *serial* growth which had marked its centuries-long history. Communication across

---

1. René Padilla, "Evangelism and the World," in *Let the Earth Hear His Voice: International Congress on World Evangelization, Lausanne, Switzerland*, ed. J. D. Douglas (Minneapolis: World Wide Publications, 1975), 138.
2. Eagleton, *Culture and the Death of God*, ix.

cultural and linguistic borders had repeatedly resulted in the reappearance of the faith in new contexts beyond its previous heartlands and Walls concluded that in the contemporary situation, "southern expressions of Christianity are becoming the dominant forms of the faith."

> This is likely to mean the appearance of new themes and priorities undreamt of by ourselves or by earlier Christian ages; for it is the mark of Christian faith that it must bring Christ to the big issues which are closest to men's hearts; and it does so through the structures by which people perceive and recognize their world; and these are not the same for all. It must not be assumed that themes that have been primary in the Christian penetration of former cultures will remain primary for all the new ones. They may not possess those points of reference which made orthodoxy, for instance, or the Christian nation, or the primacy of the individual conscience, absolutely crucial to the capture of Christ by other world views.[3]

This is a theme that would require another book in order to begin to do it justice. All that can be done here is to underline the huge importance of the global shift identified by Andrew Walls. Among the many scholars who have recognized the significance of his insights, Fernando Segovia describes the statistical evidence of the growth of non-Western Christianity as "simply astounding," and notes that the process "has only just begun." What the impact of this movement will be, both beyond the West and, as a result of migration, within it, "will not be fully grasped until a century or two from now." However, it is already clear that this paradigm shift signifies that "the past domination of the West in the formulation of the direction of Christianity will gradually but inexorably yield to a much more decentered and diversified formation."[4]

---

3. Andrew F. Walls, *The Missionary Movement in Christian History: Studies in the Transmission of Faith* (Edinburgh: T&T Clark, 1996), 24. See also William Burrows, Mark Gornik and Janice McLean, eds., *Understanding World Christianity: The Vision and Work of Andrew F. Walls* (New York: Orbis, 2011) for a series of brilliant essays on Walls's vital contribution to the understanding of Christianity in the modern world.

4. Fernando Segovia, "Interpreting beyond Borders: Postcolonial Studies and Diasporic Studies in Biblical Criticism," in *Interpreting beyond Borders* (Sheffield: Sheffield Academic, 2000), 19–23.

Christianity in the Majority World

The "diversified formation" anticipated by Segovia was already presaged in the Second Vatican Council in the 1960s and at the Lausanne Congress on World Evangelization in 1974. The groundbreaking event that was Vatican II had resulted from a series of massive shifts within Roman Catholicism, both with regard to the attitude towards the modern, secular world, and in relation to new perspectives concerning the gospel and the church resulting from the spread of Catholic Christianity beyond its European heartlands. Karl Rahner, whose theology addressed these changes, articulated the radical issues they posed with regard to Catholicism's response to modernity. He challenged Catholics in Europe as follows:

> If we once have the courage to give up our defense of the old facades which have nothing, or very little, behind them; if we cease to maintain, in public, the pretence of a universal Christendom; if we stop straining every nerve to get *everybody* baptized, to get *everybody* married in church and onto our registers . . . if, by letting all of this go, we visibly relieve Christianity of the burdensome impression that it accepts responsibility for everything that goes on under this Christian top-dressing . . . a folk religion (at the same level as folk costumes) – *then* we could be free for real missionary adventure and apostolic self-confidence.[5]

With regard to the form taken by Catholicism beyond Europe, I beg the indulgence of readers if I relate a personal experience at this point. Some years ago I accompanied an international group of students on a visit to Nairobi and we spent time with local Christians in the vast slums of Kibera. Walking out of that sprawling township on one occasion, I found myself wrestling again with the agonizing questions which inevitably arise from exposure to the poverty and disadvantage in which so many millions of people exist. I stumbled into a bookshop on the edge of Kibera and discovered a small

---

5. Karl Rahner, *The Christian Commitment: Essays in Pastoral Theology* (New York: Sheed & Ward, 1963), 34–35. Elsewhere he urges the rejection of "the tyranny of statistics" which will be against us "for the next hundred years." Then follows this statement: "*One* real conversion in a great city is something more splendid than the spectacle of a whole remote village going to the sacraments" (33). Italics original.

volume by an African theologian I had never heard about previously. His name was Jean-Marc Ela, and the book – which became like gold to me – was his *My Faith as an African*. That evening I devoured Ela's book and realized that I had discovered African theology in a completely new dimension. On the first page I read this: Christianity "has long practiced a 'deculturizing' control over African populations – forcing them brutally to sever their roots and lose their authenticity. Even today, after a hundred years of evangelization, these young forms of Christianity remain subject to the cultural tutelage of their mother churches."[6]

I discovered that the author, a brilliant scholar with a PhD from the University of Strasbourg for a thesis on Martin Luther's image of the cross, and a second doctorate in sociology (also pursued in France in quest of the analytical tools which would enable the reading of the gospel in relation to African social realities), had literally poured out his life among oppressed peasants in the north of Cameroon. Ela expressed his gratitude to "the African nuns and the young black priest" who had given him fraternal support "in the hard struggle, carried on night and day," to try to think and live an experience of liberating evangelization "without gold and silver." He described the origins of his extraordinary reflections as being "the villages of the lowlands and of the mountains where we went on foot, our only baggage a sleeping mat, a Bible, our heart, and the love of the poor."[7] In the centre of Africa this radical Catholic priest had felt the same dissatisfaction and frustration with the inherited structures of the church that we have heard Karl Rahner express, only in this context the very notion of Christendom was a completely alien concept: "I did not feel called to become the manager of a form of decaying Christianity, bound up in its doctrine and discipline, so I decided to keep my distance from a model of a church *designed elsewhere by people who do not know the conditions of the mountain people.*"[8]

It will not surprise the reader to learn that Ela was subjected to fierce criticism and marginalization by the local Catholic hierarchy; he was never invited to teach in a Catholic institution, becoming instead a lecturer in the Protestant faculty of the University of Yaoundé. His deep understanding of traditional

---

6. Jean-Marc Ela, *My Faith as an African* (Nairobi: Acton Publishers, 2001), xiii.
7. Ela, *My Faith as an African*, xix.
8. Ela, 5; emphasis added.

African cultures, and the insistence that the gospel had to be related to the fundamental concerns of the tribal peoples among whom he had lived, did not prevent him from also engaging with the challenges posed by modernity, development and urbanization. Here is a passage in which Ela's prophetic insight leads to a searching critical analysis of the plight of modern Africa:

> How can we express our belonging to God in a continent that does not belong to itself? Under the pretext of cooperation, economic and financial organizations freely quarrel over our lands and beaches, our bauxite, copper and diamond mines, and our business and tourism – without neglecting our uranium, oil, and of course, the very conscience of our people. . . . The phenomenon of recolonization in Africa is developing a new proletariat in the cities and the countryside. The capital cities grow like an enormous cancer, and are becoming a formidable powder keg ready to explode. . . . How can we express this Kingdom [of God] concretely under current conditions in our countries where the real but secret empire of financial power and capital has reduced a fabulously rich continent to a pauper?[9]

As we have seen, Ela studied in France and later, having been repeatedly warned that there was a serious threat to his life in Cameroon, he lived and died in Canada, so that he had first-hand experience of the situation in the Western world. In perhaps the most moving section of *My Faith as an African* he writes that it is the "Third World" which "carries within itself the hidden Christ," and that those who claim to be Christian must "go and rediscover Christ in the slums, in places of misery and domination, among the majority of the poor and oppressed people. *It is the Third World that allows the church to make salvation in Jesus Christ visible.*"[10] Having myself discovered the extraordinary faith of believers in Kibera, this passage struck me with enormous power, as did the following question, directed to the churches of the prosperous and privileged West:

> What God do the people of the West believe in? What is the Good News for those who live in dominating societies? . . .

---

9. Ela, 149.
10. Ela, 99.

Christians should consider the failure of decades of development to date, and design a model for life that leaves room for our daily work for whatever will create a different future. . . . In the painful march of the peoples of the Third World toward the victory of life, perhaps Christians should remember that the God of Life has lifted up the poor and fed the hungry. Today that God calls us to struggle for justice and right. Then we shall be able to sing the Magnificat, not in Latin, but in deeds, wherever faith is lived among the poor. We shall sing the Magnificat in the slums, in the villages, in the streets – wherever we are – because the truth of God is fully engaged both in the countries of hunger and in the dominating societies.[11]

The crucial issue of the influence of modern Western culture on missionary Christianity in Africa, expressed so clearly by Ela, has a parallel in the language used by Latin American evangelicals at the Lausanne Congress in 1974. If the Second Vatican Council was the harbinger of radical changes within Catholicism, the Lausanne gathering of more than two thousand delegates, the majority from the non-Western world, was to occasion the emergence of prophetic voices within Protestant evangelicalism asking the same kind of questions. The quotation at the head of this chapter is taken from the address delivered at this international assembly by René Padilla from Argentina. If any

---

11. Ela, 100. In a later volume with the title *African Cry*, Ela concentrated his critique on the sources of corruption and oppression in the post-colonial world. "In order to emerge from the fundamental ambiguity of traditional mission, the churches must always take care to observe themselves in the mirror of the gospel, lest they fall dupe to any collusion that would make them pillars of the systems dominating the human being in the world of our times. *We must rediscover the subversive power of Christianity vis-à-vis all idolatries, including those of the powers that be*" (*African Cry* [Eugene: Wipf & Stock, 2005], 26; emphasis added). I have discussed this remarkable man's work in my "Theology as a Voice for the Voiceless: Jean-Marc Ela's *African Cry*," *Theological College of Northern Nigeria Research Bulletin* 52 (2010): 19–29. In 1986 a group of 132 "Concerned Evangelicals" from the township of Soweto in apartheid South Africa published a "critique of their own theology and practice" in which they described the evangelicalism they had inherited as being "rooted in the USA and Europe" and so "blind to western domination and exploitation of the peoples of the Third World." Attitudes derived from colonial times remained prevalent in evangelical circles: "For instance they still see blacks as the 'mission field' and whites as the bearers of truth and civilization. They still see Africa as the 'dark' continent which needs the gospel when there are more 'lapsed' Christians or non-Christians in Europe and in white South Africa" (Concerned Evangelicals, *Evangelical Witness in South Africa: A Critique of Evangelical Theology and Practice by South African Evangelicals* [Oxford: Regnum Books and Evangelical Alliance (UK), 1986], 25).

public pronouncements in modern times merit the description "prophetic," this one surely belongs within that category. Pre-circulating his address to enable comments to be returned in advance of the event, Padilla responded publicly to the feedback, some of it critical and even hostile. His address on "Evangelism and the World" divided the huge audience between those who hailed it as a desperately needed corrective to Western priorities and dominance, and others who lamented it as a violation of received orthodoxy which verged on heresy! In the original paper Padilla had exposed what he called "culture Christianity," challenging the association of the gospel with "the American way of life" and condemning it as a contemporary form of syncretism which had turned faith "into a type of merchandise, the acquisition of which guarantees the consumer the highest values – *success* in life and personal *happiness* now and forever."

> The God of this type of Christianity is the God of "cheap grace," the God who constantly gives but never demands, the God fashioned expressly for mass-man, who is controlled by the law of least possible effort and seeks easy solutions, the God who gives his attention to those who will not reject him because they need him as an analgesic.[12]

The voices from Latin America that so deeply impacted the Lausanne Congress in 1974 serve to remind us that this region of the world was also the context within which liberation theology had come to birth. Its leading proponents employed forthright language in denouncing the injustices of the

---

12. Padilla, "Evangelism and the World," 126. See David R. Swartz, *Facing West: American Evangelicals in an Age of World Christianity* (Oxford: Oxford University Press, 2020) for a detailed description of this event. He concludes that Lausanne "sparked a transformative conversation about the nature of missionary work, imperialism, and social responsibility. Just beginning to understand the magnitude of global Christianity, American evangelicals in the 1970s were living in a brave new postcolonial world. The Majority World had put them on notice that missiology would no longer develop in North American isolation" (123). The critique of Western missions emanating from Latin America could take even stronger forms, as evidenced by the claim of Orlando Costas that there was a "secret alliance between the world missionary movement and the internationalist capitalist enterprise." He exempted the early Moravian missionaries from this charge, and recognized that William Carey and his colleagues had established "a genuine commune in which they shared the little that they earned with their manual labour." However, Costas argued that subsequent mission work was "so dependent on the world of free enterprise that it is practically impossible for it to exist without that support" (Orlando E. Costas, *Christ Outside the Gate: Mission beyond Christendom* [New York: Orbis, 1982], 62, 69).

world system, reflecting the righteous anger of Christians who had lived close to many of the poorest people on earth and were outraged at the indifference to such suffering within the wider human family. For example, Jon Sobrino described the "First World" as being submerged in the "sleep of inhumanity" since it continued to be wilfully ignorant of the plight of those whom he identified as "the crucified peoples." This prophetic voice from South America clearly echoes those we have already heard coming from Africa:

> People do not want to acknowledge or face up to the reality of a crucified world, and even less do we want to ask ourselves what is our share of responsibility for such a world. The world of poverty is truly the great unknown. It is surprising that the First World can know so much and yet ignore what is so fundamental about the world in which we live.[13]

Having listened to voices from Africa and Latin America, we must also hear the testimony of Christian witnesses from the vast regions of Asia and the Pacific Rim. Michael Nai-Chiu Poon has described how the claim of the historic churches in the previous heartlands of Christianity to be the guardians of universally valid forms of the faith has been invalidated by the fact that the global expansion of the religion has taken it *"beyond the European mind and experience."*[14] Churches across Asia have increasingly discovered each other as, in a context of religious pluralism, often with a particular Asian religious tradition dominant, they have recognized the irrelevance of inherited denominational divisions which originated in another place and a different time. Poon points out the role that geographical and geological factors play in the process of contextualizing faith:

> Asia's geological configuration is different from that of the transAtlantic world. . . . It rests on two stable continental platforms,

---

13. Jon Sobrino, *The Principle of Mercy: Taking the Crucified People from the Cross* (New York: Orbis, 1994), 5. See also Daniel M. Bell, *Liberation Theology after the End of History: The Refusal to Cease Suffering* (London: Routledge, 2001), 175.

14. Michael Nai-Chiu Poon, "The Rise of Asian Pacific Christianity and Challenges for the Church Universal," in *Ecumenical Visions for the 21st Century: A Reader for Theological Education*, eds. Melisande Lorke and Dietrich Werner (Geneva: WCC, 2013), 65; emphasis added. Robert Schreiter observes that although current cartography represents the Atlantic Ocean at the centre of the world, "it is likely that this old practice could soon change as the Century of the Pacific dawns upon us" (*Reconciliation: Mission and Ministry in a Changing Social Order* [New York: Orbis Books, 1992], 6).

and two major arcs of volcanic instability that stretch from the Indonesian to the Philippines islands. The region consists of a series of geographical conversations between lands and seas, highlands and lowlands, rivers and mountains. The geological and geographical configuration of the Pacific Rim contrasts sharply with that of the transatlantic world.[15]

In a most revealing analysis, Poon shows how geography influences historical, cultural and religious developments, contrasting the "stable geological conditions in Western Europe" and the east coasts of the Americas which made the creation of a shared cultural and linguistic world possible, with the "vulnerability, volatility and fragility" that are central features of social life across Asia. In such situations, "migrant workers, refugees of wars and stateless peoples testify to the fluid conditions in human life that are punctuated by the eruptions of wars, tsunamis and earthquakes." Whereas the solidity of tradition made visible in the shape of European cathedrals was related to regional topography, life becomes apocalyptic and millions of people live under the existential threat of "an impending end" in the Asian context. Poon's conclusion is enormously important:

> Ecumenical experiences in the Pacific Rim highlight the geological and geographical foundation of world Christianity. The Pacific Rim opens up spiritual horizons and awakes moral tasks *that Christendom experiences cannot reveal.* If there is a need for the church universal to rediscover a new theological grammar, syntax and semantics for today's world, the Pacific Rim may well be a fruitful arena for this theological work.[16]

Michael Nai-Chiu Poon's reference to "ecumenical experiences" alerts us to the urgent priority of the discovery of a unity-in-diversity by which a Christianity that has become multicultural might offer a dangerously divided

---

15. Poon, "Rise of Asian Pacific Christianity," 69.
16. Poon, 70; emphasis added. See the important article "Theological Method" by T. D. Gener and L. Bautista in which they comment: "Times have changed. With the collapse of Euro-American (Western) dominance in Christian theology, there is an increased recognition of a polycentric world and a polycentric world Christianity, with emphasis on many theological centers.... The future beckons for a truly catholic Christianity that honors unity-in-diversity in both church and theology" (in *Global Dictionary of Theology*, eds. William A. Dyrness and Veli-Matti Kärkkäinen [Nottingham: Inter-Varsity Press, 2008], 890).

world concrete evidence of the healing power of the gospel of Jesus Christ. Andrew Walls expresses this so well when he writes that the great ecumenical issues of the twenty-first century "will be about how African and Indian and Chinese and Korean and Hispanic and North American and European Christians can together make real the life of the body of Christ."[17] In particular, the voices we have heard demand that we ask how Christians in the dominating societies, in the places where the structures of a dying Christendom linger still, will react to the promise of what has elsewhere been described as the "new reformation."[18] To that question we finally turn.

"Come Out of Her, My People"

We have travelled a very long way in this book, from the ancient world in which urban forms first appeared in human history, through the development of a succession of imperial powers, culminating in the Roman Empire in which cities multiplied wherever the conquering legions imposed the Pax Romana. At the same time, we have recognized that this "secular" history constitutes the context within which both the story of biblical Israel and the events described in the literature we know as the New Testament took

---

17. Andrew F. Walls, *The Cross-Cultural Process in Christian History: Studies in the Transmission and Appropriation of Faith* (Edinburgh: T&T Clark, 2002), 69. Elsewhere he writes that the churches of Africa and Asia "are being forced to work out some sort of Christian response to situations where Western theology has no answers because it has no questions or any relevant experience" ("The Transmission of Christian Faith: A Reflection," in *The Wiley Blackwell Companion to World Christianity*, eds. Lamin Sanneh and Michael McClymond [Oxford: Wiley Blackwell, 2016], 697).

18. The historian Justo González argues that people will look back on our period as "the Reformation of the Twentieth Century." We are living through "a time of vast changes in the church's self-understanding, and it is possible that the consequences of those changes will be more drastic than those which took place in the sixteenth century" (*Mañana: Christian Theology from a Hispanic Perspective* [Nashville: Abingdon Press, 1990], 43). This book is a key resource in regard to this subject; elsewhere González underlines the message that we have already heard from the Global South: "It is the Christian poor of today's world that will bring salvation to the rich nations of the world, who because of the material wealth of their own nations *are too blind to see the truth of the gospel*" (14; emphasis added). Another Asian voice that must be heard is that of Vinoth Ramachandra, who warns that as long as both Western and Asian Christians remain blind "to the way their economic and political power distorts their presentation of the gospel, all their well-meaning efforts in 'global mission' will only backfire on the churches of the Third World. Once again the poor are exposed to a Constantinian Christ rather than the Christ of the cross. The alliance of 'big business' expertise with missionary enterprise will prove disastrous, as it always has in the history of the church" (*Gods That Fail: Modern Idolatry and Christian Mission* [Carlisle: Paternoster, 1996], 220).

place, and that those events cannot be properly understood apart from the rise and fall of the ever-expanding imperial powers. The language of the Bible concerning the *kingdom* of God itself indicates that the message of the Hebrew prophets and the movement begun by Jesus ultimately transcends its Jewish origins and has the future of "the nations" as its horizon. That message therefore constitutes a direct and unambiguous challenge to the idols of power and wealth which usurped the reign of God and brought social and economic division to the earth.

Beyond this, we have traced the rise of Christianity, again attempting to read its history in relation to the broad historical context in which its growth took place, especially with regard to the reappearance of cities in Europe, and the subsequent growth of money power which, with the development of the modern, industrialized world, has extended its dominance over individuals and societies, expanding its geographical reach to a scale that is completely unprecedented. As we have seen above, the empire of Mammon has been the context within which Christianity's latest missionary expansion has occurred, and once again that phenomenon has taken place far from the glittering centres of urban power and glory, among the millions of people on the underside of the modern world who have discovered in the crucified God the promise of liberation and hope.

On the final pages of his brilliant study *The City in History*, Lewis Mumford states that the future of the urban world of today will be bleak indeed unless we can recover the vision of the city as "an organ of love," a love manifested in the transformation of both society and economy, so that they become devoted to "the care and culture" of all the global city's peoples.

> In order to defeat the insensate forces that now threaten civilization from within, we must transcend the original frustrations and negations that have dogged the city throughout its history. Otherwise the sterile gods of power, unrestrained by organic limits of human goals, will remake man in their own faceless image and bring human history to an end.[19]

What role might world Christianity play in such a transformation, and what will be required for it to fulfil its calling and mission within this historical

---

19. Lewis Mumford, *The City in History* (Harmondsworth: Penguin, 1966), 655.

context? The summons which John of Patmos heard, urging the churches of Asia Minor to "come out" of the collapsing city of Babylon, "so that you will not share in her sins" (Rev 18:4), echoes down the centuries and confronts the disciples of Jesus in a globalized world with a challenge they dare not evade. While we must not ignore the differences between then and now, the parallels which exist between these contexts are striking. Revelation 18 contains one of the most detailed descriptions known to us of the extent of Roman trading links from this period, providing a picture that complements the report of Aristides which we cited earlier in this book.[20] The many products which flowed incessantly into Rome from every corner of the empire have been shown to have come from Spain, Greece and Egypt, and much further afield from distant lands, including India, China and Africa. We cannot linger over every detail, but by way of example the phrase "articles of every kind made of *ivory*" (18:12) draws attention to the excessive consumption of luxury products by the Roman elite, and to a trade which endangered the survival of Syrian elephants in the first century, and was thus "one of the earliest stages in the process which in our own time threatens the survival of the elephant" as a species![21] The list reaches its terrible climax – or rather its dreadful nadir – with the phrase "and bodies and souls of men" (18:13 NKJV). This is a prophetic indictment of the slave trade and of a socio-economic system in which nothing was beyond the reach of the Roman market. Bauckham concludes that by placing this exposure of the horrors of the slave trade at the climax of the catalogue of imports which flooded into Rome, the author of Revelation was revealing "the inhuman brutality, the contempt for human life, on which the whole of Rome's prosperity and luxury rests."[22]

It is difficult to read this text without being reminded of Max Weber's image of the "iron cage" within which, he suggested, everyone now born into "the tremendous cosmos of the modern economic order" discovers himself or

---

20. See pp. 112–13.

21. Richard Bauckham, *The Climax of Prophecy: Studies on the Book of Revelation* (Edinburgh: T&T Clark, 1993), 357. He cites Roman authors as describing how "the extravagant Roman use of ivory led to the severe depletion of elephants within the accessible areas of North Africa, and the shortage of African ivory was made up by the increasing trade in Indian ivory throughout the first century."

22. Bauckham, *Climax of Prophecy*, 371.

herself confined!²³ The parallel between now and then becomes even more stark and disturbing when we recall that something very much like that iron cage seemed to be present in Laodicea in a church which boasted, "I am rich; I have acquired wealth and do not need a thing" (Rev 3:17). The reality was that this community had become blind to its own spiritual bankruptcy, and deaf to the excluded Christ left outside and knocking on the door! Do the voices we have heard earlier in this chapter, pleading with Christians in "dominating societies" to hear their cries, function in a similar way today? Here is one Western reader of the Apocalypse who thinks so:

> For where is a first-world white male of privilege to find himself described in the Apocalypse if not in this seventh message – rich, not needing anything, neither hot nor cold, but lukewarm – the typical citizen of a reigning order that keeps the majority of the planet's inhabitants in servitude to furnish me with my comforts?²⁴

On a number of occasions Andrew Walls discussed the phenomenon of Christian expansion and decline and drew upon the work of the American historian Kenneth Scott Latourette, who had identified three tests by which the influence of Christ on human societies and cultures might be assessed.²⁵ The first test can be described as *statistical*: the attempt to quantify the number of people professing faith in Christ and forming communities to worship and follow him. This approach to the assessment of Christian growth has become popular in a technological age in which statistics reflecting expansion and success are pervasive everywhere. What Walls calls "the counting exercise" has taken sophisticated forms in the era of artificial intelligence, so that church

---

23. Max Weber, *The Protestant Ethic and the Spirit of Capitalism* (London: Counterpoint, 1985), 181.

24. Harry O. Maier, *Apocalypse Recalled: The Book of Revelation after Christendom* (Minneapolis: Fortress, 2002), 38.

25. See "A History of the Expansion of Christianity Reconsidered," in Walls, *Cross-Cultural Process*, 3–26. This was previously published by Yale Divinity School Library in 1996 as Occasional Publication No. 8. Walls also made use of Latourette's work in his Henry Martyn Lecture for the annual conference of the Evangelical Missionary Alliance in 1985. This brilliant paper was titled "Christian Expansion and the Condition of Western Culture" and was subsequently circulated with other annual Martyn lectures under the title *Changing the World*, MARC Monograph no. 8 (Bromley: MARC Europe and Evangelical Missionary Alliance, [1986]).

growth can be quantified on a global scale, enabling researchers to identify "unreached peoples" who then become the target of missionary activity. While he recognized the importance of statistical evidence, Latourette also knew its limitations and insisted that other questions had to be asked concerning the depth and socio-cultural consequences of movements of conversion. This led him to a second test which we may call the *social factor*, in which the question becomes whether or not the impact of faith in Jesus extends beyond mere profession; whether, to use biblical language, there are signs of the coming of the kingdom of God in movements inspired by faith in Christ which effect the transformation of society and culture. As Walls puts it, the church criterion alone is no guarantee of the continuing influence of Christ: "The church without the sign of the kingdom is a counter-sign of the kingdom, hiding Christ instead of revealing him to the world."[26]

Finally, Latourette went one step further and proposed a third test of Christian expansion which he described as "the effect of Christianity upon mankind as a whole." That is to say, there is a wider dimension of Christ's influence upon history, difficult to quantify, but resulting from the insistence of the gospel that the resurrection of Jesus Christ has forever changed the history of the world. Andrew Walls identifies this test as *the gospel criterion* since the New Testament declares that the rising of Jesus from the dead has created a new dimension in human history, reaching "to the depth of the individual personality" and extending through "the whole of society and environment."[27]

Elsewhere, Walls related Latourette's three tests of Christian expansion to the condition of Christianity in contemporary Western culture, concluding that with regard to the *statistical* test, "Western Europe is probably the least encouraging area in the world." Likewise, in respect of the second test concerning the *signs of the kingdom*, we look in vain today for contemporary parallels to earlier radical movements such as monasticism or the eighteenth-century missionary movement, as described previously in this book. Contemporary Western Christianity "has shown remarkably little fundamental innovation for some time past. The changes in society have been very much greater than the capacity of Christians to respond to them."[28] Walls

---

26. Walls, *Changing the World*, 15.
27. Walls, 20.
28. Walls, "Christian Expansion," 23.

concludes that at a time in which Western culture is in the grip of a hideous idolatry, Christianity "has so far issued no clear call to repentance from the cult of Mammon."

> It is possible to accommodate [Mammon's] worship very well to the apparatus of church going. It is possible to hold evangelistic campaigns that spell out the gospel in easy steps, and never breathe a word about the false gods who hold Western society in thrall. It is not that the Western world is devoid of Christian witness. . . . It is rather that *Western Christianity has ceased to have critical contact with Western culture.* It can no longer do it any harm or any good.[29]

Clearly, we have arrived at the point at which the central question posed by this study emerges with great clarity: what is required for world Christianity today to resist the juggernaut of free market forces in a technological society which appears to be beyond challenge across the contemporary world?[30] In a series of studies, Michael Budde has argued that the crucial questions which cannot be avoided today are all related to "Christian formation," which he describes as involving the "lifelong effort to push against interpretive frameworks not rooted in the word become flesh, in the Christ that brings the kingdom of God among us and calls us to live in the world as if that kingdom has already begun." Budde insists that being a Christian involves "changing the operating system of our hearts and minds":

---

29. Walls, 23; emphasis added.

30. As long ago as 1954 Jacques Ellul wrote in *The Technological Society* that, while Western civilization still attested to "a secularized Christian ideology" which valued "brotherly relations," the structures of the world increasingly represented diametrically the opposite. "The fundamental rule of the world today is the rule of economic, political and class competition" (*The Technological Society* [New York: Vintage, 1964; orig. French ed. 1954], 333). I regret that I discovered the work of Tomáš Halik too late to include reference to it in this discussion. His voice reminds us that Christians in post-communist states in central and eastern Europe have their own distinctive contribution to make to the conversation taking place within world Christianity. Here is a sample: "How can we resist the temptation to turn the Church and religion into a ghetto, a locked and fortified bunker, a mausoleum of yesterday's certitudes or a private garden for consumers of soothing and soporific drugs? Can Christianity . . . inspire the formation of a political culture capable of transforming a chaotic polyphony into a moral climate of mutual respect, communication, and shared values?" (*The Afternoon of Christianity: The Courage to Change*, trans. Gerald Turner [Notre Dame: University of Notre Dame Press, 2024], 29–30).

> It means that the process of making disciples is about taking down the scaffolding of some interpretive frames... dismantling the complexes that make nationalism seem normal, subverting the conventional wisdom that makes might right, and giving people new eyes with which to see and new ears with which to hear all that's been going on around them all the while, but to which they have been oblivious so long as they lacked the right equipment with which to catch, retrieve and act upon this God-soaked reality.[31]

The language used here points us unerringly towards the central importance of conversion in the New Testament. Early in the Fourth Gospel we are told of a man named Nicodemus, a distinguished member of the Sanhedrin, who was attracted to Jesus by the "miraculous signs" which accompanied his ministry. The reaction of Jesus, both here and in other accounts of conversations with privileged and wealthy enquirers, was not to welcome this interest and offer immediate access to the new movement, but instead to make absolutely clear the unconditional requirement for entry into discipleship: access to the kingdom of God is conditional upon *new birth*, a requirement which baffled the enquirer who responds by asking how such a thing was possible? The text might suggest that Nicodemus was thinking in rather crude, physical terms of the impossibility of beginning life anew, but it is equally possible that, like so many wealthy enquirers in the early centuries of the Christian movement, he really grasped the difficulty of divesting oneself of the habits, values and practices which become embedded by a lifetime of cultural, social and religious conditioning! In other words, Nicodemus, rather than displaying a crude literalism, actually recognized the truth of Jesus's words and grasped the immensity of the challenge of entering the kingdom of God. If confirmation of this reading of the text is needed, we have it at the other end of the Gospel when Joseph of Arimathea, another member of the Sanhedrin, requests the Roman authorities for permission to care for the body of the crucified Jesus, and, we are informed, was "accompanied by Nicodemus, the man who earlier

---

31. Michael L. Budde, *The Borders of Baptism: Identities, Allegiances, and the Church* (Eugene: Cascade, 2011), 123. See also his *Foolishness to Gentiles: Essays on Empire, Nationalism, and Discipleship* (Eugene: Cascade, 2022) and *The Two Churches: Catholicism and Capitalism in the World System* (Durham: Duke University Press, 1992).

had visited Jesus by night" (19:39). There could not be clearer evidence that the enquirer's original doubts had been overcome, the secret of kingdom life had been discovered, and genuine conversion had moved Nicodemus from anonymous enquirer to active disciple of his now crucified Lord.

What we may call the "Nicodemus question" hovers over world Christianity today. In fact, the context in which we find ourselves in the twenty-first century makes the prospect of radical conversion appear more unlikely than ever. Nicodemus had a head start over us since he knew Moses and the Prophets, whereas the world into which millions of people are born today is one in which culture and education make talk of "new birth" appear not just absurd, but potentially treasonous.

Eugene McCarraher's remarkable book *The Enchantments of Mammon: How Capitalism Became the Religion of Modernity* challenges the long-held view that the modern world became disenchanted and secular, and describes in extraordinary detail how capitalism became the new location of the sacred, creating supportive networks in the shape of business schools, capturing the imaginative realm and intellectual and political discourse, and even producing its own cathedrals in the form of the iconic buildings celebrating its triumph in every major city on earth.

> Where Weber had seen desacralization as a constituent and expansive feature of modern consciousness, [Lewis] Mumford suggested that enchantment had instead been redirected toward the paleotechnical apparatus of industrial capitalism.... Mumford underlined the religious character of machinery and of the hopes invested in its dubious guarantees of limitless mastery and wealth.... "Mechanical invention," he argued, "was the answer to a dwindling faith," a "substitute religion" that supplanted a Christianity grown stale, implausible, and subservient.... The alleged disenchantment of the world introduced, not a brave new world of secular reason and justice, but a "religion of power" embodied most frightfully and destructively in industrial capitalism.[32]

---

32. Eugene McCarraher, *The Enchantments of Mammon: How Capitalism Became the Religion of Modernity* (Cambridge: Belknap Press, 2019), 485. With regard to the significance

If this is indeed the case, then the Nicodemus question becomes more urgent and challenging than ever: how in a culture saturated by capitalist enchantment can we discover an alternative way of thinking and behaving which would enable us to actually begin life again? The question can be asked by people who are wearied by the barrenness of life in a culture without messianic hope, but it must also be of urgent concern to professing Christians who, familiar with the *concept* of "new birth," nonetheless experience tensions between what they sincerely believe, and the difficulty of translating those beliefs into praxis in a world governed by very different values and ambitions.

No one, I think, has described this dilemma more movingly than Johann Baptist Metz, who survived the Second World War and was left facing the most urgent existential questions. As a sixteen-year-old boy he and his young friends had been taken out of school and thrust into the trenches of a conflict which was then in its final weeks. Sent back by his commanding officer with a message to headquarters, he returned to discover his entire unit had been obliterated: "Now I could only see dead and empty faces, where the day before I had shared childhood fears and laughter. I remember nothing but a wordless cry."[33]

Like many young German Christians who survived the horrors of the Second World War, Metz turned to theology with agonizing questions concerning human suffering and the search for hope. *He found himself asking the Nicodemus question*, and it was to trouble him throughout the remainder of his life. Here he is addressing a Catholic Congress in 1978 and asking whether Christianity in West Germany was now "only a bourgeois religion – one of great value for society, but devoid of any messianic future?"

> The conversion of hearts is indeed the threshold to the messianic future. It is the most radical and most challenging form of conversion and revolution, and it is so because transforming situations in society never changes all that really needs to be changed. . . . If we are to trust the gospel testimonies, it goes through people like a shock, reaching deep down into the

---

of iconic buildings, see Leslie Sklair, *The Icon Project: Architecture, Cities, and Capitalist Globalization* (Oxford: Oxford University Press, 2017).

33. Johann Baptist Metz, *Remembering and Resisting: The New Political Theology*, ed. John K. Downey (Eugene: Cascade, 2022), 81.

direction their lives are taking, into their established systems of needs, and so finally into the situations in society they have helped to create; it damages and disrupts one's own self-interests and aims at a fundamental revision of one's habitual way of life.[34]

Metz's concern was that although Christians spoke the language of conversion and stressed the inward nature of faith, the radical change of heart which was indispensable to a life of genuine discipleship was not happening. His challenging critique could not be more relevant to the situation of Christians in the context we have described in our world today:

> The crisis (or sickness) of life in the church is not just that the change of heart is not taking place . . . but that the absence of this change of heart is being further concealed under the appearance of a merely *believed-in-faith*. Are we Christians really changing our hearts, or do we just believe in a change of hearts and remain under the cloak of this belief in conversion basically unchanged? . . . Do we show real love, or do we just believe in love and under the cloak of belief in love remain the same egoists and conformists we have always been? Do we share the sufferings of others, or do we just believe in sharing, remaining under the cloak of a belief in "sympathy" as apathetic as ever?[35]

Metz here shares the concerns of various contemporary thinkers that the culture of modernity not only resulted in far-reaching external changes in society, but had consequences which can be described as *anthropological*, affecting human consciousness. For example, Eric Fromm described modern, Western industrial society as populated with "notoriously unhappy people: lonely, anxious, depressed, destructive, dependent – people who are glad when we have killed the time we are trying so hard to save."[36] Fromm was in fact extending a tradition of critical analysis of modern culture which can

---

34. Johann Baptist Metz, *The Emergent Church: The Future of Christianity in a Postbourgeois World* (New York: Crossroad, 1981), 2–3.

35. Metz, *Emergent Church*, 2–3. I cannot forbear to offer a further example of this prophetic language: "It is possible that what love demands of us here may look like treason – a betrayal of affluence, of the family, and of our customary way of life. But it is also possible that *this* is the very place where the discernment of spirits is most needed in the churches of the rich and powerful countries of this earth" (14–15).

36. Eric Fromm, *To Have or To Be?* (London: Abacus, 1979), 15.

be traced back to figures such as Blaise Pascal and Søren Kierkegaard, but by the second half of the twentieth century he could write that for the first time in human history, "the *physical survival of the human race depends on a radical change of the human heart.*"[37]

Johann Baptist Metz would include professing Christians as in need of what he described as an *anthropological revolution*. It is not easy to summarize his teaching at this point but in essence he saw modern, Western people as having been locked into a worldview which resulted in a model of the human person as "an essentially dominating kind of being." The emergence of modernity, which can be traced externally to the impact of the Enlightenment and the rapid growth of a techno-scientific culture, had a profound impact on the way in which people understood themselves. The principle of subjugation "has long since permeated the psychic foundations of our total sociocultural life," so that we can speak of "a poisoning through unrestricted technical exploitation of the outer nature surrounding human beings, *but also of a poisoning of the inner nature of man himself.*"[38]

These comments related to the impact of modernity upon peoples whose history and cultures had been deeply shaped by it; however, the increasing visibility of surviving indigenous peoples at the present time, insisting both on their right to life and on the contribution which their traditional worldviews can make to global debates concerning the future of life on earth, mean that we must recognize both the source and the limits of this anthropological crisis. After almost a lifetime spent among some of the poorest people on earth, Jon Sobrino spells out this distinction with disturbing clarity:

> The Western capacity to achieve, to struggle and emerge victorious, has been so highly valued that it has enabled the westerner to feel like a Prometheus, unneedful of anything or anyone else, including grace – a subject few First World philosophies and theologies know what to do with. Western human beings have to a great extent produced an inhuman world for those in the

---

37. Fromm, *To Have or To Be?*, 19; emphasis original. See also Fromm's *Beyond the Chains of Illusion* (London: Abacus, 1980). Mention must also be made here of Viktor E. Frankl, *Man's Search for Meaning* (New York: Washington Square Press, 1984).

38. Metz, *Emergent Church*, 35; emphasis added.

Third World and a dehumanizing world in the First World. And still, no change seems imminent.[39]

It is in precisely this context that Metz glimpsed the possibility of a new kind of Christianity, one transcending the centuries-long division between Catholic and Protestant in what he called the "Second Reformation." Whereas the Protestant Reformation had occurred at the historical point at which the medieval world was fading, and represented a response to the emergence of a bourgeois culture, Christianity in the late twentieth century confronted a very different era which has elsewhere been described as "the great unravelling."[40] Metz believed that in the deepening crisis of our time the Reformation question of how to attain grace was breaking through once again and could presage a *kairos* point at which the gift of new life might result in the anthropological revolution which a broken world so desperately needed. He describes how those who discover the life which is offered by Jesus begin to travel together as a new people of the Way, nourished by the love of God, overcoming the habitual practice of domination, and exorcizing interiorized capitalism, "that attitude of grasping and struggling for advantage." Here is Metz's description of what the new birth spoken of by Jesus would entail for modern people in the Western world:

> For this revolution is not, in fact, concerned with liberating us from poverty and misery, but rather from our wealth and our totally excessive prosperity. It is not a liberation from what we

---

39. Sobrino, *Principle of Mercy*, 7. R. H. Tawney kept a diary, or as it was called then, a "Commonplace Book," up to the start of the First World War. His last entry was dated 2 December 1914 and in it he discussed the relationship between war and peace. He described the conflict, which was almost to cost him his own life, as "the natural outcome of the ideals and standards which govern Western Europe, especially Germany and England, in its ordinary every day social and economic life. . . . I mean that our whole tendency is to exalt the combative qualities, and to undervalue those of the humble and meek, and that the existing economic organization of society is a perpetual evidence that the world gives its applause to energy, pugnacity, ruthlessness. . . . Modern industry has no body of ethical doctrine to control our crude instinct to believe that success is its own justification. The types which it carries to power tend to be those not unlike those produced by war. . . . They must be undisturbed by pity for the weak, by doubts as to the value of the immediate ends at which they aim, by reverence for the finer, more delicate human qualities and achievements. . . . They are essentially a conquering race. . . . If we are to end the horrors of war, we must first end the horror of peace" (*R. H. Tawney's Commonplace Book*, eds. J. M. Winter and D. M. Joslin [Cambridge: Cambridge University Press, 1972], 82–83).

40. See Alan J. Roxburgh, *Joining God in the Great Unraveling: Where We Are and What I've Learned* (Eugene: Cascade Books, 2021).

lack, but from our consumerism in which we are ultimately consuming our very selves. It is not a liberation from our state of oppression, but from the untransformed praxis of our own wishes and desires. It is not a liberation from our powerlessness, but from our own form of predominance. It frees us, not from the state of being dominated but from that of dominating; not from our sufferings but from our apathy; not from our guilt but from our innocence, or rather from that delusion of innocence which the life of domination has long since spread through our souls.[41]

It may help us at this point to take note of someone who has been deeply involved in the modern world at the level of teaching economics in a university setting, and so has felt compelled to wrestle with the tension between the demands of discipleship and a professional career in a discipline in which neoliberalism exerts enormous influence. Her struggle to allow the lordship of Christ to become a reality, not just in personal behaviour but at the level of ideas, theory and intellect in an academic setting, may help readers who can identify with the dilemmas faced in such situations.

Jane Collier, whom we met earlier as the co-author of an important study of the church and the culture of economism, has researched the ways in which that system creates seemingly impenetrable barriers to faith-as-praxis. It is not that it prevents the *profession* of faith, but that the realization of belief in daily life involves a painful struggle to overcome the obstacles thrown up by the prevailing ideology. With refreshing honesty and candour, Collier examines the difficulties of living as a Christian and as a teacher of economics, experiencing what she calls "cultural schizophrenia" as the result of participating in a world that is "deeply opposed to the value system embedded in the Gospel."[42] The encounter with students at the commencement of their studies in economics revealed the extent to which their interpretive processes – the cultural lenses already operative in shaping the understanding of reality – were imbued with the logic of economism:

---

41. Metz, *Emergent Church*, 42.

42. Jane Collier, *The Culture of Economism: An Exploration of Barriers to Faith-as-Praxis* (Frankfurt am Main: Peter Lang, 1990), 1.

Economic issues prevail in the media, consumerism rules in the pursuit of leisure, rewards for work are seen purely in monetary terms, virtue is perceived as material success. The Gospel is then heard and interpreted through a series of filters which distort its meanings and render its values at best unacceptable, at worst ridiculous.[43]

Collier provides a detailed description of the fundamental assumptions underlying modern economic theory, including the role of science, and the central belief in "progress," equated with technological advances and conceived as "an ever greater ability to manipulate the world, rather than in terms of increasing human welfare."[44] The crucial question for her became whether the dominance of this economistic worldview meant that faith would have to be confined to the weekly visit to church and thus restricted to the private sphere. This division between the public world, in which scientifically established facts operate, and the private sphere of family and home, where religious beliefs may be retained (or confined), was the consequence of the Enlightenment worldview, but it left Collier asking whether an alternative approach to the teaching of economics in obedience to Christ was possible. She writes that as a Christian, "I believe that we cannot live in the freedom of God's kingdom if *metanoia* does not result in a praxis which is dictated by our 'option for the kingdom' *rather than by the requirements of the structures in which we live.*"[45]

It is not possible here to describe the writer's response in detail, but I notice two of the ways in which she reacted to this challenge. First, she discovered the direct relevance of references in the letters of Paul to an ongoing conflict with the dominating powers of the ancient world, powers that were completely antipathetic to the way of life which the apostle had learned from Jesus Christ. This meant that Collier recognized within the New Testament itself a clear analogy to the difficulties she was facing in the modern world, since Paul's description of the Christian life as a continual spiritual battle to remain faithful to Jesus sounded remarkably similar to her own struggle.

---

43. Collier, *Culture of Economism*, 3.
44. Collier, 121.
45. Collier, 5; emphasis added.

> Paul's view of "world" was multidimensional; he saw it not only as that which was earthly and fleshy, but also in terms of political, economic and social patterns, as well as those structural, intellectual and institutional systems which hold men in bondage – the "world rulers" who were responsible for the crucifixion (1 Cor. 2:7–8).[46]

This is a dimension of the New Testament that has been much neglected within Western Christianity, yet here we discover a modern intellectual, wrestling with the deep desire to follow the way of Jesus in practice, who finds in these marginalized texts a key to the faith that "liberates us from the tyranny of something basic, inherent and powerful in our world" (Col 2:20).[47] Indeed, Paul's autobiographical references in Romans 7 to a continuing struggle, in which he admits his frequent failure to overcome a kind of dualism in which the profound desire to do good is frustrated by the evil that "is right there with me," seemed to mirror Collier's own struggle. Although the contexts are different, the Bible clearly recognizes the reality of the conflict which takes place at an individual level, in the realm of personal desires and choices, and externally in relation to the powers and structures of the social and political realms which impact upon us in ways that are significant, although often disguised.

Collier's second reaction, which is discussed at considerable length in her book, is to insist on *the crucial importance of conversion*, conceived as a radical transformation which leaves no dimension of the person unaffected. Conversion is described as "the reality of redemption," experienced not simply in the religious sphere, but as transformative "to every aspect of thought and action." It implies a radical change, involving the redirection of both the will and desires, and a new understanding of the world as the context within

---

46. Collier, 54.

47. Collier, 54. Reference must be made here to the work of Walter Wink who, in a trilogy of studies on the meaning and significance of "the powers," recognized the crucial importance of this theme for our times. See his *Engaging the Powers: Discernment and Resistance in a World of Domination* (Minneapolis: Fortress, 1992), and *The Powers That Be: Theology for a New Millennium* (New York: Doubleday, 1998). "There is more to what goes on in the world than what newspapers or newscasters report. I was prepared to wager that our ancestors were in touch with reality when they spoke about the Powers, and that they might even know something our society has lost, spiritually blinded as it is by a materialism that believes only in what it can see, hear, taste, smell or touch" (3).

which the reign of Mammon must be challenged intellectually, affectively and ethically.⁴⁸ It is precisely this understanding of Christianity which made it impossible for Collier to accept the privatization of her faith, and led her to insist on the freedom to pose seriously critical questions with regard to economistic orthodoxy, challenging the "cultural nexus of values" underpinning contemporary economic theory.

> The point is that the advocacy of selfishness as an instrumental value serving the intrinsic value of rationality is totally at variance with the demands of the Gospel. Moral conversion must entail a rejection of this most fundamental of all economic values, and an adoption of what is normally considered to be non-rational or irrational – a commitment to the welfare of others rather than self.⁴⁹

The difficulties involved in taking such a stance, not to mention the possibility of considerable personal cost, must be obvious, but this example suggests that *coming out* of Babylon and walking in the way of Jesus Christ may mean *going into* business schools and other citadels of neoliberalist orthodoxy to challenge the reign of Mammon and bear testimony to a liberating alternative to the culture of economism.

Joining God in the Great Unravelling⁵⁰

As we draw this discussion to its close I want to remind readers of the two "pause for reflection" passages which were offered earlier in the book. The first of these dealt with "Isaiah's lament" and referenced the great Hebrew prophet's grief at the failure of biblical Israel to bring "salvation to the earth." He lamented that they had not given birth to the "people of the world" (26:18), with the result that "the shroud that enfolds all peoples" remained in place

---

48. Collier, *Culture of Economism*, 287.
49. Collier, 313.
50. I have purloined this heading from Alan J. Roxburgh's excellent *Joining God in the Great Unraveling*. He describes the personal transformation of his understanding of debates about mission among "Euro-tribal Churches" which led to the recognition that "I was living (dwelling) and practicing life and leadership within modernity's wager, within the conviction that everything depended upon my agency and my ability to function as a good technocratic rationalist. I too needed conversion" (75).

(25:7) and the hope of the fulfilment of the promise made to Father Abraham was frustrated.

The second reflection occurred at the conclusion of our study of the New Testament and focused on "Paul's lament." We discussed the great central chapters of the Letter to the Romans which commence with the apostle's confession of experiencing "great sorrow and unceasing anguish in my heart" at the renewed failure of "my people, those of my own race, the people of Israel" to recognize Jesus as Messiah (Rom 9:1–4). I commented that the glorious hope expressed in the Letter to the Ephesians of a transcultural unity resulting from faith in the crucified Christ had proved to be only a passing "Ephesian moment," rendered an unachievable ideal, not only by Jewish unbelief, but by gentile arrogance and spiritual pride! Romans 9–11 can be read, it seems to me, as Paul echoing Isaiah's lament that, even after the Christ event, the schism within the apostolic community was endangering the gospel's promise of a universal transformation, thus leaving "the sheet that covers all nations" still in place!

We have now completed the second section of this book in which we have attempted to trace post-biblical, historical developments across two millennia of Christian history, and the sobering question that cannot be avoided is whether the story we have tried to tell demands that we add a third lament: *that of Christianity itself*? In a remarkable book which I discovered during this writing, sociologist David Martin discusses the perennial tensions between the promise of restoration in the message of the arrival of the kingdom of God, and the stubborn realities of "the world." He cites Peter Brown's work on early Christianity as vividly illustrating how "the visionary perspective of Christianity concerning wealth and riches encounters the reality of the social order, especially once the body of Christians includes some wealthy people in the late fourth century." This is the point at which, as we saw earlier in this book, Christianity opts for the path of accommodation to the world, since a chasm opened up "between a non-violent community where goods are shared, and enduring economic and political realities."[51]

Later in his challenging book, Martin concludes that "In the contemporary climate we do not follow through the implications of Christian economic

---

51. David Martin, *Ruin and Restoration: On Violence, Liturgy and Reconciliation* (London: Routledge, 2016), 14.

teaching any more than we follow through its teaching about violence, *but we do accord to those teachings respect as an ideal.*"[52] As a descriptive statement of existing Christianity, especially in its Western form, this is an accurate verdict, but it is far removed from both the intention of the gospel, and from the pattern of life demanded of those who are compelled to take Jesus's words concerning the decision between the worship of God or Mammon seriously!

With regard to the "intention of the gospel," despite his moving expression of lament at the actual condition of the church, Paul refuses to accept either the legalistic nationalism of the Jewish community, or the arrogant sense of superiority of the Gentiles as the best that can be expected in a broken world! Of a retreat to a regard of the gospel as a beautiful but unattainable ideal there is not a trace. He closes the letter with a ringing reaffirmation of the gospel as commanded by the eternal God, "so that all nations might come to the obedience that comes from faith" (16:26). Robert Jewett describes Paul's conclusion that God's purpose in human history is to "regain control of a lost and disobedient world."

> Paul believed that when all the peoples of the earth accept the gospel, they will all for the first time praise God rather than themselves. The competition between the nations that had always brought war and destruction will thereby come to an end. The Pauline hope of world-transforming mission is viewed as the fulfilment of biblical prophecy, that all nations will find in the Messiah a new and peaceful destiny, including solidarity with one another.[53]

There is a further reason why, with the greatest respect, I must dissent from David Martin's reduction of the gospel to an ideal. To do so would involve ignoring the massive shift which has taken place in modern culture with the rise of neoliberalism and the socio-economic transformations we have described in the last few chapters. Indeed, we may have told only part of the story since the growing power of what is called "surveillance capitalism" presents, in the words of Shoshana Zuboff, "the fight for a human future at the new frontiers of power." Her groundbreaking study is a warning that

---

52. Martin, *Ruin and Restoration*, 59.
53. Robert Jewett, *Romans: A Commentary*, Hermeneia (Minneapolis: Fortress, 2007), 702.

the digital realm is "redefining everything familiar even before we have a chance to ponder and decide. We celebrate the networked world . . . but it has birthed whole new territories of anxiety, danger, and violence as the sense of a predictable future slips away."[54] The decision for God or Mammon has never been more urgent and the consequences of that choice never so crucial for the future of humankind and its planetary home.

Even as I write these words I catch the echo of Max Weber's question whether new prophets might arise, able to expose the cruel and destructive idolatry which shapes society, and to articulate an alternative vision of what a just and humane community might look like. As we have seen, there have been such prophetic voices raised both in protest against the foundational values of contemporary economics, and envisioning a new kind of commonwealth capable of reversing the trend towards oligarchy, and of renewing God's good creation. This would not mean a simple return to Acts 2 and 4, but the application of the principles underlying that primitive apostolic community in new and visionary ways for the world of the twenty-first century. And it would demand not only a lamenting of the moral cowardice of contemporary Christianity, but its openness to a transformation far beyond our present imagining, and shaped significantly by the cultures and dreams of the poor disciples of Jesus from the Global South, where the new heartlands of this liberating religion are now to be found.

A final question: what does it look like when the decision is made to worship God alone and his kindness becomes the foundation for life? Perhaps the answer to that question may come from an unlikely source. Navid Kermani is a Muslim scholar who wrote a beautiful book on the history of Western, Christian art. He examines a series of paintings with deep sympathy and insight, but the reader is suddenly taken by surprise when discovering a chapter devoted, not to an artistic masterpiece, but to a particular *human life*!

---

54. Shoshana Zuboff, *The Age of Surveillance Capitalism: The Fight for a Human Future at the New Frontier of Power* (London: Profile Books, 2019), 4. At the conclusion of this book, she describes what she tells her own children, and any young people willing to listen, concerning the digital world. "I tell them that the word 'search' has meant a daring existential journey, not a finger tap to already existing answers; that 'friend' is an embodied mystery that can be forged only face-to-face and heart-to-heart; and that 'recognition' is the glimmer of homecoming we experience in our beloved's face, not 'facial recognition.' I say that it is not OK to have our best instincts for connection, empathy and information exploited by a draconian quid pro quo that holds these goods hostage to the pervasive strip search of our lives" (521).

The subject is a Jesuit monk named Paolo Dall'Oglio, famous in the Middle East for re-establishing an ancient Syrian monastery as a centre of interfaith conversation and dialogue. I quote here a passage in which our Muslim writer appears to describe this man's life as a "wonder beyond belief":

> If there is one thing I admire about Christianity – or perhaps I should say about those Christians whose faith not only convinced but conquered me, robbed me of all my reservations – if I were to take just one aspect, one attribute as an example, a guideline for myself, it would not be the beloved art, or the whole civilization, music and architecture included, or this or that rite, rich though they may be. *It is the specifically Christian love, which is love not just for one's neighbour.* Other religions are loving too, exhorting the faithful to compassion, indulgence, charity. *But the love that I perceive in many Christians, and most often in those who have dedicated their lives to Jesus, the monks and nuns, exceeds what a person could achieve without God: their love makes no distinctions.*[55]

In that sincere testimony I suggest we discover an arrow pointing towards the future for world Christianity in the global context we have attempted to describe in this book. I end with the glorious benediction Paul placed at the conclusion of Romans 9–11:

> Oh, the depth of the riches of the wisdom and knowledge of
>   God!
> How unsearchable his judgments,
>   and his paths beyond tracing out!
> "Who has known the mind of the Lord?
>   Or who has been his counsellor?"
> "Who has ever given to God,
>   that God should repay them?"
> For from him and through him and for him are all things.
>   To him be the glory for ever! Amen.

---

55. Navid Kermani, *Wonder beyond Belief: On Christianity* (Cambridge: Polity, 2018), 175–76; emphasis added. The story of Paolo Dall'Oglio is told by Shaun O'Neill in his *A Church of Islam: The Syrian Calling of Father Paolo Dall'Oglio* (Eugene: Wipf & Stock, 2019).

Bibliography

Abu-Lughod, Janet L. *Before European Hegemony: The World System A.D. 1250–1350*. Oxford: Oxford University Press, 1989.

Ackroyd, Peter. *Exile and Restoration: A Study of Hebrew Thought in the Sixth Century BC*. Philadelphia: Westminster, 1968.

———. *Israel under Babylon and Persia*. Oxford: Oxford University Press, 1979.

Adorno, Theodor. *Quasi una Fantasia: Essays on Modern Music*. London: Verso, 1998.

———. *Minima Moralia: Reflections on a Damaged Life*. London: Verso, 2005.

Albright, William Foxwell. *From Stone Age to Christianity: Monotheism and the Historical Process*. New York: Doubleday, 1957.

Andrews, George Reid. *Afro-Latin America, 1800–2000*. Oxford: Oxford University Press, 2004.

Annett, Anthony M. *Cathonomics: How Catholic Tradition Can Create a More Just Economy*. Washington, DC: Georgetown University Press, 2022.

Arrighi, Giovanni. *The Long Twentieth Century: Money, Power and the Origins of Our Times*. London: Verso, 2010.

Avila, Charles. *Ownership: Early Christian Teaching*. Eugene: Wipf & Stock, 2004.

Bailey, Kenneth E. *Jesus Through Middle Eastern Eyes: Cultural Studies in the Gospels*. London: SPCK, 2008.

——— *Poet and Peasant and Through Peasant Eyes: A Literary-Cultural Approach to the Parables of Luke*. Grand Rapids: Eerdmans, 1983.

———. *Through Peasant Eyes: More Lukan Parables*. Grand Rapids: Eerdmans, 1980.

Balentine, Samuel E. *The Torah's Vision of Worship*. Minneapolis: Fortress, 1999.

Bauckham, Richard. *The Climax of Prophecy: Studies on the Book of Revelation*. Edinburgh: T&T Clark, 1993.

———. *James: Wisdom of James, Disciple of Jesus the Sage*. London: Routledge, 1999.

———. *The Theology of the Book of Revelation*. Cambridge: Cambridge University Press, 1993.

Bauman, Zygmunt. *Consuming Life.* Cambridge: Polity, 2007.

———. *Liquid Fear.* Cambridge: Polity, 2006.

———. *Liquid Love: On the Frailty of Human Bonds.* Cambridge: Polity, 2003.

———. *Liquid Times: Living in an Age of Uncertainty.* Cambridge: Polity, 2007.

———. *Mortality, Immortality, and Other Life Strategies.* Cambridge: Polity, 1992.

———. *Wasted Lives: Modernity and Its Outcasts.* Cambridge: Polity, 2004.

Bauman, Zygmunt, and Leonidas Donskis. *Moral Blindness: The Loss of Sensitivity in Liquid Modernity.* Cambridge: Polity, 2013.

Bavinck, J. H. *Between the Beginning and the End: A Radical Kingdom Vision.* Grand Rapids: Eerdmans, 2014.

———. *An Introduction to the Science of Missions.* Philadelphia: Presbyterian and Reformed, 1960.

Beaudoin, Tom. *Consuming Faith: Integrating Who We Are with What We Consume.* Oxford: Sheed & Ward, 2003.

———. *Witness to Dispossession: The Vocation of a Postmodern Theologian.* New York: Orbis, 2008.

Becker, Ernest. *The Denial of Death.* New York: Free Press, 1973.

———. *Escape from Evil.* New York: Free Press, 1975.

———. *The Structure of Evil: An Essay in the Unification of the Science of Man.* New York: Free Press, 1968.

Bell, Daniel M. *Liberation Theology after the End of History: The Refusal to Cease Suffering.* London: Routledge, 2001.

Bellah, Robert N. *Religion in Human Evolution: From the Paleolithic to the Axial Age.* Cambridge: Belknap Press, 2011.

Bellah, Robert N., and Steven M. Tipton, eds. *The Robert Bellah Reader.* London: Duke University Press, 2006.

Berger, Peter. *The Noise of Solemn Assemblies: Christian Commitment and the Religious Establishment in America.* New York: Doubleday, 1961.

Bhaldraithe, Eoin de, OCist. "Early Christian Features Preserved in Western Monasticism." In *The Origins of Christendom in the West*, edited by Alan Kreider, pp. 153–78. Edinburgh: T&T Clark, 2001.

Bock, Darrell L. "Jesus, the Poor, and Mammon." In *The Bible and the American Future*, edited by Robert Jewett, pp. 162–80. Eugene: Cascade, 2009.

Boff, Leonardo, and Virgil Elizondo, eds. *1492–1992: The Voice of the Victims*, Concilium Special. London: SCM, 1991.

Bonhoeffer, Dietrich. *Letters and Papers from Prison.* London: Fontana, 1959.

Bonk, Jonathan J. *Missions and Money: Affluence as a Western Missionary Problem.* New York: Orbis, 1991.

———. "Money, Wealth." In *Global Dictionary of Theology*, edited by William A. Dyrness and Veli-Matti Kärkkäinen, pp. 576–82. Nottingham: Inter-Varsity Press, 2008.

Booth, William. *In Darkest England and the Way Out.* London: Salvation Army, 1890.

Boyd, Gregory. *Crucifixion of the Warrior God.* Vol. 1, *The Crucifixion Hermeneutic.* Minneapolis: Fortress, 2017.

———. *Crucifixion of the Warrior God.* Vol. 2, *The Crucifixion Thesis.* Minneapolis: Fortress, 2017.

Boyle, Nicholas. *Who Are We Now? Christian Humanism and the Global Market from Hegel to Heaney.* Edinburgh: T&T Clark, 1998.

Bradstock, Andrew, and Christopher Rowland, eds. *Radical Christian Writings: A Reader.* Oxford: Blackwell, 2002.

Braudel, Fernand. *A History of Civilizations.* London: Penguin, 1995.

Briggs, Asa. *Victorian Cities.* London: Penguin, 1968.

Bright, John. *Covenant and Promise: The Prophetic Understanding of the Future in Pre-exilic Israel.* Philadelphia: Westminster, 1976.

———. *A History of Israel.* 3rd ed. Philadelphia: Westminster, 1981.

———. *Jeremiah.* The Anchor Bible. New York: Doubleday, 1965.

Brockway, A. Fenner. "James Keir Hardie (1856–1915)." In *Christian Social Reformers of the Nineteenth Century*, edited by Hugh Martin, pp. 225–39. London: SCM, 1933.

Brown, Peter. *Augustine of Hippo: A Biography.* London: Faber & Faber, 1969.

———. *Authority and the Sacred: Aspects of the Christianisation of the Roman World.* Cambridge: Cambridge University Press, 1997.

———. *The Rise of Western Christendom: Triumph and Diversity, A.D. 200–1000.* 10th anniversary rev. ed. Chichester: Wiley-Blackwell, 2013.

———. *Through the Eye of a Needle: Wealth, the Fall of Rome, and the Making of Christianity in the West, 350–550 AD.* Princeton: Princeton University Press, 2012.

———. *Treasure in Heaven: The Holy Poor in Early Christianity.* Charlottesville: University of Virginia Press, 2016.

Brown, William. *Ecclesiastes.* Interpretation: A Bible Commentary for Teaching and Preaching. Louisville: John Knox, 2000.

Brueggemann, Walter. *Divine Presence amid Violence: Contextualizing the Book of Joshua.* Eugene: Cascade, 2009.

———. *Finally Comes the Poet: Daring Speech for Proclamation.* Minneapolis: Fortress, 1989.

———. *Journey to the Common Good.* Louisville: Westminster John Knox, 2016.

———. *Living Toward a Vision: Biblical Reflections on Shalom.* New York: United Church Press, 1982.

———. *Mandate to Difference: An Invitation to the Contemporary Church.* Louisville: Westminster John Knox, 2007.

———. *Money and Possessions*. Interpretation: Resources for the Use of Scripture in the Church. Louisville: Westminster John Knox, 2016.

———. *Texts That Linger, Words That Explode: Listening to Prophetic Voices*. Minneapolis: Fortress, 2000.

———. *Theology of the Old Testament: Testimony, Dispute, Advocacy*. Minneapolis: Fortress, 1997.

Buber, Martin. *The Prophetic Faith*. New York: Macmillan, 1949.

Budde, Michael L. *The Borders of Baptism: Identities, Allegiances, and the Church*. Eugene: Cascade, 2011.

———. *Foolishness to Gentiles: Essays on Empire, Nationalism, and Discipleship*. Eugene: Cascade, 2022.

———. *The Two Churches: Catholicism and Capitalism in the World System*. Durham: Duke University Press, 1992.

Burrows, William R. "A Seventh Paradigm? Catholics and Radical Inculturation." In *Mission in Bold Humility: David Bosch's Work Reconsidered*, edited by Willem Saayman and Klippies Kritzinger, pp. 121–38. New York: Orbis, 1996.

Burrows, William, Mark Gornik and Janice McLean, eds. *Understanding World Christianity: The Vision and Work of Andrew F. Walls*. New York: Orbis, 2011.

Burrus, Virginia, ed. *A People's History of Christianity*: Vol. 2, *Late Ancient Christianity*. Minneapolis: Fortress, 2005.

Camus, Albert. *The Myth of Sisyphus*. Harmondsworth: Penguin, 1975.

———. *The Plague*. Harmondsworth: Penguin, 1960.

———. *The Rebel*. Harmondsworth: Penguin, 1971.

———. *Resistance, Rebellion and Death*. London: Hamish Hamilton, 1961.

Carey, William. *An Enquiry into the Obligations of Christians to Use Means for the Conversion of the Heathens*. Didcot: Baptist Missionary Society, 1991 [1792].

Carroll, John. *The Western Dreaming: The Western World Is Dying for Want of a Story*. Sydney: HarperCollins, 2001.

Cassidy, Richard J. *Christians and Roman Rule in the New Testament: New Perspectives*. New York: Crossroad, 2001.

———. *John's Gospel in New Perspective: Christology and the Realities of Roman Power*. Eugene: Wipf & Stock, 2015 [1992].

———. *Paul in Chains: Roman Imprisonment and the Letters of St. Paul*. New York: Crossroad, 2001.

Cavanaugh, William T. *Being Consumed: Economics and Christian Desire*. Grand Rapids: Eerdmans, 2008.

———. "Strange Gods: Idolatry in the Twenty-First Century." Commonweal. 21 January 2020. https://www.commonwealmagazine.org/strange-gods.

———. *Theopolitical Imagination: Discovering the Liturgy as a Political Act in an Age of Global Consumerism*. London: T&T Clark, 2002.

Clark, Elizabeth A. "Asceticism, Class, and Gender." In *A People's History of Christianity*. Vol. 2, *Late Ancient Christianity*, edited by Virginia Burrus, pp. 27–45. Minneapolis: Fortress, 2005.

Clark, Stephen, ed. *Tales of Two Cities: Christianity and Politics*. Leicester: Inter-Varsity Press, 2005.

Coates, David. *Flawed Capitalism: The Anglo-American Condition and Its Resolution*. Newcastle-upon-Tyne: Agenda, 2018.

Cocker, Mark. *Rivers of Blood, Rivers of Gold: Europe's Conflict with Tribal Peoples*. London: Pimlico, 1999.

Cohen, Shaye J. D. *Josephus in Galilee and Rome: His Vita and Development as a Historian*. Boston: Brill Academic, 2002.

Cohn, Norman. *The Pursuit of the Millennium: Revolutionary Millenarians and Mystical Anarchists of the Middle Ages*. London: Paladin, 1970.

Collier, Jane. *The Culture of Economism: An Exploration of Barriers to Faith-as-Praxis*. Frankfurt am Main: Peter Lang, 1990.

Collier, Jane, and Rafael Esteban. *From Complicity to Encounter: The Church and the Culture of Economism*. Harrisburg: Trinity Press International, 1998.

Collins, Adela Yarbro. *Crisis and Catharsis: The Power of the Apocalypse*. Philadelphia: Westminster, 1984.

Collinson, Patrick. *The Reformation*. London: Phoenix, 2005.

Comaroff, Jean, and John Comaroff. *Of Revelation and Revolution: Christianity, Colonialism, and Consciousness in South Africa*. Vol. 1. Chicago: University of Chicago Press, 1991.

Comby, Jean. *How to Understand the History of Christian Mission*. London: SCM, 1996.

Concerned Evangelicals. *Evangelical Witness in South Africa: A Critique of Evangelical Theology and Practice by South African Evangelicals Themselves*. Oxford: Regnum and Evangelical Alliance (UK), 1986.

"The Congregational Union at Bradford." *The British Weekly*, 13 October 1892.

Coomber, Matthew J. M. *Re-reading the Prophets through Corporate Globalization: A Cultural-Evolutionary Approach to Economic Injustice in the Hebrew Bible*. Eugene: Cascade, 2022.

Costas, Orlando E. *Christ Outside the Gate: Mission beyond Christendom*. New York: Orbis, 1982.

Cragg, Kenneth. *Christianity in World Perspective*. London: Lutterworth, 1968.

———. *The Secular Experience of God*. Harrisburg: Trinity Press International, 1998.

Craigie, Peter. *The Problem of War in the Old Testament*. Grand Rapids: Eerdmans, 1978.

Dalton, George, ed. *Tribal and Peasant Economies: Readings in Economic Anthropology*. Austin: University of Texas Press, 1967.

Decker, Michael. *Tilling the Hateful Earth: Agricultural Production and Trade in the Late Antique East*. Oxford: Oxford University Press, 2009.
Delsol, Chantal. *Icarus Fallen: The Search for Meaning in an Uncertain World*. Wilmington: ISI, 2003.
———. *The Unlearned Lessons of the Twentieth Century: An Essay on Late Modernity*. Wilmington: ISI, 2006.
Dever, William. *Who Were the Early Israelites and Where Did They Come From?* Grand Rapids: Eerdmans, 2003.
Dickens, A. G. *Reformation and Society in Sixteenth-Century Europe*. London: Thames & Hudson, 1966.
Donfried, Karl P., ed. *The Romans Debate: Revised and Expanded Edition*. Peabody: Hendrickson, 1991.
Dorrien, Gary. *Social Democracy in the Making: Political and Religious Roots of European Socialism*. New Haven: Yale University Press, 2019.
Douglas, J. D., ed. *Let the Earth Hear His Voice: International Congress on World Evangelization, Lausanne, Switzerland*. Minneapolis: World Wide Publications, 1975.
Downey, John K., ed. *Remembering and Resisting: The New Political Theology – Johann Baptist Metz*. Eugene: Cascade, 2022.
Du Bois, W. E. B. "The African Roots of War." *The Atlantic* 15, no. 5 (May 1915): 707–14. WebDuBois.org. Accessed 19 January 2023. http://www.webdubois.org/dbAfricanRWar.html.
Dussel, Enrique. "The Real Motives for the Conquest." In *1492–1992: The Voice of the Victims*, edited by Leonardo Boff and Virgil Elizondo, pp. 30–46. *Concilium* Special. London: SCM, 1991.
Dyrness, William A., and Veli-Matti Kärkkäinen, eds. *Global Dictionary of Theology*. Nottingham: Inter-Varsity Press, 2008.
Eagleton, Terry. *Culture and the Death of God*. New Haven: Yale University Press, 2015.
Edwards, Jonathan. *The Works of Jonathan Edwards*. Vol. 2. London: Westley & Davis, 1834.
Ela, Jean-Marc. *African Cry*. Eugene: Wipf & Stock, 2005 [1986].
———. *From Charity to Liberation*. London: Catholic Institute for International Relations, 1984.
———. *My Faith as an African*. Nairobi: Acton, 2001.
Elkins, Caroline. *Britain's Gulag: The Brutal End of Empire in Kenya*. London: Jonathan Cape, 2005.
Elliot, Neil. "The Apostle Paul and Empire." In *Hidden Transcripts and the Arts of Resistance: Applying the Work of James C. Scott to Jesus and Paul*, edited by Richard A. Horsley, pp. 97–116. Atlanta: Society of Biblical Literature, 2004.

———. *The Arrogance of Nations: Reading Romans in the Shadow of Empire.* Minneapolis: Fortress, 2008.

———. "The Philosophers' Paul and the Churches." In *Paul in the Grip of the Philosophers: The Apostle and Contemporary Continental Philosophy*, edited by Peter Frick, pp. 217–37. Minneapolis: Fortress, 2013.

———. "Strategies of Resistance and Hidden Transcripts in Pauline Communities." In *Hidden Transcripts and the Arts of Resistance: Applying the Work of James C. Scott to Jesus and Paul*, edited by Richard A. Horsley, pp. 97–102. Atlanta: Society of Biblical Literature, 2004.

Ellul, Jacques. *Money and Power.* Downers Grove: InterVarsity Press, 1984.

———. *Reason for Being: A Meditation on Ecclesiastes.* Grand Rapids: Eerdmans, 1990.

———. *The Technological Society.* New York: Vintage, 1964 [orig. French ed. 1954].

Engels, Friedrich. "The Great Towns." In *The City Reader*, edited by Richard LeGates and Frederic Stout, pp. 50–58. 4th ed. London: Routledge, 2007.

Fenn, Richard. *The Death of Herod: An Essay in the Sociology of Religion.* Cambridge: Cambridge University Press, 1992.

Fletcher, Richard. *The Barbarian Conversion: From Paganism to Christianity.* New York: Henry Holt, 1997.

Frank, Joseph. *Dostoevsky: The Stir of Liberation, 1860–1865.* London: Robson Books, 1986.

Frankl, Viktor E. *Man's Search for Meaning.* New York: Washington Square, 1984.

Frend, W. H. C. *The Donatist Church: A Movement of Protest in Roman North Africa.* Eugene: Wipf & Stock, 2020 [1951].

Fretheim, Terence E. "The Reclamation of Creation: Redemption and Law in Exodus." *Interpretation* 45, no. 4 (Oct. 1991): 354–65.

Freyne, Sean. "Bandits in Galilee: A Contribution to the Study of Social Conditions in First-Century Palestine." In *The Social World of Formative Christianity and Judaism*, edited by Jacob Neusner, Peder Borgen, Ernest Frerichs and Richard Horsley, pp. 50–67. Philadelphia: Fortress, 1988.

———. *Galilee and the Gospel.* Boston: Brill Academic, 2002.

———. *Jesus, a Jewish Galilean: A New Reading of the Jesus-Story.* London: T&T Clark, 2004.

———. "Jesus in Context: Galilee and the Gospel." In Lassalle-Klein [ed]: pp. 17–38.

———. *The Jesus Movement and Its Expansion: Meaning and Mission.* Grand Rapids: Eerdmans, 2014.

———. "Jesus the Wine-Drinker: A Friend of Women." In *Transformative Encounters: Jesus and Women Re-viewed*, edited by Ingrid Rosa Kitzberger, pp. 162–80. Atlanta: Society of Biblical Literature, 2000.

———. *Texts, Contexts and Cultures: Essays on Biblical Topics.* Dublin: Veritas, 2002.
Frick, Peter, ed. *Paul in the Grip of the Philosophers: The Apostle and Contemporary Continental Philosophy.* Minneapolis: Fortress, 2013.
Friesen, Steven J. *Imperial Cults and the Apocalypse of John: Reading Revelation in the Ruins.* Oxford: Oxford University Press, 2001.
———. "Injustice or God's Will? Explanations of Poverty in Proto-Christian Communities." In *A People's History of Christianity.* Vol. 1, *Christian Origins*, edited by Richard A. Horsley, pp. 240–60. Minneapolis: Fortress, 2005.
Frisby, David. *Georg Simmel.* Rev. ed. London: Routledge, 2002.
Fromm, Erich. *Beyond the Chains of Illusion.* London: Abacus, 1980.
———. *To Have or To Be?* London: Abacus, 1979.
Fukuyama, Francis. "Reflections on *The End of History* Five Years Later." In *World History: Ideologies, Structures, and Identities*, edited by Philip Pomper, Richard Elphick and Richard Vann, pp. 199–216. Oxford: Blackwell, 1998.
Futrell, Alison. *Blood in the Arena: The Spectacle of Roman Power.* Austin: University of Texas Press, 1997.
———. *The Roman Games: Historical Sources in Translation.* Oxford: Blackwell, 2006.
Gampiot, Aurélian Mokoko. *Kimbanguism: An African Understanding of the Bible.* University Park: Pennsylvania State University Press, 2017.
Gener, T. D., and L. Bautista. "Theological Method." In *Global Dictionary of Theology*, edited by William A. Dyrness and Veli-Matti Kärkkäinen, pp. 889–94. Nottingham: Inter-Varsity Press, 2008.
Georgi, Dieter. *Remembering the Poor: The History of Paul's Collection for Jerusalem.* Nashville: Abingdon, 1992.
———. *Theocracy in Paul's Praxis and Theology.* Minneapolis: Fortress, 1991.
Godet, Frédéric. *Commentary on St. Paul's Epistle to the Romans.* Grand Rapids: Kregel, 1977.
Goff, Stan. *Mammon's Ecology: Metaphysic of the Empty Sign.* Eugene: Cascade, 2018.
Goldman, Lawrence. *The Life of R. H. Tawney: Socialism and History.* London: Bloomsbury Academic, 2014.
González, Justo L. *Acts: The Gospel of the Spirit.* New York: Orbis, 2001.
———. *Faith and Wealth: A History of Early Christian Ideas on the Origin, Significance and Use of Money.* Eugene: Wipf & Stock, 2002.
———. *For the Healing of the Nations: The Book of Revelation in an Age of Cultural Conflict.* New York: Orbis, 1999.
———. *Mañana: Christian Theology from a Hispanic Perspective.* Nashville: Abingdon, 1990.

———. *Out of Every Tribe and Nation: Christian Theology at the Ethnic Roundtable.* Nashville: Abingdon, 1992.

Gordis, Robert. *Koheleth: The Man and His World.* New York: Schocken, 1967.

Gottwald, Norman K. *The Tribes of Yahweh: A Sociology of the Religion of Liberated Israel, 1250–1050 BCE.* Sheffield: Sheffield Academic, 1999.

Graeber, David. *Debt: The First 5,000 Years.* Brooklyn: Melville House, 2011.

Graham, W. Fred. *The Constructive Revolutionary: John Calvin and His Socio-Economic Impact.* Atlanta: John Knox, 1978.

Grant, Kevin. *A Civilised Savagery: Britain and the New Slaveries in Africa, 1884–1926.* London: Routledge, 2005.

Grant, Michael. *The Jews in the Roman World.* London: Phoenix Giant, 1999.

Green, Joel B. *The Theology of the Gospel of Luke.* New Testament Theology. Cambridge: Cambridge University Press, 1995.

Gregory, Brad S. *Rebel in the Ranks: Martin Luther, the Reformation, and the Conflicts That Continue to Shape Our World.* New York: HarperCollins, 2017.

———. *The Unintended Reformation: How a Religious Revolution Secularized Society.* Cambridge: Belknap Press, 2012.

Guder, Darrell L. *The Continuing Conversion of the Church.* Grand Rapids: Eerdmans, 2000.

Guthrie, Thomas. *The City: Its Sins and Sorrows; Being a Series of Sermons from Luke XIX.41.* Michigan Historical Reprint Series. New York: Robert Carter & Brothers, 1857.

Habermas, Jürgen. *Times of Transitions.* Cambridge: Polity, 2006.

Hagen, Jürgen von, and Michael Welker, eds. *Money as God? The Monetization of the Market and Its Impact on Religion, Politics, Law and Ethics.* Cambridge: Cambridge University Press, 2014.

Halik, Tomáš. *The Afternoon of Christianity: The Courage to Change.* Translated by Gerald Turner. Notre Dame: University of Notre Dame Press, 2024.

Hamm, Berndt. "'Buying Heaven': The Prospects of Commercialized Salvation in the Fourteenth to Sixteenth Centuries." In *Money as God? The Monetization of the Market and Its Impact on Religion, Politics, Law and Ethics*, edited by Jürgen von Hagen and Michael Welker, pp. 233–56. Cambridge: Cambridge University Press, 2014.

Hammond, Mason. *The City in the Ancient World.* Cambridge: Harvard University Press, 1972.

Hanson, K. C., and Douglas E. Oakman. *Palestine in the Time of Jesus: Social Structures and Social Conflicts.* Minneapolis: Fortress, 1998.

Hargreaves, Andy. *Teaching in the Knowledge Society: Education in the Age of Insecurity.* Maidenhead: Open University Press, 2003.

Harris, John. *One Blood: 200 Years of Aboriginal Encounter with Christianity – A Story of Hope.* Oxford: Lion, 1990.

Harris, Olivia. "The Earth and the State: The Sources and the Meanings of Money in Northern Potosi, Bolivia." In *Money and the Morality of Exchange*, edited by J. Parry and M. Bloch, pp. 232–68. Cambridge: Cambridge University Press, 1989.

Harrison, James R. *Reading Romans with Roman Eyes: Studies on the Social Perspective of Paul*. Lanham: Lexington/Fortress, 2020.

Hart, David Bentley. "What Lies beyond Capitalism? A Christian Exploration." *Plough Quarterly* (Summer 2019), pp. 31–38.

Hayum, Andrée. *The Isenheim Altarpiece: God's Medicine and the Painter's Vision*. Princeton: Princeton University Press, 1989.

Hengel, Martin. *Crucifixion in the Ancient World and the Folly of the Message of the Cross*. Philadelphia: Fortress, 1977.

———. *Property and Riches in the Early Church*. Philadelphia: Fortress, 1974.

Hill, Christopher. *Puritanism and Revolution*. London: Panther, 1968.

———. *A Turbulent, Seditious, and Factious People: John Bunyan and His Church, 1628–1688*. Oxford: Oxford University Press, 1989.

Hobsbawm, E. J. *Age of Extremes: The Short Twentieth Century, 1914–1991*. London: Abacus, 1995.

———. *The Pelican Economic History of Britain*. Vol. 3, *Industry and Empire: From 1750 to the Present Day*. Harmondsworth: Penguin, 1969.

Hobson, J. A. *Imperialism: A Study of the History, Politics and Economics of the Colonial Powers in Europe and America*. [N.p.]: Adansonia Press, 2018 [1902].

Hochschild, Adam. *King Leopold's Ghost: A Story of Greed, Terror and Heroism in Colonial Africa*. London: Pan, 2012.

Holland, Tom. *Dominion: The Making of the Western Mind*. London: Little, Brown, 2019.

Hopkins, Keith. *A World Full of Gods: Pagans, Jews and Christians in the Roman Empire*. London: Phoenix, 1999.

Horsley, Richard A. *Jesus and Empire: The Kingdom of God and the New World Disorder*. Minneapolis: Fortress, 2003.

———. "Jesus and the Renewal of Covenantal Economics." In *The Bible and the American Future*, edited by Robert Jewett, pp. 181–207. Eugene: Cascade, 2009.

———. *Jesus and the Spiral of Violence: Popular Jewish Resistance in Roman Palestine*. Minneapolis: Fortress, 1993.

———. *Jesus in Context: Power, People, and Performance*. Minneapolis: Fortress, 2008.

———. *You Shall Not Bow Down and Serve Them: The Political and Economic Projects of Jesus and Paul*. Eugene: Cascade, 2021.

Horsley, Richard A., ed. *Hidden Transcripts and the Arts of Resistance: Applying the Work of James C. Scott to Jesus and Paul.* Atlanta: Society of Biblical Literature, 2004.

———. *In the Shadow of Empire: Reclaiming the Bible as a History of Faithful Resistance.* Louisville: Westminster John Knox, 2008.

———. *Paul and Politics.* Harrisburg: Trinity Press International, 2000.

———. *A People's History of Christianity.* Vol. 1, *Christian Origins.* Minneapolis: Fortress, 2005.

Horsley, Richard A., and Neil Asher Silberman. *The Message and the Kingdom: How Jesus and Paul Ignited a Revolution and Transformed the Ancient World.* Minneapolis: Fortress, 1997.

Hubbard, Moyer V. *Christianity in the Greco-Roman World: A Narrative Introduction.* Peabody: Hendrickson, 2010.

Huizinga, Johan. *The Waning of the Middle Ages: A Study of the Forms of Life, Thought, and Art in France and the Netherlands in the Fourteenth and Fifteenth Centuries.* Harmondsworth: Penguin, 1955.

Hunt, Tristram. *Building Jerusalem: The Rise and Fall of the Victorian City.* London: Phoenix, 2004.

Hunter, James Davison. *To Change the World: The Irony, Tragedy and Possibility of Christianity in the Late Modern World.* Oxford: Oxford University Press, 2010.

Hurbon, Laënnec. "The Slave Trade and Black Slavery in America." In *1492–1992: The Voice of the Victims*, edited by Leonardo Boff and Virgil Elizondo, pp. 90–100. *Concilium* Special. London: SCM, 1991.

Ireland, Paddy. *Property in Contemporary Capitalism.* Bristol: Bristol University Press, 2024.

Irvin, Dale T., and Scott W. Sunquist. *History of the World Christian Movement.* Vol. 1, *Earliest Christianity to 1453.* New York: Orbis, 2001.

Jacobs, Jane. *Dark Age Ahead.* New York: Vintage, 1993.

Jay, Elizabeth. *Faith and Doubt in Victorian Britain.* London: Macmillan, 1986.

Jenkins, Philip. *The Lost History of Christianity: The Thousand-Year Golden Age of the Church in the Middle East, Asia and Africa – And How It Died.* New York: HarperOne, 2008.

Jeremias, Joachim. *New Testament Theology.* Volume 1, *The Proclamation of Jesus.* London: SCM, 1971.

Jewett, Robert. "Following the Argument of Romans." In *The Romans Debate: Revised and Expanded Edition*, edited by Karl P. Donfried, pp. 265–77. Peabody: Hendrickson, 1991.

———. *Romans: A Commentary.* Hermeneia. Minneapolis: Fortress, 2007.

Jewett, Robert, ed. *The Bible and the American Future.* Eugene: Cascade, 2009.

Joyce, Patrick. *Remembering Peasants; A Personal History of a Vanished World.* London: Penguin, 2025.

Judt, Tony. *Ill Fares the Land: A Treatise on Our Present Discontents*. London: Allen Lane, 2010.

———. *Postwar: A History of Europe since 1945*. London: Vintage, 2005.

Kahl, Brigitte. *Galatians Re-imagined: Reading with the Eyes of the Vanquished*. Minneapolis: Fortress, 2010.

Katangole, Emmanuel. *Born from Lament: The Theology and Politics of Hope in Africa*. Grand Rapids: Eerdmans, 2017.

———. *The Journey of Reconciliation: Groaning for a New Creation in Africa*. New York: Orbis, 2017.

———. *The Sacrifice of Africa: A Political Theology for Africa*. Grand Rapids: Eerdmans, 2011.

Keller, Catherine. *Apocalypse Now and Then: A Feminist Guide to the End of the World*. Boston: Beacon, 1996.

———. *Facing Apocalypse: Climate Democracy and Other Last Chances*. New York: Orbis, 2021.

———. "The Love of Postcolonialism: Theology in the Interstices of Empire." In *Postcolonial Theologies: Divinity and Empire*, edited by Catherine Keller, Michael Nausner and Mayra Rivera, pp. 221–42. St. Louis: Chalice, 2004.

Keller, Catherine, Michael Nausner and Mayra Rivera, eds. *Postcolonial Theologies: Divinity and Empire*. St. Louis: Chalice, 2004.

Kermani, Navid. *Wonder Beyond Belief: On Christianity*. Cambridge: Polity, 2018.

Kim, Seyoon. *Christ and Caesar: The Gospel and the Roman Empire in the Writings of Paul and Luke*. Grand Rapids: Eerdmans, 2008.

Kitchen, Robert A., and Martien F. G. Parmentier, trans. and eds. *The Book of Steps: The Syriac* Liber Graduum. Kalamzoo: Cistercian Press, 2004.

Kitzberger, Ingrid Rosa, ed. *Transformative Encounters: Jesus and Women Reviewed*. Atlanta: Society of Biblical Literature, 2000.

Koch, Klaus. *The Prophets*. Vol. 1, *The Assyrian Period*. Philadelphia: Fortress, 1983.

———. *The Prophets*. Vol. 2, *The Babylonian and Persian Periods*. Philadelphia: Fortress, 1984.

Koester, Helmut. *Introduction to the New Testament*. Vol. 1, *History, Culture and Religion of the Hellenistic Age*. Berlin: de Gruyter, 1982.

Kotkin, Joel. *The City: A Global History*. New York: Modern Library, 2006.

Kreider, Alan. "Beyond Bosch: The Early Church and the Christendom Shift." *International Bulletin of Missionary Research* 29, no. 2 (April 2005): 59–67.

———. *The Change of Conversion and the Origin of Christendom*. Eugene: Wipf & Stock, 2006.

———. *The Patient Ferment of the Early Church: The Improbable Rise of Christianity in the Roman Empire*. Grand Rapids: Baker Academic, 2016.

———. "Violence and Mission in the Fourth and Fifth Centuries: Lessons for Today." *International Bulletin of Missionary Research* 31, no. 3 (July 2007): 125–33.

Kreider, Alan, ed. *The Origins of Christendom in the West*. Edinburgh: T&T Clark, 2001.

Kreitzer, Larry J. *Striking New Images: Roman Imperial Coinage and the New Testament World*. Sheffield: Sheffield Academic, 1996.

Kuhn, Karl Allen. *Luke: The Elite Evangelist*. Collegeville: Liturgical Press, 2010.

Küng, Hans. *The Catholic Church*. London: Phoenix, 2002.

Lakeland, Paul. "Spiritual Resistance: Theology in the Age of Neoliberalism." *Commonweal* 144, no. 6 (June 2020): 24–29. https://www.commonwealmagazine.org/spiritual-resistance.

Lambert, Malcolm. *The Cathars*. Oxford: Blackwell, 1998.

Lampe, Peter. *From Paul to Valentinus: Christians at Rome in the First Two Centuries*. Minneapolis: Fortress, 2003.

las Casas, Bartolemé de. *A Short Account of the Destruction of the Indies*. Edited and translated by Nigel Griffin. London: Penguin, 1992.

Lassalle-Klein, Robert, ed. *Jesus of Galilee: Contextual Christology for the 21st Century*. New York: Orbis, 2000.

Leach, Edmund. *Social Anthropology*. Glasgow: Fontana, 1982.

Leeuwen, Arend Theodor van. *Christianity in World History: The Meeting of the Faiths of East and West*. Edinburgh: Edinburgh House, 1964.

LeGates, Richard, and Frederick Stout, eds. *The City Reader*. 4th ed. London: Routledge, 2007.

Léry, Jean de. *History of a Voyage to the Land of Brazil*. Translated and with an introduction by Janet Whatley. Berkeley: University of California Press, 1990.

Letter to Diognetus. CCEL.org. Accessed 11 April 2022. http://www.ccel.org/ccel/richardson/fathers.x.i.ii.html.

Lewis, Alan. *Between Cross and Resurrection: A Theology of Holy Saturday*. Grand Rapids: Eerdmans, 2001.

Lindblom, J. *Prophecy in Ancient Israel*. Philadelphia: Fortress, 1962.

Little, Lester K. *Religious Poverty and the Profit Economy in Medieval Europe*. New York: Cornell University Press, 1983.

Lochman, Jan Milič. *Christ and Prometheus? A Quest for Theological Identity*. Geneva: WCC, 1988.

Lopez, Davina C. *Apostle to the Conquered: Reimagining Paul's Mission*. Minneapolis: Fortress, 2008.

Lopez, Robert S. *The Commercial Revolution of the Middle Ages, 950–1350*. Cambridge: Cambridge University Press, 1976.

Lorke, Melisande, and Dietrich Werner, eds. *Ecumenical Visions for the 21st Century: A Reader for Theological Education*. Geneva: WCC, 2013.

Lorrimer, G. C. *Missionary Sermons, 1812–1924: A Selection from the Discourses Delivered on Behalf of the Baptist Missionary Society on Various Occasions.* London: Carey Kingsgate, 1924.

Lupieri, Edmundo F. "'Businessmen and Merchants Will Not Enter the Places of My Father': Early Christianity and the Market Mentality." In *Money as God? The Monetization of the Market and Its Impact on Religion, Politics, Law and Ethics*, edited by Jürgen von Hagen and Michael Welker, pp. 379–413. Cambridge: Cambridge University Press, 2014.

Macpherson, C. B. *The Life and Times of Liberal Democracy.* Oxford: Oxford University Press, 1977.

Magdoff, Harry. *Imperialism: From the Colonial Age to the Present.* New York: Monthly Review Press, 1978.

Magistris, Francesco de. "The 'Apiru and the Egyptian Domination of Late Bronze Age Israel." MSc diss., University of Edinburgh, 2014.

Maier, Harry O. *Apocalypse Recalled: The Book of Revelation after Christendom.* Minneapolis: Fortress, 2002.

MARC Europe and Evangelical Missionary Alliance (London). *Changing the World.* MARC Monograph no. 8. Bromley: MARC Europe and Evangelical Missionary Alliance [1986].

Marchal, Joseph A., ed. *The People beside Paul: The Philippian Assembly and History from Below.* Atlanta: Society of Biblical Literature, 2015.

Marion, Jean-Luc. *A Brief Apology for a Catholic Moment.* Chicago: University of Chicago Press, 2021.

Markus, Robert. *The End of Ancient Christianity.* Cambridge: Cambridge University Press, 1990.

———. "From Rome to the Barbarian Kingdoms (330–700)." In *The Oxford Illustrated History of Christianity*, edited by John McManners, pp. 62–91. Oxford: Oxford University Press, 1992.

Marquand, David. *Mammon's Kingdom: An Essay on Britain Now.* London: Penguin, 2015.

Martin, David. *Ruin and Restoration: On Violence, Liturgy and Reconciliation.* London: Routledge, 2016.

Martin, Hugh, ed. *Christian Social Reformers of the Nineteenth Century.* London: SCM, 1933.

Mauser, Ulrich. *The Gospel of Peace: A Scriptural Message for Today's World.* Louisville: Westminster John Knox, 1992.

Maxey, James A. *From Orality to Orality: A New Paradigm for Contextual Translation of the Bible.* Eugene: Cascade, 2009.

Mays, James Luther. *Amos.* The Old Testament Library. Philadelphia: Westminster, 1969.

McCarraher, Eugene. "Comrade Ruskin: How a Victorian Visionary Can Save Communism from Marx." *Plough Quarterly* (Summer 2019), 89–96.

———. *The Enchantments of Mammon: How Capitalism Became the Religion of Modernity.* Cambridge: Belknap Press, 2019.

McCarty, James, Matthew Tapie and Justin Bronson Barringer, eds. *The Business of War: Theological and Ethical Reflections on the Military-Industrial Complex.* Eugene: Cascade, 2020.

McGinn, Bernard, ed. *Apocalyptic Spirituality: Treatises and Letters of Lactantius, Adso of Montier-en-Der, Joachim of Fiore, the Franciscan Spirituals, Savonarola.* New York: Paulist, 1979.

McLeod, Hugh. *Class and Religion in the Late Victorian City.* London: Croom Helm, 1974.

McManners, John, ed. *The Oxford Illustrated History of Christianity.* Oxford: Oxford University Press, 1992.

Meagher, Robert Emmet. *Albert Camus and the Human Crisis.* New York: Pegasus, 2021.

Meeks, M. Douglas. *God the Economist: The Doctrine of God and Political Economy.* Minneapolis: Fortress, 1989.

Meeks, Wayne A. *The First Urban Christians: The Social World of the Apostle Paul.* New Haven: Yale University Press, 1983.

Meggitt, Justin J. *Paul, Poverty and Survival.* Edinburgh: T&T Clark, 1998.

Mendenhall, George. *The Tenth Generation: The Origins of the Biblical Tradition.* Baltimore: Johns Hopkins University Press, 1973.

Metz, Johann Baptist. *The Emergent Church: The Future of Christianity in a Postbourgeois World.* New York: Crossroad, 1981.

———. *Remembering and Resisting: The New Political Theology.* Edited by John K. Downey. Eugene: Cascade, 2022.

Miall, Edward. *The British Churches in Relation to the British People.* London: Arthur Hall, Virtue & Co., 1849.

———. *The Politics of Christianity.* London: Arthur Miall, 1863.

Miguez, Nestor O. *The Practice of Hope: Ideology and Intention in 1 Thessalonians.* Minneapolis: Fortress, 2012.

Miguez, Nestor, Joerg Rieger and Jung Mo Sung. *Beyond the Spirit of Empire: Theology and Politics in a New Key.* London: SCM, 2009.

Miles, Jack. *CHRIST: A Crisis in the Life of God.* London: Heinemann, 2001.

Miller, Patrick D. "Property and Possession in Light of the Ten Commandments." In *Having: Property and Possession in Religious and Social Life*, edited by William Schweiker and Charles Mathewes, pp. 17–50. Grand Rapids: Eerdmans, 2004.

Mishra, Pankaj. *From the Ruins of Empire: The Intellectuals Who Remade Asia.* New York: Farrar, Straus & Giroux, 2012.

Mitchel, Patrick. *The Message of Love: The Only Thing That Counts.* London: Inter-Varsity Press, 2019.

Moffett, Samuel. *A History of Christianity in Asia.* Vol. 1, *Beginnings to 1500.* 2nd ed. New York: Orbis, 1998.

Moltmann, Jürgen. *The Crucified God: The Cross of Christ as the Foundation and Criticism of Christian Theology.* London: SCM, 1974.

———. *The Spirit of Hope: Theology for a World in Peril.* Louisville: Westminster John Knox, 2019.

Morgan, Kenneth O. *Keir Hardie: Radical and Socialist.* London: Phoenix, 1997.

Mumford, Lewis. *The City in History.* Harmondsworth: Penguin, 1966.

Mumma, Howard. *Albert Camus and the Minister.* Brewster: Paraclete Press, 2000.

Murphy, Ronald G., S.J. *The Saxon Savior: The Germanic Transformation of the Gospel in the Ninth-Century Heliand.* Oxford: Oxford University Press, 1989.

Myers, Ched. *Binding the Strong Man: A Political Reading of Mark's Story of Jesus.* New York: Orbis, 1988.

Nasrallah, Laura. "The Acts of the Apostles, Greek Cities, and Hadrian's Panhellion." *Journal of Biblical Literature* 127, no. 3 (2008): 533–66.

Neusner, Jacob, Peder Borgen, Ernest Frerichs and Richard Horsley, eds. *The Social World of Formative Christianity and Judaism.* Philadelphia: Fortress, 1988.

Newbigin, Lesslie. *Lesslie Newbigin: Missionary Theologian – A Reader.* Edited by Paul Weston. London: SPCK, 2006.

———. *Proper Confidence: Faith, Doubt, and Certainty in Christian Discipleship.* Grand Rapids: Eerdmans, 1995.

———. *Signs amid the Rubble: The Purposes of God in Human History.* Edited by Geoffrey Wainwright. Grand Rapids: Eerdmans, 2003.

Nickle, Keith E. *The Collection: A Study in Paul's Strategy.* Eugene: Wipf & Stock, 2009 [1966].

Noll, Mark A. *Turning Points: Decisive Moments in the History of Christianity.* Leicester: Inter-Varsity Press, 1997.

Northcott, Michael. *An Angel Directs the Storm: Apocalyptic Religion and American Empire.* London: I. B. Tauris, 2004.

Nouwen, Henri. *The Return of the Prodigal Son: A Story of Homecoming.* London: Darton, Longman & Todd, 1994.

Oakman, Douglas E. *Jesus, Debt, and the Lord's Prayer.* Eugene: Cascade, 2014.

O'Connor, Kathleen. *Jeremiah: Pain and Promise.* Minneapolis: Fortress, 2011.

O'Neill, Shaun. *A Church of Islam: The Syrian Calling of Father Paolo Dall'Oglio.* Eugene: Wipf & Stock, 2019.

Osiek, Carolyn. "Family Matters." In *A People's History of Christianity.* Vol. 1, *Christian Origins*, edited by Richard A. Horsley, pp. 201–20. Minneapolis: Fortress, 2005.

Ott, Craig, and Harold Netland, eds. *Globalizing Theology: Belief and Practice in an Era of World Christianity*. Nottingham: Apollos, 2007.

Otto, Rudolf. *The Idea of the Holy*. London: Oxford University Press, 1958.

Owst, G. R. *Literature and Pulpit in Medieval England: A Neglected Chapter in the History of English Letters and of the English People*. Oxford: Basil Blackwell, 1961.

Ozment, Steven. *The Age of Reform 1250–1550: An Intellectual and Religious History of Late Medieval and Reformation Europe*. New Haven: Yale University Press, 1980.

———. *The Reformation in the Cities: The Appeal of Protestantism to Sixteenth-Century Germany and Switzerland*. New Haven: Yale University Press, 1975.

Padilla, René. "Evangelism and the World." In *Let the Earth Hear His Voice: International Congress on World Evangelization, Lausanne, Switzerland*, edited by J. D. Douglas, pp. 116–46. Minneapolis: World Wide Publications, 1975.

Pagden, Anthony. "Introduction." In Bartolemé de las Casas, *A Short Account of the Destruction of the Indies*, pp. xiii–xliii. Edited and translated by Nigel Griffin. London: Penguin, 1992.

———. *Peoples and Empires: Europeans and the Rest of the World – From Antiquity to the Present*. London: Weidenfeld & Nicolson, 2001.

Parry, J., and M. Bloch, eds. *Money and the Morality of Exchange*. Cambridge: Cambridge University Press, 1989.

Pelikan, Jaroslav. *Jesus Through the Centuries: His Place in the History of Culture*. New York: Harper & Row, 1985.

Perdue, Leo G. *The Collapse of History: Reconstructing Old Testament Theology*. Minneapolis: Fortress, 1994.

Pitkänen, Pekka. "Ethnicity, Assimilation and the Israelite Settlement." *Tyndale Bulletin* 55, no. 2 (2004): 161–82.

Polanyi, Karl. *The Great Transformation: The Political and Economic Origins of Our Time*. Boston: Beacon, 1957.

Pomper, Philip, Richard Elphick and Richard Vann, eds. *World History: Ideologies, Structures, and Identities*. Oxford: Blackwell, 1988.

Poon, Michael Nai-Chiu. "The Rise of Asian Pacific Christianity and Challenges for the Church Universal." In *Ecumenical Visions for the 21st Century: A Reader for Theological Education*, edited by Melisande Lorke and Dietrich Werner, pp. 65–72. Geneva: WCC, 2013.

Price, S. R. F. *Rituals and Power: The Roman Imperial Cult in Asia Minor*. Cambridge: Cambridge University Press, 1984.

Prunier, Gerard. *Africa's World War: Congo, the Rwandan Genocide, and the Making of a Continental Catastrophe*. Oxford: Oxford University Press, 2010.

Rabb, Theodore K. *The Last Days of the Renaissance and the March to Modernity*. New York: Basic, 2006.

Rad, Gerhard von. *The Message of the Prophets*. London: SCM, 1968.

Rahner, Karl. *The Christian Commitment: Essays in Pastoral Theology*. New York: Sheed & Ward, 1963.

Ramachandra, Vinoth. "Globalization, Nationalism, and Religious Resurgence." In *Globalizing Theology: Belief and Practice in an Era of World Christianity*, edited by Craig Ott and Harold Netland, pp. 213–30. Nottingham: Apollos, 2007.

———. *Gods That Fail: Modern Idolatry and Christian Mission*. Carlisle: Paternoster, 1996.

Reeves, Marjorie. "Preface." In *Apocalyptic Spirituality: Treatises and Letters of Lactantius, Adso of Montier-en-Der, Joachim of Fiore, the Franciscan Spirituals, Savonarola*, edited by Bernard McGinn, pp. xiii–xviii. New York: Paulist, 1979.

Reston, James, Jr. *Dogs of God: Columbus, the Inquisition, and the Defeat of the Moors*. London: Faber & Faber, 2006.

Ribeiro, Darcy. "The Latin American People." In *1492–1992: The Voice of the Victims*, edited by Leonardo Boff and Virgil Elizondo, pp. 13–29. *Concilium* Special. London: SCM, 1991.

Richard, Pablo. *Apocalypse: A People's Commentary on the Book of Revelation*. Eugene: Wipf & Stock, 2008.

———. "1492: The Violence of God and the Future of Christianity." In *1492–1992: The Voice of the Victims*, edited by Leonardo Boff and Virgil Elizondo, pp. 59–67. *Concilium* Special. London: SCM, 1991.

Rosa, Hartmut. *Democracy Needs Religion*. Cambridge: Polity Press, 2024.

Rowe, C. Kavin. *World Upside Down: Reading Acts in the Graeco-Roman Age*. Oxford: Oxford University Press, 2010.

Roxburgh, Alan J. *Joining God in the Great Unraveling: Where We Are and What I've Learned*. Eugene: Cascade, 2021.

———. *The Missionary Congregation, Leadership, and Liminality*. Harrisburg: Trinity Press International, 1997.

Ruskin, John. *Unto This Last and Other Writings*. London: Penguin, 1997.

Russell, James C. *The Germanization of Early Medieval Christianity: A Sociohistorical Approach to Religious Transformation*. Oxford: Oxford University Press, 1994.

Saayman, Willem, and Klippies Kritzinger, eds. *Mission in Bold Humility: David Bosch's Work Reconsidered*. New York: Orbis, 1996.

Sacks, Jonathan. *The Dignity of Difference: How to Avoid the Clash of Civilizations*. London: Continuum, 2003.

Sahlins, Marshall. *Stone Age Economics*. London: Tavistock, 1974.

Sale, Kirkpatrick. *The Conquest of Paradise: Christopher Columbus and the Columbian Legacy*. New York: Plume, 1991.

Sanghera, Sathnam. *Empireland: How Imperialism Has Shaped Modern Britain*. London: Penguin, 2021.

Sanneh, Lamin. *Encountering the West: Christianity and the Global Cultural Process – The African Dimension.* London: Marshall Pickering, 1993.

———. *Translating the Message: The Missionary Impact on Culture.* New York: Orbis, 1989.

———. *West African Christianity: The Religious Impact.* New York: Orbis, 1983.

Sanneh, Lamin, and Joel Carpenter, eds. *The Changing Face of Christianity: Africa, the West, and the World.* Oxford: Oxford University Press, 2005.

Sanneh, Lamin, and Michael McClymond, eds. *The Wiley Blackwell Companion to World Christianity.* Oxford: Wiley Blackwell, 2016.

Sartre, Maurice. *The Middle East under Rome.* Cambridge: Belknap Press, 2007.

Sassen, Saskia. *Cities in a World Economy.* 4th ed. Los Angeles: Sage, 2012.

———. *Expulsions: Brutality and Complexity in the Global Economy.* Cambridge: Belknap Press, 2014.

———. *Globalization and Its Discontents.* New York: Free Press, 1998.

Sawicki, Marianne. *Crossing Galilee: Architectures of Contact in the Occupied Land of Jesus.* Harrisburg: Trinity Press International, 2000.

———. "Magdalenes and Tiberiennes: City Women in the Entourage of Jesus." In *Transformative Encounters: Jesus and Women Re-viewed*, edited by Ingrid Rosa Kitzberger, pp. 181–202. Atlanta: Society of Biblical Literature, 2000.

Schreiter, Robert. *The New Catholicity: Theology between the Global and the Local.* New York: Orbis, 1997.

———. *Reconciliation: Mission and Ministry in a Changing Social Order.* New York: Orbis, 1992.

Schreiter, Robert, ed. *Mission in the Third Millennium.* New York: Orbis, 2001.

Schüele, Andreas. "'Do Not Sell Your Soul for Money': Economy and Eschatology in Biblical and Intertestamental Traditions." In *Money as God? The Monetization of the Market and Its Impact on Religion, Politics, Law and Ethics*, edited by Jürgen von Hagen and Michael Welker, pp. 365–78. Cambridge: Cambridge University Press, 2014.

———. "Sharing and Loving: Love, Law, and the Ethics of Cultural Memory in the Pentateuch." In *Having: Property and Possession in Religious and Social Life*, edited by William Schweiker and Charles Mathewes, pp. 51–68. Grand Rapids: Eerdmans, 2004.

Schweiker, William, and Charles Mathewes, eds. *Having: Property and Possession in Religious and Social Life.* Grand Rapids: Eerdmans, 2004.

Scott, R. B. Y. *Proverbs and Ecclesiastes: A New Translation with Introduction and Commentary.* Anchor Bible. New York: Doubleday, 1965.

Segovia, Fernando. "Interpreting beyond Borders: Postcolonial Studies and Diasporic Studies in Biblical Criticism." In *Interpreting beyond Borders*, pp. 11–34. Sheffield: Sheffield Academic, 2000.

Segovia, Fernando, ed. *Interpreting beyond Borders*. Sheffield: Sheffield Academic, 2000.

Selby, Peter. *An Idol Unmasked: A Faith Perspective on Money*. London: Darton, Longman & Todd, 2014.

Seow, Choon-Leong. *Ecclesiastes: A New Translation with Introduction and Commentary*. New Haven: Yale University Press, 1997.

———. "The Social World of Ecclesiastes." In *Money as God? The Monetization of the Market and Its Impact on Religion, Politics, Law and Ethics*, edited by Jürgen von Hagen and Michael Welker, pp. 137–58. Cambridge: Cambridge University Press, 2014.

Shenk, Wilbert R., ed. *Enlarging the Story: Perspectives on Writing World Christian History*. New York: Orbis, 2002.

Shenker, Jack. "Picking a Fight." *The Guardian*, 29 July 2023, pp. 20–27.

Shortall, Sarah. *Soldiers of God in a Secular World: Catholic Theology and Twentieth-Century French Politics*. Cambridge: Harvard University Press, 2021.

Simmel, Georg. "Money in Modern Culture." *Theory, Culture and Society* 8 (1991): 17–31.

Simpson, Leanne Betasamosake. *As We Have Always Done: Indigenous Freedom through Radical Resistance*. Minneapolis: University of Minnesota Press, 2017.

Sklair, Leslie. *The Icon Project: Architecture, Cities, and Capitalist Globalization*. Oxford: Oxford University Press, 2017.

Smith, David W. "The Forgotten 'Grandfather' of Protestant Mission: Perspectives on Globalization from Jean de Léry." *Missiology: An International Review* 34, no. 3 (July 2006): 349–59.

———. *The Kindness of God: Christian Witness in Our Troubled World*. Nottingham: Inter-Varsity Press 2013.

———. *Marx and Jesus in a Post-Communist World*. Leicester: Religious and Theological Students Fellowship, 1992.

———. *Moving toward Emmaus: Hope in a Time of Uncertainty*. London: SPCK, 2007.

———. "Reading Romans after Christendom." *Scottish Bulletin of Evangelical Theology* 40, no. 1 (Spring 2022): 61–73.

———. *Seeking a City with Foundations: Theology for an Urban World*. 2nd ed. Carlisle: Langham Global Library, 2019.

———. *Stumbling Toward Zion: Recovering the Biblical Tradition of Lament in the Era of World Christianity*. Carlisle: Langham Global Library, 2020.

———. "Theology as a Voice for the Voiceless: Jean-Marc Ela's *African Cry*." *Theological College of Northern Nigeria Research Bulletin* 52 (2010): 19–29.

———. *Transforming the World? The Social Impact of British Evangelicalism.* Carlisle: Paternoster, 1998. 2nd ed., Milton Keynes: Paternoster Digital Library, 2005.

———. "A Victorian Prophet without Honour: Edward Miall and the Critique of Nineteenth-Century British Christianity." In *Tales of Two Cities: Christianity and Politics*, edited by Stephen Clark, pp. 152–83. Leicester: Inter-Varsity Press, 2005.

Smith, Sydney. *The Works of the Rev. Sydney Smith.* London: Longmans, Green, Reader & Dyer, 1869.

Smith-Christopher, Daniel L. *The Religion of the Landless: The Social Context of the Babylonian Exile.* Eugene: Wipf & Stock, 1989.

Snyder, Timothy. *Bloodlands: Europe between Hitler and Stalin.* London: Vintage, 2011.

Sobrino, Jon. *The Principle of Mercy: Taking the Crucified People from the Cross.* New York: Orbis, 1994.

Stanley, Brian. *Christianity in the Twentieth Century: A World History.* Princeton: Princeton University Press, 2018.

———. *The History of the Baptist Missionary Society, 1792–1992.* Edinburgh: T&T Clark, 1992.

———. *The World Missionary Conference, Edinburgh 1910.* Grand Rapids: Eerdmans, 2009.

Stearns, Jason K. *Dancing in the Glory of Monsters: The Collapse of the Congo and the Great War of Africa.* New York: Public Affairs, 2011.

Stegemann, Ekkehard W., and Wolfgang Stegemann. *The Jesus Movement: A Social History of Its First Century.* Minneapolis: Fortress, 1999.

Steger, Manfred B. *Globalisms: The Great Ideological Struggle of the Twenty-First Century.* 3rd ed. Lanham: Rowman & Littlefield, 2009.

Steiner, George. *After Babel: Aspects of Language and Translation.* Oxford: Oxford University Press, 1998.

———. *Grammars of Creation: Originating in the Gifford Lectures for 1990.* London: Faber & Faber, 2001.

———. *Real Presences: Is There Anything in What We Say?* London: Faber & Faber, 1991.

Streek, Wolfgang. *How Will Capitalism End? Essays on a Failing System.* London: Verso, 2016.

Stroope, Michael. *Transcending Mission: The Eclipse of a Modern Tradition.* London: Apollos, 2017.

Swartz, David R. *Facing West: American Evangelicals in an Age of World Christianity.* Oxford: Oxford University Press, 2020.

Swift, Louis J. *The Early Fathers on War and Military Service.* Wilmington: Michael Glazier, 1983.

Tamez, Elsa. *The Amnesty of Grace: Justification by Faith from a Latin American Perspective.* Nashville: Abingdon, 1993.

———. *Bible of the Oppressed.* Eugene: Wipf & Stock, 2006 [1982].

———. *The Scandalous Message of James.* New York: Crossroad, 1990.

Tanner, Kathryn. *Christianity and the New Spirit of Capitalism.* New Haven: Yale University Press, 2019.

———. "Economies of Grace." In *Having: Property and Possession in Religious and Social Life*, edited by William Schweiker and Charles Mathewes, pp. 353–82. Grand Rapids: Eerdmans, 2004.

———. *Economy of Grace.* Minneapolis: Fortress, 2005.

Tawney, R. H. *The Acquisitive Society.* Delhi: Lector House, 2022 [1920].

———. *Religion and the Rise of Capitalism.* London: John Murray, 1926.

———. *R. H. Tawney's Commonplace Book.* Edited by J. M. Winter and D. M. Joslin. Cambridge: Cambridge University Press, 1972.

Taylor, John V. *Enough Is Enough.* London: SCM, 1975.

———. *Kingdom Come.* London: SCM, 1989.

Temple, William. *Christianity and Social Order.* New York: Seabury, 1977.

Theodoret of Cyrrus. *A History of the Monks of Syria.* Translated and with introduction by R. M. Price. Kalamazoo: Cistercian, 1985.

Thielicke, Helmut. *The Waiting Father: Sermons on the Parables of Jesus.* London: James Clarke, 1960.

Tillich, Paul. *The Shaking of the Foundations.* Harmondsworth: Penguin, 1962.

Trevor-Roper, Hugh. *The Rise of Christian Europe.* London: Thames & Hudson, 1965.

Ubieta, Carmen Bernabé. "Mary Magdalene and the Seven Demons in Social-Scientific Perspective." In *Transformative Encounters: Jesus and Women Re-viewed*, edited by Ingrid Rosa Kitzberger, pp. 203–23. Atlanta: Society of Biblical Literature, 2000.

Vajta, Vilmos, ed. *The Gospel and Human Destiny.* Minneapolis: Augsburg, 1971.

Vallance, Edward. *A Radical History of Britain: Visionaries, Rebels and Revolutionaries.* London: Little, Brown, 2009.

Veblen, Thorstein. *The Theory of the Leisure Class.* Oxford: Oxford University Press, 2007.

Von Laue, Theodore. *The World Revolution of Westernization: The Twentieth Century in Global Perspective.* Oxford: Oxford University Press, 1987.

Wall, Robert W. *Community of the Wise: The Letter of James.* Valley Forge: Trinity Press International, 1997.

Wallerstein, Immanuel. *Historical Capitalism with Capitalist Civilization.* London: Verso, 1983.

Walls, Andrew F. *The Cross-Cultural Process in Christian History: Studies in the Transmission and Appropriation of Faith.* Edinburgh: T&T Clark, 2002.

———. *Crossing Cultural Frontiers: Studies in the History of World Christianity.* Edited by Mark R. Gornik. New York: Orbis, 2017.

———. "Eusebius Tries Again: The Task of Reconceiving and Revisioning the Study of Christian History." In *Enlarging the Story: Perspectives on Writing World Christian History*, edited by Wilbert R. Shenk, 1–21. New York: Orbis, 2002.

———. *"A History of the Expansion of Christianity" Reconsidered: The Legacy of George E. Day.* New Haven: Yale Divinity School Library Occasional Publication No. 8, 1996.

———. *The Missionary Movement in Christian History: Studies in the Transmission of Faith.* Edinburgh: T&T Clark, 1996.

———. "The Transmission of Christian Faith: A Reflection." In *The Wiley Blackwell Companion to World Christianity*, edited by Lamin Sanneh and Michael McClymond, pp. 685–98. Oxford: Wiley Blackwell, 2016.

Walls, A. F., and Wilbert Shenk, eds. *Exploring New Religious Movements: Essays in Honour of Harold W. Turner.* Elkhart: Mission Focus, 1990.

Walzer, Michael. *Exodus and Revolution.* New York: Basic, 1985.

Ward, William. *Farewell Letters to a Few Friends in Britain and America.* London: S. & R. Bentley, 1821.

Ware, Kallistos. "Eastern Christendom." In *The Oxford Illustrated History of Christianity*, edited by John McManners, pp. 123–61. Oxford: Oxford University Press, 1992.

Weber, Max. *Ancient Judaism.* Translated by H. Gerth and D. Martindale. Glencoe: Free Press, 1952.

———. *The Protestant Ethic and the Spirit of Capitalism.* London: Counterpoint, 1985.

Welker, Michael. *In God's Image: An Anthropology of the Spirit.* Grand Rapids: Eerdmans, 2021.

———. "Kohelet and the Co-evolution of a Monetary Economy and Religion." In *Money as God? The Monetization of the Market and Its Impact on Religion, Politics, Law and Ethics*, edited by Jürgen von Hagen and Michael Welker, pp. 96–108. Cambridge: Cambridge University Press, 2014.

Wengst, Klaus. *Humility: Solidarity of the Humiliated.* London: SCM, 1988.

———. *Pax Romana and the Peace of Jesus Christ.* London: SCM, 1987.

Westermann, Claus. "Creation and History in the Old Testament." In *The Gospel and Human Destiny*, edited by Vilmos Vajta, pp. 11–38. Minneapolis: Augsburg, 1971.

———. *Isaiah 40–66: A Commentary.* Philadelphia: Westminster, 1969.

Williams, Rowan. *Looking East in Winter: Contemporary Thought and the Eastern Christian Tradition.* London: Bloomsbury Continuum, 2021.

Wink, Walter. *Engaging the Powers: Discernment and Resistance in a World of Domination*. Minneapolis: Fortress, 1992.

———. *The Powers That Be: Theology for a New Millennium*. New York: Doubleday, 1998.

Winter, J. M., and D. M. Joslin, eds. *R. H. Tawney's Commonplace Book*. Cambridge: Cambridge University Press, 1972.

Wire, Antoinette Clark. *The Case for Mark Composed in Performance*. Eugene: Cascade, 2011.

Witherington, Ben, III. *Jesus and Money*. London: SPCK, 2010.

Wolff, Hans Walter. *Anthropology of the Old Testament*. Philadelphia: Fortress, 1981.

World Council of Churches. "Together towards Life: Mission and Evangelism in Changing Landscapes." In *Ecumenical Visions for the 21st Century: A Reader for Theological Education*, edited by Melisande Lorke and Dietrich Werner, pp. 191–206. Geneva: WCC, 2013.

Wright, N. T. "Paul's Gospel and Caesar's Empire." In *Paul and Politics*, edited by Richard A. Horsley, pp. 160–83. Harrisburg: Trinity Press International, 2000.

Wright, Tom. *The Day the Revolution Began: Rethinking the Meaning of Jesus' Crucifixion*. London: SPCK, 2016.

———. *Paul: A Biography*. London: SPCK, 2018.

Yeo, Eileen. "Christianity in Chartist Struggle: 1838–1842." *Past and Present* 91 (May 1981): 109–39.

Zampaglione, Gerardo. *The Idea of Peace in Antiquity*. Translated by Richard Dunn. London: University of Notre Dame Press, 1973.

Zuboff, Shoshana. *The Age of Surveillance Capitalism: The Fight for a Human Future at the New Frontier of Power*. London: Profile, 2019.

Langham Literature, with its publishing work, is a ministry of Langham Partnership.

Langham Partnership is a global fellowship working in pursuit of the vision God entrusted to its founder John Stott –

> *to facilitate the growth of the church in maturity and Christ-likeness through raising the standards of biblical preaching and teaching.*

Our vision is to see churches in the Majority World equipped for mission and growing to maturity in Christ through the ministry of pastors and leaders who believe, teach and live by the word of God.

Our mission is to strengthen the ministry of the word of God through:
- nurturing national movements for biblical preaching
- fostering the creation and distribution of evangelical literature
- enhancing evangelical theological education

especially in countries where churches are under-resourced.

Our ministry

Langham Preaching partners with national leaders to nurture indigenous biblical preaching movements for pastors and lay preachers all around the world. With the support of a team of trainers from many countries, a multi-level programme of seminars provides practical training, and is followed by a programme for training local facilitators. Local preachers' groups and national and regional networks ensure continuity and ongoing development, seeking to build vigorous movements committed to Bible exposition.

Langham Literature provides Majority World preachers, scholars and seminary libraries with evangelical books and electronic resources through publishing and distribution, grants and discounts. The programme also fosters the creation of indigenous evangelical books in many languages, through writer's grants, strengthening local evangelical publishing houses, and investment in major regional literature projects, such as one volume Bible commentaries like the *Africa Bible Commentary* and the *South Asia Bible Commentary*.

Langham Scholars provides financial support for evangelical doctoral students from the Majority World so that, when they return home, they may train pastors and other Christian leaders with sound, biblical and theological teaching. This programme equips those who equip others. Langham Scholars also works in partnership with Majority World seminaries in strengthening evangelical theological education. A growing number of Langham Scholars study in high quality doctoral programmes in the Majority World itself. As well as teaching the next generation of pastors, graduated Langham Scholars exercise significant influence through their writing and leadership.

To learn more about Langham Partnership and the work we do visit **langham.org**

www.ingramcontent.com/pod-product-compliance
Lightning Source LLC
Chambersburg PA
CBHW052011290426
44112CB00014B/2205